EUROPEAN BUSINESS ETHICS CASES IN CONTEXT

Issues in Business Ethics

VOLUME 28

Series Editors:

Wim Dubbink, *Department of Philosophy, Tilburg University, The Netherlands*
Mollie Painter-Morland, *Department of Philosophy, De Paul University, USA*

Consulting Editor:

Pat Werhane, *Director, Institute for Business and Professional Ethics,
De Paul University, USA*

Former Series Editors:

Brian Harvey, Henk van Luijk[†], Pat Werhane

Editorial Board:

George Enderle, *University of Notre Dame, USA*
William C. Frederick, *University of Pittsburg, USA*
Campbell Jones, *University of Leicester, United Kingdom*
Daryl Koehn, *University of St. Thomas, USA*
Andreas Scherer, *University of Zurich, Switzerland*
Horst Steinmann, *University of Erlangen-Nürnberg, Germany*
Hiro Umezu, *Keio University, Japan*
Lu Xiaohe, *Shanghai Academy of Social Sciences, P.R. China*

For further volumes:
http://www.springer.com/series/6077

European Business Ethics Cases in Context

The Morality of Corporate Decision Making

edited by

WIM DUBBINK

Tilburg University, The Netherlands

LUC VAN LIEDEKERKE

Katholieke Universiteit Leuven, Belgium

and

HENK VAN LUIJK

Editors
Wim Dubbink
Tilburg University
Department of Philosophy, Faculty
  of Humanities
PO Box 90153
5000 LE Tilburg
The Netherlands
w.dubbink@uvt.nl

Luc van Liedekerke
Katholieke Universiteit Leuven
Centre for Economics and Ethics
Naamsestraat 69
3000 Leuven
Belgium
Luc.Vanliedekerke@econ.kuleuven.be

Henk van Luijk (deceased)

ISSN 0925-6733
ISBN 978-90-481-9333-2   e-ISBN 978-90-481-9334-9
DOI 10.1007/978-90-481-9334-9
Springer Dordrecht Heidelberg London New York

Library of Congress Control Number: 2011921121

© Springer Science+Business Media B.V. 2011
No part of this work may be reproduced, stored in a retrieval system, or transmitted in any form or by any means, electronic, mechanical, photocopying, microfilming, recording or otherwise, without written permission from the Publisher, with the exception of any material supplied specifically for the purpose of being entered and executed on a computer system, for exclusive use by the purchaser of the work.

Printed on acid-free paper

Springer is part of Springer Science+Business Media (www.springer.com)

*In memory of Henk van Luijk
(1929–2010)*

Preface

Case analysis is the cradle of contemporary business ethics. The established moral philosophers of the 1980s were so absorbed by fundamental issues that they could only make room for sketchy cases in passing. To make matters worse, these so-called examples usually had little to do with the real world: "Suppose you were to be left on a deserted island ..."; "Suppose you would pass a pond in which two people were drowning and you only had time to save one?"; "Suppose a sadistic official in a outlaw state would offer you the choice of killing two people...". The pioneer business ethicists of the 1980s distanced themselves from both establishment and fundamental issues by analysing real life cases in a real life manner; i.e. with an interest in contributing to the solution of concrete problems. In doing so, they also distanced themselves from the dominant sociological and political thought on commercial life. At the time these disciplines were enchanted by system theory. This theory looks at the market as ruled by institutional forces. Consequently, there is hardly any room left for an analysis from the action perspective.

However emancipating all this was, almost 30 years later many business ethicists have come to realize the disadvantages and limitations of an academic methodology that focuses on case analysis, especially if its aim is to provide all too concrete answers to concrete questions like: is it permissible for company A to do x in these circumstances? Some will say that with this growing awareness the business ethics world has finally come of age. Nonetheless, the business ethics world would make a serious mistake if it would believe that it can and ought to take leave of case analysis as a core methodological device. Case analysis remains important and not only for educational purposes. It is crucial for the academic advancement of the discipline. It is exactly by means of the thorough analysis of cases that today's business ethicists re-establish contact with and learn to appreciate the fundamental issues that the established moral philosophers are struggling with. Thus, paradoxically, today's business ethics may perhaps contribute most to fundamental ethics by stubbornly clinging to case analysis.

Despite its long history the need for comprehensive and well-informed case descriptions remains without abatement. Case analysis still is an excellent way of arousing people's interest in the moral aspects of commercial life as well as in business ethics as an academic discipline. And it can be used as a means to link business ethics to other academic disciplines and moral philosophy in general.

This book consists of two parts. Part I takes up three short chapters. In these chapters we provide an orientation of contemporary business ethics. We hope this context will be instructive for the analysis of the cases. The first chapter sketches a brief inside history of business ethics as an academic discipline. The second chapter touches on the skills needed to analyse and reflect on moral business ethics cases. In the third chapter we elaborate upon the important institutional turn that business ethics is going through at the moment. The institutional turn makes it clear that the organisation of morality will become a main business ethics theme in the years to come. It also shows that we must explore other themes, such as the theory on moral excuses.

The second part of the book consists of eight recent cases that were broadly discussed in Europe; in particular North Western Europe. It is characteristic of the international dimension of our contemporary world that many of these cases relate to global issues. But one way or another, European companies and the European general public were involved in all these cases. We have also tried to present a variety of industries, including pharmacy, ICT and construction. We have not only focussed on morally hard cases. We have also included a few cases that can better be categorized as problems of moral motivation. A morally hard case is a situation in which a moral agent must make a moral choice, but sincerely does not know what the morally right course of action is. There are good moral reasons for a specific course of action and good moral reasons against the same course. For example: must a company lay off child workers even if in the particular circumstances at hand, it clearly is in the best interest of the children to be employed? Morally hard cases call for reflection. A problem of moral motivation differs categorically from a morally hard case. A problem of moral motivation arises when a person knows what the morally right course of action is but finds it hard to motivate herself to act accordingly. In case of a problem of moral motivation a person has a good moral reason to do A but a good non-moral reason not to do A. For example: a person has a good moral reason not to break a promise but also a good non-moral reason to break it (e.g. because it is profitable). When a person fails to act on the moral reason, immoral conduct ensues. We have included cases that mainly concern problems of moral motivation because these cases help us to understand why and how immoral conduct arises in commercial life.

A special feature of this book is that we wanted it to be more than a collection of cases, however important that may be in itself. Each case is followed up by two expert commentaries. The experts have various backgrounds: from organisation theory to morality and from economics to philosophy. What binds them all together is that in their own way each commentary shows the extent to which case analysis in business ethics has become interwoven with and dependent upon the knowledge gathered and preserved in other disciplines. Issues such as the extent of the duty to help of the pharmaceutical industry in relation to AIDS cannot seriously be discussed without becoming acquainted with the discussion on overdemandingness in morality; The moral analysis of the accident with the ICE train requires knowledge of the "problem of many hands" and the impact of technology in contemporary society; The analysis of cases such as the rise and fall of L&H can only be meaningfully pursued if we have taken a course in leadership theory. As we see it, the multidisciplinary character of business ethics makes the field very exciting. It also is one of its greatest challenges-how can one person remain up to date in all these expanding fields of expertise? We hope to demonstrate that the growth of expert knowledge within disciplines and sub-disciplines can still be made compatible with meaningful cross-disciplinary interaction.

Half-way through the production process of the book, Henk van Luijk indicated that we had to speed up the process. Now that his wife was about to retire, the couple wanted to move to France and live a few quiet years in the country side. In fact, they had already spotted the house they wanted to buy. But it turned out differently. Out of the blue, Henk fell ill and his health quickly deteriorated. He died early 2010. We dedicate this book to his memory.

Tilburg, The Netherlands Wim Dubbink
Leuven, Belgium Luc van Liedekerke

Acknowledgements

The realization of this book was financially supported by Springer Science+Business Media; The Department of Organization Studies, Faculty of Social Sciences, VU University Amsterdam; Brabant Center of Entrepreneurship, Tilburg University and Eindhoven University of Technology; The Centre for Economics and Ethics of the KU Leuven; and the Department of Philosophy, Faculty of Humanities, Tilburg University.

The work has greatly benefitted from the skill and dedication of the administrative staff at our home universities. We would like to extend our thanks to Ann van Espen, Annette van Gemerden and Nicole van Eijndhoven. We also like to gratefully thank Neil Olivier and Diana Nijenhuijzen from Springer for the effort they put into the realization of the book.

Tilburg, The Netherlands	Wim Dubbink
Leuven, Belgium	Luc van Liedekerke

Contents

Part I   Theory

1. Business Ethics: Cases, Codes and Institutions 3
   Henk van Luijk
2. Moral Competence 11
   Henk van Luijk and Wim Dubbink
3. Institutions and the Institutional Turn in Business Ethics 19
   Wim Dubbink

Part II   Case A: The Pharmaceutical Industry and the AIDS Crisis

4. Case Description: The Pharmaceutical Industry and the AIDS Crisis   33
   Marcel Verweij
5. Commentary: The Struggle Against AIDS and the
   Pharmaceuticals Industry – Are There Limits to the Moral
   Obligation to Do Good? 47
   Mariëtte van den Hoven
6. Commentary: Special Duties and the AIDS-Crisis – A
   Commentary on the Roche Case 55
   Jan Vorstenbosch

Part III   Case B: Heineken and Promotion Girls in Cambodia – Part 1

7. Case Description: Heineken and Promotion Girls in Cambodia . . 65
   Frans-Paul van der Putten and Rosalie Feilzer
8. Commentary: Obscured Authority 79
   Raoul Wirtz, Edgar Karssing, and Gemma Crijns
9. Commentary: Heineken Between Moral Motives and Self-interest . 87
   Frank den Hond

xiii

Part IV   Case C: Heineken and Promotion Girls in Cambodia – Part 2

10 Case Description: Heineken and Promotion Girls in Cambodia, Part 2 97
    Frans-Paul van der Putten

11 Commentary: Legitimacy as Moral Exchange? 103
    Frank G.A. de Bakker

12 Commentary: How to Deal with the Side Effects of Delivering Beer? 111
    Peter Koslowski

Part V   Case D: A Disputed Contract – IHC Caland in Burma

13 Case Description: A Disputed Contract – IHC Caland in Burma . 121
    Frank G.A. de Bakker and Frank den Hond

14 Commentary: Dredgers on Land 141
    Pieter Ippel

15 Commentary: IHC Caland in Burma – An Analysis 147
    Johan Graafland

Part VI   Case E: The Ice Train Accident near Eschede

16 Case Description: The ICE Train Accident near Eschede 157
    Michiel Brumsen

17 Commentary: Collective Responsibility and the Virtue of Accuracy 169
    Bert van de Ven

18 Commentary: Technology as Material Ethics 177
    Tsjalling Swierstra

Part VII   Case F: A Matter of Involvement – Unilever and Indian Cottonseed Cultivation

19 Case Description: A Matter of Involvement – Unilever and Indian Cottonseed Cultivation 185
    Wim Dubbink

20 Commentary: The Scope of Chain Responsibility 213
    Jos Kole

21 Commentary: Child Labour, Companies, and Precautions 223
    Robert Heeger

Part VIII Case G: Rise and Fall of Silicon Valley in Flanders – Lernout & Hauspie Speech Products

22 Case Description: Rise and Fall of Silicon Valley in Flanders – Lernout & Hauspie Speech Products 233
Marc Buelens and Eva Cools

23 Commentary: Law Versus Community 245
Luc van Liedekerke

24 Commentary: Lernout & Hauspie – Chronicle of a Bankruptcy Foretold 251
Dick de Gilder

Part IX Case H: Construction Fraud

25 Case Description: Construction Fraud 261
Johan Graafland and Luc van Liedekerke

26 Commentary: The Moral Assimilation of the Market 277
Bert Musschenga

27 Commentary: Fraud, Excuse and Responsibility 285
Marcel Verweij

About the Authors 291

Index 293

Contributors

Michiel Brumsen Delft University of Technology, Delft, The Netherlands, m.brumsen@zonnet.be

Marc Buelens Vlerick Leuven Gent Management School, Ghent University, Gent, Belgium, marc.buelens@vlerick.com

Eva Cools Vlerick Leuven Gent Management School, Ghent University, Gent, Belgium, eva.cools@vlerick.com

Gemma Crijns Rotterdam School of Management, Erasmus University, Rotterdam, The Netherlands, gcrijns@rsm.nl

Wim Dubbink Department of Philosophy, Faculty of Humanities, Tilburg University, Tilburg, The Netherlands, w.dubbink@uvt.nl

Frank G.A. de Bakker Department of Organization Science, VU University, Amsterdam, The Netherlands, f.g.a.de.bakker@vu.nl

Dick de Gilder Department of Organization Science, VU University, Amsterdam, The Netherlands, tc.de.gilder@vu.nl

Frank den Hond Department of Organization Science, VU University, Amsterdam, The Netherlands, f.den.hond@vu.nl

Rosalie Feilzer Department of Social Science, VU University, Amsterdam, The Netherlands, info@nolannorton.com

Johan Graafland Tilburg Sustainability Center and European Banking Center, Tilburg School of Economics and Management, University of Tilburg, Tilburg, The Netherlands, j.j.graafland@uvt.nl

Robert Heeger Ethics Institute, Utrecht University, Utrecht, The Netherlands, rheeger@theo.uu.nl

Pieter Ippel Roosevelt Academy, Middelburg, The Netherlands, p.ippel@roac.nl

Edgar Karssing Nyenrode Business University, Breukelen, The Netherlands, e.karssing@nyenrode.nl

Jos Kole Ethics Institute, Utrecht University, Utrecht, The Netherlands, J.J.Kole@uu.nl

Peter Koslowski VU University, Amsterdam, The Netherlands, p.koslowski@ph.vu.nl

Bert Musschenga Faculty of Philosophy, VU University, Amsterdam, The Netherlands, aw.musschenga@dienst.vu.nl

Tsjalling Swierstra Faculty of Arts and Social Sciences, Maastricht University, Maastricht, The Netherlands, t.swierstra@maastrichtuniversity.nl

Bert van de Ven Department of Philosophy, Tilburg University, Tilburg, The Netherlands, b.w.vdven@uvt.nl

Mariëtte van den Hoven Ethics Institute, Utrecht University, Utrecht, The Netherlands, M.A.Vandenhoven@uu.nl

Frans-Paul van der Putten Netherlands Institute of International Relations Clingendael, The Hague, The Netherlands, fputten@clingendael.nl

Luc van Liedekerke Centre for Economics and Ethics, Katholieke Universiteit Leuven, Leuven, Belgium, Luc.Vanliedekerke@econ.kuleuven.be

Henk van Luijk Nyenrode Business University, Breukelen, The Netherlands

Marcel Verweij Ethics Institute, Faculty of Humanities, Utrecht University, Utrecht, The Netherlands, M.F.Verweij@uu.nl

Jan Vorstenbosch Department of Philosophy, Utrecht University, Utrecht, The Netherlands, jan.Vorstenbosch@phil.uu.nl

Raoul Wirtz Executive and Management Development Center, Nyenrode Business University, Breukelen, The Netherlands, r.wirtz@nyenrode.nl

Part I
Theory

Chapter 1
Business Ethics: Cases, Codes and Institutions

Henk van Luijk

Abstract No one had ever heard of business ethics until around 1970. Matters were very different 10 years later. Business Ethics had established itself in the curricula of many university programs in management and business studies, both in the US and somewhat later, in Europe. The achievement did not come about without labour. The new discipline was frowned upon from many sides. Looking back, we can discern three phases in the development of business ethics. In the first phase case discussions dominated the discipline. The case method was a welcome change from an academic practice that had stayed aloof of concrete problems for too long on the one hand and was caught up in abstract system theoretical reflections on the other. The second phase meant a shift towards organisation issues and CSR. The third phase is the future. It is to be hoped that the discipline retrieves the workmanship of morally analyzing cases and finds ways of linking this to a thorough investigation into the institutional dimension of business ethics.

Introduction

No one had ever heard of business ethics until around 1970. People had their own opinions on business practices in specific cases – good, dubious, totally reprehensible – and, of course, when they were in business, they sometimes wondered what the most responsible decision might be under given circumstances. The places (usually pulpits) from which an appeal came to do good and abandon evil also regularly addressed trade practices. But there was little question of systematic attention for ethics in business life, let alone that there was a clearly demarcated field of study known as business ethics.

Matters were very different 10 years later. Colleges and universities in the US and, somewhat later, in Europe included a course on business ethics in their curricula, sometimes required, often as an elective. Manuals and specialised periodicals followed in their wake as did congresses and associations devoted to

---

Henk van Luijk is deceased.

the subject. The Society for Business Ethics was established in the US in 1980 and the European Business Ethics Network followed a half decade later. A new specialisation was born.

But not without labour. Not everyone welcomed the young discipline. Neither the business community, nor fellow ethicists stood with open arms. We see three reasons for this reticence. The first was social. Business ethics sprouted largely from dissatisfaction with society. In the slipstream of the 1960s and 1970s, political leaders and authorities were the permanent targets of social criticism. The business community did not escape this unscathed. It was regarded as instigator behind much of the harm to people and the environment and as the natural ally of those mainly concerned with saving their own skin and furthering their own interests. This critical tone and its rejection of the business community resounded repeatedly in the new field's early years. The business community was not amused.

The second source of reticence was scholarly. Ethics as officially taught and studied at universities had long stayed aloof from daily practice, preferring to concentrate on fundamental, yet abstract, question such as "What is the nature of a moral statement"? What does it mean to say that something is morally necessary, or morally unacceptable? Is that a statement of fact, a subject opinion, an exhortation, commandment or a prohibition? In this last case, on what authority is this propounded? Important questions, doubtless, but daily practice needed something more direct. It wanted guidelines for handling practical situations and problems. Is a government allowed to use offensive cruse missiles as deterrent to contain opponents? Do a woman's rights take precedence over those of an unborn child? Does someone addicted to alcohol or tobacco have an unlimited right to medical care? What are we to think of cigarette production and cigarette producers? As society became more complex and the questions more urgent, many fields felt the need to develop applied ethics. Official ethics gradually recognised this need, yet its practitioners still did not welcome the newcomers; despite those applications' making the field more accessible, ethicists feared that these also made it more trivial. Business ethics had an additional hitch. It is quite understandable that momentous dilemmas can occur in matters of war and peace, life and death, but can we say the same about drafting the most advantageous income and expenditure statement? The ethicist that gets mixed up in such matters becomes profit's servant. She links ethics' reputation to the market's price.

The third cause was that business ethics silently shifted its view of the market to a different angle. Up to 1970, when (and if) scholars studied market activities they did so from macro-sociological, political and theoretical perspectives that treated the market as part of the social system. These analyses often originated from a Marxist view of society, which assumed a critical view of the market. Business ethics shifted from the macro level the meso and micro levels by taking the company and its representatives as methodological starting point. Traditional scholars thought that in doing this business ethics legitimated what was considered an essentially pernicious system.

Business ethics was not born under a lucky star. That made its later growth into a young adult with attendant promise and uncertainty all the more striking. It is worthwhile to describe the growth phases that led to this state. In addition to providing insight into the discipline's recent history, this will offer a better view of the questions and problems facing the modern free market and of the ways business ethics can help. In what follows we discern two clearly distinguishable phases and the contours of a third still largely on the horizon.

Case-Discussion Phase

The classroom was business ethics' first habitat. Classroom methods were the first ones the new discipline used. Case analysis is one didactic instrument frequently used in management studies and other practice-based programs. Students were asked to develop arguments leading to a position regarding an every-day situation or occurrence. The situation could be real or fictitious. A real situation is recognisable and prescriptive; a fictitious one has the advantage of being able to be refined as desired with venomous details that block escape routes. All with a view to ultimately reaching a lucid stance. This may not be the only possible stance, and certainly not the only correct one, but it will be well thought out and reasonably defensible on moral grounds, in the instance of a case in business ethics.

A careful analysis of several diverse and morally pertinent business cases will make people more alert to the ethical aspects of situations that arise daily. More often than is apparent at first glance, they learn to see that a responsible business decision also requires attention to the ethical aspects of the issue. That is a gain because it enhances the ethical quality of decision-making. In addition, case analyses strengthen ethical competence and skill. Ethical questions are open to reasoning. They rise above one-dimensional "I think" statements: "I think that is unacceptable!" "Why?" "Because it is, that's why". Rather than that, we get thought-out arguments that make people think and that may prove convincing. The timidity that often overcomes people when they must make a moral judgment disappears in a candid discussion.

But the case analysis method also had a weak point. A student at Harvard Business School, the cradle of the case study method, drew attention to the problem when he proudly stated that "We treated more than 180 cases this semester". That is the problem. The trees hide the forest. An accumulation of business cases, however telling each may be individually, is more likely to lead to intellectual indigestion than to greater culinary skills. But it took business ethics some time to discover this. It first needed to detour through a new phase in its development.

From Case to Code

The business community's initial resistance to the dreaded interference of business ethics ebbed gradually. The meddling turned out not to be so bad. Ethicists had their hands full with accumulating their own expertise. Most of them were not out to nail a company to the wall every time a new scandal broke. They had learned from the business community that incident management had a poor yield. Advancement was better served by understanding than shouting.

But this understanding did not materialise from thin air. In its early years, the European Business Ethics Network, mentioned above, requested an Advisory Council, consisting of several CEOs of international companies, to act as bridge between practice and academia. One of the members was a somewhat elderly chairman of the board of a large Italian company. He seemed rather silent for an Italian. His main contribution consisted of one repeatedly uttered sentence: "But what are your saleable goods?" What do you, ethics specialists, have to offer that is to our advantage? It was a disconcerting question. From it, scholars learned that the law of supply and demand also applied in business ethics.

Once they discovered that, things moved quickly. The field proved to have specific questions. The corresponding answers were skilfully constructed and brought to market one by one. Moral codes proved especially popular. Business codes sprouted like mushrooms to join a plethora of professional codes, industry codes and civil service codes. In the Netherlands, this development reached its public-relations apex in the Tabaksblat Code (the Dutch corporate governance code). An integrity thermometer to take a company's temperature was also on offer along with a game for tackling moral dilemmas with financial and reputational profit and loss reckoned in. "When you tackle your case this way, you end up with a pile of money, but dent your reputation". Screening methods used a series of standards to sift companies that, depending on the result, could then be included in or barred from ethical investment funds. Attention focused on a company's culture. "What elements of a company's culture need to make a code truly effective? Were people to be measured against their strict adherence to rules, or should emphasis fall on their own moral responsibility? How does one reinforce the moral competence of management and staff? Can courses in ethical problem solving help? Or is everyone knowing, yet refraining from speaking out, part of the business culture?"

The question regarding business ethics' saleable goods was actually an invitation to implement business ethics. Once there is sufficient interest to make ethics and social responsibility points for discussion in a company, the next step is to turn interest into action and implementation. This required supportive instruments. Ethicists accepted this challenge: "Show that your have these instruments, show that they help, that they work".

But ethicists were not the call's only recipients. The suppliers' market grew in numbers and skill. Organisational sciences entered and began cultivating the field of business ethics. Organisational sciences came into play whenever an organisation needed to change whenever it had to set out on new paths. How to direct a company that is entering a new phase? What risks does it encounter, what perspectives are open to it? This practice goes by a range of names: change management, transition management, risk management or reputation management, but the constant pattern in all this is that the present situation is subjected to a strength/weakness analysis and then a target situation is defined with the greatest possible precision, including potential hindrances and ways to eliminate or usefully circumvent them. Specialists in organisational studies and business ethicists became one another's privileged partners.

But, certainly in Western Europe, there was still another element, a terminological one this time. The term business ethics was looked upon suspiciously from the start. Business people too often felt that pretentious critics "who never risked a penny of their own in business" stood them up against a moral yardstick. That is not the way to make friends and influence people. However, the situation changed strikingly when the term business ethics made room for corporate social responsibility or CSR. Overnight, many felt attracted and displayed a will to join discussions and even participate in their own way. CSR proved able to do what business ethics could not: convince the business community gradually that while profit and continuity may be indispensable, ignoring the triple-p (people, planet and profit) of social, environmental effects and business dealings would be like building a company on quicksand. When you think that a general definition of ethical conduct includes "taking into account the rights and interests of all those who can reasonably claim to possess them and making sure that they are included in your decisions", in other words when you give people and planet a place in all your plans, the distance between corporate social responsibility and business ethics narrows.

But it was not merely a question of different terminology. Since the 1970s, a series of cultural and institutional shifts have played a role in the background. Two of them are

- the cultural shift in dominant market morality. The old ethics in which the entrepreneur's actions were ethically correct when he obeyed the law and made a profit withered away. In its place an ethic came into existence in which the entrepreneur must render account directly for his/her conduct.
- the institutional shift in which NGOs work directly with the business community rather than invoking links to the government when trying to bring about social change.

These two developments sensitised companies to moral criticism and stimulated them to take it seriously, yet it also led them to analyse this ethical criticism in financial and economic terms.

The inclusion of organisational and operational matters within business ethics and the shift towards CSR implied clear gains for the young field. It has made the morality of business more accessible and manageable. There is no need to explain to entrepreneurs that they must take into account critical attention from customers, media, citizenry and government, each having its own specific social expectations. The definition of CSR based on the triple-p, and the elaborate ethical and social criteria used to evaluate companies' social qualities delineate the field clearly. Companies have a bad day when they seem to sink in the Dow Jones Sustainability Index of respectable companies. At the very least, the broad range of workshops and training courses sustains awareness that moral competence and moral leadership can be acquired and must be maintained and that they are not simply inherent.

But there is also loss, practical and theoretical. A practical loss is that CSR is felt to be less demanding than developing well-considered and elaborate moral stances when faced with business dilemmas. As long as a company is able to maintain a mix of the three p's, it will normally assume that it satisfies standard ethical requirements. Manageable compromise replaced the non-negotiable fastidiousness associated with business ethics. There remained matters to discuss, of course, but there was no attempt to squeeze blood from a stone. One characteristic of this attitude is a persistent but unfortunate suggestion reflected in some statements on CSR, being that "Corporate social responsibility is voluntary but is not free of obligation". That incantation is intended to shore up ethical reputations while staving off ethical demands. Of course, CSR is not always imposed by law, but that does not make it ethically optional in the sense of not obligatory. Ethics knows no optional obligations. CSR apparently does. That is a substantial difference. Motivation also becomes shallower in the transition from ethics to CSR. The fundamental objective of much of what goes under the name of corporate responsibility is the company's reputational damage control, keeping down costs when a court case drags on, getting a step ahead by anticipating legislation that will pass sooner or later and, all by all, profiting from being known as respectable and environment-minded. Each of these motives is defensible and ethically legitimate, but not really stunning. All attention goes to sensible – not ethically well-considered – actions. We may well fear that the transition from ethics to CSR will pay for its great accessibility with a loss of profundity.

This also applies to theory. The joint venture of business ethics and organisational sciences has made change management the main expertise, even of practising ethicists. Methods and techniques take precedence over critical analysis, because the latter is not the prime foundation of market demand. The two specialisations have carried a backpack full of step-by-step plans and models to a plateau from which they see a broad field of operation, but little that is new. They can only ask "Do we stay here or continue on? If we continue on, where to and how?"

The Future: A Phase for Broadening and Deepening

From the very start, business ethics portrayed itself as a special branch of ethics, all with the best of intentions, but without much other expertise beyond general ethical tradecraft. Then it somewhat overenthusiastically joined the fast action in the market, where it imperceptibly adopted the language of change management. Now it must shed its first and second naiveté and develop the deeper expertise of analysis and reflection.

To advance from a plateau one first must descend some distance to familiar territory before ascending to new heights. What does that mean for business ethics in its present state of development? It has several meanings. Without detracting from the importance of responsible business conduct, it means above all that we must once again concentrate on conspicuous business cases, must resume the slow work of ethical analysis. Which moral judgement is defensible in specific cases? What is a well-informed moral assessment and how should it be developed? In other words, what are the technical requirements of a proper moral judgement? But we must also ask whether the business community – is willing to put energy into developing ethical judgments and what society may expect of business. Questions that pop up are e.g. How far do a company's responsibility and duty to help extend? What should market participants include in their task package? What tasks should the government shoulder? These are substantive issues with an unmistakable moral purport. The return to case analysis pursued here is more than a means against shallowness. It is also a way to draw attention to new dilemmas and issues that society and the market will have to face in the future and for which the step-by-step plans offer no solutions or on which they have reflected too little. Think of sequential responsibility and cessation of business activities. When is enough, enough? The present volume offers the basis for reflection on these issues in the form of recent European case studies on which general and business ethicists offer commentaries. Business ethics has matured to the point where it can and must follow up on questions currently under discussion in general ethics.

Although resurgent attention for case study is needed, on its own it is not sufficient. We would remain too close to the first phase of business ethics, case analysis. We must cultivate new fields, ask new questions and develop new methods. For this reason we turn to experts in other fields than ethics in this book. Ethics must recognise that it cannot do everything alone. Questions arising today along a broad horizon address institutional contexts within which business cases occur. Is it not illusory to believe that companies and entrepreneurs will freely set their own ethical standards? How much room do a company's structure, the market's laws and supranational directives, international agreements and de facto balances of power leave for an unambiguous ethical business procedure? Within which institutional configurations do companies operate? If these configurations can explain many aspects of conduct, is each explanation also a justification? In short, we must take the institutional dimension of business ethics into account. That is why, in this book, we draw attention to the institutional dimension of business ethics in the commentaries on the business cases that make up the principal part of the book. It is discernable in many of the questions business ethics addresses. Renewed attention for business cases and attention for the institutional dimension can lead to a new phase in the development of theoretical and practical business ethics.

Chapter 2
Moral Competence

Henk van Luijk and Wim Dubbink

Abstract In our modern, complex society an ever stronger appeal is made upon each person to make proper moral judgments and act on them; this also goes in commercial life. Viewed positively, this is caused by the emancipation of the citizen and the individual. Viewed negatively, it is a consequence of the growing individualization of modern society. This growing appeal demonstrates the practical moral relevance of analyzing cases. Analyzing cases can help to strengthen a person's capacity to reflect on moral issues. Moral reflection relates to the ability to recognise a moral issue when it arises in practice and then to deal with it in a deliberate and articulate manner. Still, moral reflection is not all that counts in real life – it may not even be the most important thing. A moral person also needs moral competence. A morally competent person takes her conclusions seriously, makes them part of her mental and moral life. It shifts attention from cognition to willing and acting. Moral competence presupposes self-reflection and self-control. The degree to which a person will need her moral faculties in the course of her life is partly a matter of luck. However, a person, unlucky enough, having to make tough calls in her life, cannot argue that she ought to be excused for her moral failings because of her lack of luck.

Introduction

In a discussion on Dutch construction fraud, an experienced attorney very familiar with the business community said, "Ethical awareness in the construction industry is close to zero". People found his comment was shocking. Is the whole building trade really made up of cheats and scoundrels? No, that is not so, and that is not what the speaker meant. His assertion was much more interesting. He observed that the construction industry saw no need to submit its own actions to an explicit moral judgment. "We builders do our work to the best of our ability; we know how things work; we know the customs in the trade and keep to them, because that works

---

Henk van Luijk is deceased.

best. There is not much else to say". The comment is interesting because it contains two messages. First, they do exist apparently: normal functioning adults that are seldom if ever concerned about the ethical side of what they do. Second, one often encounters this attitude as characteristic of a specific group or industry. Thus, in the coffee and tea trade, the rules of conduct are, or at least long used to be, much kindlier than in the petrochemical industry; people are more on their guard with a second-hand car salesman than with desk clerks in a public library. Apparently moral sensitivity is unevenly distributed. Apparently you can expect a greater feeling for ethics in one branch or social group then in another. Is that bad, and if so, can it be corrected?

Is that bad? Either way it is a fact of life that people do not keep their moral flame burning constantly high. A pilot light is often good enough for when it is needed, with the risk, of course, that the breeze of unexpected moral confrontation may abruptly extinguish it. That is unfortunate, but is it also a turn for the worse? It is becoming increasingly so today, for society and for individual citizens. In an increasingly complex society in which authority is fading, laws remain a step behind, religion becomes debased and contacts fragmented, morality – as separate competence – is becoming more necessary as prescriptive and cohesive factor. More than ever, people feel caught in a wave of individualisation that continuously forces them to make autonomous decisions, including in ethical matters. In many cases people find that positive, because it gives them room to live and be responsible for their lives in the manner they choose. It becomes negative when, at the same time, ethical reflection is minimal, social ties become ever more complex and room for individual initiative is cluttered with moral opportunism turning sometimes this way and sometimes that, with no discernible direction. At such times, a dearth of ethical competence can be painful.

Can it be corrected? Is it possible to reinforce moral reflection, to increase people's moral competence? Of course, and we need to look into that. A book offering several case studies with moral implications as avenue of approach for an exercise in taking an ethical stance, as this one does, may leave no uncertainty about what is needed for a mature moral position. First we must identify and define moral reflection and moral competence.

Reflection on and Competence in Ethical Questions

Moral reflection relates to the ability to recognise a moral issue when it arises in practice and then to deal with it in a deliberate and articulate manner. It is a largely cognitive skill supported by moral alertness and sensitivity, because ethical problems only become apparent to those interested in them. Yet interest alone is not enough for proper moral reflection. You have to take the trouble to analyse problems by tracing the their roots, the moral principles at issue and by determining which rights and interests of which specific persons and parties must feature in the decision. Next you must investigate the possible positions and the arguments for the various options and then decide what ultimately ought to weigh most heavily. It is a long drawn-out procedure, but one worth the effort, because it can provide a grasp on what at first seems to be an intricate tangle of considerations and claims and it can lead to a stance that you consider satisfactory and others consider convincing.

The good news is that moral reflection can be learned. Over the years, rich experience has accumulated in developing step-by-step plans that lead people through dilemmas (Van Luijk, 2000; Karssing, 2000; Bolt et al., 2003). The signposts may be different, but the route is essentially the same: delineation, analysis, argumentation, consideration and conclusion. This road appears passable and, when well-travelled, undeniably advances the cognitive skill of moral reflection. The rest of the news is that moral reflection alone is not enough. Reflection is good, competence is better.

Moral competence adds action to moral reflection. Being able to analyse, argue and draw conclusions when faced with a moral issue does not in itself make someone morally competent. This person must also be able to make the shift to willing and acting. A morally competent person takes her conclusions seriously, makes them part of her mental and moral life. She identifies with them in an act of mental appropriation. In a conclusion on a situation in which an actor actually played a part, the competent person reasons: "I see it like this, and I and my significant others are convinced there is good reason for this, so I'll do it". That is her attitude. When reaching a conclusion about a case in which she was not actually involved, the competent person truthful attitude is: "That's what I would do if I were in the same situation". Morally competent people suit actions to words. They identify with the case and the insights it produces and act accordingly. They say what they mean and mean what they say. This demonstrates the gravity of a moral viewpoint. An outsider's viewpoint is never sufficient in ethical matters. One cannot say that "He or she must act in this or that way under those circumstances, but when I am in those circumstances I have another option". People passing a moral judgment on another also commit themselves. This means that moral competence presupposes two things: *self-reflection* and *self-control* (Doris, 2002). Moral self-reflection implies linking your conclusion ("this is how one should act") to your motive and subsequent actions ("so I shall do it, because that's how I want to be"). Self-control is a guidance mechanism that ensures that your will to do what you feel is right does not weaken. Self-reflection and self-control are necessary and sufficient conditions for moral competence. After all, ethics is about serious matters and makes serious demands.

Moral reflection can be learned, in part it is a skill that can be practised. You can even take exams in it and, if you pass, earn a diploma as trained analyst in moral matters. But what about self-reflection and self-control? Can you learn or improve self-reflection (being willing and able to adopt what you consider required, as motive for your own behaviour) and self-control (your inner defence line against weak will)? How do you acquire moral competence? Earlier on, when we mentioned moral reflection, we encountered several conditions that a moral judgment must satisfy to quality as a well-made judgment. There we discussed procedural requirements such as precision in stating the problem, attention for the rights and interests of all parties, careful argumentation that takes counter-arguments into account, unbiased deliberation and an unambiguous conclusion. Here we are speaking about factors that affect character building. What makes one a morally competent person?

Can moral competence be engineered or influenced? If so, by whom or what? Is a person the sole influence on her moral competence? Cannot other people or surrounding circumstances impact on a person's moral competence? This is basically an empirical question that psychologists and sociologists study. It teases out the operation and weight given to the circumstances or personal disposition that turn someone into a moral personality. But a normative question follows quickly on its heels. What level of moral competence may we expect a person or organisation to have? How far does a person's or company's moral obligation extend? What may we reasonably expect in ethical terms from a properly functioning adult, from a participant in market transactions, from a company? That is what ethics asks. Let's take a closer look at each of these.

What is the source, what are the sources, of morally competent behaviour? How does it happen that people act ethically? Opinions differ, as do experiences. One important view in moral psychology stresses personality, the character that prompts someone's action. This virtue approach says that people's actions reflect what they are; a person's action flows from her dispositions. Carl is quiet at a party because he is shy; Carla is successful in her profession because she is disciplined; Conrad is not open to persuasion because he is resolute. Dispositions that produce morally competent action are called virtues. Someone who is virtuous does not let circumstances catch him off guard. Moral conduct is a question of personality, disposition, character, virtue. Character explains conduct.

Other moral psychologists object to a character-based explanation of moral conduct (Doris, 2002). Situationalists explain moral behaviour by appealing to a person's circumstances. They cite experiments that show that character offers less purchase and predictability than is often presupposed. One such from the 1960s is the famed Milgram experiment on tractability and obedience; Milgram and others have reproduced it numerous times. Subject A was told that he was participating in a study on how punishment affects learning. He had to administer a word association test to subject B. He could hear B but not see him. Each time B made a mistake, A was to administer an electric shock. As the errors accumulated, the shock became more forceful. B groaned distressingly to the point of mortal terror, but the experimenter told A to continue for the sake of the experiment. What A was not told was that B was part of a plot. He pretended. Nearly every psychology manual contains detailed descriptions of the experiment. Psychologically all subjects were reasonably well-balanced individuals. It is disconcerting that while a third of the subjects refused to administer an increasingly strong shock, two-thirds obeyed instructions to the bitter end. Conclusion: when under pressure, everything becomes fluid, even character and resolution. In scientific terms, character's influence on conduct is grossly overestimated.

Another objection concerns virtue theory's generalising character, which suggests that whoever has one virtue has them all. She is honest, so she will also be loyal and courageous. That would make character building very effective. Reinforcing one element directs all. But the facts contradict this optimism. A dutiful civil servant can be an unfaithful husband. Fragmentation is as frequent as consistency when it comes to disposition and personality. Utterly virtuous people stick out from the crowd. But do not people often display an outspoken stability in their responses, which makes their conduct reasonably predictable? Does that not point to virtue and character as morality's main substructure? Not necessarily. Often repetitive conduct will prove to be linked to systematically comparable situations. Opportunity, not character, makes the thief.

Moral psychology's situationists find support among sociologists who study the circumstances in which social conduct occurs and who are thus professional situationists even though some of them also stress the negative effects of nasty character traits and a dubious company culture. Business cases are excellent objects of research into the factors that influence the behaviour of individuals, groups and organisations. How could anyone even think of launching the Challenger space shuttle after repeated and express warnings about the dangers of a cold-weather launch? What went wrong to cause the ferry accident with the Herald of Free Enterprise in Zeebrugge seaport? Sociological analysis produces a multitude of factors running from technical defects and bureaucratic glitches over unadulterated greed and craving for status to collective pressure from the organisation's culture in the sense that "What is right in the corporation is what the guy above you wants from you" (Jackall, 1988; Punch, 1996). Sociological studies led to very revealing, sometimes disconcerting insights, but there were also weak spots. The search tended to concentrate on the dark pages, while morality is not restricted to difficult moments and contestable decisions, either in business or elsewhere. A description of possibly influential factors gains force when it surpasses the mere incidental. It should organise and reveal links rather than just providing an inventory.

We need not try to settle here the controversy separating personality psychologists and virtue ethicists from empirical moral psychologists and sociologists. Such an attempt would probably end on an indulgent middle road in which the situationist had to recognise that earlier experiences, genetic features and character traits do influence conduct and the personalist will have to appreciate that situations and circumstances have an extraordinarily great impact on behaviour and decisions. While such broad statements make few enemies, they also cultivate few friends. Much more important for the purposes of this book is being able to resist the lure of either of the reductionist views. A view that denies virtue its proper place is as unfruitful as a view that only vindicates virtue. A view that denies the impact of institutions and circumstances is as out of touch with the reality of human existence as one that turns human beings into playthings of circumstance.

Moral Luck, Praise and Blame

People with strongly opposing views fight over basic assumptions but at some level they usually also are in agreement with each other on basic assumptions. That is why they are so well able to discuss their disagreements. This also holds for the virtue ethicists and the sociologists. It is striking that both assume that our moral actions are linked to systematic causes that we can understand and control, even if the causes differ by being internal (virtue) or external (environment). But what about the moral meaning of chance circumstances? These are matters that one cannot foresee and can scarcely direct because chance plays a dominant role in them. Yet they can influence whether conduct is ethical. Does chance have moral consequences? Ethics discusses this last point under the heading moral luck or luck in circumstances (Nagel, 1979; Williams, 1981). They do not mean that an ethical life can make a person happy, however true this may be. The point is more trivial. You can be lucky from an ethical perspective in that circumstances turn out to your advantage. There is personal luck, e.g. you are healthy, talented, well off, socially gifted and have a pleasing character. All these factors can spark others' jealousy, make them think, "Who couldn't stay respectable under those circumstances". There is also physical and institutional luck, e.g. your company/organisation operates in an environment with a temperate climate, an advantageous location, high economic and industrial development, a stable government and political constellation, properly functioning legal system, a reliable system for maintaining law and order and fair social provisions. Those operating there are clearly lucky, certainly in comparison with many others. Does this luck have moral consequences? Does it create specific moral obligations? Moral luck also has to do with watching other people or companies come under nearly irresistible pressure. You do not know what you would do under the same circumstances, but luckily, you do not have to confront them. War turns some people into heroes and unmasks others as lackeys or malingerers. The lucky ones do not live in a war zone. Of course, the more worldly wise will warn you to "Make no mistake, doing business is war". But its easy to see the bombast in this. It is more prudent to count your blessings, acknowledge your good luck and realise that morality does not arrive on the wings of chance but must always be won against hotbeds of resistance.

We do not consider a lucky star and favourable circumstances to be the result of ethical merit. Being lucky will not earn you moral praise. But will you, likewise, earn no blame when unfavourable circumstances knock you off balance? That is less obvious. People tend to quote Jean-Paul Sartre, who once said that "The question is not what circumstances have made of us. The question is what we make of what circumstances have made of us". In other words, each person ultimately writes his/her own life story. Modern-thinking Western individuals nearly take that for granted and certainly see it as an encouraging, even heroic, idea. Sartre voices the idea of our inalienable and indestructible inner core as source of our decisions and guardian of our freedom. But can we always count on this inner core and are we always accountable for it? That is the question. As human beings we cannot cease believing in this highly personal inner core, at least not without surrendering fundamental ideas of, and denying our essential experience of, what it means to be human.

References

Bolt, L.L.E., Verweij, M.F. and van Delden., J.J.M. 2003. *Ethiek in praktijk*. Assen: Van Gorcum.
Doris, J.M. 2002. *Lack of Character. Personality & Moral Behavior*. Cambridge, New York, NY: Cambridge University Press.

Jackall, R. 1988. *Moral Mazes. The World of Corporate Managers*. New York, NY: Oxford University Press.
Karssing, E. 2000. *Morele Competentie in Organisaties*. Assen: Van Gorcum.
Nagel, T. 1979. *Mortal Questions*. Cambridge, New York, NY: Cambridge University Press.
Punch, M. 1996. *Dirty Business. Exploring Corporate Misconduct*. London: Sage Publications.
van Luijk, H. 2000. *Integer en verantwoord in beroep en bedrijf*. Amsterdam: Boom.
Williams, B. 1981. *Moral Luck*. Cambridge, New York, NY: Cambridge University Press.

Chapter 3
Institutions and the Institutional Turn in Business Ethics

Wim Dubbink

Abstract Business ethics is in the midst of an institutional turn. This carries over into many dimensions of business ethics, including the organisation of morality. What institutional measures must be taken to ensure that the human representatives of the corporation do not act morally wrong or reprehensible – thereby causing corporations to act morally wrong or reprehensible? The theories on the psychological and sociological causes of human misconduct within the corporation are insightful but still fragmented. We suggest installing order by considering the basic reasons explaining why human agents morally succumb in an organisational context. The institutional turn also has important consequences for the moral analysis of wrong and reprehensible conduct, in particular the validity of moral excuses. It seems that we must conclude that immoral conduct can result from decisions that are all too human and perfectly explainable. We certainly do not have to presuppose sheer evilness on the part of the agent. However, the institutional turn must not lure us into thinking that an immoral deed can be excused simply because it can be explained from a sociological or psychological perspective. There is a categorical distinction between a moral justification and a moral excuse and the conditions under which moral excuse fully exculpates a person are still stern.

Introduction

Let us take a look at a Hollywood TV series, one that follows the standard formula. The A-Team is a good example. The A-Team is about a group of Vietnam veterans mistakenly accused of war crimes committed under the command of Colonel John "Hannibal" Smith. The group supports itself by helping people in need, especially elderly men or couples with beautiful daughters of a marriageable age. Every

W. Dubbink (✉)
Department of Philosophy, Faculty of Humanities, Tilburg University, Tilburg, The Netherlands
e-mail: w.dubbink@uvt.nl

episode follows the same pattern. Some needy person contacts the A-Team because he urgently requires help in escaping the machinations of a wealthy, powerful person who is after his land/business/orchard/daughter or any combination thereof. The A-Team agrees to help this needy person, which usually requires constructing some strange kind of car/tank/machine to ram through a door or wall.

Armed with this vehicle, the A-Team sets out after the rich, powerful person, gains access to his home and engages in fisticuffs. The villain decides to flee and there is a happy ending, in which the beautiful daughter plays a role. The A-Team series contains, implicitly, a clear view of the origin of "morally bad states of affairs" (i.e., injustice). Morally bad states of affairs arise as a result of people's evil deeds. The series has an equally clear view of the origin of evil deeds. Evil deeds are perpetrated by people with evil character traits, such as greed, tyranny or jealousy. Furthermore, far from resisting these character traits, the villain wallows in them.

The views on the causes of morally bad states of affairs and the origin of people's immoral behaviour as depicted in The A-Team series are diametrically opposed to the interesting development in business ethics over the past decade. Business ethics is in the midst of an institutional turn. There is a general recognition that the origin of moral action has institutional roots and that its explanation must be sought in these roots. Human behaviour (moral or otherwise) does not occur in vacuum; rather, people's actions are structured or mediated by their institutional context (Scott, 1981; see also Powell and Dimaggio, 1991).

The idea that action is *mediated* by institutions falls midway between two other, more extreme, views on how human beings act. One alternative is that action is *fully* determined by institutions; the other is that individual agents are completely free to act. People endorsing the former idea assert that people's actions are totally determined by heteronomous forces. Choice and free will, then, are extraneous or illusory. At the other end are those who think that people act with all their options open, in complete freedom; they believe that choices are in no way predetermined. The idea that action is mediated by institutional forces takes a central position between these two extremes. It conceptualises human action as the consequence of a choice, but at the same time recognises that in every situation there are strong forces at work which make one option much more attractive than any other. Deep or radical views on the way institutional forces mediate action will maintain that the framing of the choice situation itself is mediated by cultural forces.

The notion of institutionally mediated action refines what it means to act freely. It is certainly not contradictory to the idea of freedom of action. These two ways of viewing human action are compatible. An average or normal individual acts rationally in letting institutional powers determine his/her choice. A typical example of institutionally embedded action in the marketplace is that people buy products at the lowest price they can find. Various institutional market forces – competition being one – usher human choices in that direction. A different example is that people on the market usually keep their promises. Here, again, many institutional forces are at play. Think of socialisation, in which people develop a conscience, of the presence of the judiciary as an institution, and of social forces, such as the fear of exclusion should others discover that one has behaved unacceptably.

Institutions and Institutes

So, what is an institution? Ever since the late nineteenth and early twentieth centuries, academics have been interested in institutions, although early sociologists like Emile Durkheim and Max Weber did not always use that term. They referred to systems of shared values, norms and convictions that were identifiable in, and that regulated, the social behaviour of groups, classes, religious communities and unions. Economists also turned their attention toward the notion of institutions quite long ago. One example was Gustav Schmoller's nineteenth-century German Historical School, which stressed the social context of economic processes. The laws of supply and demand were not the sole determinants of economic relations and transactions. Schmoller emphasised that the idea of free enterprise owes its success to more than just conformity with the market and high economic efficiency. The market is rooted in an aggregate of political, cultural and social institutions that has a profound influence in terms of channelling economic behaviour.

While the idea that institutions are important is a broadly shared view, this has not resulted in a univocal use of terminology. Some people use the term "institution" in reference to the informal structures of society (Fukuyama, 2006), while others use it to refer to formal aspects of the societal structure, such as the police services and the judiciary (Rawls, 1999). Similarly, sometimes we use the term to refer to a material entity, like a building with an impressive entrance and all. In such cases the term "institution" is actually identical to the term "institute", as when we refer to the International Labour Organisation (ILO) in Geneva as an institution. But at other times the term is used to refer to intangible objects, such as culture or a particular way of thinking. The concept of an institution has multiple meanings; that much is clear. Recurrent elements in the various ways the concept is used are that institutions are long-term, polyvalent social structures consisting of symbolic elements, social activities and material sources. They are relatively immune to change and transferable to subsequent generations. They provide solidity within social systems. And they monitor and restrain behaviour, while also creating opportunities for, and supporting, activities.

Scott (1995) made an important contribution to this discussion by pointing out that institutions are built – to varying degrees – of regulatory, normative and cultural-cognitive elements. Where the emphasis is on the *regulatory* aspects, usefulness, rules and sanctions come to the fore (e.g., as market constraints). Economists interested in institutions tend to focus primarily on regulatory aspects. The *normative* aspects of institutions are in play when reciprocal social obligations, binding expectations and accepted suitability of behaviour are emphasised. The early sociologists were partial to normative institutions. Anthropologists and cognitive psychologists tend to find themselves attracted to the *cultural-cognitive* elements of institutions as these become manifest in modes of thought, implicit truisms, cognitive patterns and frameworks that sustain meaning, discernment and insight.

Scott's categorisation can be supplemented with a classification in terms of the *levels* on which institutions operate. It is quite customary to distinguish between the micro, meso and macro levels, which correspond to the individual, organisational and societal levels. While this division is often helpful for clarifying matters, there is also the problem of its lack of specificity. An alternative classification, which does greater justice to the place and function of institutions within our historical context, distinguishes among the levels of the *world system*, the *political society* in which one lives, the *organisational field* in which one operates on the basis of shared cultural-cognitive and normative frameworks (e.g., the educational system), the individual *organisation*, and finally the *organisational subsystem* (e.g., staff, line management and leadership).

The Dimensions of the Institutional Turn

The institutional turn carries over into many dimensions of business ethics. One of these is the relationship between business ethics, political theory and macro sociology. One of the most striking aspects of business ethics as it developed in the 1980s was its radical break with the system-theoretic view of the market dominant at the time. Under that tradition, the action perspective was almost completely absent. Actors' conduct was merely the outcome of institutional variables and there was no hope that actions by single individuals could make any difference. This view fitted in well with a modernist, liberal political theory that made sharp distinctions between the political and the economic, the public and the private sphere.

Nascent business ethics flouted that dominant tradition by making a radical choice for a case-oriented approach. This approach gave pride of place to the action perspective of human conduct. A typical case might focus on the question of what Company A should do when faced with dilemma B. The individual conducting business suddenly became the focus of attention and the system perspective would usually be completely absent in analysing the case. The institutional turn acknowledges that focusing exclusively on the action perspective also has its limitations. It challenges business ethics to develop thinking on morality in the domain of the market that does justice to the need to take into account both the action perspective and the system perspective.

Two other dimensions of business ethics for which the institutional turn has been relevant are the organisation of morality and the theory on moral excuses. We will elaborate on these two dimensions in somewhat greater depth, as these seem particularly relevant for the analysis of cases. Case studies often spin out of situations in which an economic agent acted morally reprehensible or even morally wrong, thereby creating a morally bad state of affairs (i.e., burdening third parties with bad consequences).

One preliminary remark may be in order. It may seem a bit odd to focus on the behaviour of *human* agents when we live in a world in which corporations are the dominant agents, also acting morally right or wrong. Still, regardless of how important corporations are, they can not, by their very nature, act without a human being's agency. That is the crucial distinction between a robot and a corporation. This means that corporate moral misbehaviour cannot arise without at least one human agent acting morally wrong or reprehensible, with negligence perhaps being the most common form of morally wrong behaviour. Hence, even if we were solely interested in explaining and modifying *corporate* misbehaviour, we still would have to focus our attention on understanding *human* behaviour within the corporate context.

The Organisation of Morality

The institutional turn greatly heightened interest in the ways that morality can be organised within organisations. It has led to a recognition that the relationship between a human agent's deeds on behalf of the organisation and the impact of the organisation's deeds on third parties is usually only indirect. There is a breach between the severity of the consequences of organisational actions and the severity of the agent's deeds that gave rise to those consequences. The institutional mediation works as a lever magnifying the consequences that result from an agent's deeds. The mechanic who either made a mistake or conducted an act of sabotage at the chemical factory in Bhopal, India, thereby releasing an enormous cloud of poisonous gas, was clearly in the wrong, technically and morally. Even if he was not a saboteur, as has been suggested, he should never have agreed to perform maintenance work while the safety system was not up to standard, as was usually the case. At the same time, these misdeeds were not in proportion to their consequences for third parties.

Still, the fact that there is no evil genius at the controls behind many immoral deeds in the marketplace does not make the consequences any less severe. This generates attention for the organisational aspects of morality. That attention has led to what we might refer to as a more technical approach to the immoral deeds of organisations and the reprehensible and immoral deeds of people within organisations, an approach less concerned with moral categories like responsibility and culpability and more with taking simple but effective precautions with regard to the reprehensible immoral conduct of human agents in an organisation. The starting point for this technical approach is that it is much more important to ensure that the consequences of organisations' deeds do not impact third parties than to be able to ascertain afterwards exactly who bore responsibility and blame for what. An ounce of prevention is better than a pound of cure. The focus of the technical approach falls on two questions: What specific institutions within organisations give rise to morally unacceptable effects? And what institutional design for organisations is best able to prevent these effects?

Recent years have been productive for the technical perspective. A multitude of institutional mechanisms to explain immoral behaviour within organisations has been uncovered. There is, for instance, the influence of aspects of the formal institutional structure, such as misdirected wage-related stimuli (Paine, 1997). Many studies also draw attention to the impact of organisational culture and other informal aspects of the organisational structure (Vaughan, 1982), institution-based communication problems – e.g., a strong hierarchy that hinders bottom-up communication (Waters, 1978) – and a lack of moral education among employees (Trevino and Weaver, 2003).

However valuable all this theory may be, it also has its limitations; it is very fragmentary. Given the current state of the theory, we cannot offer practitioners much more in terms of advice than to say that in some cases organisational culture can explain immoral deeds, while in other cases the formal structure or some other cause plays an important role. This article is not the place for engineering a great synthesis. We will merely try to create a modicum of order by abstracting from the institutional mechanisms and consider the basic reasons given to explain why human agents go along with institutional pressure and consequently succumb morally in an organisational context.

There seem to be four basic motives (i.e., four types of human agents in the danger zone). Several authors (e.g., Boatright, 2004) stress that some people are pretty much nothing more than economic actors, who can do nothing but respond to economic stimuli. Morality as a distinct reason for action is either a weak force or lacking entirely. This means that these people will only do the morally right thing if there is also a non-moral (i.e., economic) reason for doing so. It also means that they will succumb morally as soon as the action dictated by economic stimuli diverts from the morally right course. Moral failure in the banking crisis is sometimes explained by this model. The bankers did not comply with morality because it simply was not economically rational for them to do so. Other authors point out that some people are unable to free themselves from a natural tendency, or culturally determined norm, to follow orders at whatever cost (Bauman, 1989). Still other authors point out that some people working in organisations are morally immature. Their education included reading, writing and arithmetic but left them stuck at a stage of moral development that is not commensurate with their age or responsibilities (Trevino and Weaver, 2003). The last group of people has a natural or culturally determined tendency to sidestep responsibility whenever they have the chance.

This bleak summary of human ineptitude demonstrates its value primarily when we ask how we can prevent actions by or within organisations from having a morally unacceptable impact on third parties. If we want to take full precautions, then we must design organisations to accommodate the fact that in morally demanding situations, at least some of the people within an organisation will act like those spurred by purely economic calculations or like morally immature actors or like someone who takes advantage of every opportunity to sidestep responsibility. Over the last 20 years, business ethics' answer to the question of how to take this into account has grown enormously. The business ethicists' initial answer on how to prevent immoral conduct was to develop a code. It became quickly clear, however, that a code on its own had little effect. "Coding" proved to be much more suitable. Coding is what happens when an entire company, from top to bottom, is made aware of the importance of morality, of establishing specific rules and of the ease with which these rules can be broken in an organisation (Kaptein and Wempe, 1998). These days, coding is making way for the more comprehensive idea that organisations need ethical management programmes. These comprise several components, such as drafting a code, appointing ethics managers, providing permanent, or at least periodic, schooling, clearly delineating responsibilities, establishing unambiguous rules and control systems, and protecting whistleblowers (Crane and Matten, 2004; see also Trevino and Weaver, 2003).

The Organisation of Morality: The Future

The challenges facing the organisation of morality can be divided into those related to refining the diagnosis of immoral and reprehensible conduct by agents in an organisation and those related to refining the precautionary organisational design (therapeutic suggestions). Diagnostically speaking, the greatest challenge is to work out a unifying sociological theory of moral action. Prerequisites for this are determining how the various explanations (like culture or formal structure) relate to one another and determining the conditions under which they are valid. The moral presuppositions for these explanations will also have to be included.

Therapeutically speaking, the greatest challenge is to align two theories regarding prevention that have been drifting farther and farther apart. At one end, many authors still reason along the lines of improving codes, coding and ethical management programmes (Trevino and Nelson, 2004; see also Trevino and Weaver, 2003). These authors keep looking for clever new institutions that would be useful, or even indispensable, in preventing immoral behaviour within organisations. At the other end, we have a handful of authors who are critical of this line of thought (MacLagan, 1998). They do not disagree with the idea of prevention but object to the implicit assumption of the dominant prevention strategy. This assumption is that increasing the level of monitoring and supervision will some day lead to an organisational design less prone to inducing agents to commit reprehensible or morally wrong conduct. The opposing authors have important moral and strategic objections to this assumption. From a moral perspective, they have observed that the ultimate goal of ethical programmes should be for people in organisations to adopt a more moral stance. To their minds, the greatest danger of ethical management is that people will simply factor ethics into their plans as if it were one more variable in a formula. The means would then defeat the end. From a strategic perspective, these authors observe that despite all efforts, ethical management programmes always fall short when their implicit strategy is one of ever-increasing supervision. Surveillance alone will not get organisations to toe the ethical line.

Accordingly, these authors argue that organisational design should devote more attention to enhancing the moral autonomy of human agents within the organisation. Compliance with an ever-growing number of rules and procedures should not be the objective and is not going to work. Moral autonomy – at least that of some people – ought to be given room to manoeuvre. Freedom of speech for people within organisations and reciprocal critical examination are often mentioned as key instruments for attaining this goal. Seen in this way, the organisation that encourages its employees to search honestly for and disclose skeletons in the closet – with due regard for procedure – will be the organisation that does the most to prevent immoral behaviour. As yet, though, not many organisations dare to put their trust in their employees' moral autonomy in such a radical fashion. Controlling the workforce and enforcing compliance is considered the safer option.

Moral Excuses

The institutional turn has important consequences for the analysis of morally wrong and reprehensible conduct, in particular the validity of moral excuses. The acknowledgement of moral excuses implies that we distinguish between the immorality of a given *act* and the immorality of the *agent* performing it. When a person puts forward a moral excuse, she tries to show that she should not be held morally accountable, in full or in part, for the morally wrong deed she committed because of certain morally significant circumstances. When a moral excuse is accepted as valid, people acknowledge that there are indeed reasons to separate the deed from the person involved. The person should not be held fully accountable for the wrongness of the deed. Consequently, she is either not blamed at all or blamed less for the morally wrong deed. Some typical exculpatory conditions are ignorance and compulsion. We do indeed we find it unreasonable to blame a person for the unforeseen and unexpected consequences of a deed; in a similar vein, we exculpate a mother, at least in part, for not protecting her children from a incestuous father if it turns out that she was terrorized herself and kept in isolation in the house without the social capital needed to stand up against her husband.

The institutional turn in business ethics is relevant for our thinking regarding excuses because it greatly increases our ability to understand the behaviour leading up to immoral deeds as the actions of a normal person ("one of us") under particular circumstances. Sensitivity to the normality or prosaic nature of the conduct leading up to immoral deeds is a primary, and crucial, condition for the applicability of moral excuses. Hannah Arendt's analysis of the life and character of Nazi criminal Adolf Eichmann (1963, see also Bauman, 1989) has, of course, greatly contributed to this sensitivity. Arendt introduced the concept of "the banality of evil". Evil does not originate in inherently evil people; it originates in normal – but ambitious – people led astray by an institutional structure. Arendt's conclusions have been criticised and are controversial because she applied her analysis of the normality of evil to the incomprehensible context of the Nazi government. Could it really be that totally normal people were operating in a totally normal way where evil of such magnitude was concerned?

Interestingly, the present-day marketplace may well present a better context for examining the notion of evil reduced to banality. Businesses are geared toward profit, not evil. Their evils are seldom intentional; they are usually the by-product of an allowable, morally neutral action. Indeed, descriptions of morally wrong or reprehensible behaviour in the marketplace contrast sharply with the horrifying stories of morally bad states of affairs throughout European history, such as those of Cortez, who ravaged the indigenous populations of South America, killing women and children just for the fun of it. Whereas we find it hard not to attribute pure malignancy to such people, we are usually struck by the normality or prosaism of the agents involved in contemporary business ethics cases (though there are still some cases where the coarseness of the agents' calculated heartlessness makes a normal person's hair stand on end, viz. Bernie Madoff).

In most cases the business ethicist is tacitly grateful that she was not at the wheel. It is all too uncertain whether she would have acted any differently under the given circumstances. Morally wrong and reprehensible behaviour arises in the grey zones where ordinary people have to make their decisions. Not that improper behaviour is totally unexpected or that those concerned are taken by surprise in most business ethics cases. There are often signals ahead of time and an awareness of minor abuses. But there are also strong forces compelling people to just go along with it. People do not want to lose their jobs; they have ambitions that they don't want to upset; they don't want to be ostracised by the group; they are easily intimidated – just to name a few. What makes matters worse is that people have a strong tendency to underestimate both the risk, on the one hand, and their power to change the course of things, on the other. At the same time, they tend to overestimate their ability to influence a structure or process at the very last minute, just before things really go wrong (as in a Hollywood movie).

A case that illustrates all this quite nicely is the shipwreck of the *MS Herald of Free Enterprise* off the coast of Belgium in the 1980s. The immediate cause of the ship's capsizing was that it left the port of Zeebrugge with its bow doors open; as a result, it quickly took on water and sank even before it was well clear of the harbour. The ship's captain doubtless committed a variety of juridical and moral errors. However, he and his colleagues had repeatedly raised the issue of the departure procedure with management, especially the fact that there was no mechanical indicator to show whether or not the bow doors were open. The management thought this would be too expensive and offered the captains a simple choice: sail or resign. It was left up to an assistant to keep watch and make sure that the doors were shut. To make matters worse, the management relied on a positive feedback system for this. In the interest of time, the departure procedure required the captain to leave on schedule unless he was told there was something wrong with the bow doors. On the day in question, the assistant had fallen asleep and the captain set sail because he had not received any notice not to do so.

What all this teaches us is that immoral conduct can come about from decisions that are all too human and perfectly explainable, without any sheer evilness on the part of the agent. It is therefore only natural to consider the possible validity of moral excuses in most business ethics cases. In fact, nothing seems more natural. In the aftermath of the financial crisis, bankers and financial experts came up with one moral excuse after another: "everybody was doing it"; "bankers are no worse than anybody else" and "the rules and monitoring agencies failed, too".

It is exactly because there seems to be such a natural overflow in terms of emphasising the institutional aspects of human conduct and acknowledging the validity of invoking moral excuses that it is imperative that we qualify our thinking regarding moral excuses. The first important comment is that the institutional turn should not lure us into thinking that an immoral deed can be excused simply because it can be explained from a sociological or psychological perspective. Moral evaluations must be kept separate from sociological and psychological explanations. Just because we understand everything does not mean we ought to condone it. All the institutional turn shows is that it happens to be relatively easy to place normal people in situations where they will ultimately decide to do something immoral. In many institutional contexts, moral behaviour may require extraordinary courage and alertness. This is something we must take to heart in developing theories on organisational design.

Still, we must persist in making a sharp distinction between situations in which someone's behaviour is quite understandable (but no more than that) and situations in which someone can justifiably appeal to a moral excuse. In the case of someone whose behaviour is quite understandable, we may well conclude that we would have done more or less the same thing. But in doing so, we are saying more about our own assessment of our meagre strength of character than about the validity of a moral excuse.

The second important comment is that we must guard against the tendency within commercial life to use moral *excuses* as moral *justifications* of conduct. A morally justifiable deed is a deed that is morally right. Agents performing morally justifiable deeds do nothing wrong. Sometimes when we are called on to judge an unusual act, we sometimes conclude that the deed was nevertheless justifiable: given the circumstances and complexity of the situation, the person acted correctly, even if it seemed odd at first instance. One example might be a mother who kills her fully paralysed child, who she knows did not want to live like that. By contrast, a morally excusable deed is still wrong. Price-fixing, environmental pollution, human rights violations are all morally unacceptable. Hence, even if the agent performing the deed ought to be excused, the deed should be viewed as reprehensible and not to be repeated. If deeds like that are structurally prompted in a domain of action, there is something wrong with that domain. What is more, the agent who has been excused usually bears a strong responsibility to make sure it does not happen again. That is part of the deal of being excused. If a person is excused for lack of knowledge in one particular instance, she ought to make sure that she knows everything she needs to in a second instance.

The distinction between a justified action and an excusable action is also important because excuses rarely *fully* excuse a person. The bank employee handing over money to a bank robber at gun point may be the rare example. We tend to absolve her completely from blame. However, in most cases, the excuse only partly excuses the agent. Hence, the agent is not morally off the hook because of the excuse. She still acted morally wrong to some extent and ought to face the consequences, in terms of guilt and a responsibility to change (e.g., become more knowledgeable) and to preclude a repeat of the circumstances that led her to perform the morally wrong act. Once again, business people seem to have a tendency to interpret the slightest, partial excuse as a full excuse that absolves them from blame. The bankers' reactions to the financial crisis serve again as a nice example.

Furthermore, we must guard against the tendency in today's business practices to think excuses are valid far too easily. There are only a few reasons that can possibly count as valid excuses and the conditions under which they apply are limited. Many arguments that are presented as moral excuses are actually quite lousy or should only apply under very strict conditions. They may help us understand a decision, from a sociological and psychological perspective, but they are morally insignificant. Examples of such arguments are that a decision was necessary for making or preserving one's career, that others were also to blame, that "everybody was doing it" or that "the government did not ensure proper regulation". Even "ignorance" cannot be used too quickly in the business context –

much less quickly than many upper-echelon managers who get into trouble think. They often claim to have known remarkably little of the things that went on in their companies. Still, in many situations – especially in organisations – morality does not depend on what someone actually did or did not know. The morally relevant issue is what a person was *supposed* to do or *should have known* given her role.

One important reason that business ethics, in particular, must be on its toes in terms of guarding the limits of using moral excuses is the justifiability of the free market as a social institution. If we want to avoid the conclusion that the market has an inherent proclivity toward evil, we will have to assume that ordinary people are normally able to withstand the pressure put on them by the discipline of the market, even if it tests their strength of character. Difficulty in legitimating the market as a sphere of action increases in direct proportion to our abandonment of this assumption. If immoral deeds are to be excused all too easily in the market, it will become hard to reject the conclusion that the market is an evil institution itself – or at least an institution unfit for coordinating human conduct. In terms of political theory, that is a huge problem. No political theory can legitimate the market if it has an inherent proclivity to evil. It is irrational for a society to permit an inherently immoral sphere of action to persist.

Moral Excuses: The Future

Looking toward the future, there is still some interesting work to be done in terms of the thinking on moral excuses in commercial life. There remain many uncertainties and ambiguities about the validity and meaning of specific excuses and the possibilities for using them. A case in point is "compulsion" as a moral excuse. When we define compulsion very narrowly as "use of physical force", then there is little question of compulsion in a market context. The major form of compulsion on the market is economic compulsion but that does not involve physical threats. Still, it seems unreasonable to exclude this type of compulsion completely. Sometimes people can fall under such heavy economic pressure that their actions can be excusable – at least in part. Think of a farmer in an emerging country who shoots an endangered animal because it is the only way to get food for his family.

At the same time, recognising economic compulsion as a moral excuse poses an enormous danger. The market is by definition a domain where institutions (competition and rewards) put people under economic pressure. Markets ought to be competitive and ought to discipline agents, on the one hand, while constantly inciting them to pursue profit, on the other. Where is the borderline between acceptable compulsion and enticement (which can not be cited as an excuse) and unacceptable compulsion (which may be grounds for moral excusableness)? What should we think of the situation that mechanics working for Sears found themselves in the 1990s (see Paine, 1997)? The management had made their wages largely dependent on their personal turnover. That gave them a strong incentive to decide to replace parts in cars brought in for repair sooner than was strictly necessary; not to do so would have meant a big cut in pay. Is this a case of compulsion? Can the mechanics correctly invoke a moral excuse to cast off some of the blame? Or is it merely an enticement in which case that would not be allowable? The answer requires a moral theory on market compulsion that we do not possess. The same kinds of questions can be posed about a case in which a person knowingly and willingly overextends her budget to take out a heavy mortgage to buy a house. Is it reasonable for such a person to use her precarious financial situation as an excuse for going along with the ride because she cannot take the risk of being dismissed, when her company puts pressure on her to compromise moral standards? Is that compulsion or a case of tying a noose and then inserting one's head in it? These and other questions prepare us for the case analysis in the following chapters.

References

Arendt, H. 1963/1994. *Eichmann in Jeruzalem. A Report on the Banality of Evil*. Harmondsworth: Penguin Books.
Bauman, Z. 1989. Introduction: Sociology After the Holocaust. In: Bauman, Z. (ed.), *Modernity and the Holocaust*, 6–28. Cambridge: Polity Press.
Boatright, J.M. 2004. *'Individual Responsibility in the American Corporate System: Does Sarbanes-Oxley Strike the Right Balance?' Working Paper*. Chicago, IL: University of Chicago.
Crane, A. and Matten, D. 2004. *Business Ethics*. Oxford: Oxford University Press.
Fukuyama, F. 2006. 'After Neo-Conservatism'. The New York Times 02 June 2006. http://zfacts.com/metaPage/lib/Fukuyama-2006-After-Neoconservatism.pdf
Kaptein, M. and Wempe, J. 1998. Twelve Gordian Knots When Developing an Organizational Code of Ethics. *Journal of Business Ethics*, XVII: 853–869, Dordrecht: Springer.
MacLagan, P. 1998. Developing Organizations: Towards the Moral Community. In: MacLagan, P. (ed.), *Management and Morality. A Developmental Perspective*, 156–173. London: Sage Publications.
Paine, L.S. 1997. Cases in Leadership, Ethics and Organizational Integrity. In: *A Strategic Perspective*. Chicago, IL: Irwin.
Powell, W. and Dimaggio P.J. (eds.) 1991. *The New Institutionalism in Organizational Analysis*. Chicago, IL: University of Chicago Press.
Rawls, J. 1999. *The Law of Peoples*. Cambridge, MA: Harvard University Press.
Scott, W.R. 1981/1995. *Organizations. Rational, Natural and Open Systems*, 4th edition. Upper Saddle River, NJ: Prentice Hall International.
Scott, W.R. 1995. *Institutions and Organizations*. Thousand Oaks, CA: Sage Publications.
Trevino, L.K. and Nelson, K.A. 2004. Managing Business Ethics. In: *Straight Talk About How to Do it Right*, 3rd Edition. Hoboken, NJ: Wiley.
Trevino, L.K. and Weaver, G.R. 2003. Ethical Decision Making and Conduct in Organizations: Individuals, Issues and Context. In: Trevino, L.K. and Weaver, G.R. (eds.), *Managing Ethics in Business Organizations. Social Scientific Perspectives*, 159–184. Stanford: Stanford University Press.
Vaughan, D. 1982. 'Toward Understanding Unlawful Organizational Behavior.' Michigan Law Review LIII/7: 1377–1402.
Waters, J.A. 1978. 'Catch 20.5: Corporate Morality as an Organizational Phenomenon.' Organizational Dynamics. X/x: 3–14.

Part II
Case A: The Pharmaceutical Industry and the AIDS Crisis

Chapter 4
Case Description: The Pharmaceutical Industry and the AIDS Crisis

Marcel Verweij

Abstract Since 1996 AIDS patients can be treated effectively with combinations of antiretroviral drugs. From the beginning this treatment has been very expensive and therefore unaffordable and unavailable for millions of patients in developing countries. As a result, pharmaceutical companies have been criticised because for their price policies and for holding on to patents that ultimately impose constraints to access to lifesaving treatment. On the other hand, pharmaceutical companies have developed various programs as part of their corporate social responsibility policies. Some of these programs indeed aim to expand access to treatment for AIDS patients. Examples are price reduction programs, donations, but also decisions to refrain from enforcing patent protection in developing countries. The question remains however to what extent pharmaceutical companies have moral obligations to make their lifesaving products affordable for people who need them. The problem is illustrated with policies of one of the leading pharmaceutical producers, Roche.

Fatal Illness, Expensive Medicines, Wealthy Pharmacists?

During a demonstration in March 1987, an activist group called ACT UP (AIDS Coalition to Unleash Power) managed to halt trading on Wall Street for a few minutes. The demonstration drew an enormous amount of attention. ACT UP's most important objective was to speed up patients' access to experimental AIDS medicines. The focus was on a medicine called AZT, the only AIDS inhibitor available at that time. Shortly after the demonstration, the American Food and Drug Administration (FDA) announced that it would speed up its procedure for approving new medicines. In subsequent years, ACT UP played an important role in the struggle to increase availability of and access to anti-AIDS medicines. Highly visible,

M. Verweij (✉)
Ethics Institute, Faculty of Humanities, Utrecht University, Utrecht, The Netherlands
e-mail: M.F.Verweij@uu.nl

non-violent actions successfully exerted pressure on the pharmaceutical industry to lower the price of AIDS inhibitors.

AIDS treatment has improved dramatically since 1987. A cocktail of antiretroviral drugs (ARVs) can effectively control the illness, allowing AIDS patients to live reasonably normal lives. Although there is no cure in sight, persons with HIV, who consistently follow a strict course of treatment in which they take various medicines several times a day, can keep the illness under control with a very low virus level in their blood. However, this treatment is not destined for all AIDS victims around the world. The treatment is complex and expensive; it is accessible and affordable for health care insurers in many Western countries; it is not available or affordable for most patients in developing countries. A large majority of all people with AIDS is deprived of AIDS inhibitors.

The AIDS crisis in Africa and Asia is giving a new dimension to the pressure on companies to provide better access to medicines. On one side, criticism is levelled at GlaxoSmithKline (GSK), Merck Sharp & Dohme (MSD), Roche, Novartis and other large multinationals that sell their medicines at high prices despite their wealth and profitability. On the other, the World Health Organisation (WHO), UNAIDS and many non-governmental organisations (NGOs) work with these same pharmaceutical companies to set up programmes aimed at increasing access to anti-AIDS treatment and lowering prices in developing countries.

Roche

The most important manufacturers have drastically lowered their prices in recent years. They sell their antiretroviral drugs in developing countries at prices that are up to 90% lower than the price in developed countries. In 2004, Roche took a step that none other at that time seems to have taken. Roche announced that it would not take out patents in least developed countries for existing and new antiretroviral HIV therapies. It would also refrain – in those countries – from taking action against generic versions ("copies") of its products.[1] This offered developing countries a legal option to manufacture generic medicines or to import them from India, Brazil or other countries subject to less strict patent regulations. Roche contributes in this way to increasing access to much-needed AIDS medication.

This case study focuses on how this course of action should be viewed from an ethical perspective. If we accept that lowering prices and maintaining a flexible approach to patents does, indeed, help more AIDS patients gain access to the medicines they need, that would seem to be morally praiseworthy at the very least. (CoreRatings, 2003). But one could also posit that Roche is simply doing what is to be expected of a company with its expertise, abilities and profitability. This would then have nothing to do with benevolence but with a moral *obligation* – a duty to help or an obligation to do good. Roche considers its course of action one

---

[1] Roche, "Removing Barriers; Increasing Access", brochure, www.roche.com.

part of its corporate responsibility. But this understanding leaves open whether we can consider this to be a strict obligation. If, when viewed from the perspective of benevolence, Roche or another pharmaceutical company has a duty to increase access to medicines, that means that this obligation also applies to other pharmaceutical companies – at least to the extent that they are in a similar position. A strict obligation raises many ethical questions: How far does it go? Is lowering prices or waiving patent rights sufficient? There is also the question whether an obligation to help might not be stretched so far that it demands that the company make too great a sacrifice. In short: Does an obligation rest upon Roche and similar pharmaceutical companies to help this group of patients and, if so, how far does this obligation extend? We should also note that while the central issue here concerns the moral duties of a pharmaceutical company, there is no doubt that combating AIDS is not only, and not even in the first place, the business community's responsibility. An effective response to the AIDS epidemic is only possible when many parties contribute (national governments, UN, WHO, NGOs, civilians). As we will see, this also plays a role in the arguments for the pharmaceutical industry's moral duties.

AIDS: More than an Illness

HIV (Human Immunodeficiency Virus) is the cause of AIDS (Acquired Immune Deficiency Syndrome). This virus destroys the immune system, which leaves a patient susceptible to numerous types of infections and varieties of cancer – illnesses against which healthy people are normally well protected but which are ultimately fatal for AIDS patients. HIV is transmitted through unprotected sex, transfusion of infected blood products and sharing needles when taking drugs. Infected mothers can also infect their babies during pregnancy, birth and breast-feeding. In the early 1980s, AIDS seemed to touch mainly homosexual men in the West. However, in time HIV proved to spread more broadly and rapidly in developing countries in Africa and Asia. There, unprotected heterosexual contact and mother-child transmission are the most important avenues for spreading the virus.

By 2004, nearly 40 million people around the world were infected with HIV. In 2004 alone, 3.1 million people died and nearly 5 million became infected. Most of these live in Africa. In sub-Saharan territories, 28 million people are thought to be infected with the HIV virus. The percentage in some countries is extremely high. In Botswana, an estimated 40% of the entire population is seropositive. Life expectancy in these countries has fallen sharply (UNAIDS, 2004).

The high morbidity and mortality in southern Africa is not merely a public health crisis. Since fatalities are mainly among young adults, children are growing up orphaned. The working-age population in these countries is falling sharply. Infection, illness and death are affecting the age category that is most essential for the labour market. The public health crisis is becoming an economic disaster that is pushing emerging economies in southern Africa into a still deeper crisis. The struggle against the AIDS epidemic is coming up against a variety of problems. Proactive HIV prevention (information, safe sex, proactive testing, etc.) is needed, but difficult. Having HIV is often a taboo, unmentionable between partners. This makes practicing safe sex difficult. The Roman Catholic Church and other religious organisations reject the use of a condom during sex. Often no condoms are available. Poverty forces women into prostitution, where unsafe sex is the rule. In some countries, the spread of AIDS goes hand in hand with war and rape. Sometimes people even deny that AIDS results from sexually transmitted HIV infection.

At the same time, the total number of people with HIV has remained relatively stable in most developed countries. At least, the epidemic is under control there. The number of new cases is relatively small and most patients respond to treatment with antiretroviral drugs. These medicines do not cure, but they effectively slow the virus' reproduction and thus its destructive impact on the immune system. However, AIDS inhibiting therapy is complex. Treatment normally consists of a cocktail of three drugs, each of which combats the virus in a unique manner. The complexity lies in the number of medicines that must be taken daily at set times according to a fixed schedule. Furthermore, regular monitoring is needed. As soon as effectiveness declines, a different combination of drugs is required. The fixed schedule is extremely important: if the therapy is not followed meticulously, the virus can become resistant to the drugs used. The therapy is also expensive. In the Netherlands, a cocktail of antiretroviral drugs for an AIDS patient can cost €10,000 per year. Standard health insurance reimburses the cost of the treatment, making it accessible to patients in the Netherlands.

The situation is different in developing countries. In Zambia, Congo, Burkina Faso and similar countries, the per capita health care budget is under $55 a year.[2] Few, if any, are able to afford regular treatment at Western prices. It is true that pharmaceutical companies sell AIDS inhibitors to developing countries at sharply lowered prices; but even then, these drugs remain beyond the means of most patients. In developing countries, only 7% of all people infected with HIV have access to AIDS inhibitors (UNAIDS, 2004).

Patents, WTO and TRIPS

One important element in the discussion on the accessibility of antiretroviral drugs is that these medicines are patented. The objective of patenting is to allow inventors and companies to market their discoveries, but this often leads to high prices for patented products. Allowing every competitor to produce generic versions of new discoveries would undermine the economic motive for research. Patenting innovations gives the "owners" a temporary monopoly that allows them to profit from their discoveries. The patent recognises and protects the innovator's intellectual property.

---

[2]For the year 2002. In comparison: the Dutch average expenditure on health care is $2554 per capita. www.who.int/countries. Last viewed October 25, 2005.

Although, in granting monopolies, patents place restriction on the "free market", they are primarily intended to promote the development and dissemination of innovations. That is why international patenting regulations (Trade-Related Aspects of Intellectual Property Rights, TRIPS) fall under the jurisdiction of the World Trade Organisation (WTO), the organisation that monitors (free) trade agreements and regulation.

The AIDS crisis sparked much discussion on the specific consequences that TRIPS regulations had on public health. After all, as long as pharmaceutical companies could enforce their patents, the medicines were seldom if ever available for developing countries. TRIPS regulations allow patents to run for 20 years. Only after that may others manufacture a generic version – which would have a drastic effect on the price. However, the TRIPS agreement states that the government of a country with a public health crisis can compel a pharmaceutical company to licence a local manufacturer to produce the medicines needed. The patent holder must, of course, receive reasonable compensation (royalties) for the medicines that can then be produced more inexpensively. As of August 2003, countries that do not have production facilities are allowed to import such medicines from countries that have wrested this licence. Nevertheless, developing countries and pressure groups sometimes complain that although the ability to obtain compulsory licences may exist on paper, Western countries exert pressure not to use this option. The United States, for instance, imposes extra restrictions on bilateral free trade agreements. [3]

For several years, Brazil and India have been major producers of generic version of antiretroviral medicines. India is also a major exporter of these drugs to countries with many AIDS patients. Both countries have legislation that diverges from the TRIPS regulations; their legislation permits producing copies of patented medicines under certain circumstances. Until recently, Indian legislation allowed only production processes to be patented. That law did not forbid producing copies using slightly altered production methods. In Brazil, a patent expires when its developer does not produce the drug in Brazil within a few years. Brazil also makes energetic use of compulsory licences.

All things considered, we can say that the options that TRIPS regulations offer for compulsory licences and import have not led to large-scale accessibility of anti-AIDS drugs for people in developing countries. One possible response is to criticise WTO and TRIPS and to seek innovation in patent regulations. A group of scientists around philosopher Thomas Pogge is working on a proposal. They are attempting to develop a parallel patent system in which pharmaceutical companies receive income based on how their drugs affect global health. As of 2010, the projected *Health Impact Fund* is still to be established. (Hollis and Pogge, 2008; see also Pogge (ed) 2008). Meanwhile, whether pharmaceutical companies could do more, or even should do more, to increase access to these medicines remains controversial.

---

[3] Free Trade Agreement Between the USA and Thailand Threatens Access to HIV/AIDS Treatment, Oxfam Briefing Note, July 2004. www.oxfam.org/eng/pdfs/bn_USThai_FTA_HIVAIDS.pdf

That is why pressure groups and other stakeholders address their criticism to the pharmaceutical industry as well as to the WTO.

Criticism of Pharmaceutical Companies

AIDS inhibitors are unaffordable and inaccessible for most people with AIDS. At the same time, pharmaceuticals belong to one of the most profitable industries. In the first half of 2005, Roche's profits reached CHF 4.2 billion, which equal 30% if the company's turnover. ACT UP and other organisations often use the contrast between the impossibly high price of medicines and the companies' profits to sway public opinion and, with it, the companies' behaviour.[4]

Many other pressure groups and NGOs choose a more argumentative path. They seek publicity in the mass media or professional journals; they write directly to companies or take legal action. The high price of medicines is a major target. Pressure groups often emphasise that these prices are not in proportion to production costs. TAC (Treatment Action Campaign) is one leading South African pressure group. In 2003, TAC took action against GlaxoSmithKline (GSK) and Ingelheim to get them to lower prices. TAC took out ads (see figure) and lodged a complaint with the South African competition commission. The complaint was substantiated with personal stories of people with AIDS. TAC argued that the price of these companies' antiretroviral drugs was two to three times higher than that of generic drugs. TAC concluded that these were excessively high prices – which is forbidden in South Africa.

> The excessive pricing of ARVs [by GSK and Boehringer Ingelheim] is directly responsible for premature, predictable and avoidable deaths of people living with HIV/AIDS, including both children and adults.[5]

Médecins Sans Frontières (MSF, Doctors Without Borders) is another major organisation. Increasing access to AIDS inhibitors is one of MSF's objectives. Although MSF emphasises that governments bear primary responsibility for increasing access, it also points a finger at the pharmaceutical industry. One of its arguments is that medicines should not be regarded as luxury goods in a free market. In an article in the *British Medical Journal* Nathan Ford of MSF puts it this way,

> The director of the International Pharmaceutical Manufacturers Federation recently said: "For people with no income or little income, price is a barrier. I mean I can't afford certainly a car of my dreams, you know, which might be a Jaguar XJE." But medicines are not the same as sports cars, and patients are not consumers: they cannot choose between AIDS and leukaemia, and few can move from Guatemala to Switzerland. Over 90% of the world's medicines are produced in Western countries by companies that develop drugs according to profit prospects, not health needs. This needs to change. (Ford, 2003)

---

[4] Act Up, an NGO based in New York, challenges the price policy of Abbot and in between also the income of its chairman.

[5] TAC, The main complaint against GlaxoSmithKline and Boehringer Ingelheim. www.tac.org.za

4   Case Description: The Pharmaceutical Industry and the AIDS Crisis   39

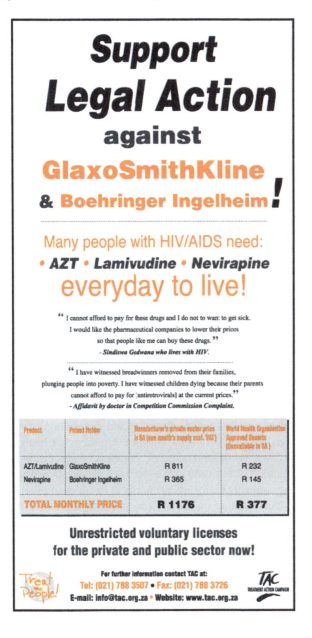

In an editorial in the *Washington Post*, Donald Berwick, President and CEO of the Institute of Health Care Improvement, suggested that AIDS medication should be *free*; he believes that the directors of pharmaceutical companies have the power to bring this about:

> The devastated nations of the world need AIDS medicines... at exactly their marginal costs of manufacture... Here is how it could happen: the board chairs and executives of the

world's leading drug companies decide to do it, period... No one could stop them; none would dare try. For the small profit they would lose, they would gain the trust and gratitude of the entire world. (Berwick, 2003)

We can distil from these actions and publications various arguments for thinking that a strong obligation to help rests on pharmaceutical industries. All arguments start from the presupposition that there is an extremely great need for good AIDS inhibitors, especially in Africa. On this there is no dispute. But why is this the pharmaceutical industry's responsibility? According to the critics:

(1) When pharmaceutical manufacturers keep the price of AIDS inhibitors high to generate maximum income, these companies share responsibility for the sickness and premature death of many people with AIDS. This argument does not explicitly refer to a duty to help; but it did imply that companies caused serious harm to AIDS patients. The (negative) obligation to avoid doing harm is often considered a norm more stringent than the duty to help. This argument gives rise to several questions. First, it is not evident that maintaining high prices can be considered a case of *doing harm* permitting the pharmaceutical industry to be held responsible for AIDS deaths. In addition, this argument presupposes that the industry has an obligation to supply medicines. After all, only then could the industry rightfully be held responsible for the consequences of a lack of medicines. However, it is still unclear whether companies are subject to this moral obligation. In short, this argument presupposes what it wants to demonstrate.

(2) Medicines are not luxury goods whose development and commercialisation can best be left to the operation of the free market. Patients are not consumers that can opt for one product rather than buying another. AIDS inhibitors and other life-saving medicines are really "priceless goods" – goods whose value cannot and must not be expressed in money. Leaving the sales and distribution of medicines to the market opens the door to great social injustice. On the other hand, imagine that it would be reasonable to consider medicines "priceless goods" that were not to be distributed via the market; that would still leave open the question whether this would lead to moral requirements being laid primarily at the door of pharmaceutical companies that definitely operate on the market. In practice, many countries curb the market's influence on their health care systems; examples are universal health insurance and imposing budgets on health care providers and insurers. In such systems, the burden of expensive medicines rests on many shoulders. When countries with a minimal health care budget also have to deal with many cases of HIV, such steps are out of the question. Any solidarity that comes into play will have to be on an international level. In practice, the many price reductions in developing countries are only possible because (and to the extent that) pharmaceutical companies can charge a higher price in developed countries.

(3) Extreme price reductions and the waiver of patent rights – steps that only the pharmaceutical industry can take – will serve as catalyst in the struggle against AIDS and will help overcome other blockages (e.g. lack of infrastructure and basis health care). This is the essence of Donald Berwick's plea. The argument makes

crystal clear that the responsibility for tackling the AIDS crisis does not rest solely with the pharmaceutical industry.

The Pharmacists' Defence

Responses from Roche, GSK, MSD and other companies to the criticism that the high price they charge for their antiretroviral drugs shares responsibility for AIDS crisis are largely as follows. These responses, too, elicit questions and subtleties.

(1) Medicines are expensive, but the price should not be regarded only from the perspective of production costs. While the final production cost can probably be kept down, the cost of development and testing drugs is immense. The cost of scientific research (laboratory research, animal tests, large-scale experiments with patients) and registration can run to hundreds of millions of euros before a drug actually reaches the market. Moreover, this development is very risky. Roche issued a brochure on its approach to patents:

> As a research-based organisation, the prices of products reflect not only the costs of research and development, but also the risks associated with such research and development. (Roche, 2004)

Patents allow only a circumscribed period to earn back the cost of developing a new medicine. That earn-back is essential for a commercial company. Seen from that perspective, the high price of new medicines is far from unreasonable. A counter-argument is that universities and teaching hospitals do a lot of research with public resources and that this research also ultimately leads to the development of new medicines (Angell, 2004). However, it is debatable whether that last is a reason to believe that pharmaceutical companies should set lower prices. It could however lead us to believe that pharmaceutical companies cannot simply focus on maximising profits. By piggybacking on the research of universities which is sponsored by public money they receive indirectly public support and therefore should focus also on public or social responsibility. There are few companies that would dispute that (see the section on Roche at the end of this chapter). A second counter argument brought against invoking development costs is that while these are high, they do not far outpace the sums that companies invest in marketing and advertising.[6] While this argument may be true, it does not lower development costs. The argument seems to be aimed more at stressing the pharmaceutical companies' great financial potential (that can conceivably be used to provide assistance or lower prices) than at underpinning the argument that antiretroviral drugs are unreasonably expensive.

---

[6]Marcia Angell claims in the above mentioned article that the budgets for marketing are two and half times as large as those for research and innovation. This is denied by the Pharmaceutical Research and Manufacturers of America (PhRMA). The marketing budget that Angell refers to contains according to them a number of activities which have nothing to do with marketing. See: www.phrma.org/publications/policy/15.09.2004.1078.cfm

(2) Donations are not a real answer. Although it is obvious that, from the perspective of the duty to help, prosperous companies should donate a portion of their medicines to countries that are unable to pay for them, such action is also not without its problems. Donations are sometimes meaningful, for instance in starting up a pilot project; but they are not a systematic answer to the AIDS problem. Since patients must be treated for the remainder of their lives, the industry must be committed to continue supplying the drugs – and so must be able to charge at least the manufacturing cost. This last argument draws attention to an important aspect – the need for help to be continuous. However, this concern cannot be sufficient reason to restrict donations. After all, even temporary help can be very worthwhile – if not morally obligatory – when the sickness can be halted for a time in a group of patients. That it is not certain whether the same assistance will be available in 1 year or 2 year's time does not detract from this.

(3) The price of antiretroviral therapy has fallen drastically over recent years. In 2002, Richard Sykes, chairman of the board at GSK, noted that six of GSK's AIDS medicines were available in developing countries at prices 90% lower than in the Western world (Sykes, 2002). At the same time, however, he saw that price reductions have had little effect on the use of these medicines in developing countries. That brings us to the next argument.

(4) The price of medicines is ultimately not the core problem. Countries in central and southern Africa simply do not have the infrastructure and health care needed to treat patients adequately. The infrastructural problems and the many other problems implicated in the AIDS epidemic are so large that it is not correct to think that a greater effort by pharmaceutical companies is the primary requirement for turning the tide. The primary responsibility lies with the governments of the countries concerned, even when it is a question of greater access to anti-AIDS medication. Many steps are needed and many problems need to be removed before AIDS patients can receive proper care. The first requirement is a properly working health care system, including infrastructure for testing, monitoring and treatment. The second is that local governments must create the conditions needed for proper care, among which is curbing stigmatisation of, or discrimination against, AIDS patients. The pharmaceutical industry has but a small role to play in many of these problems. At the same time, the industry cannot simply invoke these problems to ignore what it can and must do. Médecins sans Frontières and other NGOs play an important role in setting up pilot projects that demonstrate that the complex routine of treating AIDS is indeed possible in the least developed countries. Donald Berwick's thesis that an extreme price reduction for (or even free) medicines can be an enormous stimulus to overcome all the other problems can be seen as a refinement of the pharmacists' argument that lowering prices does not make medicines more accessible.

It can be concluded that the pharmaceutical industry is not the only one to bear responsibility for providing AIDS patients with greater access to medicines. At the same time, it is reasonable to assert that they should contribute – and to that extent that they have an obligation to help. But the question remains: How far does this duty extend? Is it possible to situate the border between duty and charity with precision? We can illustrate this with the steps that Roche took to increase access to care.

Roche, Social Responsibility and AIDS

Roche, a Swiss company, describes its primary contribution to society as follows:

> Our principal contribution to society is to continue committing substantial resources to long-term research and development aimed at creating diagnosis and treatment options to address the many unmet health needs facing mankind.[7]

The company also states that, in as far as its financial means allow, it is prepared to make significant contributions to the reduction of suffering. Roche has a patent and pricing strategy that helps patients in the poorest countries gain access to its products.

Roche produces three antiretroviral drugs for directly treating AIDS: Invirase (saquinavir), Viracept (nelfinavir), and Fuzeon (enfuvirtide). Fuzeon is a relatively new drug administered intravenously. That makes it (still) difficult to administer this medicine in least developed countries. The WHO recommends the other two medicines as secondary treatment options (when other primary drugs prove insufficient).

Roche has sharply reduced the price of these antiretroviral drugs. Invirase and Viracept are available at "no profit" prices in sub-Saharan countries. According to Roche, these prices are the lowest possible for medicines with a sustainable production method; they are also lower than those of generic versions of the drug (Roche, 2005). In addition, Roche supports numerous public health projects around the work. One example is "Phelophepa": a "health-care train" that traverses parts of South Africa 36 weeks a year, going to places where people have little if any access to normal health care. The train does not offer anti-HIV medication, but does provide other types of basic medical, dental, ophthalmic and psychiatric care. Since 2004, Roche has taken out no patents in countries on the UN's "least developed" list. This holds for current and new medicines, for all illnesses; so it also covers HIV/AIDS. For HIV/AIDS this course of action has been expanded to all sub-Saharan countries. No action is taken against the production or sale of generic versions of Roche's medicines in these countries. That means that no licence is needed to produce generic versions of Roche's antiretroviral drugs (i.e. Saquinavir) in these countries. These countries may also import generic versions from Brazil, India or elsewhere. *CoreRatings* praised this flexible attitude toward patents in a report on social responsibility in the pharmaceutical industry.[8] Of course, not compelling respect for patents still falls short of making medicines directly available in developing countries. But as the supply of generic antiretroviral drugs grows, prices will fall further.

---

[7] www.roche.com/home/sustainability/sus_comm.htm

[8] CoreRatings, 2003: "In 2001, Roche was forced to cut its prices in Brazil after the Brazilian government threatened to licence a government company to reproduce Roche's HIV/AIDS drug. Roche has responded to that, and other recent intense pressure over access to medicines, by introducing one of the most flexible policies on patenting in the sector. Having already donated its

Given the worldwide AIDS crisis, is Roche's approach to patents morally praiseworthy while remaining morally *optional*, or can it be considered a moral *obligation*? If Roche does have a moral obligation to help African AIDS victims, then much farther-reaching help could also be offered. After all, passively tolerating the manufacture of generic versions of its medicines is still far from doing something to help these countries; before these countries can manufacture medicines they need expertise, technology and investment. In January 2006, Roche took steps to transfer knowledge and expertise. CEO William Burns announced that Roche would help companies in least developed countries to manufacture copies of Saquinavir.

> We want to use the knowledge we have developed to help strengthen local manufacturing capability and hope to help as many manufacturers as possible in these hardest hit countries by sharing our knowledge, so that they can learn and benefit from our knowledge.[9]

Once again we must ask whether this is an act of charity or a moral obligation.

Concluding Remarks

These examples of Roche's course of action show that there is no limit to the help that can be given to AIDS patients. That makes it difficult to draw a line between moral obligation and charity. It is reasonable to state that the answer to the moral question "how much help should Roche give" depends in part on the degree to which other parties, companies, governments and civilians work to contain the AIDS crisis. The WHO started its "3 by 5" campaign in 2003. Its goal was to provide antiretroviral treatment for 3 million people with advanced HIV by the end of 2005. By the end of 2005 it was obvious that this goal had not been reached. A report by the International Treatment Preparedness Coalition (ITPC) drew attention to the most important blockages: inadequate leadership in countries suffering from the AIDS crisis where too little priority is given to AIDS and health; insufficient international coordination; and an insufficient and uncertain financial basis

---

malaria patents to the WHO, the company has also said it will not be seeking new patents on HIV/AIDS drugs in the least developed countries or sub-Saharan Africa. Roche no longer has a drugs donations programme as it believes such programmes are not sustainable. Instead the company has strengthened its procedures on differential pricing by changing the packaging on low-priced drugs and monitoring supply and distribution on the ground in Africa. This maximises the social benefit of the programmes and reduces the risk of parallel importation. The company recently adopted differential pricing for HIV/AIDS drugs which it supplies at manufacturing cost plus transportation costs. Roche has said it will not act against infringements of patents of its HIV/AIDS drugs in sub-Saharan Africa (SSA) and UN defined developing countries. If other companies develop generic versions of Roche's HIV/AIDS drugs, Roche will not take any action if they distribute them through SSA and developing countries. However, those companies will not be able to file patents on Roche's products since it owns the intellectual property rights in developed countries. If such companies export outside of these regions, then Roche states it is obliged to take action to protect these rights." www.coreratings.com/site/products/sector_reports/CoreRatings_Pharma_Report.pdf

[9] Press report see: www.roche.com/med-cor-2006-01-12b

for international programmes. In many countries, the stigma of HIV infection hinders access to medicines (International Treatment Preparedness Coalition, 2005). The price of antiretroviral drugs is not the greatest stumbling block. This report shows once again that the criticism that some launch against pharmaceutical companies is simplistic. ("Despite their profits they keep prices for antiretroviral drugs high, which makes them responsible for AIDS patients' premature death".) But this does not answer the moral questions of how far these companies' obligation to help extends and whether they adequately meet this moral obligation.

References

Angell, M. 2004. The Truth About the Drug Companies. *The New York Review of Books*, 51(12), 15 July, 2004.
Berwick, D.M. 2003. "We all have AIDS". *Washington Post*, 26 Jun, 2001, A17.
CoreRatings 2003. Philanthropy or Good Business? Emerging market issues for the global pharmaceutical industry. May 2003.
Ford, N. 2003. "Public Health and Company Wealth." *BMJ* 326:1296 (full text: www.bmj.com).
Hollis, A. and Pogge, T. 2008 *The Health Impact Fund: Making New Medicines Accessible for All*. Incentives for Global Health http://www.yale.edu/macmillan/igh/.
International Treatment Preparedness Coalition. 2005. "Missing the Target." *A Report on HIV/AIDS Treatment Access from the Frontlines.* http://www.aidstreatmentaccess.org/itpcfinal.pdf
Pogge, T. (ed.) 2008 Special Issue: Access to Medicines *Public Health Ethics* ;1(2).
Roche. 2004. "Committed to Making a Difference." *Roche Activities to Increase Access to Healthcare Globally.* www.roche.com/pages/downloads/sustain/pdf/comm_diff_rep.pdf
Roche 2005. *Committed to Making a Difference: Roche Progress in Global Efforts to Increase Access to HIV/AIDS Health Care.* Basel: Roche.
Sykes, R. 2002. Commentary: The Reality of Treating HIV and AIDS in Poor Countries. *BMJ*, 324: 216–217.
UNAIDS. 2004. *Report on the Global AIDS Epidemic.* www.unAIDS.org

Chapter 5
Commentary: The Struggle Against AIDS and the Pharmaceuticals Industry – Are There Limits to the Moral Obligation to Do Good?

Mariëtte van den Hoven

Abstract Anyone presupposing that pharmaceutical companies have a moral obligation to help curb the AIDS crisis challenges us to think about the outer limits of this obligation and about the substance what can reasonably be obliged. The idea that the outer frontier of the moral obligation to render assistance is reached only when one encounters a threat to the actors' fundamental interests runs contrary to our healthy common sense. The borderline with the reasonable seems to be much closer. A need to define the boundaries of reasonable moral obligations and to justify the grounds for putting them there lies at the core of the demandingness objection in philosophy. I show that the Roche case is well suited for launching a discussion on the reasonableness of the moral obligation to render assistance. In doing so I present several arguments and how they could be applied to this case. I did not define what would be a tangible and reasonable obligation for Roche. This cannot be done in isolation for Roche or any other company. It must be done in conjunction with the moral community and in the light of normative theories. What I have tried to show in this article is that extreme positions are untenable. The moral obligation to render assistance in curbing AIDS may not elicit an all or nothing answer. The reasonable may perhaps be negotiable.

Introduction

Today a strong call has gone out to pharmaceutical companies to help contain the AIDS crisis. That is not strange when we consider that pharmaceutical companies hold the key to the medicine chest and can offer an answer to this worldwide and very urgent problem. Therefore, it is often argued that pharmaceutical companies are not being *charitable* when they waive patent rights or even lower the price of medicines, but that they have a *moral obligation* to do so. In this commentary,

---

M. van den Hoven (✉)
Ethics Institute, Utrecht University, Utrecht, The Netherlands
e-mail: M.A.Vandenhoven@uu.nl

I argue that whoever accepts that this is a moral obligation cannot avoid asking whether there are limits to the moral obligation placed on pharmaceutical companies. The answer requires more discussion on the reasonableness of moral obligations.

The Obligation to Do Good

Let us first briefly address the nature of the moral obligation attributed to these pharmaceutical companies and the reason for assigning it. We can interpret this moral obligation as a general moral duty to do good. This obligation is often based on the argument known as the life-saving analogy. This analogy, as Peter Singer introduced it, compares the responsibility for misery in the world with saving a child from drowning (Singer, 1972). Imagine that you are standing near a lake in which a child has fallen. He is in danger of drowning and you are the only one around. In this case you have a moral obligation to save the child because wet clothing counts for little when compared to saving a life. This leads to a more general principle of doing good which states that you must help someone when this costs relatively little effort. This principle is universal as it does not only apply to the child in the lake but also to people dying of hunger and illness in emerging countries. Even more, when you make relatively little effort, you misinterpret the requirements that your obligation to do good places on you when you do not work to alleviate affliction in the world (Cullity, 2004).

The obligation to do good, as universal obligation, applies to everyone that can be considered a moral actor. What does this mean for Roche and other companies? The case study shows that Roche already assumes responsibility by not taking out patents in least developed countries; this permits the development and distribution of generic products in those countries. In addition, the company works with NGOs to provide medicines at cost. Other pharmaceutical companies do similar and/or other things. If we regard these acts as an extension of their obligation to provide help, we encounter an important question: Can we construe the things done as matters about which Roche may decide independently and arbitrarily or must we regulate the substance of a pharmaceutical company's obligation to help? Given the way pharmaceutical companies' actions are being so avidly discussed, we must take the last viewpoint seriously. The consequences for Roche and other pharmaceutical companies could be very extensive. We hear told that these companies should not take out any more patents or should distribute medicines free of charge. The main question, however, is whether that is reasonable. In other words: If we think that companies have a universal obligation to help, then this automatically raises the question how this obligation can and must be met in all reasonableness. This question will certainly arise at Roche and other companies. Given the fact that the company is primarily a commercial business – that its primary interest is to make a profit and to keep its shareholders satisfied – it will want to curb any unreasonable demands drastically. That makes it meaningful for us to explore moral views on reasonable moral claims. Philosophy calls this the demandingness objection. In practice, this subject elicits extreme positions. NGOs sometimes claim that companies should not take out any patents at all or should set up large-scale distribution of free medicines, whereas companies sometimes claim that the obligation to render aid imposes no responsibility upon them. Can a discussion on demandingness shed light on the substance of the obligation to help or about these two extreme positions?

A Close Look at Demandingness

Discussions on demandingness focus on the question whether there are or can be limits to the sacrifices that may be demanded of moral actors. They presuppose that the actors share a strong, intuitive view that some moral obligations lead to disproportionately great sacrifices and therefore that they obviously cannot be imposed. Saving a child from drowning in a lake at the cost of one's clothing is different from pulling a child from a burning building at the risk of one's own life. However, a shared intuitive view cannot justify curtailing the moral obligation to render assistance. The discussion focuses on the grounds for limiting moral obligations and on how these limits should be set.

It is important to know that the demandingness objection was raised in response to consequentialist theories[1] that measured the moral value of deeds against the value of the consequences of these deeds. It states that a morally correct act is that act that results in the greatest attainable good (usefulness, well-being, health, happiness...). It is said that, if anything it is our *duty* to perform those acts and *only* those acts, except for acts that demand extreme sacrifices from the actors, such as danger to life and limb (mutilation, death,...) (Cullity, 2004). In several very critical essays, Bernard Williams has spoken out against the inhuman and alienating ramifications of consequentialist theories (Williams, 1973 and 1981). He thought it troublesome that these theories make no distinction between someone's relations with loved ones and those with (distant) strangers. This denied the importance of special relations and commitments and that put a burden on the actors. Because of their demand to maximise good, consequentialist theories can also lead to unsuitable or immoral suggestions, such as intentionally hurting someone, via torture, or even willingness to kill if this would save or benefit more human lives. Such suggestions are unreasonable and distressing for the actors.

Criticism from B. Williams and others resulted in a discussion on demandingness. One view is that *too much* can be demanded in some cases. This implies that the requirements that we make of an actor on the strength of a specific obligation can be unreasonable and thus must be adjusted or modified. Not all philosophers recognise that demands can be too heavy. They often draw attention to the fact that an

---

[1] The present discussion clearly goes further than criticism of consequentialist theories. Contractualism and the care ethic can put great burdens on actors. Some authors even assert that every ethical theory can be too demanding. See Ashford (2003) and Hoven v.d. (2006).

ethical theory centres on a normative view of how we should deal with one another. They claim that the potential burden on actors comes not from the theory but from our not living in an ideal world. Moreover, it is suspect to claim that some sacrifices are too demanding, because of the enormous observable differences in the degree to which people are willing to exert effort to do good. Despite these sceptics, scholars take very seriously the basic claim of the demandingness objection that there can be limits to what can be asked of moral actors. It is interesting to explore how this objection can be developed in the Roche case.

Ethical Demandingness in the Roche Case

Imagine that Roche would want to defend itself against extreme claims sometimes made during a discussion of the obligation to do good. The most logical, or most frequently used, strategy is to refer to formal responsibilities or bring up practical objections. After all, governments in emerging countries also have an obligation to do more. Western governments share responsibility for containing the AIDS crisis. Furthermore, medicines alone often do fairly little. AIDS inhibitors require a stringently hygienic routine in which health care infrastructure is very important. When that is lacking, providing free medicine brings little solace. The problem with these arguments is that it seems to shift the moral responsibility, or at least to avoid addressing the scope of the moral obligation to render assistance. The underlying idea is probably that a moral obligation to render assistance is an all or nothing question. Whoever is presupposed to be morally responsible must do the utmost possible. I will demonstrate here that Roche and similar companies have no need of this defence. They can invoke the general intuition behind the demandingness objection, i.e. that there are limits to the moral obligation to render assistance and that one cannot demand that pharmaceutical companies be required to do just anything.

Therefore, I do not agree with the idea that appealing to actors' extreme sacrifices is the only way to curb a moral obligation to render assistance. For Roche this would mean that it has an obligation to help contain the AIDS crisis up to the point that its fundamental business interests were put at risk. It is difficult to determine exactly what a company's fundamental interests are short of bankruptcy, but this would be to impose a far too radical moral obligation. It is striking that this type of radical moral obligation to render assistance goes against our common sense intuition and that many think that the limits of what is reasonable were reached much earlier. B. Williams' criticism is a good example of this, because he posits that it is important for people to make their own choices and to carry out their own ground projects. Autonomy and integrity are important values for moral actors; this puts a check on the moral obligations that can be expected of an actor. I call this the argument based on a "chance to live one's own life", which is more than a conservative argument to justify laziness (Unger, 1996) or the normative status quo (Murphy, 2000). It expresses what many people consider valuable and important. Actors must be allowed to flourish as people and that means more than just fulfilling your moral obligations.

5 Commentary: The Struggle Against AIDS and the Pharmaceuticals Industry   51

Roche could appeal to this argument by pointing out that commercial companies must follow several important rules such as keeping shareholders happy, making a profit and exploring new markets. These actions are essential if a commercial company is to prosper. If a moral obligation to render assistance demands sacrifices that have a negative impact on the company, then the situation is no longer reasonable. Roche can certainly try to find a balance between what is and is not directly in conflict with the company's interests. If AIDS medication costs so much that patenting seems necessary to earn back the amount spent, then the demand to waive patents quickly becomes less reasonable. But when waiving patents in the poorest countries has little or no effect on the company's turnover and profit, it cannot be considered either a heavy sacrifice or something unreasonable. In that case, the argument based on a chance to live one's own life does not apply.

However there are other grounds for considering a given action too demanding. Whoever is continually overburdened with moral responsibility could start wondering whether it makes any difference what anyone contributes to moral good. If I encounter a homeless person or beggar every other step I take along the High Street, I'll soon stop donating. An infinite stream of responsibilities and requests for help not only make efforts seem for nought, they leave the actor frustrated. If you no longer feel that you have been able to help because whatever you do it is not enough, then your motivation to act morally is quickly eroded and left barren. This can lead people to become morally indifferent. This is the frustration argument. This argument can quickly surface when we expect Roche to dispense free AIDS inhibitors. Expecting Roche to provide an endless stream of people with medicines for the rest of their lives while new cases of HIV infection keep appearing can quickly overtax the company. Is this a reasonable expectation? To make matters worse, if this is true for AIDS, would it not also be true for malaria and a long list of other diseases? It seems that the frustration argument would label this request unreasonable.

These are two examples of arguments that support the intuitive view that morally reasonable demands can lead to demands that in practice are too heavy to bear. However, there are important objections against this intuition and against the arguments that I have presented. I will discuss three of them.

The first shows that the demandingness objection brings to light a conflict of interest between the actor and his moral duties. It is not a priori obvious why the interests of an actor should be taken so seriously that one can speak of his being overburdened. If morality speaks of what is just and an actor makes a subjective estimate of whether that might not demand too much, it is not obvious that a complaint from the actor can cast doubt on the correctness of the moral obligation. Imagine that the actor's objections can outweigh a moral obligation. Sceptics claim that in that case, the demandingness objection would quickly loose its meaning because the more someone's personal interests deviate from the moral interest, the stronger the experienced conflict will be. This does not at all justify complaints from actors that ethics demands too much of them. An example: Imagine that the environmental norm for emission of a given substance is tightened. This will cause more difficulty for and require greater sacrifice from a company that causes much pollution than it will from an organic farmer. But is that reason enough for the company to claim that the more stringent measures are unreasonable while the organic farmer has already done so much to adjust his own interests. It is often said that because of their commercial drive and patenting system, pharmaceutical companies' interest conflicts with the moral obligation to render assistance in curbing the AIDS crisis. But this rift does not justify lowering the standard of the moral obligation to render assistance.

This argument seems convincing, but has limited scope. The arguments presented above show that there is more at stake than just a conflict of interest. The frustration argument is not so easily put aside. In short, the argument that too much is being asked has not been countered, despite the restraint it imposes.

The sceptics' second objection is that our world is not ideal. It is simply so that we live in a world with great disparities, a world with an enormous rift between rich and poor, healthy and sick, the privileged and disadvantaged. This explains why the obligation to render assistance is so radical, because in an ideal world actors would not be asked to make big sacrifices. We must not complain about the moral principle, but about the circumstances in the world. We might consider this argument impossible to ignore were it not that our daily experience shows that it is very difficult to reach an ideal world. Given that our world is not ideal, we will have to put limits on actors' responsibility. From the perspective of daily morality, it would be too much to expect each person to take up the problems of the whole world. In the end, the argument from a chance to live one's own life and the frustration argument are founded on this idea.

The third objection points out that a definition of an unreasonable contribution is lacking. It is extremely difficult to establish criteria and thus to define what is truly reasonable or unreasonable, hence make claims of unreasonableness arbitrary and suspicious. The sceptic would observe that the relatively well-off will be the first to complain that too much is being asked because they are the ones that can contribute a lot to relieving need without being much worse off for the effort. But why is donating an extra €100 so unreasonable if this can save the lives of several people? Will it diminish our own comfort in any way? How do I decide whether €100 is reasonable or not? What do I use as criterion? Is it my present situation in comparison with the ideal situation (e.g. do nothing vs €1000) or is it €100 (actual request) vs €1000 (ideal donation)?

If we apply this to Roche, we see parallel problems arise. Should Roche weigh its duty to alleviate the AIDS crisis against the way it has contributed thus far to combating other diseases, against what competing companies actually do or against what is ideally necessary to defuse the crisis as quickly as possible? Or may Roche measure every contribution against a company baseline, i.e. not accepting any obligation to render assistance, which would mean that any contribution at all can quickly be labelled enough and reasonable. All standards have important pros and cons, with the greatest risk being that taking one's own status quo or that of a competitor as primary criterion can turn into an excuse for not making any effort at all to satisfy the moral obligation to render assistance. And that would be the worst conclusion to draw from this discussion.

A Final Word

Anyone presupposing that pharmaceutical companies have a moral obligation to help curb the AIDS crisis challenges us to think about the outer limits of this obligation and about the substance what can reasonably be obliged. The idea that the outer frontier of the moral obligation to render assistance is reached only when one encounters a threat to the actors' fundamental interests runs contrary to our healthy common sense. The borderline with the reasonable seems to be much closer. A need to define the boundaries of reasonable moral obligations and to justify the grounds for putting them there lies at the core of the demandingness objection in philosophy. I have tried to show that the Roche case is well suited for launching a discussion on the reasonableness of the moral obligation to render assistance. In doing so I have presented several arguments and shown how they could be applied to this case. I did not define what would be a tangible and reasonable obligation for Roche. This cannot be done in isolation for Roche or any other company. It must be done in conjunction with the moral community and in the light of normative theories. What I have tried to show in this article is that extreme positions are untenable. The moral obligation to render assistance in curbing AIDS may not elicit an all or nothing answer. The reasonable may perhaps be negotiable.

References

Ashford, E. 2003. The Demandingness of Scanlon's Contractualism. *Ethics*, 113: 273–302.
Cullity, G. 2004. *The Moral Demands of Affluence*. Oxford: Oxford University Press, Chapter 2.
Hoven van de, M.A. 2006. *A Claim for Reasonable Morality: Commonsense Morality in the Debate on the Limits of Morality*. Utrecht: Zeno.
Murphy, L.B. 2000. *Moral Demands in Nonideal Theory*. Oxford: Oxford University Press.
Singer, P. 1972. Famine, Affluence and Morality. *Philosophy and Public Affairs*, 1(3): 229–243.
Unger, P. 1996. *Living High and Letting Die: Our Illusion of Innocence*. Oxford: Oxford University Press.
Williams, B. 1973. A Critique of Utilitarianism. In: Smart, J.J.C. and Williams, B. (ed.), *Utilitarianism: For and Against*. Cambridge: Cambridge University Press.
Williams, B. 1981. Persons, Character and Morality. In: Williams, B. (ed.), *Moral Luck, Philosophical Papers*. Cambridge: Cambridge University Press, 1973–1980.

Chapter 6
Commentary: Special Duties and the AIDS-Crisis – A Commentary on the Roche Case

Jan Vorstenbosch

Abstract This comment concerns the question whether with respect to the AIDS-crisis in Africa waiving legally acquired and economically important patents, and other actions on the part of pharmaceutical company Roche, can and/or should be understood as a matter of moral duty. More specifically, the question is whether it is a case of a special duty on the basis of which pharmaceutical companies such as Roche, ought to take certain actions. Four possible foundations of a special duty of Roche are examined: (1) the voluntary, self contracted duties of the company, (2) the special bond that the company has with the victims on account of other causes than self contracting, (3) the special character of the good or the need that the products of the company provide for, (4) and the catastrophic character of the situation we are dealing with. It is concluded that in none of these ways a special duty can be successfully argued for. There may, however, be a case to make on the basis of the general principle that anyone in "Samaritan" circumstances, is bound to do what is in his power to improve the situation of others, at reasonable costs.

Introduction

In this commentary I examine whether waiving legally acquired and economically important patents and other actions of the pharmaceutical company Roche, in response to the AIDS-crisis in Africa can and/or should be understood as a matter of moral duty. More specifically, I inquire whether it is a case of a special duty on the basis of which pharmaceutical companies such as Roche ought to take certain actions. For a clear understanding of what follows, it is important to specify the notion of a *special duty*.

The first specification concerns the *special* character of the duty. Its speciality does not reside in the fact that in special circumstances this moral duty falls to a particular agent, for example because the agent happens to be on the site of the

---

J. Vorstenbosch (✉)
Department of Philosophy, Utrecht University, Utrecht, The Netherlands
e-mail: jan.Vorstenbosch@phil.uu.nl

event or action which invites action, and is in a position to help – such as saving a child which has fallen into a pond. Such a duty can be well understood as the application of a universal principle of a general moral theory. For its application, by individual agents, such a principle or theory is in general *always* dependent on contingent, empirical circumstances. In this comment I am concerned with the supposition that there are relations of duty which follow from a special *relation* that the holder of the duty has with another party, and that is founded on a more fundamental ground. Examples of such relations are friendship, parentship and citizenship. The question that I want to address is whether such a type of relation can be pointed out in the AIDS-case between the victims of AIDS (all victims or some victims) and a pharmaceutical company such as Roche, on the basis of which a special duty can be ascribed to Roche.

The second specification concerns the idea of a duty. With the philosopher Kant we can make a distinction between perfect and imperfect duties. Perfect duties are marked out by the fact that they correlate with a right of another party, which can be identified. Moreover, perfect duties have a relatively precise content. My right of property to this car obligates others to the "perfect" duty to not use it without my consent. Imperfect duties are much more "open": the duty to fight hunger in the world is very general and it can be filled in by different agents in different ways. I will not go into the reasons why imperfect duties are called duties at all. I just want to observe here that for the purposes of this contribution, the duty of Roche to combat the AIDS-crisis is less open and vague than an imperfect duty is. Especially those, to whom the duty is owed, are clearly identifiable and this goes contrary to the idea of an imperfect duty.

An action which expresses an imperfect duty is also to be distinguished from an action in which more is done than what reasonably can be demanded from some agent. These actions are usually called "supererogatory".

If someone gives one or two dollar to a collector of Amnesty International, the same amount as several million of other people, this surely is a way of acting in line with an imperfect duty – Amnesty International cannot claim a right to the money. But it is farfetched to call it a "supererogatory" action. Probably because for that the contribution is too slight and not exceptional.

I will scrutinize four possible foundations of a special duty of Roche in a thus specified sense: the voluntary, selfcontracted duties of the company (paragraph 1), the special bond that the company has with the victims, on account of other causes than selfcontracting, (paragraph 2), the special character of the good or the need that the products of the company are concerned with (paragraph 3), and the catastrophic character of the situation we are dealing with (paragraph 4).

In all four cases my conclusion will be that there are no good reasons to assume a special strict duty for Roche as a particular (collective) agent.

Duties and Obligations

There seems to be a difference between special *duties* and special *obligations*. Obligations the agent – which can also be a collective or an institution, which is the more important case for business ethics – has more or less voluntarily incurred. If I borrow 100 euro from someone, I have a special obligation towards this person, which I have not towards anybody else. This obligation, moreover, takes generally priority over other morally positive actions, which I could take with that amount of money, even if those alternative actions would bring about more good. I am for example not permitted, referring to this greater good, to give the 100 euro, if I have them, to a poor beggar instead of to my creditor, even if this creditor has no need for the money.

The example is not difficult to translate to the Roche case. Companies most of the time work with the money of shareholders, money that has explicitly been given with the objective that it will be used to make profit. So there is a clear special relation of obligation between the management and/or board of the company on the one hand and the shareholders on the other. In a well-known article Milton Friedman has stated unambiguously that this relation is central to business ethics (Friedman, 2004). The problem of Friedman's position is that he is not very clear about the factual and normative position of shareholders. In most cases, the idea that shareholders want to see their money increased, without any further ceremonies, moral or otherwise, is more of a normative assumption than a thesis for which there is factual evidence. Often, there is room for managers and Board of Directors to have strategic and also moral views of their own. In fact, the special obligation which the company has incurred relative to the shareholders seems to be one obligation among others. Nevertheless, the corporation is not permitted to change its policy, under the influence of pressure groups and without support of the shareholders, in such a way that its financial situation changes for the worse, let alone that the continuity is put at risk.

There are additional special obligations of a company which fit better into what has been called a stakeholders approach of business ethics, and which is posed against the shareholders approach of Friedman. An example is the obligation which the business man, implicitly or explicitly, contracts with the sale of a product to his customers. Under this title fall all kinds of obligations such as the obligation to deliver in time.

The main problem to deal with the Roche case along these lines is that it doesn't deal with *real* customers, but with *potential* customers, which because of their weak financial position will never be real customers, *unless* Roche lowers its prices. Because we are dealing with potential customers, it is also difficult to hold that Roche has caused the problems.[1] One could still hold that in view of her role and means, Roche can and ought to improve the situation for the victims of the AIDS crisis. But this comes very close to the thesis which we have excluded from consideration, that under contingent factual circumstances – the child which is in danger of drowning – a special duty falls to a suitable and able agent which happens to be

---

[1] The paradox is that in the case of pharmaceuticals there is less reason to assume that the industry has created the need (apart from absurd ideas such as that the pharmaceutical industry itself has caused AIDS). In the case of all kinds of more trivial needs such as the need for chocolates the influence of companies in the need for it is much more plausible.

around. But this duty to help is not founded on a voluntarily incurred obligation, but derives from a different moral principle. Moreover, this situation raises the question why this special duty should fall to Roche and to Roche alone. Other companies, which operate in the market of AIDS medication, or even other agents who can buy the medicine, seem to be similarly positioned.

Duties and the Market

The concluding remarks of the previous section set us on the track of three important issues. The first is that research, development and production of pharmaceuticals in general is dependent on a complex economic system which, thanks to several interdependent mechanisms and parameters, binds the players on the market to rather strict laws, roles and moral norms. This is a matter of "bounded rationality" the general positive effects of which are only brought about in case of relatively strict compliance. Only strict compliance results in the certainties and predictabilities which make the risk of enterprise manageable. Without compliance pharmaceutical companies would no longer be prepared to run the risks of developing new and cheaper medicines, because the patent could turn out to be worthless in the end.

This implies, for that matter, that if all producers of AIDS-inhibitors would enter into a covenant, or if on a worldwide basis a duty would be imposed on all players, equality of conditions under which companies compete, would be restored. But in that case there is no longer a special moral duty for Roche specifically.

Second, a possible way to get around this conclusion is offered by the stakeholders model. A special duty can perhaps be grounded on the particular relation with a special group of people. For instance, if Roche should have a production plant in Gabon, the workers of this plant in Gabon, or the people of Gabon, would be the beneficiaries of the special duty. In that case, the special duty would have two sides: it would be a special duty for Roche and it would involve the special rights of a particular group of AIDS victims, those in Gabon. But this situation is not referred to in the description of the case. It also becomes clear from this example that in view of the limited capacity to do good in this case, it could only involve a so-called imperfect duty: a duty which largely may be filled in according to one's own views and preferences and towards selected others. Such an imperfect duty, however, can not – one is tempted to say: by definition – be called a special duty, in any case not in that sense that the special character concerns the group or the person against whom the duty is owed. The special character would then have to be based on the fact that Roche disposes of means, patents or medicines, by which specifically Roche can choose to act in accordance with its imperfect duty. But, if it involves medication, these products can always be bought by other agents, such as individuals, NGO's, governments, the WHO, which in this way could realise their imperfect self-contracted duty to reduce the suffering in the world as well. Their actions would, moreover, be independent of the morality of the market.

A third issue is that the measures which Roche up until now has taken, could also and perhaps more correctly be considered as "supererogatory", that is to say that

Roche has done something to which the company is not morally obligated, but which is a sign of a special kind of beneficence (Roche, 2004). From the perspective of what players in a market system are bound to, this seems to be the right qualification.

The Special Character of the Goods as a Rationale for Special Duties

I continue the exploration of possible rationales for a special duty for the Roche company with a new hypothesis: the special duty could reside in the specificity of the good, or the specificity of the need to which the pharmaceutical industry, i.c. Roche, answers. In the ethics of economics there is a huge debate going on about the commoditization of things which for one reason or another do not lend themselves for commercial processes. In this case, it would not concern limits *to* commercialisation, but limits *within* commercialisation. These limits would have to do with the kind of *good* (I take this to be the product *and* the use value, the consummation of the good), that is produced and distributed according to market principles. The barman who refuses to pour out the drunken man another glass, does not in general give up his commercial disposition, but he considers it to be here and now his special duty to do something in relation to this special customer, that is to protect the drunkard in his own interest and to accept the minor costs that he incurs by refusing to serve his customer.

To do justice to this view, we would need an analysis of the relation between the use value of a good – the consumers side, which derives from a particular want or need – and the exchange value of a good – the producers side, which derives from the pursuit of profit. At what point does the second ambition, the pursuit of profit, meet a limit which is caused by the first, the nature of the need or the good, and what sort of limit is this?

This analysis would take us very far for this occasion. Besides, it is clear beforehand that in view of our interest in finding a rationale for a *special* duty for Roche, any result would have two important limitations.

The first limitation is that the issue is not whether the good or the category of goods – AIDS-inhibitors – should be withdrawn completely from the market process, a step that is defended in case of, for example, organs, or babies, or votes. So there is no question of an absolute "blocking" of market transactions or market principles. We are talking about an exception to the rule, an exception that is based on the situation of the producer and the exceptional circumstances of the needy, rather than on the good and the need itself. In the rich Western countries nobody thinks about putting the market out of action in the case of AIDS inhibitors specifically.

The second limitation is that a special duty is more a matter of the role and the relation of the agent, and how the relation has come about, than of the kind of good or need involved. The fact that I, as a parent of this child, have a special duty to take care of its wellbeing, can not be derived from the kind of need or the wellbeing itself of the child – there are, for that matter, so many other children with the same needs, or whose condition is much worse than that of my child. The duty has to do with the fact that I bear a special responsibility for this child, because it is *my* child, and because I have taken upon me this responsibility by accepting to become a parent. The most plausible foundation for the duty is that I have chosen or accepted the role of a parent. But Roche does not stand in such a kind of relation to the AIDS-victims, as we saw above. I conclude that this analysis, again, confirms that special duties derive from special relations and the way they originate, and that a specific kind of good as such does not create a special relation. At the most does it create, if one has this good at its disposal, a special position and duty to use it in a morally right or best way, on account of general moral principles of doing well.

Normal and Catastrophic Conditions: The Contingency of Our Moral Duties

It looks as if we'd do best to base an eventual special duty of Roche on the fact that the AIDS crisis in Africa is a catastrophic condition, which cancels all usual or normal moral relationships, which can be expressed in mutual and/or correlative rights and duties. The contingency is not based in the isolated fact itself, but in the fact that the agent is in a special position because he disposes of special means to meet the catastrophe and on that account incurs a special duty. In this sense the condition is different from the situation in which we are an accidental bystander in a situation in which someone is in danger of drowning (which we have understood as not giving rise to a *special* duty). The agent is special because he has special properties, such as the possession of certain means, and these properties are the result of a more or less conscious process, such as starting a company of a certain character, in which the agent has acquired these properties, not just by accidentally being at the place of incidence.

I take the difference between normal and catastrophic situations from Fried, who introduces it in a discussion of utilitarianism (Fried, 1978). Fried argues that utilitarianism as an ethical theory leads to moral paralysis, because each and every situation is "moralized". The reason is that what I will do will always make a difference, however small, for the resulting state of the world, in a positive or negative way. To impose on each and every situation in which we act, a duty to bring about the best state is paralysing and senseless. What we need, according to Fried, is a much more modest and demarcated system of morality that leaves (or creates) a considerable space in which persons may act on other grounds, on grounds of pleasure or self-interest, but also on other moral grounds such as the duty to care specially, to show love for their neighbours and loved ones, and to be admired for doing things that are not strictly their duty. This moral core system is founded, according to Fried, on a deontological principle of respect for persons, which forbids such things as sacrificing the rights of persons for a greater collective good. The market mechanism, with its underlying principles such as freedom, transparency and accountability, is an example of a system that is compatible with this deontological principle, and does not hold self-interest to be immoral in itself.

But Fried recognizes that this moral system is developed and primarily suitable for normal situations and for stable societies. When catastrophes occur, such as in conditions of war or disasters of nature, or in case of serious social crisis, then a situation sets in, in which the norms of the standard moral system do no longer apply, because they are not developed for these conditions. In those cases the deontological principles perhaps will have to be put aside in favour of a consequentialist approach or criterion for right action, in favour of answering to what we are bound to do to alleviate the worst needs and to reduce harm as much as possible. In those cases, it can be inevitable to sacrifice the life of someone to save many others, and in those cases it certainly can be our duty sometimes to put aside our relatively trivial self-interest and our own rights.

A problem is that Fried does not explain how to identify "normal" and "catastrophic" situations. For our case this is a relatively minor problem because it is not disputed that the AIDS crisis in Africa is a catastrophe (UNAIDS, 2004). But there are other respects in which Fried does not explain the implications of his position. One of these is whether, and when, in case of a catastrophe that happens to befall the neighbours. I am morally bound to give up the stable morality and the duties that it involves, and to accept a different, superior moral framework. A greater problem, for the purposes of this article, which is to clarify the special character of the duty of the Roche company (and eventually other pharmaceutical companies), is that this duty is not justified by a special relation, but by the *general* principle that anyone in "Samaritan" circumstances, is bound to do what he or she can to improve the situation of others, when this requires relatively minor, reasonable costs. How serious the situation must be for such a duty, how reasonable the costs are, and, relatively to the answers to these questions, how obligatory or admirable the actions taken by Roche are, these questions can not be answered on the basis of an ethics of special relations in itself, which is part and parcel of the common system of morality.

References

Fried, Ch. 1978. *Right and Wrong*. Cambridge, MA: Cambridge University Press.
Friedman, M. 2004. The Social Responsibility of Business is to Increase its Profits. In: Beauchamp, T.L. and Bowie, N.E. (eds.), *Ethical Theory and Business*, (7th edition), 50–55. New York: Pearson Prentice Hall.
Roche. 2004. Committed to Making a Difference: Roche activities to increase access to healthcare globally. www.roche.com/pages/downloads/sustain/pdf/comm_diff_rep.pdf
UNAIDS. 2004. Report on the Global AIDS Epidemic, www.unAIDS.org

Part III
Case B: Heineken and Promotion Girls in Cambodia – Part 1

Chapter 7
Case Description: Heineken and Promotion Girls in Cambodia

Frans-Paul van der Putten and Rosalie Feilzer

Abstract In Cambodia so-called promotion girls (PGs) working in bars and restaurants play a large role in marketing beer. PGs' work and the circumstances in which they work are far from ideal. The situation is made more complicated by the fact that some PGs have sexual contact with pub customers after hours to earn more money. Among the most frequently cited dangers to which PGs are exposed is the risk of becoming infected with HIV. Although many parties are involved in the circumstances in which PGs work – chiefly the local pub owners, local distributors and the Cambodian government – foreign media focus mainly on the role of international brewers. Heineken is one of the companies operating on the Cambodian market. This brewer developed a programme for PGs that promote its brands. This case study describes Heineken's position in Cambodia, PGs' position in Cambodia, the way the PGs' relation to foreign brewers drew international attention and, finally, Heineken's policy on the PGs' working conditions.

Introduction

In several Asiatic countries PGs or promotion girls are used to sell alcohol and cigarettes. Cambodia is one of the countries where these women play a large role in marketing beer. Local distributors of domestic and foreign brands use PGs to sell their beer at entertainment spots. PGs working for various beer brands customarily work in pubs where they try to get customers to order their beer brand.

PGs' work and the circumstances in which they work are not ideal. According to CARE Cambodia, part of the worldwide NGO of the same name that fights poverty, it often happens that PGs are subjected to unwelcome sexual advances during their working hours.[1] In addition, many PGs have sexual contact with pub customers after

---

F.-P. van der Putten (✉)
Netherlands Institute of International Relations Clingendael, The Hague, The Netherlands
e-mail: fputten@clingendael.nl

[1] www.asianlabour.org/archives/000627.html 12 Feb. 2004.

hours to earn more money.[2] Some media report that PGs are exploited (Sauviller, 2004) and that through their role as indirect sex workers some PGs contribute to the spread of HIV (Bouma, 2003). Although many parties are involved in the circumstances in which PGs work – chiefly the local pub owners, local distributors and the Cambodian government – foreign media focus mainly on the role of international brewers. Heineken is one of the companies operating on the Cambodian market. This brewer developed a programme for PGs that promote its brands. This case study describes Heineken's position in Cambodia, PGs' position in Cambodia, the way the PGs' relation to foreign brewers drew international attention and, finally, Heineken's policy on the PGs' working conditions.[3]

Social Context in Cambodia

Cambodia has thirteen million inhabitants, nearly half of whom are under age fifteen.[4] The country is predominantly agrarian, three-quarters of the population work in agriculture, silviculture or fishery. One consequence of the country's past history of political instability is that Cambodia is one of the poorest countries on the planet. Cambodia has been the scene of wars and occupations since its independence in 1953. The nadir came with the communist Khmer Rouge's reign of terror. Its leader Pol Pot came to power in 1975 after a bitter struggle. The new regime abolished medical facilities, postal services, telecommunication, money, private property and education and restarted the calendar. The urban population was banished to the countryside where it was compelled to establish an agrarian culture. Potential political opponents and ethnic minorities were persecuted. An estimated two million Cambodians, a quarter of the population at that time, died of hunger, torture or by execution. In 1978, a Vietnamese invasion drove the Khmer Rouge into a few isolated parts of the country where it carried on guerrilla warfare for years. In the early 1990s, the parties allowed the UN to mediate to end the civil war. Mines were cleaned up and the infrastructure for tourists was improved under the supervision of the UN. Hotels, restaurants and pubs sprouted everywhere. That was when the sex industry started its rapid rise.[5]

The rise of new industries and tourism contributed greatly to the enormous exodus from poverty-stricken rural areas to the cities. The tourist industry is the fastest

---

[2]One study by the Cambodian government says that 40% of PGs report doing this (see also Stecklow and Marshall, 2000).

[3]This case study reflects the situation at the start of 2005. Heineken helped with the study by granting access to internal company information and offering advice on its incorporation in the text.

[4]General information on Cambodia taken from John Kleinen and Tara Mar, *Cambodja*. Amsterdam: KIT publishers, 2004.

[5]www.visit-mekong.com/cambodia/background/history.htm 25 October 2004; www.ncbuy.com/reference/country/backgrounds.html 25 October 2004.

growing economic sector. Many young people hope to find a job there; men generally have a better starting position. 85% of women are illiterate and have had little or no schooling. Men are often better educated which gains them access to better jobs in the tourist industry. Given the modest size of the textile industry, the urban job market for unskilled women from rural areas is very small. Some work in bordellos as "direct" sex worker or in the entertainment branch, e.g. as dancer, masseuse, karaoke singer or PG. Some of these women are considered "indirect" sex workers because they earn extra money after hours by going with customers they met while at work. These women do not consider themselves prostitutes because they can decide whether or not to accept a customer's offer (Luyn, 2004 and Lubek et al., 2002).

Heineken in Cambodia

Heineken NV is a Dutch company that brews beer in 65 countries and that markets it in over 170.[6] It has been in business since 1864 and has its headquarters in Amsterdam. The founder's descendents control Heineken via two holding companies. 49.995% of the shares in Heineken are traded on the Amsterdam stock exchange. The company produces many brands of which *Heineken* is the most important.[7] The name of the most important product is thus identical with the name of the company. Although Heineken operates around the world, Europe is by far the brewer's most important market. In 2003, the company derived 73% of its sales in Europe. Heineken was one of the largest brewers in the world. Internationally it competed with Anheuser-Bush, InBev en SABMiller. The company said that its primary goal was to strengthen its competitive position and ensure its independence.

In 2003, the Asian Pacific market represented only 4.4% of Heineken's company sales. But this market's population, demographic development, economic growth and low per capita beer consumption means it has enormous potential for sales growth. There is fierce competition in China and Southeast Asia among large international brewers seeking to increase their market shares. Heineken, too, is trying to slip into a leading position in the region. It is not a question of fast profit, but of building an abiding position. That means that Heineken has to invest in marketing its own brand and in building a network of local brewers and distributors. Finding vigorous and reliable local partners is of prime importance in the Asian market. Without good local allies, Western brewers are unable to arrange mass distribution of their products because long-standing personal contacts play a more essential role in Asian business life than they do in the West.

Heineken's primary Asian partner is a Singaporean company, Fraser & Neave Ltd (F&N). Originally, F&N was a British company, now Singaporean Chinese own it.

---

[6] General information on Heineken is taken from the company's annual report for 2003 and the company web site.
[7] In 2004, the brand came in 99th in BusinessWeek's global brand scoreboard: *BusinessWeek.* 2 Aug. 2004.

F&N and Heineken have run Asian Pacific Breweries Ltd (APB) in Singapore since 1931. It sees to the production, marketing and distribution of beer in China, various Southeast Asian countries (Singapore, Cambodia, Malaysia, Thailand, Vietnam and Laos) and New Zealand and Papua New Guinea (Korthals, 1948; Jacobs and Maas, 2001). Heineken owns 42.2% of APB, and F&N owns 37.9%.[8] APB is proportionally consolidated in Heineken's annual figures, which indicates that Heineken and F&N have formally agreed that each would control half of the joint venture.[9] Heineken's relation with F&N is of great strategic importance and is the mainstay under Heineken's position in Asia; APB and, by extension F&N, play a major role in all growth plans. This implies that Heineken's plans in Asia can only be realised with F&N's consent and that Heineken cannot manage joint venture APB as flexibly as it can its fully-owned subsidiaries (Smit, 1996). Of course, F&N's interests and Heinekens do not always coincide. An important example of this is that social expectations have less impact on Asian companies than on a Western company. Heineken is more sensitive to negative media attention for the working conditions at subsidiaries in emerging countries than is F&N. So Heineken feels sooner than its Singaporean partner the need to invest in improving working conditions.

Beer Distribution in Cambodia

Expressed in beer volume, the total Cambodian beer market was good for 15,982,409 gallons in 2002.[10] By way of comparison: that is approximately 0.55% of the 2,879,475,370 gallons that Heineken sold worldwide in 2003.[11] While Cambodia's 13 million inhabitants comprise a modest market, it is one with growth potential. In 2000–2002, APB's sales in Cambodia grew by approximately 35%. Beside the local population, tourists are an important target group for beer vendors. Heineken reported that APB held 47.1% of the Cambodian market in 2003.[12]

APB's Cambodian organisation is called Cambodia Brewery Ltd (CBL). It brews and distributes beer for the local market. APB owns 80% of CBL.[13] APB's brand *Tiger* is this brewery's most important beer brand. Heineken brand beer is sold in Cambodia, but is not brewed locally. Heineken outsourced the import, marketing and distribution of Heineken beer in Cambodia to a Cambodian company Attwood

---

[8] www.apb.com.sg/profile/profile.html 4 Nov. 2004.

[9] See also Heineken, *Annual Report 2003* (Amsterdam: Heineken NV, 2004) 77: "Proportionally consolidated participating interests: The companies listed below [among which are APB and CBL] are proportionally consolidated because control of [sic] these companies is exercised jointly and directly by virtue of an agreement with the other shareholders." See also www.heinekeninternational.com/content/live/files/downloads/InvestorRelations/H_ENG_JV2002_07_tcm4-4466.pdf. Last viewed 11 Oct. 2009.

[10] www-nl.heinekeninternational.com/about/who/breweries/cambodia_brewery.jsp.20 May 2005.

[11] For Heineken NV's total beer volume in 2003 see www-nl.heinekeninternational.com/images/NVNLjaarverslag_tcm7-10002.pdf. 20 May 2005.

[12] www-nl.heinekeninternational.com/about/who/breweries/cambodia_brewery.jsp.

[13] APB, *Annual Report 2003* on www.apb.com.sg. 4 Nov. 2004.

Import Export Co. Ltd. It did so via Interlocal, a subsidiary of Singaporean company Kong Siang (Pte) Ltd. Keeping the distribution chain for Heineken brand beer separate from that for Tiger prevented a conflict of interest for CBL that, like APB, was primarily responsible for supporting and selling Tiger brand beer.[14] Moreover, Attwood is well positioned to protect Heineken beer's "premium" image; it also imports and distributes other exclusive liquor brands (Hennessy Cognac en Moët & Chandon champagne). Heineken had to keep up its ties with Attwood and, via APB, CBL as long as these distributors provided product promotion if it wanted to retain its place as market leader in Cambodia.

PGs in Cambodia[15]

Much of the beer sold is sold via bars and restaurants. It is customary in many such businesses for promotion girls to sell beer. They work for the distributor or local brewery and are used to stimulate consumption of a given brand. The pub or restaurant owns the beer that they sell. The owners of the establishments where promotion girls work have a great impact on the girls' working conditions. The pub owner and not the distributor or brewer is directly present when the women do their work.

Whenever he orders, a customer can choose from among the beer brands that the promotion girls who are present at the time pour. The brands compete via the PGs for every bottle and can of beer sold. In many other countries, licensed establishments have exclusive contracts with distributors to purchase only one or a few beer brands. There brands compete by trying to have the greatest possible number of sales points under exclusive contract. In Cambodia this system is not or hardly in operation; whoever does not use PGs does not sell any beer in pubs or restaurants.

All major distributors of alcoholic beverages in Cambodia use PGs. If Heineken is to maintain its market position, it is essential that CBL and Attwood ensure massive presence of promotion girls in the entertainment districts. Large numbers alone are not enough. It is also essential that the women be highly motivated and popular with customers. That gives them the best chance to stimulate beer sales. The women wear uniforms in the colours of the brands they promote and with the brand name clearly visible. CBL uses around 600 PGs. Attwood has around 150 PGs for promoting Heineken beer.[16] It is important for Heineken that Attwood and CBL have

---

[14] This did not always run smoothly in the past: Jacobs & Maas (1991).

[15] Barring indications to the contrary, data in this section on the general situation of PGs in Cambodia date from 2001 to 2004. The situation of PGs that sell Heineken and APB brands may diverge from this, or may have changed in the meantime.

[16] Care Cambodia (2004). See www.fairtradebeer.com/reportfiles/CARE/CAREendlinereport2005.pdf. Last viewed 22 Oct. 2009.

their PGs sell as much beer as possible. In this sense, Heineken has a clear interest in the way distributors manage the women. They, in their turn, are dependent on cooperation from the pub and restaurant managers for the women's immediate working conditions.

The promotion girls working for Attwood and CBL are over age 18 and average age 25.[17] Other distributors also use PGs under age 18. In Cambodia, most distributors give PGs a little training when they start work. This usually has to do with pouring beer.[18] Often in exchange for a deposit (Bainbridge and Nara, 2002) PGs are given a uniform with the name and in the colours of the brand they promote. Their workday often starts at noon in their employer's office where they change into their uniforms and get instructions on where they will work. Then a bus brings them to a bar or restaurant where they will stay until closing time. Most of the women work seven evenings a week for an average of US$40 to US$60 per month. PGs in Cambodia are often paid by commissions or in a wage system with financial bonuses and disincentives. All or part of their pay depends on how much beer they can sell. The payment structure differs from one distributor to the next.[19]

PGs and Prostitution

Having sexual contact after hours is a fast and easily accessible way for PGs to earn an average of US$25 extra per month. That helps the women contribute to the care of family members back home; that was usually the women's initial motive for coming to the city to find work.[20] Research shows that between 30 and 60% of women have regular sexual contact after their work as a PG.[21] These contacts are usually without protection; various sources indicate that rape is frequent (Stecklow & Marshall 2000). Most employers, including the distributors working with Heineken and APB, stipulate that after-hours sexual contact with pub customers is forbidden on pain of dismissal. Moreover, distributors often provide transportation to and from work. However, it is unclear whether PGs are required to use it.

The growth of sex tourism and direct and indirect prostitution in Cambodia lies at the heart of a serious social problem: the rapid rise in HIV infections. The AIDS virus followed upon the heels of the UN and the tourists. The first cases

---

[17] Heineken provided this information.

[18] Data in this section are based on Stecklow and Marshall (2000); Mc Court (2002); Shine (2003); van Luyn (2004).

[19] In 2003, CBL used a standard wage annex bonus system for sales over a given limit as well as a disincentive. That was an amount, up to 10%, deducted from wages when sales were under a given minimum. The monthly wage for a CBL PG was then US$50. Heineken provided this information.

[20] www.actionaid.org/asia/325_1_31.html. 25 Oct. 2004.

[21] One study by the Cambodian government says that 40% of PGs report doing this: Stecklow & Marshall (2000). A Behavioral Sentinel survey by the National Centre for HIV/AIDS reports 30–60%: Bainbridge & Nara (2002).

were reported in 1991. Cambodia now has one of the highest AIDS rates in all of Southeast Asia.[22] While drug-related infection is significant in China, Vietnam, Thailand and Burma, sexual contact is the main cause in Cambodia (Jansen, 2000). Because no family was spared during the Khmer Rouge period, the genocide led to the dissolution of social norms and the disintegration of social and family life. Many men express this in extreme dissipation linked to excessive drinking and unprotected sexual contact. Excessive alcohol consumption results in aggression and sexual audacity.[23] In pubs the PGs are the targets. The expressions range from pawing to request for paid sexual contact, sometimes even rape.[24] The Cambodian culture encourages young unmarried men to engage in sex, since they are expected to enter marriage experienced. Other rules apply to women. A woman's family suffers shame when she has frequent sexual contact with a variety of partners. A well-known Cambodian saying puts it this way: "A man is a diamond and a woman a piece of cotton; when they fall in the mud, the diamond can be washed clean, but the cotton remains dirty forever" (Pheterson, 1996, Giebels 2003).

The urban sex industry ensures a rapid transmission of HIV. PGs who have paid, after-hours sexual contact are a particularly vulnerable group because they are not considered direct sex workers and do not want to consider themselves sex workers. That means that they fall outside the government's public information campaigns (Lubek 2002). Customers also perceive sex with a PG as safer than with direct sex workers. All this leads to condom use among PGs being the lowest of all groups in the direct or indirect sex industry. Only 10% of these women have safe contacts; in some cities, 20% of PGs are infected with HIV (McCourt 2002). An additional problem relating to low condom use is that many PGs looking for work move from city to city, since the demand for PGs depends heavily on the tourist season. That increases the risk of transmitting the virus. Moreover, married men then transmit the virus to their wives. In Cambodia, AIDS and sex workers are taboo. AIDS patients and sex workers are shunned and discriminated against. They keep out of sight, which further augments the risk of transmitting HIV/AIDS (Jansen, 2000, McCourt 2002).

Social Criticism

Ian Lubek, a Canadian psychology professor, played a major role in drawing international attention to the position of PGs in Cambodia. Prof. Lubek is not the only one campaigning to improve the working conditions and health of beer promotion girls. Several national and international NGOs have been working within Cambodia for some years. Still, it is useful to draw attention to this person. In the international

---

[22] www.unaids.com. 1 Nov. 2004.
[23] www.state.gov/g/drl/rls/hrrpt/2000/eap/681.htm. 25 Oct. 2004.
[24] www.alterbusinessnews.be/nl/index.php. 16 Nov. 2004.

media, Lubek is the most often cited critic of the brewers' role in Cambodia. He is keenly single-minded and has forcefully articulated his view on many occasions.

In 1999, when he was passing through on the way to Australia, Ian Lubek got to talking with a young Cambodian who told him about the AIDS problem and the PGs in his country. Back in Canada, he decided to take steps. On 2001, the Canadian helped set up an AIDS prevention project in Siem Reap, the epicentre of tourism in Cambodia (Bouma, 2003). Here Lubek joined various national and international organisations to take up the cause of the PGs with help from a modest donation from the Elton John AIDS Fund. The programme focussed on distributing information on how to prevent the HIV virus from spreading.[25]

However the project's scope was too narrow for Ian Lubek: Cambodia lacked proper medical infrastructure; AIDS inhibitors are scarce and expensive. This led to many HIV patients' dying from complications. Lubek believed that the Cambodian government did too little to help PGs. In addition, financial support did not always reach its intended recipients due to corruption and dysfunctional infrastructure. Without the help from (international) employers, charity organisations and NGOs, it was likely that more and more Cambodians would die from AIDS-related diseases. That is why Lubek thought that support from and participation of large international brewers was essential for improving the PGs' health situation (Landsberg, 2002). He published an article on Heineken's and other brewers' role in PGs' HIV/AIDS infection, but did not state explicitly why he thought that international brewers had a responsibility to make up for the Cambodian government's inadequate health care (Lubek, 2004).[26] However, the article did imply that brewers, as producers of the products that the PGs sell, must use their influence as employer or the employer's business partner. This referred to salary level and assistance with health care. In mid-2002, Lubek contacted several large breweries and kept pursuing them with letters and e-mails. Most did not respond or simply stated that they had not hired any PGs.

Heineken and other international brewers were very important targets for the Canadian professor because they and APB controlled a large share of the Cambodian market and had internationally known names. Moreover, Heineken had set up a HIV/AIDS programme for its own personnel. Heineken first developed this policy in Africa. Its purpose was to make medical help available for employees and family members infected with HIV. Lubek hoped that Heineken would feel called upon to take the first steps and become a model for other brewers to follow.

In 2002, Ian Lubek asked Heineken whether its HIV/AIDS programme also applied to Cambodian PGs.[27] The brewer, feeling it owed Prof. Lubek an answer, said that its HIV/AIDS programme at that time was restricted to Africa and that later it would use the experience gained to introduce it elsewhere. Furthermore, Heineken told Lubek that it was still studying options for a programme for those

---

[25] www.psycholoy.uoguelph.ca/research/lubek/cambodia/aidsep.html. 25 Oct. 2004.

[26] See www.fairtradebeer.com/reportfiles/lubekheineken2004.rtf.

[27] Heineken NV, in-house documentation.

7 Case Description: Heineken and Promotion Girls in Cambodia

not on its payroll (e.g. Cambodian PGs) and that in any case every programme must become operative throughout the world.[28]

Lubek thought that things could be done more quickly. Moreover, he believed that in this context there was no difference between an employee and an off-payroll worker. In either case their work directly benefitted the brewer (Lubek, 2004). He did not want to make this distinction because the PGs felt that they worked for Heineken since their uniform bore the beer brand's name and since they poured only Heineken beer and competed with PGs representing other brands to capture the largest market share for Heineken.

In 2002, Lubek sent two letters to Heineken with copies to the Cambodian government, NGOs, international dignitaries and the international press (Lubek, 2004). In them, Lubek claimed that Heineken's attitude in Cambodia conflicted with its international approach to HIV/AIDS. He thought that Heineken was dragging its feet when it came to helping the PGs in what he considered an epidemic situation that cost lives daily. In the meantime Lubek helped set up two web sites (www.fairtradebeer.com and www.ethicalbeer.com) that monitored brewers' course of action regarding PGs. Lubek's correspondence with and about brewers (often sent to many recipients), his two web sites and his lectures on PGs' working conditions drew international attention. The media took this up and published articles on the subject in several newspapers and periodicals (Sauviller, 2004; Bouma, 2003). They were often distinctly negative regarding the circumstances in which PGs worked and considered the major brewers, including Heineken, as accessories to this. Several individuals and investors and the Dutch Trade Union Federation FNV contacted Heineken with questions about the PGs.

Lubek made three demands of Heineken and other international brewers in his letters and articles. First he demanded that salaries be doubled from around US$55 to US$110 per month. He believed that this would remove the women's need to accept after-hours sexual contact. Second, he broached the importance of providing efficacious health information to bring about a change of behaviour and so to prevent the spread of HIV/AIDS virus. Finally, Lubek wanted the brewers to distribute AIDS inhibitors free to those PGs who had already become infected.[29]

Lubek's campaign focused heavily on the relation between the PGs work and the spread of HIV/AIDS. Newspaper articles were also quick to lay the link with HIV/AIDS (Stecklow & Marshall 2000). Yet, while HIV infection was a serious problem for those immediately involved and for the health situation in Cambodia, it is important to remember that this was only one of the possible consequences of the PGs working conditions. Research showed that many PGs were sexually harassed during their work.[30] This shows that even apart from HIV/AIDS, the PGs' working conditions posed fundamental problems.

---

[28] Heineken NV, in-house documentation.
[29] www.fairtradebeer.com/reportfiles/lubekheineken2004.rtf. 10 Jan. 2005.
[30] www.asianlabour.org/archives/000627.html. 12 Feb. 2004.

Heineken's Answer and Stance Toward PGs

Although Heineken cut off all direct communication with Lubek after 2002, the company did take steps to adopt a course of action toward PGs. Representatives from Heineken's international medical service paid an initial visit to Cambodia in December 2002. Their purpose was twofold. First, Heineken wanted to investigate the PGs' situation and how local stakeholders would respond to a course of action regarding PGs. Next, they wanted to obtain local partners' (APB/CBL and Attwood) cooperation in improving the PGs working conditions. After the visit, the parties undertook additional steps. They worked to build contacts with NGOs and local government bodies.[31] CARE is an NGO operating in several countries; one of its specialisations is HIV/AIDS prevention. After being contacted by Heineken, CARE suggested setting up a training programme for PGs in Cambodia on selling beer safely. In April 2003, Heineken representatives visited Cambodia again to contact all parties to evaluate the results of the steps taken so far for PGs and to get them to agree to cooperation with a plan of action that CARE would carry out. In early 2004, CARE set up its Selling Beer Safely programme in Cambodia. The programme contained information on alcohol and its effects, behaviour training on how to deal with difficult customers, health information, information on sexually transmissible diseases (STDs), information on how to prevent STDs including HIV/AIDS, training and information for outlet owners, training for trainers, introduction and supervision of supervisors and creation of better working conditions with attention for transport and changing rooms.[32] This test project, set up at Heineken's request, focussed on developing a course of action regarding PGs that Heineken could use for all promotion girls throughout the world.

The CARE pilot study ended at the close of 2004. Heineken then drafted a policy on PGs worldwide. It continued the approach developed in conjunction with CARE. It contained provisions on hiring, contracts, working conditions, medical care and privacy. In addition, it contained a programme to educate, instruct and train PGs. Heineken stated that the policy would apply to all PGs working for Heineken companies and for business partners working with Heineken brands. Heineken's HIV/AIDS policy will only apply when PGs have no other source of care and when they are on Heineken's payroll, which is not the case in Cambodia.[33]

Heineken's arguments for setting up a worldwide PG policy were that PG work entails serious risks and that Heineken felt it has a responsibility when these risks could lead to HIV infections. Heineken said it had this responsibility as owner of the beer brand that the PGs promoted, even when the PGs sexual contact was not limited to pub customers and even when the company had no control over what PGs did in

---

[31] Heineken NV, in-house documentation.
[32] Heineken provided this information.
[33] Heineken NV, in-house documentation.

their free time. The responsibility that Heineken acknowledged in a document entitled "Promotion Girls Policy" tried to keep PGs' work-related risks to a minimum by providing information and training and seeing to safe working conditions.

Ian Lubek's response to this programme had positive notes. The project satisfied one of his demands (information). At the same time, he noted that it did not satisfy his two other requirements, to wit doubling the PGs' income and distributing AIDS inhibitors for free (McDonald-Gibson 2003). Apart from that, Lubek acknowledged that Heineken was the first brewer to take steps to set a course of action for PGs in Cambodia. His criticism was very pragmatic. Other brewers did less, but Prof. Lubek and other activists probably thought that criticising them at that point would have had a potentially smaller effect. Lubek and others gave little attention to the Asian brewers that operated on the Cambodian market.

However, Heineken is not planning to raise the PGs pay. The brewer believes that the income is sufficient to cover living expenses, which Heineken defines as providing for oneself and contributing to the maintenance of a family. According to its own word, Heineken, in Cambodia, is one of the best payers in the beer industry. When compared to other occupational groups, the women also earned a very decent wage. That is why Heineken thinks that raising PGs' income would seriously disturb the organisation's pay structure in Cambodia.

The brewer also comments that Heineken's most important business activity is brewing and selling beer and that local governments are the one's primarily responsible for health care. Only when the local governments are unable to meet these responsibilities and when this affects its own employees would Heineken see itself obliged to offer conditional assistance. Heineken's progressive HIV/AIDS programme, set up within the same framework, focuses only on its own employees and their families. In Cambodia, the PGs are not on Heineken's payroll. Rather they work for the distributors. CBL's PGs are subject to a policy that APB set up. Heineken has no direct influence on this. In addition, providing AIDS inhibitors would also require complex treatment and guidance that does not fit well with the rapid turnover in staff and many temporary workers as is the case for PGs in Cambodia.[34] Neither Heineken nor Lubek suggested terminating the use of PGs completely. This would probably lead to a smaller market share, which conflicts with Heineken's objective in Asia.

Conclusion

The working conditions of the PGs in Cambodia are far from ideal even when the AIDS issue is disregarded. In a society where women were traditionally required to behave and dress modestly and where men display depraved behaviour in entertainment areas, PGs draw sexually tinted attention from males in bars. Because these women's income is dependent on their ability to get men to purchase a specific

---

[34]Heineken provided the authors with this information.

brand, some customers feel free to paw and sexually harass PGs. Any kind of friction with customers or pub owners has a negative impact on PGs' turnover, which puts them in a weak position.

As market leader in Cambodia, Heineken is very dependent on PGs' work. As for turnover, the company benefits from a system in which the women are encouraged to sell as much beer as they can. But increased turnover is not the brewer's only concern. In the long term, Heineken wants to continue operating in Cambodia; a great deal is at stake in other countries, as well. The Heineken and Tiger brands are sold in many other countries and the first brand is identical with that of the company. The brand value and reputation of the entire company play a large role in the manner in which the company deals with the situation in Cambodia.

At the same time, Heineken's influence in Cambodia is restricted in several ways. Many competing brewers also use the promotion system. They would like nothing better than to see Heineken recede. The women work either for a local distributor or for a subsidiary of the joint venture. Heineken has to take the competition and local partners into account in all that it does. They do not always share the same interests as Heineken.

In 2003 and 2004, Heineken set up a pilot project in Cambodia to train promotion girls. The training is primarily intended to contribute to preventing HIV infections, but is also aimed at improving general working conditions. NGOs and Heineken's local partners also support the training programme. The company used the results of the pilot project to set up and publicise a worldwide project for promotion girls. The company has chosen to be proactive, while competitors ignore it. There is no data on the effectiveness of Heineken's policy. It is clear that Heineken and its local partners have no plans to do without PGs. This would lead to a loss of market share unless the entire industry did the same. As yet there is no question of competitors joining forces to improve the situation. This would appear difficult to achieve given competitors' passive attitude and Asian brewers' apparent invulnerability to social pressure to improve PGs' working conditions.

References

Bainbridge, B. and Nara, L. 2002. 'The Cost of Living: Research Suggests More Beer Girls are Being Forced by Poverty to Provide Clients with Sex'. Phnom Penh Post, July 19 – Aug 1.
Bouma, J. 2003. 'Biertje?', Trouw, 23 May 2003.
Care Cambodia, 2004. *'Selling Beer Safely: A Woman's Health Initiative'*, Care International in Cambodia. http://www.fairtradebeer.com/reportfiles/CARE/ingridquinnCARE2003.pdf
Giebels, R. 2003. Seks met maagd maakt man sterker. *NRC Handelsblad*, 19 Aug.
Heineken. 2004. Annual Report. Amsterdam: Heineken N.V. http://www.heinekeninternational.com/content/live/files/downloads/InvestorRelations/Full%20Annual%20Report_tcm4-12793.pdf last viewed 6 Nov. 2009.
Jacobs, M.G.P.A. and Maas, W.H.G. 2001. *De magie van Heineken*, 57–58. Amsterdam: Heineken.
Jansen, A. 2000. 'Alleen andere moraal houdt tegen'. *Reformatorisch Dagblad*, 6 Dec.
Kleinen, J. and Mar, T. 2004. *Cambodja*. Amsterdam: KIT publishers.
Korthals, H.A. 1948. *Heineken's Bierbrouwerij, 1873–1948*, 387. Amsterdam: C.V. Allert de Lange.

Landsberg, M. 2002. 'One Canadian's Dedication to AIDS Education'. *Toronto Star*, 17 Nov.

Lubek, I., et al 2002. Collaboratively Confronting the Current Cambodian HIV/AIDS Crisis in Siem Reap: A Cross-Disciplinary, Cross Cultural 'Participation Action Research' Project in Consultative, Community Health Change. *Asian Psychologist*, 3(1): 21–28.

Lubek, I. 2004. *Just Dying for a Heineken? A Case Study of Cambodian Beer Promotion Women, Corporate Caution, Recalcitrance or Criminal Neglect?*. Canada: University of Guelph.

Luyn, F.-J. van 2004. 'Ze zijn jong, verkopen bier en verspreiden aids'. *NRC Handelsblad*, 6 February.

Mc Court, M. 2002. *Grassroots Empowerment for Beer Girls*. Canada: University of Guelph, Thesis for the degree of Honours Bachelor of Arts.

McDonald-Gibson, C. 2003. 'Ethical beer campaign to target Western drinkers'. *Phnom Penh Post*, Issue 12/07, March 28 – April 10.

Pheterson, G. 1996. *The Prostitution Prism*. Amsterdam: Amsterdam University Press.

Sauviller, R. 2004. 'De handel in bier en seks: Interscrew'. 53–55. *Deng,* May.

Shine, R. 2003. 'Aids in Asia: the Continents Grwong Crisis/Workers at Risk/Cambodian Beer Grils Add to HIV Epidemic: Activists Say Brewers Must Get Involved'. *Chronicle Foreign Service*, 15 Jan. URL http://www.unaids.com, 1 Nov. 2004.

Smit, B. 1996. *Heineken: Een leven in de brouwerij*, 272. Nijmegen: Sun.

Stecklow, S. & Marshall, S. 31 May 2000. 'Asian "Beer Girls" Sell Western Brew, End Up with AIDS'. *Wall Street Journal*.

Chapter 8
Commentary: Obscured Authority

Raoul Wirtz, Edgar Karssing, and Gemma Crijns

Abstract In the case discussion of Heineken and the promotion girls in Cambodia we address the question to what extent Heineken is responsible for the well-being of promotion girls in Cambodia. Heineken's authority in Cambodia is obscured: at best it has a shared authority, in this case with Heineken's Asian partners, the Cambodian government and the establishment owners. In examining Heineken's responsibilities, we rely on two fundamental moral principles: the first is to do no harm and the second is the principle of autonomy. Furthermore we examine the extent of Heineken's authority and the significance of its obscured authority. Our conclusion is that the fact that authority is primarily indirect, does not relieve Heineken from all moral responsibility.

Introduction

Heineken is trying to gain a leading position in Asia. That is why Heineken has a strategic interest in maximising consumption of Heineken and Tiger beers in Cambodia. Competition is heavy. To build up and maintain this market position Heineken needs reliable and long-term business partners in the region. Even by Asian standards, Cambodia is a poor country. It has all the basic characteristics of an underdeveloped country: its national government is weak, its level of prosperity lies far below that of Western Europe and there is a large, impoverished underclass for which an income from employment can make the difference between life and death.

The question we address in discussing the case of Heineken and the promotion girls (PGs) in Cambodia is: To what extent is Heineken responsible for the well-being of PGs in Cambodia in a situation where its authority is obscured? We will

---

R. Wirtz (✉)
Executive and Management Development Center, Nyenrode Business University, Breukelen, The Netherlands
e-mail: r.wirtz@nyenrode.nl

gear this specifically to Heineken's responsibility to improve PGs employment conditions and to ensure good working conditions. We define obscured authority as the fact that Heineken has no direct managerial influence on the PGs' terms of employment or working conditions. The urgency of this question can clearly be inferred from the case-study. Promotion girls run a risk of encountering (sexual) intimidation during their working hours and being exploited as indirect sex workers. Moreover, because of their low pay or pressure from pub owners, some PGs are obliged to have sexual contact with customers during working hours, which entails a risk of HIV/AIDS infection. The central question in this reflection goes beyond the case of the Cambodian promotion girls. Many companies that operate internationally, encounter the question of moral responsibility in a situation where their authority is obscured.

Moral Principles

For the integrity of the argumentation, we will first discuss an employer's moral responsibility to do something about the PGs' working conditions or the institutions in Cambodia. In examining employers' responsibilities, we rely on two fundamental moral principles: the first is to do no harm and the second is autonomy. These are generally seen as fundamental moral principles. They have a great prescriptive force and are universally accepted (Bernard et al., 1997). In addition, we discuss the extent to which Heineken is responsible in a situation where its authority is obscured.

Do No Harm: The Non-maleficence Principle

The principle of doing no harm, or the non-maleficence principle, states that people may not do one another harm or evil. It is a fundamental moral principle because without it social intercourse would be impossible. For an employer the principle means that its employees must not be exposed to avoidable risks. The PGs' working conditions entail the risk of sexual intimidation and abuse. Serious harm can issue from infection and transmission of the HIV virus. Sometimes, the customers dissipated sexual behaviour also directly violates the PGs' physical integrity. In the Netherlands, prevention of this type of harm is considered so important that respect for physical integrity is a provision established in the constitution. International treaties also speak of the inviolability of the person.[1] The non-maleficence principle requires employers to make PGs' working conditions safer (by reducing the risk of HIV infection). Moreover, employers must see to it that the PGs run no increased risk of sexual intimidation and abuse during and because of their work.

---

[1] Art. 13 of the *Universal Declaration of Human Rights* states "Everyone has the right to life, liberty and security of person (..)" and Article 5: "No one shall be subjected to torture or to cruel, inhuman or degrading treatment or punishment".

The Autonomy Principle

One could argue against the preceding by saying that every PG must be free to chose this type of work (and accept the accompanying risks). Respect for another's free choice, for his or her autonomy, is also a fundamental moral principle. However, it is not easy to answer the question whether an employer does enough to respect the PGs' autonomy. On one side, we note that working as PG can be a source of income for young women in Cambodia, one they would otherwise not have, with all that this implies for themselves and their families. On the other, there is a condition for the autonomous choice for this work, i.e. that the women know of all the dangers and risks that the work entails and that they freely accept this. The case study shows that many people (in Cambodia and beyond) are not acquainted with the risks of HIV/AIDS infection. In addition, it is debatable whether there is much voluntary consent involved in the decision to become a PG. The case study describes how working as a PG is one of the few options available to earn an income in Cambodia. Beyond that, others (family members) are often dependent on the PGs' income. This implies a degree of compulsion to take up this work.

The PGs' autonomy is also assailed during working hours. Even if we assume that a PG chooses to accept the risks that the work entails, it still cannot be asserted that she *chooses* to be sexually intimidated or assaulted or to be infected with HIV. We might even argue that one should protect women from such risks, that they should not even be offered the choice. An apparently autonomous choice for this work in the present, could lead to much less freedom of choice in the future due to the consequences of sexual abuse or HIV infection. To the extent that there is any question of coercion or encouragement from the PG's employer to have sexual contact with customers, the PG's autonomous choice (whether or not to allow this type of contact) during working hours is further eroded.

A PG's relationship of dependence with her employer is unbalanced. An employer (be it the distributor or establishment owner) can easily find another PG, while for a PG it is much more difficult to find another job. This puts her in a very weak position when negotiating her own working conditions with her employer. If she wants to raise the question of intimidation or other types of harm or danger in her work, she will be ignored and even run the risk of being sacked. PGs thus have very few modalities for improving their working conditions.

What Is the Extent of Heineken's Responsibility?

Were employees at Heineken in the Netherlands to be exposed to the risks described above or to similar risks, Heineken would certainly do something immediately, and thus satisfy the moral principles described. The question whether Heineken must do something for the wellbeing of the PGs and the institutions in Cambodia is more difficult to answer. Heineken is not their employer. We could speak of Heineken's *obscured* authority.

This is a situation of obscured authority because Heineken has no direct managerial influence on the PGs' working conditions. At best there is shared authority, in this case with Heineken's Asian partners, the Cambodian government and the establishment owners. The situation in which an international company does business in a host country, but cannot exert direct (managerial) influence is common.

Generally, the moral *obligation* to do something increases or decreases in proportion to one's *ability* to do something. In addition, one's moral responsibility grows in proportion to one's *involvement* with the other, i.e. because one profits from the other's situation. It follows that we must first examine the extent of Heineken's authority and the significance of its obscured authority. Second, we must examine the extent of Heineken's involvement with the PGs and the institutions in Cambodia.

To start with we will describe three factors that curtail Heineken's authority over the Cambodian PGs well-being. The managerial stratification of Heineken's operations in Cambodia limits its authority. It shares ownership of Asia Pacific Breweries Ltd. (APB) that produces, markets and distributes beer in Cambodia, with Fraser en Neave Limited (F&N). Heineken's authority is further obscured in that the distribution of APB's Tiger Beer and Heineken is outsourced; Tiger Beer to Cambodia Brewery Ltd (CBL), 80% of which APB owns and Heineken to Atwood, over which Heineken has no formal authority. In addition to managerial stratification, Heineken's authority over the situation of the Cambodian PG is limited by the fact that although the PGs work for the distributor or local brewer, the owners of the establishments where they work exert great influence on their immediate working conditions.

Three questions will help us understand the scope of Heineken's responsibility for the PGs' working conditions and the restoration of social institutions: To what extent does Heineken put PGs at risk?; To what extent does Heineken profit from the PGs' employment in the primary tasks or company goals?; To what extent can Heineken influence working conditions or institutions?

To What Extent Does Heineken Put the PGs at Risk?

PGs do not work directly under Heinekens authority as defined by labour law; at most they fall under that of a subsidiary (in this case, CBL) over which Heineken has only partial authority. Moreover, the cause of the PGs' risks does not lie in the production or distribution of beer, but in the circumstances in which the PGs must work, i.e. the intimidating, violent and unsafe behaviour of pub customers. Heineken is thus not the direct cause of the PGs' risky employment position or of Cambodia's weakened social structure. This lessens Heinekens involvement with the situation and thereby its moral responsibility to do something about it.

However, we must also take into account that consumption of beer and other alcoholic beverages can increase the risk that visitors to the establishments where it is sold will intimidate or behave aggressively toward the PGs.

To What Extent Does Heineken Profit from the PGs' Employment Position in the Primary Tasks or Company Goals?

Does Heineken profit from the situation in Cambodia? Does the distribution of beer by PGs offer a business opportunity? The case study shows that the use of PGs does not bring any competitive advantages, but it is a prerequisite for Heineken's retaining its present position.

There is no direct employment relationship between Heineken and the PGs, yet Heineken depends on their performance for the success of its strategic objectives. The case states that the distributor cannot sell beer without using PGs. This shows how dependent the beer manufacturer is on PGs. Without effective alternatives for beer distribution (e.g. promotion *men*) the burden of this type of distribution is born exclusively by the promotion girls.

In short, the PGs are an indispensable link in Heineken's production and distribution chain. The risks that PGs run during their work are only partially inherent to their task in the distribution chain, i.e. only to the extent that alluring behaviour sells more beer. However, this seductive behaviour could have the same effect without the attendant risks of sexual intimidation or abuse and without pressure to have to perform as indirect sex worker, e.g. by supervising the safety of PGs' working conditions and by paying an hourly wage that removes the financial motive for after-hours sexual contact.

To What Extent Can Heineken Influence Working Conditions or Institutions?

By and large, we can say that responsibility for a situation increases in proportion to one's influence on the situation. This also applies to Heineken. Generally speaking we can identify three spheres of influence attributable to an internationally operating company, i.e. its own operations, its immediate business environment and the broader political and cultural environment (Jeurissen and van der Putten, 2006: 253–254). The company bears full responsibility for its own operations. In its immediate environment, the company is responsible for using its influence to work with others to promote human rights. The responsibility for advancing the company's political and cultural environment is – at least for now – the weakest.

Because Heinekens authority over the PGs' working conditions is layered, the operations cannot be considered completely its own. PGs' working conditions belong to the indirect, not the immediate, business environment because they are an important link in the distribution of beer. The fact that authority is primarily indirect does not relieve Heineken from all moral responsibility. Here Heineken is subject to the moral principle of transference (Van Luijk, 1993: 193–140). In this case, this principle implies that when Heineken can exercise no direct influence on the PGs' working conditions, it has the moral obligation to shift this influence to the next higher level where influence *can* be exercised. The first way in which this can be done is by invoking CBL's (indirect) authority. Contracts with distributors and selling points could also contain provisions relating to the PGs' employment and working conditions. Heineken could also help develop codes of behaviour or more stringent prescriptions that could ensure the well-being and safety of PGs while at work.

It is clear from the case-description that the PG's problems are at least partly caused by weak institutions in Cambodia. Must Heineken also assume some of the responsibility for this? Does Heineken have a responsibility to strengthen Cambodia's social structure and contribute to improving the country's weak (social) institutions? We should note first that there is a limit to this responsibility. Normally we look upon this as an governmental task. We expect companies to be reticent rather than interfering. Furthermore, Heineken's influence is more indirect than its possible influence over working conditions. Heineken has little means to exert influence over e.g. education or housing conditions. However, The idea that multinational companies operating in poor countries with weak social structures always have some obligation to contribute to improving local structures is gaining ground. It also seems reasonable, because companies should do more to behave as global corporate citizens and should enter into dialogue with stakeholders (including lobbies like Ian Lubek's, Care International and Amnesty International) (Daboub and Calton, 2002: 85–98 and 92; see also: Donaldson, 1992). Like other companies, Heineken is expected to render account over more than annual figures and competitive position (*profit*) in Asia. It must also report on the consequences that obtaining these results has on the natural environment (*planet*) and the social environment (*people*). For Heineken, this could offer a basis for a growing concern with PGs and the social structure in Cambodia.

Conclusion

Given the answers to the three questions that we posed on the degree to which Heineken bears moral responsibility, we can conclude that Heineken is indirectly involved with the PGs' circumstances. However, rather than releasing Heineken from moral responsibility, this confirms that it can exercise indirect influence, via its partners, and that it can and should use this influence to improve the PGs' working conditions.

A complicating factor in Heineken's obscured authority is that the partners in the joint venture have different interests. The case description shows that Heineken, most of whose sales are generated in Europe and the US, is far more vulnerable to the harmful results of negative publicity regarding the PGs' working conditions than are its Asian partners. The moral judgment about working conditions is much less vigorous in Asian countries. Still, we should not overestimate this differing influence. Both partners, Heineken and the Asian companies, benefit from a stable relationship. If Heineken's image in the West were to be damaged, this could have a negative impact on its partners. The case description names another common objective, i.e. *motivated* promotion girls. The motivation of PGs is directly proportionate to the safety of their workplace; wage level will also have a positive effect. In this sense Heineken does have some residual responsibility even in a position of obscured authority.

References

Bernard, G., Culver, C. and Clauser, K.D. 1997. *Bioethics. A Return to Fundamentals*. New York, NY: Oxford University Press.

Daboub, A.J. and Calton., J.M. 2002. Stakeholder Learning Dialogues: How to Preserve Ethical Responsibility in Networks. *Journal of Business Ethics*, 41(1–2): pp 85–98.

Donaldson, T. 1992. *The Ethics of International Business*. Oxford: Oxford University Press.

Jeurissen, R. and van der Putten, F.P. 2006. Ethiek en internationaal zaken doen. In: Jeurissen, R.J.E. (ed.), *Bedrijfsethiek een goede zaak*. Assen: Van Gorcum.

Luijk, H. van 1993. *Om redelijk gewin: Oefeningen in bedrijfsethiek*, 139–140. Amsterdam: Boom.

Chapter 9
Commentary: Heineken Between Moral Motives and Self-interest

Frank den Hond

Abstract Why did Heineken respond as it did to the mounting criticism? This commentary seeks to appraise whether or not a moral motive can be assumed to have played a role in explaining Heineken's response. As moral motives are hard to empirically trace in behaviour, the question is approached from the other side, by means of elimination: if all alternative, non-moral motives are implausible, then a moral motive remains as the sole explanandum.

Heineken is a company that wants to do more than just make a profit. It strives toward corporate social responsibility (CSR), or at least it wants to be known for doing so. "Heineken is committed to conducting business responsibly and ethically. We continuously take our initiatives to combat alcohol abuse, misuse and focused resources and energy on setting even higher standards in the social and environmental areas of our business" (Heineken, 2004: p. 6). Can this objective be invoked to explain the way Heineken acted in the case of the beer promotion girls (PGs)? Properly considered, no. Heineken defines CSR in terms of achieving certain publicly and ethically desirable standards. Simply listing these morally edifying standards says nothing about *why* Heineken wants to achieve them.

Moral philosophy makes an important distinction between moral and non-moral motives for actions. In a market context, we can equate non-moral motives with long-term economic self-interests. Moral motives go beyond these. Morally motivated behaviour is usually associated with costs unrelated to any direct or indirect benefit. Friedman (1970) referred to this distinction when he said that most of what passes for companies' socially responsible behaviour should not bear this name. When CSR arises from self-interest, or at least the interest of the company's shareholders, the company is being hypocritical when it tries to link these to moral motives. But when CSR is pursued at the expense of the shareholders, Friedman considers this unacceptable because it is a waste of their property.

F. den Hond (✉)
Department of Organization Science, VU University, Amsterdam, The Netherlands
e-mail: f.den.hond@vu.nl

Could a moral motive – be it conscious or unconscious – have played a role in Heineken's considerations? I certainly do not want to exclude this possibility, but the problem with this type of statement is that it is difficult to substantiate empirically. On one side, it is difficult to determine the exact motive that prompts any actor's action. We often do not even know what prompts our own actions. On the other, we distrust people who are too eager to announce that their deeds are based on high ideals (and therefore we see that companies seldom appeal to moral motives, because they are quickly distrusted). One way that outsiders can learn something about an actor's moral motives is by excluding all non-moral motives. We can justifiably presuppose the presence of moral motives once we have shown that all imaginable, non-moral motives are unlikely, i.e. that in the long term the costs do not have any adequate corresponding benefits. This is the method I use in this article. I try to determine whether we should presuppose that Heineken has a moral motive by examining the plausibility of non-moral motives. In what follows, I shall use "the prudent motive model" to refer to morally edifying behaviour. In my analysis I will first demonstrate that the perspective of prudence does not fully account for Heineken's actions when only the local Cambodian market and institutions are taken into consideration. We are better able to understand Heineken and other multinational concerns operating in local markets when we take into account that Cambodian PGs are not isolated from the interdependent, globalised world order. Second, I will show that we nevertheless cannot understand the case from the perspective of prudence when we look only at Heineken's relationship with Western consumers. Only when we have thoroughly studied the network of actors in which Heineken operates and the mechanisms that move them will we come within sight of an explanation.

The case study focuses on Heineken. Still, it is not clear to what extent international protests are directed only at Heineken. After all, the question of the PGs is a matter that should affect all beer (and cigarette) distributors in Cambodia. A quick search on internet shows that the problem is not restricted to Cambodia. PGs are also deployed to stimulate the sale of beer in other southeast Asian countries (Vietnam, Thailand, Malaysia, Burma,...) and China.[1] Ian Lubek sent letters to various Western brewers, but Heineken was the only one to answer. "Most did not respond or simply stated that they had not hired any PGs." (case description, p. 72).

At first sight there are three possible reasons why Heineken took up the criticism and developed a programme to improve the situation. The first reason is that Heineken was worried about its reputation on the Cambodian market, since the company's Tiger and Heineken brands hold a dominant market share. But we can quickly reject this reason. The deployment of PGs to sell beer seems generally accepted in Cambodia where nearly all distributors use them. Until this practice looses its

---

[1] www.fmg.uva.nl/amidst/object.cfm/objectID=BAC91C21-724F-4F7E-826B3FF7043AD302, www.sba.muohio.edu/abas/2000/Paper10.pdf, www.fairtradebeer.com/reportfiles/engtrouw230503.html. Last viewed 22 December 2005.

legitimacy in Cambodia, brewers and distributors will have no reason to abandon it. Moreover, I would expect that the first player to stop deploying PGs will lose market share.

The other possible reasons have little to do with the situation in Cambodia. The first of these two is related to Heineken's brand reputation and to a lesser extent that of Tiger beer in other, Western countries. Earlier, in the mid-1990s, Heineken came under fire in the Netherlands and the US for investing in Burma. In the end, Heineken reversed this decision. One reason was that it ran the risk that its products would be boycotted in the US (Vergouw and den Hond, 2000). It is not unimaginable that Heineken's management learned from these prior events and wanted to prevent a commotion around its brand. However, the case did not state clearly whether North American or other consumers played a role in Heineken's decision. Nor did it say why other brewers, e.g. Carlsberg, were not targeted. Distributors of Carlsberg beer also hire PGs and the company left Burma at the same time as Heineken after being put under similar pressure.

Finally, Heineken may have felt that the company's proactive course of action against HIV/AIDS infection among its employees and their families in Africa created a precedent. Heineken invoked the latter to substantiate its claim to exercising corporate social responsibility. After this policy was publicised as applying to the whole company, finding oneself accused of having a double standard can be a great blow. The accusation of using a double standard usually arises when working conditions or the implementation of environmental regulations in the West differ from those in emerging countries. This case shows – and I find this interesting – that this accusation can also be made when company policy differs from one emerging country to the next. Indeed, the authors of the case description note that Heineken considers it very important to apply the same policy around the world, apparently with a view to avoiding this accusation.

Similar reasons are found in the literature. Generally speaking, authors seek motives for corporate social responsibility in supply and demand (McWilliams and Siegel, 2001; Spar and La Mure, 2003). Supply factors include the company's characteristics and those of the industry in which it operates. On the demand side, McWilliams & Siegel (2001) note that there are two important sources: consumers and other stakeholders. This case shows that we must distinguish between local and supra-local or international supply and demand factors.

Heineken is vulnerable to supply factors. Its product, beer, is an "experience good"; comparable products are available at competitive prices. Moreover, it operates in an industry noted for expensive advertising. In such situations, there is a real chance that consumers will show their protest by shifting to other brands. Producers will choose to define their products by stressing attributes that denote social responsibility (McWilliams and Siegel, 2001; Spar and La Mure, 2003). In any case, Heineken seems to want to profile itself in the West as a socially responsible company. It is not clear to what extent that is the case in Cambodia.

Other supply factors include transaction and other costs incurred to comply with demands (Spar and La Mure 2003). Although data is lacking, I would be surprised if the cost involved in setting up and implementing the intended training programme were to prove to be high, for a profitable company like Heineken. However, it is not certain whether, in the end, Heineken will bear the cost or whether its local partners, which produce and distribute the beer, will do so. If the latter is the case, there is less chance that the programme will have a long and effective life. Although the cost in absolute figures is not high, it can be substantial for a Cambodian company because it is not easy to earn back. The production of beer is relatively capital intensive. An increase in the fixed costs has a relatively heavy influence on profitability, certainly when market competition keeps margins low.

A final supply factor mentioned is that a company can obtain a strategic advantage over competitors by proactively anticipating NGOs' demands (Spar and La Mure 2003). There seems to be no question of that in this case study.

Among the demand factors in this case, we must also distinguish between the local, Cambodian market and the European and North American markets that are much more important for Heineken. In Cambodia, beer consumers are not particularly interested in the lot of PGs, but it is not clear how open consumers are for this issue in the European and North American markets. The demand that Heineken do something in this case comes mainly from other stakeholders, e.g. NGOs connected with Ian Lubek. Apparently Heineken wants to play it safe by setting up and implementing a training programme to prevent damage that could arise should Lubek's campaign gain momentum. At the same time, Heineken can use the programme to sustain and even strengthen its reputation as a socially responsible corporation.

All in all, reviewing supply and demand factors does not bring us much closer to an explanation for Heineken's behaviour. One reason is the paucity of information needed for an in-depth analysis. Still, it would seem that Heineken derives few advantages from tackling the problem of PGs in Cambodia; it is also unclear whether all this would provide any benefit for Heineken in the West. But that does not mean that we must abandon the prudent motive model, i.e. this does not mean that we have no other option than to presuppose ethical motives as explanation for Heineken's actions. In our modern globalised, interdependent and complex world, Heineken's apparent need to present itself as a "decent" company that feels responsible for the conditions under which its products are sold only becomes manifest in a social context and situation in which NGOs play a pivotal function. In the rest of this article I would like to address the interplay between activist NGOs and Heineken to understand how Western NGOs can bring about change in emerging countries.

The case study focuses on Ian Lubek more than on other activist NGOs. This Canadian professor does research, publishes articles in newspapers and on his own website and writes to brewers. The case states that Lubek hopes that other brewers and distributors will follow Heineken's example. He hopes to encourage this by publishing the addresses of brewers whose products are distributed in Cambodia (see: www.fairtradebeer.com/). However, it is not certain whether consumers will, indeed, put pressure on brewers.

Heineken took steps in 2002; and at the same time it "cut off all direct communication with Lubek" (case description, p. 74); the reason remains uncertain. The company studied the issue. It examined the PGs' working conditions and tried to understand how a course of action aimed at these women would be received. In any event, local partners' cooperation is essential to the impact of any potential course of action. Heineken cultivated contacts with NGOs and local government institutions and, in the end, set up and implemented a training programme for PGs with Care Cambodia. Heineken would have to introduce the programme everywhere where PGs stimulate beer sales. However, Heineken's approach to HIV/AIDS applies only to employees on Heineken's payroll and thus not to the Cambodian PGs, whom the local distributors employ.

Of course, we could ask about the fairness of Heineken's policy – broadly speaking and in terms of this one programme. However, I will not go into that question here. I prefer to concentrate on understanding the mechanism that prompted Heineken to develop a training programme for the PGs. How can we understand the underlying mechanism?

To understand this, I will draw on a now classic study of "transnational advocacy networks" (Keck and Sikkink, 1998). Keck and Sikkink argue convincingly that NGOs increasingly join forces in international networks to influence institutions in which they often have no immediate material interest. This is more than just cooperation between NGOs in emerging countries; it is a combination of NGOs in developed and emerging countries working together. One familiar pattern is when a development organisation travels to an emerging area to dig wells, set up schools or organise medical assistance. A less well known pattern is when Western NGOs campaign and lobby *in industrialised countries* to improve an undesirable situation in an emerging country. Keck and Sikkink analysed this latter pattern and described it as a boomerang effect. Subjects can include improving human rights situations, strengthening the position of women and preventing and resolving environmental problems. Although the original model analysed institutional change via government interference, the model can be broadened to include other powerful entities. "Powerful entities" here refers to actors with high impact on, and the power to change, the living conditions of specific groups in society. Large companies certainly fit this description.

The model (See Fig. 9.1a) explains how in emerging countries local groups that cannot directly sway local rulers to organise the institutional change they desire can try another approach. Access to local rulers can be blocked because the ruler is an authoritarian or semi-authoritarian state or an unscrupulous profit-grabbing company that could not care less about the needs of local groups. In other situations, conflicts of interest or lack of interest can frustrate access to local rulers. Local groups join networks with Western NGOs to apply pressure. If Western NGOs decide to work for the needs of such local groups, they can provide advice and support, information and resources and can move Western rulers to apply pressure on the local rulers. Local rulers can be sensitive to Western pressure, e.g. because of the latter's moral authority or because the local rulers depend on the West for legitimacy or resources. Western rulers can use such factors to exact institutional change. This mechanism – the boomerang effect – can be found in many case studies. Armbruster-Sandoval (2003) explains how the Korean management finally improved working conditions in a Honduran *maquiladora* factory; their US

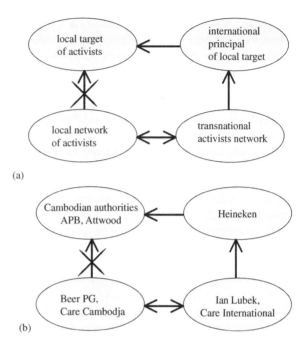

Fig. 9.1 Boomerang effect, **a** general model, **b** applied to the PG in Cambodia (adapted from Keck and Sikkink, 1998: 13)

principals forced it to do so after US pressure groups inundated the US principals with letters and a media campaign.

We can discern a similar pattern in the case of PGs (see Fig. 9.1b). Those in Cambodia who could improve the PGs' working conditions – local pub owners, local distributors, Cambodian governments and other power holders – are doing nothing. Lubek believed that the Cambodian government did too little to help PGs (case description, p. 72). We can also imagine reasons why these parties are not very interested in tackling the issue. Pub owners and local distributors might see their profits slide and the Cambodian government, its tourist industry were PGs to be better protected. Lubek's chance meeting with a young Cambodian led to the creation of a transnational advocacy network. Lubek aimed at Western public opinion and Western brewers. Lubek and others gave little attention to the Asian brewers that operated on the Cambodian market (case description, p. 75). For its own reasons, Heineken decided to do something to help the PGs; earlier on in this article I speculated on the question why the focus was on Heineken and not on other brewers. On one side, Heineken investigated the PGs' situation and finally joined with Care Cambodia to set up a programme. On the other, Heineken met with its partners and the Cambodian government. We can only interpret Heineken's interest as the result of pressure to do something. APB and Attwood, the PGs' employers, will have to get involved in carrying out the programme. Furthermore, I think it probable that – given Heineken's stance – the responsibility for the programme will ultimately be placed with the Cambodian partners.

In fact, although such may well have been its underlying ambition, Heineken did not work directly to improve the Cambodian PGs working conditions but to develop a standard that, in time, could be made obligatory for all Heineken partners working with PGs. In doing this, Heineken gave a new dimension to the long-standing codes of behaviour that Western companies use when working in emerging countries. Most such codes were drafted to impose Western norms for working conditions, wage and environmental quality on suppliers in emerging countries – upstream in the chain of production. In this situation a Western company is trying to influence the distribution and marketing conditions of its product in an emerging country – downstream – in the production chain. This, too is an interesting point.

All things considered, the case of Heineken and the Promotion Girls in Cambodia has several interesting points. Did Heineken have ethical motives? Who knows? It is certainly not impossible, but despite the absence of some information, the case offers a few clues for evaluating the plausibility of other statements using the prudent motive model. Setting up and implementing a programme to prevent HIV/AIDS infection among PGs seems to produce no advantages for Heineken in Cambodia. Nor does it appear to produce any immediate advantages for Heineken in the West. But there may be indirect advantages. One can speculate that Heineken wanted to prevent damage to its reputation that could arise from a discrepancy between the conditions under which its products were sold in Cambodia and its ambition to apply high moral and publicly desirable standards. However, it seems that a NGO's prompting was needed to get it moving. It is more generally true that NGOs draw companies into their struggle to improve the world. Even when the companies have moral motives, the NGOs' activities remove these from sight with their direct or indirect attempts to influence the company by appealing to its self-interest. After all, the point is: would Heineken have acted to improve the PGs' lot without Lubek's pressure to do so? But that is also speculation.

References

Armbruster-Sandoval, R. 2003. Globalization and Transnational Labor Organizing. The Honduran Maquiladora Industry and the Kimi Campaign. *Social Science History*, 27(4): 551–576.
Friedman, M. 1970. "The Social Responsibility of Business is to Increase its Profits." in New York Times Magazine, (13 September): 22–26. http://smba03.furchescompany.com/files/Social_Responsibility_of_Business.pdf
Heineken. 2004. Annual Report. Amsterdam: Heineken N.V. http://www.heinekeninternational.com/content/live/files/downloads/InvestorRelations/Full%20Annual%20Report_tcm4-12793.pdf last viewed 6 Nov. 2009.
Keck, M. and Sikkink, K. 1998. *Activists Beyond Borders. Advocacy Networks in International Politics*. Ithaca, NY: Cornell University Press.
McWilliams, A. and Siegel, D. 2001. Corporate Social Responsibility. A Theory of the Firm Perspective. *Academy of Management Review*, 26(1): 117–127.
Spar, D.L. and La Mure, L.T. 2003. The Power of Activism: Assessing the Impact of NGOs on Global Business. *California Management Review*, 45(3): 78–101.
Vergouw, J. and den Hond, F. 2000. Actiegroepen als nieuw bedrijfsrisico. Over de invloed van actiegroepen op het beleid van ondernemingen. *Management en Organisatie*, 54(1): 21–44.

Part IV
Case C: Heineken and Promotion Girls in Cambodia – Part 2

Chapter 10
Case Description: Heineken and Promotion Girls in Cambodia, Part 2

Frans-Paul van der Putten

Abstract In the spring of 2005, CARE presented a research report at a congress in Phnom Penh. It showed the case of Heineken and the promotion girls (PGs) from a largely new perspective. The approach to PGs that Heineken developed in 2003–2004 was mainly aimed at reducing the PGs' risk of becoming infected with HIV and other sexually transmitted diseases (STDs). However, CARE's new report shows that the girls' working conditions – not the chance that a minority of them will become infected with HIV as a result of after-hours sex with customers – are the greatest threat to the PGs' well-being. The most serious consequences of the PGs' working conditions appear to be that they are daily exposed to violent types of sexual intimidation.

Introduction

In the spring of 2005, CARE presented a research report at a congress in Phnom Penh. It showed the case of Heineken and the promotion girls (PGs) from a largely new perspective. The approach to PGs that Heineken developed in 2003–2004 was mainly aimed at reducing the PGs' risk of becoming infected with HIV and other sexually transmitted diseases (STDs) (Heineken International, 2004).[1] However, CARE's new report shows that the girls' working conditions – not the chance that a minority of them will become infected with HIV as a result of after-hours sex with customers – are the greatest threat to the PGs' well-being.[2] The most

---

F.-P. van der Putten (✉)
Netherlands Institute of International Relations Clingendael, The Hague, The Netherlands
e-mail: fputten@clingendael.nl

[1] See also www.heinekeninternational.com/selling_beer_safely.aspx and www.fairtradebeer.com/reportfiles/heinekenaidspolicy2002.pdf. Both last viewed 26 Oct. 2009.

[2] Hawkins (15 June 2005) See: www.camnet.com.kh/cambodia.daily/selected_features/cd-15-6-05.htm (last viewed 26 Oct. 2009). In addition, even before May 2005 several other articles based on

serious consequences of the PGs' working conditions appear to be that they are daily exposed to violent types of sexual intimidation.

CARE's Research[3]

In early 2005, CARE carried out a survey among 640 PGs in Cambodia. The study addresses the situation in the capital and in six other cities. Its purpose was to ascertain the extent to which sexual harassment and abuse played a role in PGs' working conditions. The participating PGs worked for the five largest employers of beer promotion girls. Combined, they employ around half of the approximately 4000 PGs at work in Cambodia.

CARE's study shows that sexual harassment and abuse occur frequently in beer promotion. Sexual harassment at work entails being confronted with unwelcome sexual advances in a work situation.[4] Abuse is when this is accompanied by manifestations of physical or verbal violence. Of the PGs interviewed, a large majority (80%) has been pawed by customers in the pubs where they worked. More than a quarter of this group said it happened every day. In addition, many women (60%) received occasional threats of violence from a customer when they did not do what he wanted. It did not stop with threats. More than half the women said they had been physically abused by pub or restaurant customers (17% reported that this occurred daily), and nearly one in three of all those interviewed occasionally required medical treatment as a result of work-time abuse.

According to CARE, beer promotion is a dangerous activity. This is not a matter of being beaten or treated roughly. A considerable portion (38%) of those questioned stated that customers in the pubs or restaurants where they worked had occasionally forced them to engage in sexual acts or had raped them (the study made no distinction between these two). Nearly 4% of all those questioned had undergone this more than 10 times.

The owners of the pubs and restaurants where the PGs work can hardly be called supportive. More than a third (37%) of the respondents had been forced by the owner to be more intimate or friendly with a customer than they wanted to be. 15% of respondents reported that the location owner tried to force women to engage in

---

less systematic research than CARE's showed that sexual intimidation was a substantial element of the circumstances in which PGs work in Cambodia. See ActionAid, "Hand in my Pant: The Life of a Beer Promotion Girl in Phnom Penh" (ActionAid 2003) on www.actionaid.org/asia/337_5_31.html (1 Aug. 2005). However, the best-known critic, Ian Lubek, still emphasised HIV/AIDS in early 2005. See: www.fairtradebeer.com/reportfiles/Lubek2005.pdf (last viewed 29 Oct. 2009) and www.fairtradebeer.com/reportfiles/lubekheineken2004.rtf (last viewed 26 Oct. 2009).

[3] All the data in this section are taken from Louise Bury (2005). See www.fairtradebeer.com/reportfiles/CARE/louiseburyCARE2005.pdf. Last viewed 24 Oct. 2009.

[4] See also the ILO's description at www.ilo.org/public/english/employment/gems/eeo/tu/cha_4.htm. 1 Aug. 2005.

sex with customers. A portion (17%) of the PGs who reported needing medical treatment said that they were abused by the owner or his/her staff. In some cases, their own organisation – not the pub or restaurant but the distribution company – was directly involved in the abuse. Eight percent of respondents reported that colleagues (managers, salesmen, drivers, etc.) had forced them to have sex.

CARE notes that in many cases the wage structure probably contributes to the GPs weak position vis-à-vis aggressive customers. Three quarters of the PGs in the study work on commission. Their wage is totally dependent on their sales. This system increases the customer's hold over a PG. The product subject to the promotion, beer, is also a large part of the problem. Not only may we assume that a customer's aggression increases in proportion to his alcohol consumption, it appears that nearly all PGs also drink beer during working hours. A quarter drinks more than five cans or bottles per evening. The women interviewed report that the reason for their beer consumption was that customers forced them to drink or that they did so to sell more beer. According to the study, PGs' alcohol consumption results in behaviour toward the customers that is more intimate and less prudent than otherwise.

The expressiveness of the figures in the study is heightened by the fact that many of the women questioned were but recently employed as PGs. Nearly half of those questioned had been working less than 6 months. The study showed that the employer or length of service as PG made no difference in the intensity or gravity of the sexual harassment and abuse. Although pubs (beer gardens and karaoke bars) are more dangerous than restaurants, sexual harassment occurs everywhere where PGs work.[5]

Local Standards

The CARE study's findings provide evidence of a social problem. First, it is important that CARE's researchers focused on the types of sexual harassment that the PGs considered unacceptable. The women who had undergone them considered all the investigated types of sexual harassment undesirable. Second, CARE also studied the most pertinent Cambodian legislation.[6] Unlike rape or attempted rape, unwelcome sexual advances are punishable by 1–3 years imprisonment. When these advances are accompanied by violence or threats, the punishment is doubled. Rape and attempted rape are prohibited on pain of 10–20 years imprisonment. Cambodian

---

[5]For the rest, CARE advises against using the terms promotion girls and indirect/direct sex work. They contribute to the public's negative image of PGs and further downgrade an already weak position. Promotion women is preferable. Bury (2005). See www.fairtradebeer.com/reportfiles/CARE/louiseburyCARE2005.pdf Last viewed 24 Oct. 2009.

[6]Bury (2005), Annex 2. See www.fairtradebeer.com/reportfiles/CARE/louiseburyCARE2005.pdf Last viewed 24 Oct. 2009.

law thus clearly prohibits the kind of sexual harassment and sexual violence that many PGs experience at work.[7]

Cambodian labour law also forbids all types of sexual harassment at work. According to this law, "all employers and managers of establishments in which child labourers or apprentices less than 18 years of age or women work, must watch over their good behaviour and maintain their decency before public".[8] So the beer distributor is not alone. The owner or manager of the pub or restaurant where the PGs work are obliged to see to it that the women are not exposed to sexual harassment.

In practice, this legal protection is meaningless for the promotion girls. Laws do exist but few people know about them, and faith in the judiciary system is almost non-existent. According to CARE, "Reporting a serious matter [to the police or their employer] is not even an option in the eyes of most BPs [beer promotion women], and even to report an incident to an outlet manager is not encouraged for fear of reprisal [by the owner of their workplace]".[9]

Impact on the Case

CARE's report does not mention the names of the beer producers, but does say that the abuses documented apply to the entire beer promotion industry in Cambodia. However, two earlier CARE studies were based solely on data about PGs who worked for Heineken partners CBL and Attwood.[10] Although these two studies were primarily aimed at PGs' attitude toward HIV/AIDS, they also collected data on safety at work. According to CARE, these show that the women considered harassment and violence a more serious problem than HIV infection (Quinn 2003).[11] Data from these earlier studies support the more recent CARE report and show that working conditions at Attwood and CBL are no different than elsewhere in the industry.

CARE believes that brewers as well as other parties (including the Cambodian government) have a role to play in improving working conditions. It has addressed recommendations to brewers and their distributors.[12] There will have to be a code of behaviour toward PGs that penalises pubs and restaurants that abuse these women.

---

[7] Licadho (2004), 7. See www.licadho-cambodia.org/reports/files/48Rape%20briefing%20report%202003%20English.pdf. Last viewed 24 Oct. 2009.

[8] www.cchr-cambodia.org/Laws/English/LaborLaw.htm (28 July 2005).

[9] Bury (2005), 51–52. See www.fairtradebeer.com/reportfiles/CARE/louiseburyCARE2005.pdf Last viewed 24 Oct. 2009.

[10] Care Cambodia (2003). See www.fairtradebeer.com/reportfiles/CARE/ingridquinnCARE2003.pdf (last viewed 24 Oct. 2009). Klinker (2005). See www.fairtradebeer.com/reportfiles/CARE/CAREendlinereport2005.pdf Last viewed 24 Oct. 2009.

[11] See also www.fairtradebeer.com/reportfiles/CARE/ingridquinnCARE2003.pdf. Last viewed 24 Oct. 2009.

[12] Bury (2005), 13 and 62–64. See www.fairtradebeer.com/reportfiles/CARE/louiseburyCARE2005.pdf Last viewed 24 Oct. 2009.

International companies should ensure that their local partners comply with local and international standards. Brewers and distributors should provide a training programme aimed at combating sexual harassment. These parties would have to investigate others channels for beer promotion.

As follow-up to the information already given on Heineken's organisational relation to the way beer is distributed in Cambodia, we note that Heineken has broad experience with the Cambodian beer market. Heineken opened a representative office in Cambodia in 1993, shortly after the arrival of the UN troops that put an end to the political chaos in the country (Gersdorf 1994). Construction of CBL's brewery was the first major foreign investment to which the Cambodian Investment Board granted approval in 1994 (Christern 1997). This brewery – the first to brew international brands in Cambodia – commenced operation in 1996. Upon its establishment, CBL took over distribution operations from Progress Import and Export Ltd (PIE), a Cambodian company that had formerly distributed Tiger beer (Algemeen Dagblad 1994).[13] Heineken's long presence in Cambodia is pertinent because CARE's report clearly shows that the issues concerning PGs are work-related – sometimes even the distributors' male employees are involved. This is not out of the distributors' sight as was assumed to be the case for the HIV/AIDS issue. Apart from that, the fact that pub and restaurant customers sometimes force PGs to engage in sex shows that the HIV/AIDS issue is not a totally after-hours matter.

CARE's report on sexual harassment and abuse, now available on internet, had not been published directly upon release, although it was distributed among concerned parties, including Heineken. Although CARE financed its own research and concomitant thorough and extensive report it was not clear at the time why the report was not published.

Finally

By the summer of 2005, Heineken's PG policy, made public in 2004, had brought about no visible improvement. The reasons that the company gave in 2004 for drafting a worldwide PG policy concerned the co-responsibility it felt for the risks of HIV infection that the PGs ran (Heineken International, 2004).[14] One consequence is that while this policy aimed at reducing risks, it did nothing to crack down on sexual harassment and abuse. CARE drew Heineken's attention to these abuses in the PGs' working conditions in 2005. Thus far, no protestors have set up public campaigns or made specific demands of Heineken. However, there is no reason to expect that the negative attention generated earlier on to the HIV/AIDS issue could not flare up once again by the work-related sexual harassment of and violence against PGs.

---

[13] PIE bought a 20% stake in CBL, the remaining 80% went to APB.

[14] Heineken International (2004), 2. See also www.heinekeninternational.com/selling_beer_safely.aspx and www.fairtradebeer.com/reportfiles/heinekenaidspolicy2002.pdf. Both last viewed 26 Oct. 2009.

References

ActionAid. 2003. 'Hand in my Pant: The Life of a Beer Promotion Girl in Phnom Penh.
Algemeen Dagblad, 1994. "Heineken bouwt brouwerij in Cambodja." *Algemeen Dagblad*, 13, 18 October.
Bury, L. 2005. *A Report on the Situation of Beer Promotion Women in the Workplace, Cambodia: Results of a Harassment and Abuse Survey,* 15–17. Phnom Penh: CARE International Cambodia.
Care Cambodia. 2003. *Selling Beer Safely: A Baseline Survey & Needs Assessment of Beer Promoters in Phnom Penh*. Phnom Penh: CARE International in Cambodia, Sept. 2003.
Christern, M. 1997. Nederlandse ondernemingen in Azië-Pacific: Heineken; De beste ontwikkelingshulp. *NRC Handelsblad*, 14: 27.
Gersdorf, F.V. 1994. Lange reeks tegenslagen kenmerkt Azië-avontuur bierbrouwer Heineken. *Het Financieele Dagblad*, 11.
Hawkins, K. 2005. NGO Seeks Cultural Makeover for "Beer Girls". Cambodia Daily, 1–2, June 1.
Heineken International. 2004. *Promotion Girls Policy: Selling Beer Safely*. Amsterdam: Heineken International.
Klinker, C. Feb. 2005. *Selling Beer Safely: A Cambodian Women's Health Initiative; Endline Evaluation*. Phnom Penh: CARE.
Licadho. 2004. *Rape and Indecent Assault*. Phnom Penh: Licadho.
Lubek, I. Spring 2005. Cambodian "Beer Promotion Women" and Corporate Caution: Recalcitrance or Worse?. *The Psychology of Women Section Review*, 7(1): 2–11.
Quinn, I. Sept. 2003. *Selling Beer Safely: A Baseline Survey & Needs Assessment of Beer Promoters in Phnom Penh*. Phnom Penh: CARE International Cambodia.

Chapter 11
Commentary: Legitimacy as Moral Exchange?

Frank G.A. de Bakker

Abstract The sequel to the controversy between Heineken and several NGOs raises questions on how far a company must go toward satisfying the demands and expectations of external stakeholders, in this case NGOs. In this commentary I discuss two elements of the case: the role of legitimacy as important factor in the advancing demands made of the company and the value of an institutional perspective for analysing such controversies. Legitimacy plays a significant role in such controversies, both for companies and NGOs and that a moral perspective on legitimacy could offer companies a way out of the struggle for legitimacy.

Introduction

Frans Paul van der Putten's article discusses the second phase in the controversy between Heineken and several NGOs[1] on the way in which companies should handle the use of promotion girls (PGs) to sell beer in Cambodia. Recent research led to a change in the interpretation of the issue. This sequel to the controversy raises questions on how far a company must go toward satisfying the demands and expectations of external stakeholders, in this case NGOs. In this commentary I will discuss the role of legitimacy in advancing demands made on the company and the value of an institutional perspective for analysing such controversies. Before I discuss these two points, I would first like to consider the course of the controversy thus far.

F.G.A. de Bakker (✉)
Department of Organization Science, VU University, Amsterdam, The Netherlands
e-mail: f.g.a.de.bakker@vu.nl

[1] Although there are extensive discussions on the definition, I use the term NGO here to refer to any of the various organisations that try to defend the interests of promotion girls.

A Brief Review

Although Heineken is not directly involved in deploying PGs and regularly draws attention to this fact, NGO's put pressure on the company. From 2002 the company developed a policy to curb the dangers of HIV infection. This policy is built on providing information and setting up courses, mainly for women not in Heineken's direct employ. A programme was set up in conjunction with Care Cambodia, the Cambodian branch of the NGO Care International. Care International is a "global humanitarian organisation working with over 45 million people in 70 of the world's poorest countries".[2] The programme is presented as part of Heineken's international social responsibility policy. Even Ian Lubek and other critics met it with enthusiasm.[3] Heineken believes that in setting up this programme it has met the NGOs' most important demands with regard to the PGs. Yet, Van der Putten examines a recent research report that puts the earlier analysis of the problem in a new light. Care International reported in 2005 that according to the PGs HIV infection is not the greatest threat to their well-being. Their working conditions pose a still greater threat to their health and well-being. According to this report, activities that take place *during* and not after their working hours are the main problem.

These new findings can have immediate consequences for Heineken. While the programme that Heineken set up is mainly aimed at preventing HIV infection, the new report shows that the PGs interests would be better served with other accents in company policy. Given the new research results, the company could face new demands, partly because Heineken's local distributors are also involved in the PGs working conditions. This would bring the problem closer to Heineken and its local subsidiaries. The legitimacy of the earlier solution would come under discussion. Basically, the company did not change the way it promoted beer. The new findings could lead to a new round in the controversy in which NGOs try to move Heineken to take further-reaching measures. Now that the training programme for after-work activities is "safe", it's time to tackle the actual working conditions. How should we understand the NGOs' attempt to broaden the field of interest? Are there problems with this discussion on legitimacy and can its rise be explained? Can multinationals arm themselves against being entangled in this type of discussions or, if that is impossible, against loosing this battle? These are the questions treated in this commentary.

---

[2] Homepage Care International, www.careinternational.org.uk/. Last viewed on 8 December 2005.

[3] Evidence for this can be found in two articles on Heineken's position toward PGs in *P-Plus* a journal on corporate social responsibility, "Heineken beschermt Beer Promotiongirls voor prostitutie", www.p-plus.nl/artikel.php?IK=306; "Redden levens biermeisjes kost Heineken 100.000 euro", www.p-plus.nl/artikel.php?IK=502 Last viewed on 23 December 2005.

Legitimacy – From Whom, for Whom?

As Van der Putten points out, no action has been taken thus far in response to the new report, either by Heineken or the NGOs.[4] Although the report was not widely distributed immediately upon release, such reports can still pose a threat to a company if the demands or those that make them can exert enough pressure on that company. In his commentary on the first part of this controversy, Frank den Hond lists a few reasons why Heineken is a suitable target for activists in this case. Heineken's response to earlier pressure shows that the company apparently considered the NGOs and their claims as legitimate, powerful and urgent (Mitchell et al., 1997). In this commentary, I want to examine the legitimacy aspect and the dispute around it because this plays a pivotal role in this controversy. I will show that in the end many potential claims arise from the degree in which the present method of promoting alcoholic drinks is accepted socially.

The concept legitimacy has several meanings depending on the context. When an action is considered morally legitimate, it means that adequate argumentations show this action to be correct or at least permissible apart from what some or even a majority of people may actually think. Of course, this does not mean that determining the legitimacy of an action in a specific situation poses no ethical issues. There are many, contradictory, views on the legitimacy of actions, among them the relativistic, utilitarian or Kantian views. However, all these approaches consider legitimacy a normative – judgmental – concept. Economic, sociological and strategic research often has a different approach to legitimacy. For these descriptive and explanatory perspectives, legitimacy can be termed a social good that companies need to survive. Customers and the general public must view companies as legitimate if these companies are to survive. Seen in this way, we can view legitimacy as determined by the degree to which customers and the general public approve or accept a company's actions, apart from the question whether these can be adequately justified. The emphasis in this commentary lies on the second perspective. Suchman (1995: 574) defined legitimacy in this sense as "a generalized perception or assumption that the actions of an entity are desirable, proper, or appropriate within some socially constructed system of norms, values, beliefs, and definitions."

Legitimacy is thus socially desirable, is a product of its time and place, and is subject to negotiation (Mitchell et al., 1997). Legitimacy is important for companies if they are to operate within a given social context over the long term. At the same time, what is legitimate in one, Cambodian, context need not be legitimate in another, e.g. Dutch, context. Discussion on which values and standards should govern Western companies' actions in emerging countries has therefore been going on for quite some time. Obtaining and retaining legitimacy in the many different institutional environments in which multinational companies operate is an important theme for such companies (Kostova and Zaheer, 1999). Questions that can be raised

---

[4]Here, again, information on the case is incomplete; perhaps some unpublicised action has been taken in the meantime.

include: What does legitimacy of such a complex organisation actually mean? In what context should it be judged? How does the legitimacy of local branches relate to that of the parent company? The NGOs that turned against Heineken and other brewers in the first part of this case study used the argument of the double standard. They asked why these companies should operate differently in Cambodia than in other countries. This seems to be an important argument, certainly for Heineken, that wants to take social responsibility as guiding principle and that became known for its progressive approach toward HIV/AIDS in Africa. That is why this argument provides NGOs with reasons to call Heineken rather than other brewers to account for its behaviour in Cambodia and elsewhere.

In this case NGOs use legitimacy instrumentally. To use Rodgers' words (2000: p. 48), "NGOs in both adversarial and advisory relationships with corporates are increasingly becoming primary agents in the stakeholder dialogue process and are able to significantly affect the perceived legitimacy of corporate activities." They use what Suchman (1995) calls pragmatic legitimacy: a type of legitimacy based on informed self-interest. NGOs have what one could think of as a moral exchange to offer in negotiations on the claims they make, because they can influence customers' and the general publics' perception of the legitimacy of a company's actions. Care Cambodia's cooperation in the development of a training programme for Heineken gave legitimacy to the programme and its initiator, Heineken. The programme was given moral approval while it was also instrumental in reaching Care Cambodia's objective: improving the promotion girls' well-being. NGO and company were both aware that they used legitimacy as an instrument of payment.

Yet this way of treating legitimacy as moral tender can also cause a company problems. Now that Care International had presented additional research findings that differed from those on which Heineken's training programme was based, there could ensue a battle for legitimacy. Was the programme that the company developed in response to earlier claims a good answer after all? It is striking that it took Heineken a while to respond publicly to Care International's report and that the NGO did not distribute it widely as soon as it was completed. Does that mean that, upon closer inspection, there is no real support for the conclusions? Does Care Cambodia understand matters differently than Care International? Is there fear that this report will adversely affect Heineken's training programme? Van der Putten does not say. A Heineken spokesperson has stated that the company rarely distributes information on subjects other than its core activities. One reason for this is that such programmes arise partly from self-interest.[5] Perhaps more is being done here than is immediately visible.

Nevertheless, the report was a potential threat to Heineken. In the time between its unofficial and official releases, the company had to decide how to deal with Care International and the new report. If Care International were to decide to draw attention to the information and gather allies for the new analysis, it could confront

---

[5]"Heineken beschermt Beer Promotiongirls voor prostitutie", www.p-plus.nl/artikel.php?IK=306. last viewed on 23 December 2005.

Heineken with additional demands. Although, or perhaps because, the company opted for a progressive response within the Cambodian market,[6] it had become an attractive target for follow-up campaigns or claims. The company had already shown its sensitivity is to the arguments used. Now that additional research produced new facts, the company could again be put under pressure to respond to these facts. Whether and to what extent that would actually happen depended in part on the NGO's objectives. The NGO's institutional strategies play a role in this. I will address that in the next section.

An Institutional Perspective

Heineken is regularly recognised as a front-runner in this controversy and, as was said, this can provoke additional claims. The claims' stake varies. Ian Lubek visited Heineken's headquarters for the first time in September 2005. He complemented Heineken but called upon the company to take the next step by ensuring a better wage for the promotion girls. In his newsletter[7] he put it this way, "Heineken executives were asked to take an even more vanguard role in the improvement of the lives of the women selling alcohol in Cambodia, beyond their current efforts with a 'Selling Beer Safely' educational program." Lubek is thus striving to improve the lives of the promotion girls, reasoning within the present institutional structure in which the deployment of these girls is taken for granted.

Care International shows evidence of having far-reaching aspirations, given the way in which it discusses the treatment of promotion girls and ultimately the promotion of alcoholic beverages. An article[8] in *The Cambodia Daily* in June 2005 states that Care International is aiming at a "cultural change". Care International wants to change the way the Cambodian public regards PGs. They are not "indirect sex workers". To reach this, project advisor Louise Bury, who also authored the report, says that various parties must be approached. "It's about sensitizing all stakeholders". According to the newspaper article, PGs, NGO staff, government representatives and representatives of the breweries and distributors attended the conference at which the report was presented to discuss ways to make PGs' work safer. This shows that this NGO ultimately seeks an institutional change that would lead to a transformation of accepted standards, values and practices (Scott, 2001). At the same time, we see an important shift in what is at stake in the controversy. Care International pursued a broad, comprehensive social outcome – an institutional change – while Heineken was primarily interested in an organisational solution. It wanted to resolve

---

[6] See: Bopha, C. 2005. "Beer Brands Ignoring Risks to Women Promoters", www.ipsnews.net/news.asp?idnews=31126, last viewed on 19 December 2005.

[7] SiRCHESI's Newsletter, Fall 2005, www.psychology.uoguelph.ca/research/lubek/cambodia/siemreapnewsletter.pdf. Last viewed on 23 December 2005.

[8] Hawkins, K. 2005. "NGO Seeks Cultural Makeover for 'Beer Girls'". *Cambodia Daily*, June 15, www.camnet.com.kh/cambodia.daily/selected_features/cd-15-6-05.htm. Last viewed on 19 December 2005.

the acute problem with PGs and, if possible, prevent new problems that could call its own organisation's legitimacy into question. When that last goal has a positive effect on local society, so much the better; but that was most likely not the company's main objective. When speaking of efforts to combat HIV/AIDS in Africa, Heineken's spokesperson explicitly drew attention to the company's self-interest. The company risked losing its middle management to the disease.[9] These efforts targeted the company's own organisation but had a positive side effect on local society. Lubek's efforts seem also to be less oriented toward institutional change than those of Care International. Ultimately, Heineken and Care International have conflicting interests.

Still, a company will have to be aware of the broader social implications if it is going to set its strategy. In the much-discussed controversy between Shell and Greenpeace on the sinking of the *Brent Spar*, Greenpeace was mainly interested in setting clear limits to what was and was not permissible, to what could and could not be considered legitimate. Greenpeace wanted to make clear that the ocean could not be used as a dumpsite (Grolin, 1998). Greenpeace's objectives went beyond the specific case; Greenpeace used casting doubt on the legitimacy of Shell's intentions as instrument to reach its own institutional objectives. Partly due to these experiences, Shell's CEO spoke regularly in the years after this controversy of the importance of having a licence from society to operate. Shell responded by developing structures for stakeholder dialogue and by presenting itself as a transparent company.

Similar patterns are visible in the case of Heineken and the promotion girls. Although it is difficult to assess the importance of Care International's report due to a dearth of information on the way in which the report has been used, the NGO's strategy does seem to be to bring about a stakeholder dialogue. Given the institutional context in Cambodia, that would probably be an important step forward. Not all NGOs seem to pursue the same goals – there is little evidence of cooperation between Lubek and Care International in this case – but both NGOs' ideal is a more or less drastic change in the institutional context. A company can respond in several ways when confronted with such institutional change or the intention to bring it about. These responses vary from denial and letting things be to steering and manipulation (Oliver, 1991). If a company, in this case Heineken, has a reputation for being progressive, the desire to retain or reinforce its legitimacy will prompt it to use such strategies consciously. Capitalising on the NGOs' claims and expectations can confer an advantage over other actors. As large market player and progressive company, Heineken can also offer legitimacy. When Heineken puts its support behind a plan or standard, this sends out a powerful signal to other stakeholders like NGOs and the general public. Heineken could use early involvement in stakeholder dialogues and elsewhere, to help shape institutional change and in this way remain a step ahead of the competition. The fact that, after years of refusal, Heineken met with Lubek

---

[9]"Redden levens biermeisjes kost Heineken 100.000 euro", www.p-plus.nl/artikel.php?IK=502 Last viewed on 23 December 2005.

in September 2005 also shows that the company is devoting greater attention to discussions with stakeholders on this subject. In controversies like this one, claims will continue to follow upon one another because the pursued ideals and the actual situation are so far apart. However, engagement in stakeholder dialogue offers a company an opportunity to assess the value of these claims, to judge their consequences for the company's legitimacy and its actions and to choose a suitable strategy. It may even be possible to set conditions in this type of dialogue: sometimes it is best to let matters be, but in other situations it may be more advisable to do something (for a discussion on this see Oliver, 1991).

Finally

Legitimacy – of company and NGO – plays a significant role in such controversies. Company and NGO both benefit from acquiring and retaining legitimacy for themselves and for their proposed measures. In addition, another view of legitimacy – one based on a moral perspective – could offer companies a way out of this type of battle for legitimacy. After all, when a company can provide adequate arguments to substantiate why a particular course of action is followed regardless of what people actually think, it can probably reduce its dependence on the ability of other stakeholders to confer legitimacy. At the same time, it is important to recognise that ethics, too, enlists several key criteria and that other schools of thought think that ethics without context is meaningless.

Many questions remain unanswered. It would be interesting to know the extent to which the NGOs in this controversy actually speak for the PGs. How great is the NGO's legitimacy in this case? At the same time, such questions lose importance when a (Western) company concludes that disputing the NGO's legitimacy is not an option or that doing so probably has more disadvantages than advantages (see the discussion on supply and demand and corporate social responsibility in Den Hondt's commentary). The subject has become so salient (Mitchell et al., 1997) that the company feels called to respond. Its response will nevertheless depend on the assessment that the company makes of the impact this response will have on the company's legitimacy on the local level (Cf. Kostova and Zaheer, 1999), or of the degree to which the response is self-serving (e.g. because the company can set a standard and can profit from a first mover advantage). The way legitimacy is actually used as moral exchange is an interesting subject for a follow-up study.

References

Grolin, J. 1998. Corporate Legitimacy in Risk Society: The Case of Brent Spar. *Business Strategy and the Environment*, 7: 213–222.
Kostova, T. and Zaheer., S. 1999. Organizational Legitimacy Under Conditions of Complexity: The Case of the Multinational Enterprise. *Academy of Management Review*, 24: 64–81.
Mitchell, R.K., Agle, B.R. and Wood, D.J. 1997. Toward a Theory of Stakeholder Identification and Salience: Defining the Principle of Who and What Really Counts. *Academy of Management Review*, 22: 853–886.

Oliver, C. 1991. Strategic Responses to Institutional Processes. *Academy of Management Review*, 16: 145–179.
Rodgers, C. 2000. Making it Legit. New ways of Generating Corporate Legitimacy in a Globalizing World. In: Bendell, J. (ed.), *Terms for Endearment. Business, NGOs and Sustainable Development*, 40–48. Sheffield: Greenleaf.
Scott, W.R. 2001. *Institutions and Organizations*, (2nd edition). Thousand Oaks, CA: Sage.
Suchman, M.C. 1995. Managing Legitimacy. Strategic and Institutional Approaches. *Academy of Management Review*, 20: 571–610.

Chapter 12
Commentary: How to Deal with the Side Effects of Delivering Beer?

Peter Koslowski

Abstract The following commentary focuses on the difference between immediate and indirect consequences of deeds and on the difference between immediate and indirect responsibilities proceeding from this division. We defend the position that Heineken must refrain from business practices that have immoral behaviour as highly predictable side effect; the trade agreements under which Heineken works may not cause or tolerate these practices. That would make these negative side effects a habitual consequence of doing business. We conclude with some reflections of the intercultural facets of this case study.

Introduction

As we read in the study on "Heineken and the Promotion Girls in Cambodia", Heineken is not the beer promotion girls (PGs) employer. Rather, it delivers beer to the girls' employers. The promotion girls work for the pub owners, drinking establishments and the like. Because Heineken is not the PG's immediate employer, Heineken bears no immediate responsibility for their working conditions. The question is whether Heineken bears indirect responsibility and what obligations proceed from this indirect responsibility.

The following commentary focuses on the difference between immediate and indirect consequences of deeds and on the difference between immediate and indirect responsibilities proceeding from this division. People and companies bear immediate responsibility for the consequences of deeds thought to be the result of immediate intentions. They are indirectly responsible for the indirect consequences of their conduct when it is thought to be the result of indirect intentions. The vendor's product responsibility proceeds from his immediate responsibility for trade as stipulated in the contractual agreement and the nature of the relationship between vendor and buyer. The vendor is responsible for the quality of the goods sold and

---

P. Koslowski (✉)
VU University, Amsterdam, The Netherlands
e-mail: p.koslowski@ph.vu.nl

for delivering them as agreed. The buyer is responsible for paying the agreed price under the agreed conditions on the agreed date. Because Heineken's relationship with the pubs was a customer relationship, the first question to arise was what kind of responsibility Heineken had on the basis of the contractual agreement with the pubs operating on the Cambodian market.

Obligations: More than Mere Product Responsibility

A vendor that holds a strong market position and can exert considerable influence on his customers is indirectly responsible for certain of the customer's habits when these habits relate to the normal conduct of affairs within their commercial relationship. Although product responsibility is the vendor's first and most important responsibility, vendors can bear indirect responsibility for promoting the moral aspects of the conditions under which customers do business with third parties. The product responsibility theory is a controversial subject in ethical theory building. Some ethicists believe that this theory goes too far in limiting the vendor's responsibility. Nevertheless, it is the first step toward establishing the vendor's obligation because the product is the most important element in the business relationship. The ethical analysis must start with the specific nature of the business relationship. According to the sales contract, the product sold – and not any other types of possible relationships between the two parties – determines the relationship between vendor and buyer.

In terms of product responsibility theory, Heineken bears little responsibility. But given the moral principles contained in the consequentialist theory, Heineken must accept a degree of responsibility for the side effects related to its repeated sale of beer to the customers who develop their own routine within this repeated transaction. We should not concentrate solely on the main effects of Heineken's beer sales, but also on this activity's side effects, on its impact on the routines Heineken's customers develop in dealing with their own customers and employees. A complicating factor in this and similar cases is that Heineken's activities take place in a business environment with work and business standards that differ considerably from those in Heineken's native culture. The case study has an intercultural facet to which I will return at the end of this commentary.

Heineken's position in the tripartite business relationship between pub keepers, PGs and brewers is sufficiently strong economically to allow it to insist on contract conditions. Because Heineken supplies an internationally known beer brand, because in the case of follow-up orders it does so in a repetitive contract and because it can exert influence on the way in which the beer is served, as is customary in the beer industry, Heineken can exert some influence on the working conditions in his customers' establishments, although it is not directly responsible for them. Heineken's twofold position within the business relationship – as supplier with a strong market position and as partner in a long-term business relationship – makes the case more awkward than in a normal sales relationship between vendor and buyer. More is involved than a simple question about the vendor's responsibility for what the buyer does with the purchased merchandise. The vendor can influence what the buyer does with the merchandise and how the buyer serves the product in this pub. That Heineken is the strongest party in the business relationship is a complicating factor that makes the case suitable for studying the limits of companies' individual and social responsibility and their direct and indirect responsibility. Had Heineken employed PGs directly, it would have had direct responsibility for ensuring that its employees were not subjected to sexual harassment. What responsibility does Heineken bear as supplier to the PGs' employers?

Because Heineken supplies only beer, one might wonder whether Heineken is the only one responsible for the working conditions of those working for his customers. A trader is not usually responsible for the way in which the buyer uses the merchandise. The responsibility for correct use lies with the buyer. However, the general rule on the division of responsibilities changes when the vendor can clearly envisage that the buyer will use the merchandise for immoral purposes or, in the case when this prospect is lacking, that there is at least a serious chance that the buyer will do something immoral with merchandise because the buyer has done so in the past.

The rules on the distribution of responsibility and on the increased responsibility when there is a serious chance the merchandise will be misused do not imply that Heineken can be held liable for incidental violent harassment of PGs when pub keepers normally see to it that their employees are protected against sexual intimidation as Cambodian law requires.

Matters are different when the sexual intimidation of PGs becomes a side effect of serving Heineken beer in the pubs. The figures in this case arouse the impression that the latter is the case. Is Heineken indirectly responsible for sexual intimidation in pubs to which it supplies beer? Does Heineken bear indirect responsibility for the sexual intimidation even when it does not manage these pubs?

Direct and Indirect Causality

There are two reasons why Heineken is indirectly responsible. The first relates to the merchandise, beer. The second is that it permits its customers to behave in a manner that would be unacceptable within its own company. If we accept Heineken's indirect responsibility, we must distinguish two different courses of action with moral causality and indirect responsibility. Heineken could bear indirect responsibility for the sexual harassment: first because this is the result of serving beer and second, because it results from the way pub keepers do business and Heineken tolerates this.

Case 1: If Heineken's merchandise, beer, is always accompanied by improper behaviour by the pub's customers, the beer drinkers, because the product, beer, encourages intimidation and abuses and neutralises inhibitions, then Heineken should see to it that beer is served in a different way. Ethical rules for the sale of alcohol apply here. The pub keepers and PGs should not sell alcohol to customers that show signs of already being drunk or of being unable to behave properly after drinking even a small amount of alcohol. The pub keepers and PGs are not required to refuse all sales, but they are obliged to refrain from serving alcohol to customers clearly unable to hold it. As supplier of the beer, Heineken is indirectly responsible for the conditions under which it is served because it is required to ensure that its business customers, the pubs, comply with the rules. Heineken must stop its deliveries to pubs that repeatedly and customarily disregard these rules.

Case 2: Does Heineken become indirectly responsible for pub customers' unsuitable behaviour when it sells to those supplying services to these customers, i.e. to the pub keepers? This second case of Heineken's indirect responsibility for the sexual intimidation PGs is more complicated. This situation falls under second-tier indirect responsibility. The pubs are indirectly responsible for their customers' behaviour. Heineken is indirectly answerable for its customers' behaviour and they are indirectly responsible for that of their customers; the pub's customers are, in turn, directly liable for their own behaviour. The presupposition that Heineken is indirectly answerable for its customers' indirect responsibility for their customers' behaviour cannot be taken for granted. In this case, rather than being immediate Heineken's responsibility is very indirect. The first precondition for Heineken's indirect responsibility is that the company is either the indirect cause of its customers' behaviour and that this behaviour is, in its turn, the indirect cause of the pub customer's behaviour or that Heineken tolerates its customers' practices by supplying beer to these unsuitable pubs even though their owners' behaviour is morally unacceptable.

Erotic Favours Within Working Relationships

We presuppose that Heineken does not intentionally encourage unacceptable behaviour in beer drinkers and that Heineken in no way encourages pub keepers to allow this unsuitable behaviour. Heineken, we assume, has no direct or indirect intention to stimulate or tolerate unsuitable behaviour in beer drinkers with a view to selling more beer. Does Heineken expect that the PGs will undergo beer drinkers' erotic advances simply to sell more beer and does this indirectly foster beer drinkers' unsuitable behaviour?

The pubs and Heineken will certainly sell more beer when the PGs acquiesce to beer drinkers' advancers. They would sell more beer by letting beer drinkers believe that they could expect "something extra" from the PGs e.g. erotic favours on site or sexual servicing after hours. It would be dishonest for pubs to hire PGs and then expect them to supply these extra, unpaid erotic services for beer drinkers. This would mean that the employers add extra, unpaid services to the employment contract. The wage for the work PGs do does not cover these services. Their pay is therefore not a just price when compared to the work that they do when they are expected to provide extra erotic services. Heineken and the pubs could answer that tips cover the cost of these extra services. But tips do not solve the problem because the PGs are still providing extra services for their employers, the pubs, and the brewer Heineken, while neither the employer nor brewer pay for them. As for tips, it is also possible that the customers may not leave any. All customary services must be paid as wages and not as uncertain tips.

The next question concerns the sexual services that the PG may provide after hours. There is no causal connection between these services and the working relationship. They are purported to be the PGs' private matter. An employer can stipulate in an employment contract that an employee is not allowed to use knowledge obtained on the worksite, in this case in contact with potential customers. Prohibiting PGs from taking home beer drinkers met while at work falls under a normal provision prohibiting the use of knowledge acquired on the worksite. According to the case description, the PGs' employment contract contains what can be considered a prohibition against use of knowledge. However, the question is whether this prohibition is enforceable or whether it is only rhetoric.

Whether the employer has the right or duty to protect his/her employees from prostitution depends on the question whether prostitution is immoral and illegal or whether it is to be tolerated. This question is beyond the scope of this paper. However, pub keepers may not tacitly assume that the PGs are open to prostitution intended to serve as extra enticement for beer drinkers to come to their pub.

A Deed with "Double Effect"

Vendors may not sell to a buyer when the vendor can be certain that the buyer will use the merchandise inappropriately. An arms dealer may not sell arms to juveniles or to patently aggressive and dangerous customers or in a situation where it is probable that the weapons will be misused, as in times of crisis and war. In these cases, ethical theory assumes that the vendor knowingly and willingly accepts and approves the consequences of his/her actions. When people accept the harmful consequences of their deeds, it is assumed that they act with an indirect intention and that they are indirectly responsible for the consequences. They do not directly intend the consequences of their deeds, but they intend them by accepting them as a side effect of their main objective.

That an action can have a double effect or main effect and several side effects was and is a key ethical principle in the history and theory of ethics, although we must admit that ethicists disagree on this principle (See: Koslowski, 2001: 137ff). The principle applies to our case because the immoral practices in employing the PGs are not the consequence of Heineken's direct intentions or action, but a side effect that Heineken tolerates in pursuing its intention to sell beer. If subjecting PGs to sexual intimidation is a predictable and repeated side effect of the conditions under which Heineken and the pub keepers sell beer, then Heineken would have to be thought to accept and indirectly intend this side effect. In that case, Heineken would have indirectly intended and thus would bear indirect responsibility for the sexual intimidation of PGs.

The double-effect principle can be put as follows: An act with negative side effects is permitted when the following four criteria have been met:

- The objective of the action must be good and honest (i.e. the actor does not intend to produce bad and impermissible effects). The side effects should not be intended. Heineken should not intend or accept the sexual intimidation as side effect of its commercial activities.
- The type or class of activity must be good. Heineken should supply the beer in a sensible way.
- The negative side effects must, however, be true *side* effects. When regarded objectively, they must display the character of accidental effects proceeding from the pursuit of other objectives and must not serve as means for a better result. Sexual intimidation may not be a normal and customary side effect or a means to sell more beer in pubs.
- There must be a comparatively important reason for performing the action. There must be good reasons for Heineken to supply beer to these pubs. In judging the actual situation, it should be impossible to conclude that it would be better to stop completely with supplying beer to pub keepers and to focus on other activities in Cambodia.

The double-effect principle is not the same as an uncritical and general comparison of good and evil that concludes that of all possible actions that which results in the greatest good and the least evil must be chosen. The double-effect principle does not differ from the principle of the greater good in that the double-effect principle simply by weighing the good and bad consequences of actions be they of direct and indirect intentions; rather it differs by distinguishing primary from secondary effects. Good and bad consequences and side effects are not treated as equally important and ethically relevant. The primary effects of actions are of greater moral importance than their secondary effects. In distinguishing between side effects of direct intentions and the side effects of indirect intentions, the double-effect principle takes into account the different levels of intentionality and consequence and distinguishes between the direct intention of the main effect and the indirect intention of the side effect. The principle does not treat all consequences in the same way. From the perspective of the double effect principle, Heineken cannot hide behind the principle of good and evil. Heineken cannot excuse itself by saying that this way of doing business just happens to have habitual but nasty side effects in its customers' pubs, but that this has to be overlooked for the sake of Heineken's chief goal, selling beer. Although Heineken cannot exclude all cases of sexual intimidation within businesses to which it delivers beer, it must cease delivering to businesses where it has become customary to infringe the rules of correct business behaviour. Heineken must refrain from business practices that have immoral behaviour as side effect; the trade agreements under which Heineken works may not cause or tolerate these practices. That would make these negative side effects a habitual consequence of doing business.

Heineken may not sell beer to pubs whose practices or strategy permit immoral acts. Beer deliveries help sustain businesses that should not be allowed to continue because these businesses customarily sell beer under circumstances that violate the human rights of their employees and their customers. Heineken is indirectly responsible for these practices. Heineken is co-responsible for ensuring that the brand is not misused in circumstances that conflict with normal employee and consumer behaviour and where there are serious chances that these circumstances will arise.

One reason, but not the sole reason, that Heineken should do this is to protect the reputation of its brand name. Looking at the effects of this case on Heineken's good name changes the perspective from ethical to commercial. Reputation management cannot replace morality and ethics. It is, however, an extra argument alongside the moral and emphasises concern for possible negative side effects of beer deliveries for the company. When Heineken beer is repeatedly sold under circumstances that violate standard business ethics, the brand name becomes identified with these circumstances and with a sleazy moral level. Again, the predictability and habitude of its customers, the pub keepers' unsuitable behaviour and business practices with regard to the PG are of importance.

That the way of selling the beer reinforces the link between beer and erotic adventures complicates Heineken's reputation management even more. Some target groups will consider this link a stimulus for drinking Heineken. The beer industry's target group is not uniform. Its members are driven by a variety of desires which makes it difficult for a brewer to chart a single course when it comes to its morality and reputation.

The intercultural dimension makes the PGs' case more eloquent. Heineken and other Western companies face a dilemma when Western tourists visit Cambodian pubs in search of "erotic extras". May a Western company offer its goods under morally questionable circumstances? Should Heineken withdraw from such business or should it "cleanse" the companies with which it deals of such improper customs? A company need not play watchdog over its customers' behaviour. But a company can also see its reputation damaged and run a moral risk when it permits drinking and pleasure habits abroad that are unacceptable "at home" in the West. In remaining passive, Heineken can harm its reputation at home. Heineken will have to find a middle way between giving its customers a moral education and doing harm to its reputation at home because of the unacceptable moral side effects of its business operations.

The case on "Heineken and the Promotion Girls in Cambodia" is a good example for displaying the need for, and outer limits of, corporate social responsibility. Heineken cannot be expected to bear the brunt of the corporate social responsibility for ensuring that an entire industry protects PGs from unsolicited behaviour. This would shift full responsibility for the pubs and their Western customers to Western brewers. We cannot expect that company to apologise for its customers' poor behaviour and then to give these customers a lesson in good manners. On the other side, Heineken cannot withdraw from its indirect responsibility for its commercial partners' business operations. Heineken must work with its customers to develop a style of operational management that ensures that the principles of just pricing and correct business behaviour are not violated in the companies to which it delivers.

Reference

Koslowski, P. 2001. *Principles of Ethical Economy*. Dordrecht, Boston, MA: Springer, Kluwer.

Part V
Case D: A Disputed Contract – IHC Caland in Burma

Chapter 13
Case Description: A Disputed Contract – IHC Caland in Burma

Frank G.A. de Bakker and Frank den Hond

Abstract IHC Caland designed, built and operated material, ships and complete systems for offshore oil and gas, dredging and shipping industries. The relatively strong economic growth in Southeast Asia offered opportunities for IHC Caland and other specialised suppliers. In the summer of 1998, an IHC Caland subsidiary contracted for an offshore project in Burma's territorial waters. The order was for several hundreds of millions euros, hence of considerable interest to the company. The contract led to public stir because it involved work in a country controversial for its human rights situation. Many human rights, environmental and union organisations expressed their outrage and tried to move IHC Caland to cancel the contract. A controversy was born. It took IHC Caland long resisted the claims made by the NGOs. It maintained that the morality of commercial agents is limited to abiding with all legal laws and regulations. It therefore argued that it had not committed any moral wrong and was allowed to do business with the Burma government.

In the summer of 1998, an IHC Caland subsidiary contracted for an offshore project in Burma's territorial waters.[1] The order was for several hundreds of millions euros, hence of considerable interest to the company. The contract led to public stir because it involved work in a country controversial for its human rights situation. Many human rights, environmental and union organisations expressed their outrage and tried to move IHC Caland to cancel the contract. A controversy was born. At the time of the contract Burma seemed to have become inextricably associated with the name "IHC Caland". Finally, in the summer of 2003, the Dutch Trade Union Federation (FNV) and the Christian Trade Union Federation (CNV) reached a compromise with

---

F.G.A. de Bakker (✉)
Department of Organization Science, VU University, Amsterdam, The Netherlands
e-mail: f.g.a.de.bakker@vu.nl

[1] This chapter uses the name "Burma". The military government has since changed the country's name to Myanmar, but dissidents continue to use Burma; (Myanmar) or Myanmar (Burma). We chose Burma for ease of reading.

IHC Caland regarding its operations in Burma. Nevertheless, the two trade unions and other players in the controversy stressed that they preferred to see the company leave Burma.

Before discussing the company's motives and the responses to them, we will first present a brief description of the situation in Burma and of the company in question. After that we will devote a few sections to the course of the controversy, focussing explicitly on the various arguments presented by the parties to the conflict and to compromise ultimately achieved.[2]

The Situation in Burma

Burma is situated in Southeast Asia. The country borders on India, Bangladesh, China, Thailand and Laos. It is home to more than 52 million people divided over 135 different population groups. The country is rich in natural resources and has a long history. The Union of Burma gained its independence from Great Britain in 1948. The country was governed as a Western-style parliamentary democracy (Zarni, 2000). Although after the Second World War Burma was considered one of the non-aligned countries with the best chances for development and growth, by 1987 it had become the UN's "least developed country". In the interval, General Ne Win had put aside the civilian government (1962) after which (1974) the country was transformed into a socialist, one-party state under the Burma Socialist Programme Party (BSPP). Ne Win sealed the country off hermetically from the outside world; the Burmese population was as good as forbidden to travel abroad and visas for foreigners were either refused or restricted to a brief period. Ne Win stayed in power for 26 years, partly as the result of a highly centralised economic policy, military might and extreme repression by military intelligence and other services (Spit, 1995).

Social and political unrest grew in the spring of 1988 and culminated in massive strikes that summer. Protestors demanded economic and democratic reforms. The army crushed the rebellion by force (Ferrara, 2003). After the summer, Ne Win withdrew and there was a partial change of government. The new government proclaimed martial law and adopted a new name: State Law and Order Restoration Council (SLORC). Summer saw the birth of a liberation movement, the National League for Democracy (NLD). Aung San Suu Kyi, daughter of one of the heroes of the struggle for independence against the British, returned from abroad to become leader of the NLD. In 1989 the military regime changed the country's name to the

---

[2]This chapter uses newspaper articles, press releases, annual reports and other documents to sketch developments relating to IHC Caland's operations in Burma. In addition, we used conversations with Peter Ras, coordinator of Burma Centrum Nederland (BCN) and Jeremy Woodrum, a campaign leader in the US Campaign for Burma. We improved the factual accounts in the text using IHC Caland's and BCN's comments to earlier versions of this chapter. To aid readability, in this chapter we did not refer to each individual newspaper article. A fully annotated version of this chapter can be requested from the authors.

Union of Myanmar and opened the country to foreign investment in an attempt to deregulate the Burmese economy and attract more foreign currency. But the authoritarian stranglehold on the population did not diminish (Zarni, 2000). Amnesty International (AI), Human Rights Watch (HRW) and other organisations regularly drew attention to the military regime's many flagrant and systematic human rights violations that were aimed especially against ethnic minorities.

In 1990, SLORC organised free elections in which several parties participated. The NLD, led by Aung San Suu Kyi, who had been placed under house arrest well before 1989, gained 62% of the votes, good for more than 80% of the parliamentary seats. However, the SLORC refused to acknowledge the NLD's victory. In 1991, Suu Kyi was awarded the Nobel Peace Prize for her years of non-violent struggle. She was released from house arrest in 1995, but it was reimposed from 2000 to 2002. She was arrested once again in 2003 and held in secret detention for more than 3 months before being returned to house arrest. The house arrest continues today (2010), this in clear violation of international and Burmese law.

Calls for a Boycott

Although the events in 1988 and 1989 received relatively little attention in the Western media, groups of activists in Burma, Thailand and the United States exchanged information, maintained a political lobby and worked for democracy. From this grew several online list servers with news on Burma. The best known is BurmaNet, set up in 1994 with support from the Open Society Institute. The first calls for a boycott were heard in the early 1990s:

> By the time BurmaNet was created, there was already a small number of individuals, primarily in the United States, Thailand, and Canada, who were advocating consumer boycotts and were engaged in shareholder, campus and community activism against foreign investors with economic interests in Burma (Zarni, 2000: 76).

In September 1995, the Free Burma Coalition (FBC) was established at the University of Wisconsin at Madison in the USA.[3] The organisation was established to combine, streamline and give strength to thus far uncoordinated information and protest actions. FBC used internet and other channels to disseminate its views widely (Danitz and Strobel, 1999). Its most important objectives were:

> (1) to end foreign investment in Burma under the current military dictatorship through economic activism and (2) to build a genuinely grassroots international Free Burma movement in support of Burma's freedom struggle (Zarni, 2000: 78).

Suu Kyi adopted the call for a boycott. From the mid 1990s, she regularly called upon foreign companies to withdraw from Burma.[4] Her appeal gained worldwide

---

[3] There are similar specialised protest groups in other countries (www.freeburma.org, last viewed on 20th February 2010).
[4] See the French website *Info-Birmanie* (www.info-birmanie.org/birmanie/rep.htm, last viewed on 9 December 2004) or Suu Kyi's interview for the European Parliament in which she says "Now

attention. Thanks to the FBC and others a dozen multinational companies decided over a relatively brief period to withdraw from Burma. In the US, nearly 20 communities and the Commonwealth of Massachusetts adopted regulations that deterred or forbid companies from having anything to do with Burma. In May 1997, US President Clinton prohibited new investment in Burma. The campaign's impact probably benefitted from the momentum that accompanied the release of Suu Kyi in 1995, 2 months before the FBC was established (Zarni, 2000).

FBC and other organisations saw investment in and trade with Burma as support for the military regime. Because foreign companies could only invest in the company through the military junta, part of the yield would accrue to the junta directly or indirectly through taxes. The junta could use these resources to strengthen its position. On IHC Caland's contract, *Burma Centrum Nederland* (Dutch Burma Centre BCN) noted:

> IHC Caland paid taxes to the Burmese junta through various channels, including local taxes, income tax for its own staff and tax on operational costs. In doing so the company supported the actions of the Burmese military regime.[5]

Most protest groups chose an approach that focused on the political and humanitarian situation in the country. Protest groups explained companies' economic activities as political acts.

Partly in response to Aung San Suu Kyi's call, many protest groups and organisations – often united in coalitions – put companies around the world under pressure not to invest in Burma or to halt their operations in that country (Shaw, 2004; Spar and La Mure, 2003; Vergouw and den Hond, 2000). Persistent criticism from protest groups led a few dozen companies to decide to withdraw from the country. They include Heineken (June 1996), Interbrew (October 1996), Philips Electronics (November 1996), PepsiCo (January 1997), Hewlett-Packard (November 1996) and Ericsson (September 1998).[6] Other companies had left Burma earlier. Among them were Levi-Strauss (June 1992), PetroCanada (November 1992) and Amoco (March 1994). The companies offered differing explanations for their actions. Some pointed directly or indirectly to protest threats, others spoke of a shift in priorities. Examples are: preventing reputational loss (Levi-Strauss) or pressure from local groups like the Chicago Coalition for a Democratic Burma and the Coalition for Corporate Withdrawal from Burma. Sometimes, companies invoked the protest groups' arguments. Levi-Strauss, for instance, stated in 1992 that

---

is not yet the time for investment. It is more important that there is the right social and political climate which will ensure the right structural changes that are necessary for good economic recovery and sustained development. Until then I think investment is too early." (www.tni.org/archives/vervest/burma.htm, last viewed on 9 December 2004).

[5] www.xs4all.nl/~bcn/campagne-ihc.html, last viewed on 26 November 2004.

[6] For a survey of companies that have left Burma, see the Canadian Friends of Burma (CFOB) website (www.cfob.org/CorpComplicity/CorpComplicity.shtml) and *The Irrawaddy Online* (vol. 12, no. 9) (www.irrawaddy.org/aviewer.asp?a=457&z=14, both last viewed on 14 December 2004).

under current circumstances, it is not possible to do business in Myanmar without directly supporting the military government and its pervasive violations of human rights.[7]

In the Netherlands, too, the 1990s witnessed protests against new investment in Burma. Heineken's decision to withdraw from the construction of a new brewery and to halt exports to Burma was partly due to protests and the threat of a consumer boycott in the Netherlands and the US (Vergouw and den Hond, 2000). Furthermore, in 1997, the Dutch Labour Party (PvdA), the Dutch Socialist Party (SP), the European Parliament Green Party, and the Dutch trade unions FNV and CNV signed an appeal to the business community to withdraw from Burma. So, the commotion around IHC Caland's contract did not fall out of the blue. Still, the company seemed surprised at the vehemence of the criticism, as we will see further on. This controversy lasted longer than the protests against Heineken's presence in Burma. One important reason can be that IHC Caland could not be hard hit by a consumer boycott. It supplied the offshore oil and gas industry, rather than the consumer market (Vergouw and den Hond, 2000).

IHC Caland

IHC Caland NV was the public holding company of a group of companies that "design and supply tools, ships, complete systems and services to the offshore oil, dredging, shipping and undersea mining industries around the world".[8] IHC stands for *Industriële Handels Combinatie* or Industrial Trade Combine. The company was founded on a cooperation agreement that several Dutch shipyards entered into in 1943. This agreement was concluded in the expectation that together they would be able to accept large orders from Billiton when the Second World War was over. The companies in the combine merged in 1965. The merger was first of all a financial merger, in which the participating companies continued to operate under their own names, but organisational cooperation gradually increased and more companies were added. Finally, the various subsidiaries joined together to form IHC Caland holding company. The company has been listed since 1965 and has been part of the AEX index since 2003.

At the close of 2003, the company was good 4,100 jobs; its six subsidiaries operated in 29 countries. At that time its activities were spread over its offshore oil and gas operations and dredger-shipbuilding divisions. In its 2003 annual report, IHC Caland claimed to be worldwide market leader in most of its niche markets. Tables 13.1, 13.2, and 13.3 show that offshore operations are more systematically profitable than shipbuilding. For that reason, the company announced in August 2003 that it was examining several options for splitting the concern. Shipbuilding operations could be sold, or they could be floated in a separate company. In 2004 IHC Caland split its shipbuilding from its dredging operations. In 2005, after the

---

[7] See www.perc.ca/PEN/1994-03/s-freeman.html, last viewed on 2 March 2005.

[8] IHC Caland. Press release, 5 August 2004 (www.ihccaland.nl/html/News/05aug04.htm, last viewed on 1 December 2004).

Table 13.1 Nett annual turnover, in millions (source: annual reports IHC Caland 1993–2003)

	1994	1995	1996	1997	1998	1998	1999	2000	2001	2002	2003
Nett turnover	Euro					Euro					USD
Dredging and shipbuilding	257	237	305	367	337	336	679	555	653	566	569
Off-shore	145	185	387	261	311	311	550	273	312	364	1.280
Total	*402*	*422*	*692*	*628*	*648*	*647*	*1.229*	*828*	*965*	*930*	*1.849*

Table 13.2 Annual profit in millions (source: annual reports IHC Caland)

	1994	1995	1996	1997	1998	1998	1999	2000	2001	2002	2003
Profit	Euro					Euro					USD
Dredging and shipbuilding	11.6	10.2	12.4	13.2	30.3	30.3	34.9	32.3	20.7	−50.0	−81.7
Off-shore	23.3	25.2	30.9	54.7	55.1	55.0	56.2	71.8	97.6	130.0	148.8
Total	*34.9*	*35.4*	*43.3*	*67.9*	*85.4*	*82.7*	*85.7*	*99.7*	*113.8*	*74.8*	*64.4*

The contributions of the holding are taken into account in the total profit calculations.

Table 13.3 Annual total number of employees, per 31 December (source: annual reports IHC Caland)

	1993	1994	1995	1996	1997	1998	1999	2000	2001	2002	2003
Dredging and shipbuilding	n.a.	n.a.	n.a.	n.a.	2.066	2.130	2.589	2.706	2.789	2.775	2.289
Off-shore	n.a.	n.a.	n.a.	n.a.	779	809	890	855	1.237	1.542	1.838
Total	*1.819*	*1.840*	*1.935*	*2.004*	*2.845*	*2.939*	*3.479*	*3.561*	*4.026*	*4.338*	*4.148*

The employees of the holding are included in the totals.

sale of its shipbuilding operations, IHC Caland continued operating under the name SBM N.V., already in use for its offshore division.

The Contract

On 13 July 1998, IHC Caland announced that its Swiss subsidiary SBM Production Contractors signed a contract with Premier Petroleum Myanmar Ltd., a British-Burmese joint venture that is partly owned by British Premier Oil. The contract was for the construction, lease and maintenance of a floating storage and off-loading system (FSO) for development of the Yetagun gas field, 180 km off the coast of southern Burma in the Andaman Sea. FSO systems are moored permanently above or near offshore oil and gas fields to receive and temporarily store oil and gas for transfer to tankers for transport to purchasers. High prices make oil and gas extraction in deeper waters profitable, so the demand for such capital-intensive systems was expected to increase as oil prices rise. The installation was planned to be in operation by the end of 1999. The immense contract was intended to run for 15 years and would reach several hundred million euros. In a first response to this, and a few other orders in Vietnam and China, Dutch financial newspaper *Het Financieele Dagblad* wrote:

> The Asian crisis seems to have had little impact on IHC Caland new-build dredging ships and oil platforms. (Het Financieel Dagblad 1998a)

Premier Oil acquired the gas field from US company Texaco because this company could no longer operate it after the US government forbade new investment in Burma in May 1997.[9] Officially, Texaco withdrew after an asset review, but it is generally assumed that political pressure in the US and a desire to polish the company's image were important factors (Knott, 1997). Other partners in the operation of the field were Malaysian Petronas, Japanese Nippon Oil, Thai PTT-EP and the Burmese government-owned company MOGE (Myanmar Oil and Gas Enterprises).

Commotion

Because it involved economic activities in Burma, the contract elicited a storm of protest in the media. Burma Centrum Nederland (Dutch Burma Centre BCN), Amnesty International, XminY Solidarity Fund, Novib (Oxfam Netherlands), and the trade unions FNV and CNV expressed surprise and outrage at the delivery because it indirectly supported the military junta's oppression of the Burmese people. Foreign currency from the Yetagun project would be an important buttress for Burma's weak economy and so, claimed BCN's spokesman, European money would be perpetuating the Burmese regime.

> The income ends up with the generals, not the population. (NRC Handelsblad 1998a)

Moreover, protest groups pointed out that other companies were just leaving Burma. In addition, Friends of the Earth Netherlands drew attention to alleged problems with the installation of the adjoining land-based infrastructure. A pipeline, some 60 km long was being laid right through the tropical rain forest. The construction of the pipeline would have an adverse effect on biodiversity; villages would be forced to move and the construction would use forced labour.[10] IHC Caland repeatedly

---

[9]This boycott struck several US oil companies; Spar and La Mure (2003) described the conflict between Unocal and the US Free Burma Coalition. See also *Trouw* (1998).

[10]Friends of the Earth Netherlands, "IHC Caland doet nog steeds zaken met Birma" (www.milieudefensie.nl/earthalarm/alarm77birma.htm, last viewed on 9 December 2004). See also *The Independent* (2000). Similar discussions were held earlier about laying a gas pipeline for another large gas field, the Yadana field; see *The Financial Post* (1996).

stated that it dealt only with offshore infrastructure and not with whatever may be taking place on land. IHC Caland's CEO noted repeatedly:

> We are far away at sea. (Het Financieele Dagblad, 1998b)

BCN – one of the main Dutch players in the protest against the presence of IHC Caland in Burma – is a foundation whose goal is to inform Dutch society on developments in Burma and to instigate and coordinate activities that promote democracy and sustainable development in Burma. In addition, the centre seeks to contribute to a constructive dialogue between the various factions in Burma.[11]

After various trade unions, development and environmental organisations set up regular discussions on the situation in Burma, BCN was established in the early 1990s to satisfy the need for systematic action in response to the Burmese opposition's call to support all activities that would benefit democracy in Burma. With financial support from Novib and the Open Society Institute, BCN set up and coordinated activities intended to promote democracy and sustainable development in Burma. To achieve these goals, BCN zealously advocated democracy and human rights; it informed the public about the situation in Burma via consumer campaigns; it tried to exert pressure via campaigns against European companies; and it lobbied the European Union and the Dutch government to adopt economic sanctions against Burma.

Other important players were Friends of the Earth Netherlands (Milieudefensie), the trade unions FNV and CNV, XminY Solidarity Fund and the Dutch Socialist Party (SP). Most of these organisations were co-founders of BCN and as such aware of and involved in BCN's activities. But they also sought individual publicity in some campaigns. These organisations are BCN's main support base.

The storm also raged in political circles. A majority of the members of the House indicated that the government should set guidelines that hinder companies from doing business with controversial regimes. The European Parliament had scheduled a debate on Burma for the same week that the order was announced. The leader of the Dutch Christian Democratic Party (CDA) stated in Brussels that "Respectable companies no longer invest in Burma" (NRC Handelsblad, 1998b). But just at that moment France vetoed a European prohibition against investment in Burma.

Jan-Diederick Bax, then CEO at IHC Caland, said he did not understand the vehement commotion around the contract. He stated in *Het Financieele Dagblad* that gas extraction took place far off the Burmese coast so that the company had nothing to do with internal political problems.

> We're not doing anything illegal. Neither the Dutch government nor the Lower House has forbidden investment in Myanmar. So why shouldn't we do it? (Het Financieele Dagblad, 1998b)

At the same time, Bax said that the decision would have been different had it involved inland investment in Burma. He called the contract a normal business agreement, one floating storage site like many that IHC Caland operates.

---

[11] Burma Centrum Nederland (www.xs4all.nl/~bcn/, last viewed on 26 November 2004).

13 Case Description: A Disputed Contract – IHC Caland in Burma   129

> We have nine such installations in Brazil, Congo, Vietnam and elsewhere. As of next year there will be one in Myanmar. (Het Financieele Dagblad, 1998b)

After that, Bax invoked the fierce competition in the industry as argument. If he did not carry out the contract, Bax would fail to do his duty as CEO, i.e. to earn money for the company's shareholders. The company repeated these arguments regularly.

IHC Caland's deal remained prominent in the news. On 17 July 1998, in an interview in *Het Financieele Dagblad*, Bax reported that Dutch banks did not want to finance this specific contract because they considered the political risk too high. Moreover, they claimed to be afraid that such financing could harm their interests in the US because of its 1997 prohibition against new investment. In the same interview, Bax said that he was overwhelmed by all the commotion around the order.

> We have to see everything in its correct proportions. What good will it do me to start acting proud here in Schiedam. That would have no impact at all. Someone else would just step in and do the project. (Het Financieele Dagblad, 1998c)

In a discussion with two PvdA MPs and a director of FNV, Bax indicated several days later that he was willing to talk about the company's setting up its own code of conduct. He stressed, however, that this code would not address the issue of with which countries IHC Caland may do business; as far as he was concerned the company would follow the Dutch government's guidelines (Het Financieele Dagblad, 1998d).

On 4 August 1998, the trade unions BCN, XminY Solidarity Fund and Novib met with IHC Caland's management. The discussion proved fruitless. BCN wanted the order cancelled but that was out of the question for IHC Caland.

> They repeated their position, we ours,

according to Bax, who had already spoken with PvdA MPs and was scheduled to meet with Amnesty International.

> No one may have a say about whether we accept or reject an order, but we are willing to discuss a code of conduct on human rights. We do not infringe these. (NRC Handelsblad, 1998c)

After these meetings, BCN, speaking for itself and XminY, announced in an op-ed article in the 8 August issue of *Het Financieele Dagblad* that a range of actions would be undertaken. The groups wanted to approach IHC Caland's employees via the unions as well as contacting the board of directors, the council of supervisors and the larger shareholders. In addition, the groups planned to purchase one share in IHC Caland to obtain a right to address the shareholders' meeting. They also made preparations for public protests. Later that month, the Dutch government announced in a letter responding to various questions from MPs that it would investigate possible economic sanctions against Burma. Such sanctions would have to be imposed as part of a broader European campaign.

When IHC Caland announced its mid-year figures on 24 August 1998, BCN held a protest action at the entrance to IHC Caland's headquarters in Schiedam. Three bloodied "victims" of the regime in Burma lay there. Because this protest action had been announced in advance, the meeting drew much media attention. During the meeting, Bax stressed that he was unable and unwilling to withdraw from a contract that had already been signed, even when the Dutch government should announce a boycott.

> If we break this contract, we will get a bad reputation. We do not do such things. (Het Parool, 1998)

During the same meeting, Bax said he received no comment on the contract from the company:

> I didn't hear a word of concern from a single employee, shareholder or supervisor. They understand how we work. (Het Parool, 1998)

At the same time, Bax also stated that the situation would be different if IHC Caland's operations were to require dealing with the public.

> Like Heineken, then matters would be different. But we work business-to-business. And in our network it's just not an issue. (Het Financieele Dagblad, 1998e)

A month later, the Dutch government indicated in response to MPs questions that it disapproved of IHC Caland's investment in Burma but that there were no juridical grounds for taking steps against individual companies at that time.

At that point the controversy disappeared from the media, although "the IHC-Burma question" was cited regularly in relation to investment. On 7 October 1998, for instance, the company had a meeting with the Dutch Association of Investors for Sustainable Development (VBDO) on the risks to investors of investing in Burma. Other publications on sustainable investment and discussions on corporate social responsibility generally often referred to IHC Caland's disputed contract in Burma.

Toward a Code of Conduct

In April 1999, Bax announced that IHC Caland was working on a code of conduct but that it would probably not be presented at the next shareholders' meeting. Drafting a code is labour intensive, Bax noted. ABP pension fund, owner of a few percent of the share capital demanded that the company draft such a code. The Dutch ABN-AMRO Fund also let it be known that it was not happy with the contract in Burma. Nevertheless, Bax stressed that none of the major shareholders disinvested in the company after it accepted the order from Burma. Just before the annual meeting, it was announced that IHC Caland would, indeed, not be presenting a code of conduct on human rights. CEO Bax said that he preferred to wait for draft texts from the EU or the Ministry of Economic Affairs. During the shareholders' meeting, ABP appeared willing to give the company more time. Bax resigned as CEO during this annual meeting. Aad de Ruyter took his place.

Chairman of the supervisory board Langman announced on behalf of IHC Caland that the company would present a code of conduct that same year. However,

13 Case Description: A Disputed Contract – IHC Caland in Burma

Langman added that the company did not intend to act differently in similar circumstances unless it would risk government sanctions:

> If we should again find ourselves in such a situation, we would again accept the order. We work in many countries that infringe human rights. We do not think that we should act more circumspect when the government does not forbid investment in these countries. (Het Financieele Dagblad, 1999)

After the meeting, an ABP director said he was satisfied with the promise:

> We prefer that they take their time for this difficult task than that they make hasty decisions. (De Telegraaf, 1999)

However, a policy officer at FNV wrote in June 1999:

> IHC Caland is using its willingness to develop a code to stave off discussion on investing in Burma and on being an accessory to serious human rights violations (van Wezel, 1999: 58).

Directly related to ABP's concern, CNV chairman Terpstra referred a few months later to pension funds' social responsibility; he presented an investment code for pension fund managers containing guidelines for how pension funds should handle their social responsibility. This code is based in part on International Labour Organisation (ILO) guidelines. The two trade unions have seats on the boards of many pension funds, including ABP.

A Second Contract and a Code

By the end of 1999, IHC Caland was again in discredit when it became known that the company had accepted a second order from Burma. Although this was a much smaller order – for delivery of a dredging ship – again commotion arose. In response to parliamentary questions to the Minister of Foreign Affairs, the new CEO De Ruyter said that the board of IHC Caland had never spent as much time discussing any other order as it did this one. However, there were no international rules; for that reason IHC Caland again requested a clear governmental guideline. BCN also rejected this order, since the ship would be purchased directly by the military regime which could then improve the country's infrastructure. IHC Caland objected that a dredging ship could not be used to infringe human rights. At the same time, De Ruyter said that the promised code of conduct was nearly finished.

On a political level discussions were held on the desirability of a code of conduct. The employers association VNO-NCW opposed a national scheme because international discussions on responsible business conduct were then ongoing in the EU; they were intended to culminate in agreements. At the same time the labour party (PvdA) worked on a private member's bill that would have companies demonstrate accountability and responsibility in their annual reports. All these discussions regularly refer to IHC Caland's controversial contract in Burma.

In May 2000, right before IHC Caland's annual meeting, ABN-AMRO, one of the largest Dutch banks, announced that it had closed the office that it had maintained in Burma since 1995 and sold its shares in IHC Caland. Although the bank denied that this was intended to express a moral judgment, it did refer in a letter to BCN to IHC Caland's investment in Burma. In the same period, Gerrit Ybema (of D66, a liberal Dutch political party), then state secretary for economic affairs, said that he wanted to discourage irresponsible social conduct on the part of the business community by withholding export and investment grants.

IHC Caland's code of conduct was officially presented at a shareholders' meeting held on 26 May 2000. Responses were mixed. The ABP pension fund pointed out that the code did not repair the reputational damage associated with investment in Burma. The pension fund wanted to reassess its ownership of IHC Caland shares. A few months later, the FNV trade union demanded in a policy document that pension funds would engage in socially responsible investment. In this regard, the trade union also raised the issue of ABP's investment in IHC Caland. In March 2001 it became known that ABP did, indeed, sell its participation in IHC Caland in 2000 because of the company's investments in Burma; toward the end of 2001 a group of large European pension funds warned companies operating in Burma that they should carefully weigh the risks of such activities. Dutch pension fund PGGM was one of that warning letter's signatories. Together, the signatories represented a large percentage of the capital, which added weight to their warning.

Escalation and "a Different Tone"

De Ruyter resigned as CEO at the shareholders' meeting held 26 May 2000; it is rumoured that this was due to a difference of opinion on the company's strategic direction. Sjef van Dooremalen succeeded him. When Van Dooremalen, in his turn, left in August 2004, *Het Financieele Dagblad* reported that he had played an important role in discussions on IHC Caland's activities in Burma; this was not so much the result of a new direction for the company, but because he adopted a different tone from his predecessors, Van Dooremalen was able to blunt the edge of the conflict (Het Financieele Dagblad, 2004a). However, an escalation had preceded this "different tone".

In June 2000, ministers of OECD member countries agreed on a revision of the *Guidelines for Multinational Enterprises*. These guidelines are a collection of voluntary rules of behaviour for multinational companies. OECD member states drafted a first version in 1976 as part of the *OECD Declaration and Decisions on International Investment and Multinational Enterprises*. The guidelines contain recommendations relating to labour relations, consumer protection and combating bribery, but also on human rights and environmental protection. The Dutch government recommended the OECD guidelines to the business community and planned to use these guidelines as criteria in allocating grants. Responses were mixed. Employer's organisation VNO-NCW is not at all interested in national agreements because in their view only international agreements could guarantee that Dutch companies would be able to compete on a level playing field, while various NGOs preferred to see the guidelines made universally binding on the entire business community. According to Van Luijk (2000b), however, the new OECD guidelines were a

13 Case Description: A Disputed Contract – IHC Caland in Burma

major step forward toward doing international business responsibly. One element in the OECD agreement is the chance to submit a complaint to a national contact point (NCP). There are no sanctions attached to this complaints procedure beyond the publication of whatever contraventions may occur, although unions and other stakeholders hope that an NCP decision will provide grounds for legal action. At the end of 2001, FNV and CNV trade unions announced that they had submitted a complaint to the NCP that summer against IHC Caland on the grounds that the company contributed to the prolongation of the military regime in Burma. The complaints procedure would be rounded off in the summer of 2004.

2002 was a turbulent year in the controversy; pressure on IHC Caland increased. In early 2002, another large company left Burma partly as a result of actions by BCN, Novib, the Clean Clothes Campaign (CCC) and trade union FNV. Triumph, a large Swiss lingerie producer left Burma because of the public discussion in Europe (NRC Handelsblad, 2002). In a new series of actions, BCN called upon 89 Dutch provinces, municipalities and companies not to award contracts for dredging ports to IHC Caland, stressing that IHC Caland is one of the last Dutch companies still involved in economic activities in Burma. In April 2002, Friends of the Earth Netherlands sprayed IHC Caland's headquarters with 6,000 l of (ecological) dredged mud to draw attention to the filthy business that this company does (Rotterdams Dagblad, 2002). Van Dooremalen responded in an interview with the Dutch daily *De Telegraaf* at the end of March 2002. In the interview, he said that the military regime in Burma was no good, but that it was a governmental duty to demand accountability for this, especially on the part of the EU. He repeated the position that IHC Caland had long held. Still, IHC Caland slowly started to change it attitude. When it published its annual figures a few days later, Van Dooremalen announced that the company would accept no new orders in Burma, although it would not break its current contracts. Van Dooremalen said that this decision was reached at the urgent request of then state secretary of Economic Affairs, Gerrit Ybema (D66 party). BCN spoke of an empty gesture because the current contracts would be served out. In a later letter in *Het Financieele Dagblad* BCN's coordinator pointed out that the state secretary had not caused this "modest shift in the right direction" but that increasing social pressure had (Het Financieele Dagblad, 2002).

Despite this change of direction, the protests did not stop. For instance, Friends of the Earth Netherlands presented the results of a study on IHC Caland's financial flows; it showed that over the previous years, five Dutch financial institutions had supported IHC Caland with large long-term loans.[12] The presence of one of these institutions, NIB Capital, was striking because NIB is owned by ABP and PGGM pension funds that had earlier spoken critically about IHC Caland.[13] In May 2002,

---

[12] The banks in question are ABN-AMRO, ING, Fortis, Rabobank and NIB Capital. See also Friends of the Earth Netherlands, "Bagger Rapport Birma" (www.milieudefensie.nl/globalisering/publicaties/Bagger_Rapport_Birma_deel_voor_website.pdf, last viewed on 26 November 2004).

[13] An ABP spokesman responded with surprise, but as a shareholder he was unfamiliar with the loan from NIB Capital. The subject would be treated in ABP's next meeting with NIB Capital.

BCN responded to the report by Friends of the Earth by calling on these banks to stop extending loans to IHC Caland; in June 2002 BCN campaigned during IHC Caland's annual meeting to draw attention to Burma's being the world's largest opium producer and to the Burmese government's involvement in drugs trade via whitewashing drugs money through state-owed companies. The message to shareholders was: IHC Caland not only helps keep the military regime in power, it also helps the Burmese junta whitewash drugs money (BCN, undated). In September 2002, British oil company Premier Oil announced it would leave Burma and transfer its holdings there to Malaysian Petronas. Premier Oil stated that it was a purely commercial decision, but British and international pressure groups certainly saw the departure as the result of their campaigns. Dutch pressure groups also saw Premier Oil's departure as a good occasion for IHC Caland to withdraw from Burma; after all, its contracting partner had now left. IHC Caland's Van Dooremalen announced that there was little reason for the company to change its stance toward Burma. A contract is a contract and breaking a contract would be expensive and could damage the company's reputation.

On 11 December 2002, BCN and Friends of the Earth Netherlands issued the following press release:

> many civil society organisations and most of the Dutch House of Representatives urgently request five banks to halt their support for offshore company IHC Caland.[14]

The call received support from a broad range of organisations and several companies, varying from BCN and Friends of the Earth Netherlands to Pax Christi, XminY Solidarity Fund and several political parties.[15] In addition, the ASN Bank, which took a different stand from the rest of the Dutch banking community also signed the call. In February 2003, the five banks to whom the call was addressed agreed not to finance any more of IHC Caland's Burmese projects. However, the banks did not comply with the call's request to put pressure on IHC Caland to terminate its contract in Burma. ABN-AMRO wrote that it does not normally provide information on its contacts with customers, but that it would make an exception in this case,

---

[14] BCN and Friends of the Earth Netherlands press release, 11 December 2002. Civil society organisations and parliamentary parties asked the banks to cut off financial support for IHC Caland (www.milieudefensie.nl/persber/globalisering/021211.htm, last viewed on 26 November 2004).

[15] BCN, Vereniging Milieudefensie, Novib, de Stichting Interkerkelijke Organisatie voor Ontwikkelingssamenwerking (ICCO), Humanistisch Overleg Mensenrechten (HOM), Both Ends, the International Union for Conservation of Nature and Natural Resources (IUCN), Greenpeace, Justitia et Pax, Multatuli Travel, Body Shop, Pax Christi, Interkerkelijk Vredesberaad (IKV), Transnational Institute (TNI), Stichting Onderzoek Multinationale Ondernemingen (SOMO), XminY Solidarity Fund, Evert Vermeer Stichting, several parliamentary parties (CDA, VVD, PvdA, GroenLinks, D66, SP and ChristenUnie) and ASN Bank all signed the appeal (www.milieudefensie.nl/persber/globalisering/021211.htm, last viewed on 26 November 2004).

given the gravity of the situation. In a detailed explanation, the bank noted that it respected IHC Caland's decision to serve out its contract, but it would not finance any contracts in Burma. Van Dooremalen responded by saying that ICH Caland's Burmese operations were financed by Japanese banks but, given that the company had already decided not to accept any new orders from Burma, he thought the banks' announcement superfluous.

Campaigns continued in early 2003. In January 2003, the Socialist Party (SP) organised an action around an informal meeting of IHC Caland shareholders at Sliedrecht shipyard. Because SP and BCN each held one share of IHC Caland, two protesters also had access to the meeting where they posed critical questions. BCN and Friends of the Earth Netherlands again protested during the presentations of IHC Caland's figures and at its meetings. Once again an appeal was launched to IHC Caland's principal bankers to have them demand that IHC Caland terminate its operations in Burma. Speaking for the company, Van Dooremalen repeated that the company would not accept any new assignments in Burma but that it would serve out its current contracts and in doing so would follow OECD guidelines. A few weeks later, Van Dooremalen announced that this new stance toward Burma had cost the company a six-million-euro contract for the construction of three dredging ships. The order went to a Chinese company.

Toward a Solution?

In the summer of 2003, IHC Caland announced that it wanted to address the human rights situation in Burma by speaking regularly to the Burmese ambassador in London (there is no Burmese embassy in the Netherlands). Calling the ambassador to account is a conscious act, flowing from a desire to comply with OECD guidelines and from talks with Dutch trade unions, BCN and Friends of the Earth Netherlands. In talks with the ambassador held on 11 June 2003, the management of IHC Caland and a representative of the trade union expressed their concern about the human rights violations in Burma, especially forced labour, and requested that their concern be passed on to the Burmese government. In the same press release, IHC Caland announced that it would ask the Malaysian oil company Petronas, which had become the new principal after Premier Oil's departure, to comply with OECD guidelines when working in Burma.

A year later, in July 2004, the trade unions' complaint, lodged in 2001 with the National Contact Point for Corporate Social Responsibility, was formally completed. FNV and CNV trade unions and IHC Caland reached a compromise on the company's economic involvement in Burma. The trade unions would check in a year's time whether the company's operations in Burma complied sufficiently with the OECD guidelines. Although the trade unions still thought that IHC Caland should withdraw from Burma, a policy staffer at FNV said that the union had to moderate its demands because the OECD guidelines did not offer sufficient grounds for it to demand that the company leave (Rotterdams Dagblad, 2004). Referring to the NCP's hearing of the complaint, NGO representatives nevertheless wondered how effective OECD guidelines were, when there was no control over Dutch multinationals' compliance with these guidelines. Moreover, they point out that the OECD guidelines applied only to investments and not to trade relations and that, in addition, the guidelines were not enforceable. For these reasons they argued for making them less voluntary (Het Financieele Dagblad, 2004b).[16]

Epilogue: Dialogue or Sanctions?

Meanwhile, the situation in Burma remains controversial and the call for pressure and sanctions continues. In May 2002, Suu Kyi was released from house arrest. On that occasion she stated that the NLD still opposed foreign investments, aid and tourism to Myanmar as long as the military held power; she said she hoped that dialogue with the regime on national reconciliation could now resume. In the spring of 2003, the military regime again tightened its control over Burma; in May 2003 Suu Kyi was again placed under house arrest.

After this deterioration in the situation in Burma, the Bush government decided at the end of August 2003 to impose additional economic sanctions, in part as response to the expanded lobbying by the US Campaign for Burma (USCB) and with agreement of the government in exile. The "Burmese Freedom and Democracy Act" prohibits imports from Burma, freezes the assets of the Burmese government in the US, denies entry to the US to SPDC (the State Peace and Development Council, SLORC's successor) members and offers general support to those working for freedom, democracy and peace in Burma. Congress must reconfirm the act annually. In September 2004, the European Parliament also adopted proposals for heavier sanctions against Burma because the country did not do enough to respect human rights. This measure ensured that European companies could no longer do business with Burmese state-owned companies. One important condition to which companies and political leaders regularly referred seems to have been met. Shortly after the European decision in November 2004, the Dutch parliament adopted a motion calling for sanctions and political pressure. That motion called on the government to work for further EU measures such as prohibiting investment, prohibiting the import of teak wood, and to try to have the human rights situation in Burma placed on the agenda of the UN Security Council.

It is hardly possible to predict what turn campaigns against Western companies operating in Burma will take. Arguments presented in this discussion concentrate on weighing economy and market regulation against arguments of political morality (fostering democracy, respecting human rights). Sometimes other voices can be heard; the advantages and disadvantages of boycotts and investment in Burma

---

[16]This is an op-ed article written by a staff-member at the Centre for Research on Multinational Corporations (SOMO) and a staff member at Irene, an international organisation monitoring the strategies of international companies and employees' rights.

13 Case Description: A Disputed Contract – IHC Caland in Burma 137

have been discussed in other publications (e.g. White, 2004) and newspaper articles (Financial Times, 2004a).[17] Since the summer of 2003, the US Free Burma Coalition (FBC) seems to have chosen for a radically different course. In articles on its website, the organisation notes that it is no longer convinced that Western sanctions and isolating Burma are an effective way to stimulate democracy. FBC now argues for greater cooperation and openness. The background of the publications on the FBC website is not known. Jeremy Woodrum, current USCB campaign leader and former FBC staff member, explained in a telephone conversation on 4 February 2005 that the FBC imploded in 2003 after an internal conflict; all but one of the staff members left FBC and set up the USCB in September 2003 to continue their activities. Since then, FBC has fallen still. Woodrum notes that since that time the Burma movement no longer takes the FBC seriously.

In response to the question what BCN thought of the FBC's changed position, the BCN answered that the legitimacy of their pro-sanction position would dissolve were the Burmese population to turn unanimously against sanctions, but there are no indications that this will happen. BCN has had insufficient contact with FBC to be able to explain its apparent change of course, but it also says that there are still many Burma groups that do support the pro-sanction position,[18] among these are the USCB as is apparent from its leaders' letters to newspapers (Financial Times, 2004b). The government in exile also continues to favour sanctions. Protests against companies operating in Burma seem not to have been suspended yet. In addition, at the end of 2004, there was a power struggle within the Burmese regime which resulted in a stronger position for the hardliners. The situation in Burma remains controversial and Western companies operating in that country continue to run the risk of being called to account.

All things considered, the Dutch parties grew closer together in 2003. IHC Caland visited the Burmese ambassador in London to discuss the human rights situation in Burma while BCN and Friends of the Earth Netherlands suspended their campaigns in anticipation of IHC Caland's next steps. The trade unions FNV and CNV will check whether the company's operations in Burma comply sufficiently with the OECD guidelines. As far as Dutch protest groups are concerned, whether IHC Caland's compromise has really warded off all commotion on its presence in Burma will depend on whether the company rides out its current course and continues to call the Burmese government and its business partners in the Yetagun project to order for their part in the human rights situation.[19]

---

[17] Similar discussions about the announcement of US sanctions took place in Dutch media in the summer of 2003.

[18] BCN oral communication from coordinator P. Ras (12 January 2005).

[19] IHC Caland's shipbuilding has since split from its dredging operations. After the sale of its shipbuilding operations, IHC Caland continued operating under the name SBM N.V., already in use for its offshore division.

References

Burma Centrum Nederland. 2002. *Baggeren in Burma wast vieze handen wit.* Folder distributed in the spring/summer of 2002. Amsterdam: BCN.

Danitz, T. and Strobel., W.P. 1999. The Internet's Impact on Activism: The Case of Burma. *Studies in Conflict & Terrorism*, 22(1): 257–269.

De Telegraaf. 1999. "IHC Caland komt critici maar nauwelijks tegemoet." *De Telegraaf.* 5 June.

Ferrara, F. 2003. Why Regimes Create Disorder. Hobbes's Dilemma During a Rangoon Summer. *Journal of Conflict Resolution*, 47(3): 302–325.

Financial Times. 2004a. "Myanmar: Sanctions Won't Work." letter to the editor from Jefrrey Sachs, and follow up letters dated 30 July, and 1, 2, 9, 13 August. *Financial Times.* 28 July.

Financial Times. 2004b. "Sanctions against Burma Help Domestic Activists Regain Freedom," Letter to the editor from Aun Din, USCB Policy Director. *Financial Times.* 9 August.

Het Financieele Dagblad. 1998a. "IHC Caland sleept order olieopslag Birma binnen." *Het Financieele Dagblad.* 14 July.

Het Financieele Dagblad. 1998b. "IHC Caland snapt niets van dreiging met boycot", *Het Financieele Dagblad.* 15 July.

Het Financieele Dagblad. 1998c. "Ik kan geen verantwoordelijkheid nemen", *Het Financieele Dagblad.* 17 July.

Het Financieele Dagblad. 1998d. "IHC overweegt invoeren code", *Het Financieele Dagblad.* 21 July.

Het Financieele Dagblad. 1998e. "Gedane zaken nemen geen keer bij IHC", *Het Financieele Dagblad.* 25 August.

Het Financieele Dagblad. 1999. "ABP geeft IHC nog een jaar tijd voor gedragscode", *Het Financieele Dagblad.* 5 June, 1999.

Het Financieele Dagblad 2002. Op-ed article by BCN coordinator. *Het Financieele Dagblad.* 2 August.

Het Financieele Dagblad. 2004a. "Van Dooremalen zet stap terug in de tijd". *Het Financieele Dagblad.* 9 August.

Het Financieele Dagblad. 2004b. "Verantwoord ondernemen binden aan heldere internationale regels", *Het Financieele Dagblad*, 13 August.

Het Parool. 1998. "IHC Caland ziet in Birma geen weg meer terug." *Het Parool.* 25 August.

Knott, D. 1997. Exiting Myanmar. *Oil & Gas Journal*, 95(50): 25.

NRC Handelsblad. 1998a. "Birma gunt IHC Caland grote order; fel protest organisaties." *NRC Handelsblad.* 14 July.

NRC Handelsblad. 1998b. "Parijs blokkeert sancties Birma." *NRC Handelsblad.* 15 July.

NRC Handelsblad. 1998c. "Acties op komst tegen IHC-order in Birma." *NRC Handelsblad.* 5 August.

NRC Handelsblad. 2002. "Triumph weg uit Birma door acties." *NRC Handelsblad.* 29 January.

Rotterdams Dagblad. 2002. "IHC Caland met modder besmeurd." *Rotterdams Dagblad.* 5 April.

Rotterdams Dagblad. 2004. "Compromis met IHC over Birma." *Rotterdams Dagblad.* 28 July.

Shaw, J. 2004. Out of Burma. Grassroots Activism Forces Multinationals to End Ties with the Burmese Dictatorship. *Multinational Monitor*, 25(1/2): 17–19.

Spar, D.L. and La Mure, L.T. 2003. The Power of Activism: Assessing the Impact of NGOs on Global Business. *California Management Review*, 45(3): 78–101.

Spit, W.J. 1995. *Birma (Myanmar): mensen, politiek, economie, cultuur.* Amsterdam: Koninklijk Instituut voor de Tropen.

The Financial Post. 1996. "Burma Gas Pipeline Rouses Opposition", *The Financial Post.* 26 January.

The Independent. 2000. "Minister Blocks Burma Oil Project over Rights Abuse". *The Independent.* 12 April.

Trouw. 1998. "Nederlands IHC Caland neemt opdracht over van Texaco dat zich onder publieke druk terugtrok." *Trouw.* 14 July.

van Luijk, H. 2000a. *Integer en verantwoord in beroep en bedrijf.* Amsterdam: Boom.
van Luijk, H. 2000b. Wereldwijd fatsoenlijk. *Het Financieele Dagblad* 27 June 2000.
van Wezel, A. 1999. Verantwoordelijkheid kent geen grenzen. *Zeggenschap*, 10(2): 56–58.
Vergouw, J. and den Hond, F. 2000. Actiegroepen als nieuw bedrijfsrisico. *M&O*, 54(1): 21–44.
White, J. 2004. Globalisation, Divestment and Human Rights in Burma. *Journal of Corporate Citizenship*, 14: 47–65.
Zarni, K. 2000. Resistance and Cybercommunities: The Internet and the Free Burma Movement. In: De Vaney, A., Gance, S. and Ma, Y. (eds.), *Digital Communications and New Coalitions Around the World*, pp. 71–88. New York, NY: Peter Lang.

Chapter 14
Commentary: Dredgers on Land

Pieter Ippel

Abstract Holland's glory has long had a maritime character. Navigators, explorers and admirals speak to the imagination of many. Today, their heroism is disputed. Critical observers point out that these so-called heroes were often indistinguishable from robbers and pirates. Dredgers like IHC Caland seem to fit well in this tradition of hard-boiled go-getters. They perform their activities in open sea or on the edge of the land, without much interest in legal or humanitarian considerations. This does not mean that they maintain no moral code, but it is a "business is business" and "a contract is a contract" morality. Following this narrow but uncomplicated moral attitude IHC Caland had no qualms about contracting for an offshore project with the Burma rogue state in 1998. During the 5 years extending from 1998 to 2003, IHC Caland hesitatingly but unmistakable changed its business strategy and expanded its definition of its moral domain. This outcome will leave many feeling satisfied. Still, the case raises at least three issues. (1) Is not the dredger's initial defence really quite plausible? (2) Are there enforceable international standards? Is there a general consensus on the subject? and (3) Is the final result defensible in all respects? Each of these three questions will be commented upon in this commentary.

Introduction

Holland's glory has long had a maritime character. Navigators, explorers and admirals like De Ruyter speak to the imagination of many, although their heroism is disputed in modern-day Netherlands. The Hollanders may well have been at their best at sea: level-headed, resourceful, undaunted. Critical observers will immediately add that these traits were often indistinguishable from robbery and piracy and that Hollanders and Zealanders grew rich from the slave trade. At first sight, our ancestors were not overly interested in rules of law and moral standards. Perhaps we should say that they bent legal standards to clear the way for their own interests.

P. Ippel (✉)
Roosevelt Academy, Middelburg, The Netherlands
e-mail: p.ippel@roac.nl

As we know, Hugh Grotius, one of the founding fathers of classic international law, wrote *Mare Liberum*, a famous treatise on the freedom of the sea that tended to lean heavily in a direction that would guarantee his own country's interests.

Dredgers seem to fit well in this tradition of hard-boiled go-getters. They perform their activities in open sea or on the edge of the land, without much interest in legal or humanitarian considerations. This does not mean that they maintain no moral code, but it is a "business is business" and "a contract is a contract" morality.

We encounter this narrow but uncomplicated moral attitude in the first phase of the dispute on dredging company IHC Caland's contract with an oil company operating on the continental plate within Burmese territorial waters. The case description shows that during the 5 years extending from 1998 to 2003, IHC Caland, under pressure from various interest groups, hesitatingly but unmistakable changed its business strategy and thus – albeit with aversion – expanded its definition of its moral domain. The outcome of this transformation will leave many feeling satisfied because it puts pressure on a country that it would not be an exaggeration to call a rogue state. The regime in Burma operates brutally, grossly violates its citizens' human rights, tries to smother opposition and is not too fussy about compliance with recognised international environmental standards.

Still, the case raises at least three issues. (1) Is not the dredger's initial defence really quite plausible? (2) Are there enforceable international standards? Is there a general consensus on the subject? and (3) Is the final result defensible in all respects? I would like to offer a few comments on these three aspects.

Is a Contract a Contract?

At the start, the IHC Caland's management was standoffish and defensive. The CEO Jan-Diederick Bax was plainly irritated. "We're not doing anything illegal" and "A contract is a contract". What are we to make of this line of defence?

Every legal scholar quickly learns the aphorism from Roman law that states *pacta sunt servanda* [agreements must be kept]: once you have made an agreement, you have to keep your word. Without that principle, all of private law would be built on quicksand. The ideal of contractual freedom was widespread in the nineteenth century. Parties at law had a great deal of latitude in giving shape to their juridical relationships in a contract, but once a contract was agreed, it became a strict rule with whose letter all parties did their utmost to comply. A dominant theme in nineteenth-century private law was the pursuit of legal certainty and predictability. Legal certainty and predictability can flourish only when contracts are respected and interpreted strictly.

Contractual freedom is still an important principle in the property law section of private law and we still speak of an "open system" in the law of obligations, where, in practice, leasing and franchise contracts have become highly developed and only later were interwoven in the fabric of private law. Still, it is naive and incorrect to regard contractual freedom as undisputed fact. First, private law has long set standards for the establishment of contracts. For instance: information must be properly and honestly provided before a contract can be made; the Dutch Code of Civil Law explicitly forbids compulsion, fallacy, deceit and undue influence. Second, an agreement may not contravene basic moral standards. A contract to sell oneself as slave is invalid; the same is true for an agreement aimed at more effective discrimination. Penalty provisions and nationally and internationally recognised human rights restrict – at least on a national level – opportunities to apply contractual freedom nonchalantly. Third, during the twentieth century, mandatory rules were established in many areas of contract law to protect the weaker or more vulnerable parties. Well known examples are to be found in labour and tenancy law; more recent are segments of health law and consumer law. The protective provisions are legally binding and may not be departed from. That restricts the parties' contractual freedom. Finally, there is a whole range of rules in public law that tighten contractual freedom. Someone wanting to build or renovate a house will usually have to get a permit from the municipal authorities before signing an agreement with a contractor.

These changes have been well described as the socialisation of private law. There is a connection between social context, moral views and legal standards (Hessel and de Graaf, 1998).[1] Of course there are zones where the link between moral and legal is fairly loose, but occasionally there is close and intense interplay and overlapping considerations. In both cases, the initial response from IHC Caland's CEO that "We're not doing anything illegal" and "A contract is a contract", is contestable from a juridical perspective. Moral notions have long influenced and sometimes put restrictions on contractual freedom's operational territory. Anyone leafing through the Dutch Code of Civil Law will regularly encounter the terms social propriety, conscientiousness or good employment practices. The law of legal entities imposes requirements on what a company may consider acceptable corporate governance. That means that the law of agreements is open in two senses. On one side, the law of contracts honours the potential of parties in society to create and adopt law; on the other, it ties this bottom-up creation of law to morally-tinted standards.

International Rules and Standards

Compared with national law, international (public) law is underdeveloped in some ways and often displays deficiencies. This is mainly due to the lack of a central, supranational authority that can maintain and enforce compliance with rules. Present international law has developed from the international law of autonomous and sovereign states that put their own national interests first.

Still, international law changed its character markedly in the post WWII period. Internationally recognised human rights have been incorporated in binding treaties and not just in declarations. International organisations have gained power, certainly since the end of the Cold War.

While the classic law of nations as good as ignored the individual and his/her rights, individual persons are now seen as actors and subjects within the framework of international law. Individuals can appeal to human rights because these rights

---

[1] For a discussion of the relation between ethics and law in environment law, health law and privacy law, see Ippel (2002).

are considered universally applicable, although their chances of success can vary dramatically. However, in some part of the world there is a reasonably effective institutional structure that one can call upon to protect personal human rights. The *Convention for the Protection of Human Rights and Fundamental Freedoms* is directly applicable in most European countries; the European Court of Human Rights sees to its enforcement. There is a second way in which individuals have legal rights. Criminal courts can call individuals to account for heinous crimes like genocide or "crimes against humanity". The tribunals on former Yugoslavia and Rwanda and the International Criminal Court in The Hague are manifestations of a shift, the meaning and basic principles of which can hardly be overrated.

Although protection of human rights for millions of people is still inadequate or totally illusory, it has become generally recognised that this is a problem that affects the entire world community. The foreign policies of the governments of sovereign states take into account the human rights situations in countries where they do business and try to exert pressure on them (even if often hypocritically). Many internationally operating companies have been forced to change tack, have adjusted their strategy and have recorded in a code of behaviour their intention to respect human rights.

Also striking is that the OECD, WTO and other organisations that mainly target economic development and the deregulation of world trade have begun to play a role in protecting human rights and other morally-tinted interests. Apparently, the vocabulary of human rights has an expansive force even in areas known to be "hard". The case of IHC Caland in Burma refers to new OECD guidelines. These are the guidelines that the company "adopted" in time. It did so reluctantly because critical stakeholders needled banks and investors so that they, in their turn, would lean on the dredgers.

Seen juridically, the OECD directives have no formal force of law. This is an example of soft law, i.e. non-enforceable standards that presuppose a degree of consent. It is possible to put indirect and political pressure to compel compliance with the directives. In words adapted from Henriëtte Roland-Holst we could say, "sometimes a gentle touch wins out in the end". Soft law can be the cradle of new, "real" international rules.

The dredgers were forcibly run aground. Initially, they thought they could afford to leave international business ethics and human rights protection to the landlubbers and, being mighty mudslingers, they could get away with a stripped-down version of business ethics. It took years to get IHC Caland to that point because a consumer boycott of a company without national customers is futile. However, when pressure groups keep hammering on a theme indirectly and in the media, it can lead to success.

A Satisfactory Outcome?

How really successful was this success? IHC Caland did not immediately leave Burma, but promised not to accept any new assignments from that country. Heineken, Philips and Levi-Strauss had already left the controversial Asian country.

Under Aung San Suu Kyi, the opposition called for ties to be cut, committees in the Netherlands and other countries increased pressure.

The intention was to isolate the repressive regime as protest against the rulers and to use this isolation as a coercive tool to compel the regime to adopt a different and morally acceptable approach to the country's citizens which would also allow a democratic form of government to develop. The price that apparently had to be paid for this course of action was that the quality of life of everyday residence of Burma initially became worse, that their suffering in all likelihood became heavier to bear. One could put it this way: the duty to work for human rights, democracy and ecological sustainability is so imposing that a temporary (albeit for a long time) increase in normal people's suffering must be accepted. Proponents of a simple, utilitarian calculus realise that when this measure is used, the chosen policy line will have to be rejected. Only in the long term can we expect improvement in the wellbeing and happiness of the inhabitants of Burma, but *whether* this will really happen is difficult to predict.

But non-utilitarians (like myself) can feel uncomfortable when asked if this outcome can really be called good. In short: I'm of two minds. Although I too feel that working to protect and promote basic human rights for all the world's population is a very important moral orientation point, I am not convinced that this instrument – breaking all economic ties – is the best way to achieve this. Even when we accept that internationally operating companies have a moral obligation to work for human rights – and I think there are strong arguments for doing so – then we would still have to discuss the method they will use. That the opposition movement in the country urges this is an important element, but it need not always be a decisive argument. The discussion on the moral responsibility of internationally operating companies will have to address means as well as goals. A careful and empirically informed evaluation could also lead to a company's digging in its heels and remaining so it can work for recognition of basic human rights in other ways.

An internationally operating company's moral domain is undoubtedly broader and more complex than the management at IHC Caland thought in its initially chosen minimalistic and stripped-down attitude (See van Luijk, 2000). But I do not think it impossible that another outcome might have been more morally exemplary. Leaving an evil (or nearly evil) and poorly governed country as a way to "kick a conscience into its leaders" can be too easy in some situations.

References

Hessel, B. and de Graaf, P. 1998. *Over recht en bedrijfsethiek. Pleidooien voor samenwerking.* Nijmegen: Ars Aequi Libri.
Ippel, P. 2002. *Modern recht en het goede leven. Over gezondheid, milieu en privacy.* Den Haag: Boom Juridische uitgevers.
van Luijk, H. 2000. Wereldwijd fatsoenlijk. *Het Financieele Dagblad* 27 June 2000.

Chapter 15
Commentary: IHC Caland in Burma – An Analysis

Johan Graafland

Abstract In this commentary I analyze whether IHC's policies in Burma can be explained by the institutional setting in which IHC operated. Using reputation theory, I find that IHC Caland (IHC) withstood societal pressure to withdraw from Burma, because powerful stakeholders were more interested in continuation of its operations in Burma. We find no evidence of a lack of transparency or a short term horizon. Next, we evaluate IHC's policy from an ethical point of view. Using utilitarianism, if it is assumed that IHC Caland operated in a highly competitive market, we might conclude that it did what it could: it obeyed the law while upholding its reputation with its most powerful stakeholders. The present analysis regards the case first from an economic perspective, giving particular attention to the case's institutional setting in relation to the workings of what will be called "the reputation mechanism". This will help us to explain how IHC Caland was able to withstand societal pressure to withdraw from Burma for such a long time. It will also provide insight into the conditions that must be present for the reputation mechanism to help achieve social goals and into the ways institutional changes affect these conditions. It then evaluates the case from a moral perspective, discussing whether IHC Caland's policy has a utilitarian defence. Compared to other ethical theories (e.g. deontological and virtue theories), utilitarianism is closest to an economic style of thought because it considers the moral value of an action solely from its consequences for total welfare.

The Reputation Mechanism

Today, many companies are concerned about values and develop ethical codes to foster responsible behaviour. They find it increasingly important to behave like good corporate citizens, because they need a "licence to operate". To be granted this permission, they must satisfy stakeholders' expectations regarding their contribution to

---

J. Graafland (✉)
Tilburg Sustainability Center and European Banking Center, Tilburg School of Economics and Management, University of Tilburg, Tilburg, The Netherlands
e-mail: j.j.graafland@uvt.nl

the triple-P: profit, planet and people (Graafland, 2002, 2004). Those companies not meeting these expectations may find their reputation harmed and their market shares and profitability slump (McIntosh et al., 1998).

IHC-Burma is an interesting case because it provides a good illustration of the way companies can withstand societal pressures when there is no strain on their reputation. Why did the reputation mechanism fail to work here in response to the criticism of NGOs?

Several conditions must be met before the mechanism will work (Graafland and Smid, 2004; see also Fig. 15.1). First, all other potential trading partners must have access to information on the company's (past) behaviour. The transparency of a company's operations depends on the visibility of its market operations (and this depends on the complexity of its product), on society's alertness and on the company's openness. If a company is not very visible, information about its operations will only become publicly available when either society proactively monitors the company or the company voluntarily discloses information about its operations. One important element in the first, external, factor is the role of the media, NGOs and ICT. ICT is turning the world into a global village where the media can keep people up to date about what a given company is doing anywhere on the globe. Improved communication networks also strengthen NGOs' positions, making it easier for them to pass information to the media. That makes the market less anonymous. An important internal factor is company transparency. External stakeholders often require this for obvious reasons. When a company does not provide information about its operations (e.g. in an annual social report) or principles (in a code of conduct), it is much harder for NGOs and market parties to gather information on the company's economic and social impact.

A second prerequisite for the reputation mechanism to operate effectively is that the company must envisage a sufficiently long time horizon. A good reputation is a long-term benefit that entails short term expenses. The more a company focuses solely on short term profits, the fewer are its incentives to build a good reputation.

The third condition is that the company must believe that its potential market partners' strategies depend on its own decisions. The company must believe that a good reputation will reap its own reward and lead to the company's financial

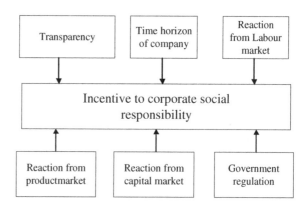

Fig. 15.1 Conditions affecting reputation

success, while a bad reputation will incur penalties and harm the company's interests. This depends on the way the various stakeholders (labour, product and capital markets, government) respond to the company's conduct.

An examination of each of these conditions will shed light on why IHC Caland was able to withstand the societal pressure for so long. First, lack of transparency cannot explain it all. IHC Caland's operations in Burma were well known. Moreover, many well-organised NGOs monitored IHC Caland's operations closely. Nevertheless, lack of transparency explains part of IHC Caland's stakeholders' responses to social protest against the operations of the company in Burma. Major Dutch financial institutions kept lending money to IHC Caland, despite public criticism of the company. They only stopped lending money when their activities became publicly known.

Second, there is no evidence that a short-term horizon caused IHC Caland's slow response. On the contrary, IHC Caland seems to have taken a long-term view that took its reputation into account. However, even in the face of unexpected social protest, IHC Caland believed that its reputation among powerful stakeholders was better served by honouring its Burmese contracts than by withdrawing from Burma. IHC Caland's financial performance showed no indication that its decision to continue its operations in Burma damaged its long-term reputation. Its financial performance did not fall after 1998 or in the longer run. Hence, there is no evidence that IHC Caland succumbed to a short-term focus on profitability when disregarding social pressure to withdraw from Burma. Yet it does appear that IHC Caland failed to anticipate the social protest's strength, insistence and impact on its stakeholders (pension funds and the banks).

The two first conditions – transparency and commitment to long-term profitability – being met, we must seek the explanation for IHC Caland's policy to stay in Burma in the third condition. Indeed, there are many indications that IHC Caland had little need to fear negative feedback from stakeholders on the labour, product and capital markets or from the government when it continued its operations in Burma. First, its own employees did not join the protest. The case gives no reason for this; it may have had to do with the business-to-business nature of IHC Caland's operations and the technical level of its market. This market context will have impacted on IHC Caland's business culture and the type of employees it hired. The selection process will have presumably given greater weight to technical expertise than to social skills or great sensitivity to social issues. Whereas IHC Caland's employees did not protest against their employer, Dutch labour unions did offer substantial criticism despite not getting IHC Caland's employees to join them. Labour unions were able to exert pressure on IHC Caland's Burma policy only after business declined in the ship building division and the jobs of employees came under threat. IHC Caland needed the labour unions' cooperation to make structural changes in this market segment. Apart from their involvement with IHC Caland's employees, the unions could also exert influence as shareholders in pension funds and via direct talks with IHC Caland board.

The nature of IHC Caland's business also explains why there was little or – if we may believe CEO Bax – no negative feedback from customers. Heavy impact stakeholders like Shell and Exxon did not object to IHC Caland's involvement in

Burma. IHC Caland thought that these powerful stakeholders were more interested in its reputation for reliability than on whether or not it worked for Burma. This argument seems quite realistic. Shell and Exxon also operated in countries where political regimes showed little concern for human rights. Shell and Exxon were thus also vulnerable to pressure from NGOs. Were IHC Caland to submit, this would offer a precedent for when NGOs dealt with large oil companies. Shell and Exxon would know this. IHC Caland would risk losing the preferential treatment they gave it if it withdrew from Burma. Loosing Shell and Exxon as clients would have a major impact on IHC Caland's financial position and could even threaten its continuity.

Social protest also seems to have had little effect to IHC Caland's reputation on the capital market. Most US shareholders were insensitive to NGOs' criticisms. A few Dutch stakeholders on the capital market did concur with criticism of IHC Caland's operations. ABP thought IHC Caland should develop a code of conduct. ABN AMRO bank communicated its uneasiness to IHC Caland. Furthermore, the Foundation of Investors for Sustainable Development (*Vereniging van Beleggers voor Duurzame Ontwikkeling*, VBDO) warned IHC Caland for the risks this operation entailed. Still, all this did not shake IHC Caland's confidence. It drew strength from the fact that no major shareholder went so far as to sell its shares. Financial stakeholders increased their pressure only after IHC Caland signed a second contract with Burma in 1999. It was then that ABN-AMRO publicly announced that it had sold its shares and that ABP pension fund reconsidered and then sold its holdings in IHC Caland. The financial stakeholders' response was too indeterminate to force IHC Caland to leave Burma. Of course we should also note that some major Dutch financial institutes (including ABN AMRO and ABP-owned NIB Capital) still extended loans for IHC Caland's operations. They also confirmed their support for its refusal to break its past contract; they were not willing to do more than stop financial support for future contracts in Burma.

Finally, the Dutch government was unable initially to alter IHC Caland's strategy. Although Dutch political parties clearly and consistently protested against trade with Burma, the government did not forbid investment in Burma or impose any other sanctions on IHC Caland (e.g. turning down applications for export- or investment grants). OECD guidelines also proved to be inadequate for moving IHC Caland, since they applied only to investment and were not enforceable by law.

However, growing pressure from NGOs, unions, financial institutions and government was not completely in vain. In 2002, after Dutch state secretary for economic affairs, Mr. Ybema, met in person with IHC Caland's CEO in an attempt to get IHC Caland to halt operations in Burma, IHC Caland announced that it would not accept new orders there. Pressure increased further in 2003 and 2004, when also other governments (USA, EU) took measures to discourage trade with Burma; in 2003 IHC Caland promised to discuss human rights with Burma's ambassador in London.

Note, however, that in a different institutional context IHC Caland would probably have been much more responsive to social concerns about Burma's violation of human rights. One example concerns the loans Dutch financial institutes extended to IHC Caland. If these had been more transparent and known earlier, then

ABN-AMRO and ABP would probably have had to give a clearer signal to IHC Caland; and not just the ambiguous one that led it to believe that financial institutions would not divest. Another example is the OECD guidelines' legal foundation. Had the national contact point (NCP) been able to impose sanctions on companies that violated OECD guidelines, government and NGOs would probably have had a stronger hold over IHC Caland.

A Moral Evaluation

So far we have only explained why IHC Caland did what it did, using an economic theory. Our analysis has not determined whether IHC Caland was morally right in doing what it did. This requires a moral analysis. In the scope of this brief commentary we cannot include all normative standards that might be useful in ethically evaluating IHC Caland's actions. We will focus on just one ethical standard: utilitarianism. We chose utilitarianism because this ethical theory is most closely aligned to the economic analysis in the first part of this article. We focus particularly on IHC Caland's decisions to sign contracts with Burma in 1998 and 1999, when the Burmese government's human rights violations were already broadly known.

Before applying the theory of utilitarianism here, we must first investigate the consequences of IHC Caland's strategies on welfare. Within the bounds of this paper we can include only the most important effects on the welfare of IHC Caland's shareholders, of its employees and of the Burmese people. Attempts to apply the theory of utilitarianism are hampered by uncertainty about impact on IHC Caland and on the Burmese people had IHC Caland forgone business opportunities in Burma. Therefore, we will consider the certainty of the effects explicitly. Utilitarianism requires the greatest expected total utility. A more fundamental methodological problem here is the difficulty in comparing the impact of IHC Caland's various options on Burmese people's welfare to their impact on IHC Caland's stakeholders' welfare. A utilitarian analysis cannot provide more but a very crude qualitative survey of major effects.

First, Table 2 in the case description indicates that IHC Caland's acceptance of Burmese orders did not harm its business. IHC Caland's share value increased from € 36.25 in 1999 to € 43 in 2003. Taking into consideration that IHC Caland signs relatively few contracts each year, it is fairly certain that refusing these contracts would have resulted in lower profitability and lower share prices, to the shareholders' detriment. However, the marginal utility for shareholders of the rise in IHC Caland's share value is limited. Since most shareholders have a diversified portfolio, we suspect that a fall in IHC Caland's share value would not have caused a dramatic decline in their wealth.

Lost profitability that would have resulted had IHC Caland refused the Burmese order might well have threatened employment at IHC Caland. It could have cost IHC Caland clients (like Shell and Exxon) and would have benefited IHC Caland's competitors. One possible result of a decline in its offshore activities might have been that IHC Caland might have had to dismiss at least some – and in the case of bankruptcy, all of its employees. This would have caused a drastic reduction in these workers' utility. Economic research shows that loosing a job has a dramatically negative effect on declared subjective wellbeing (Lane, 1994). However, it remains uncertain whether turning down the offer to operate in Burma would really have threatened jobs at IHC Caland in the long run.

The third stakeholder that we consider in our utilitarian evaluation of the IHC Caland case is the people of Burma (and related to this, the utility of the NGOs and the people they represent). There is no doubt that the violation of human rights in Burma is severe and has a detrimental impact on welfare. Improving the political situation would yield a rise in wellbeing for the Burmese people that would substantially outweigh the rise in welfare that IHC Caland's shareholders and other stakeholders would derive from high profitability. There are two reasons for this. First, the number of people benefiting from a political change is larger than the number of people benefiting from IHC Caland's economic success. Moreover, as Rawls (1999) argued, respecting basic rights to freedom is much more important for human beings than the economic welfare of Western citizens. However, it is unlikely that abstaining from doing business would have improved the political situation. By that time, many companies had already wound up their business in Burma, without visible improvement in Burma's political situation. Furthermore, the argument that other companies would have accepted the orders if IHC Caland had refused them should be considered when evaluating the case from a consequential perspective. If this is true, it is indeed highly unlikely that IHC Caland's withdrawal from Burma would have improved the human rights situation there. In addition, IHC Caland could argue that its talks with the Burmese ambassador could have helped improve the situation. Table 15.1 below rounds up the consequentional argument in a concise manner.

Utilitarianism thus confronts us with several diverging effects, incomparable in magnitude or probability and difficult to quantify. We look to Van De Ven and Jeurissen (2000) for a more definite conclusion. They argue that operating in a fierce competitive market – as IHC Caland said it did – limits the company's options for responsible strategy. In fierce competition, there are only two options: complying with the law and reputation management. Van de Ven and Jeurissen argue (2000: 110) that IHC Caland did both these. Their operations were legal under Dutch and international law; they also strengthened IHC Caland's reputation among the most powerful and needed stakeholders (i.e. IHC Caland's customers). Van de Ven and Jeurissen argue that the Dutch or European governments should have prohibited these transactions with Burma.

Table 15.1 Welfare consequences of IHC Caland's 1998 and 1999 contracts

Consequence	Stakeholder	Marginal utility	Degree of probability
Higher profitability	Shareholder	Low	High
Employment at IHC Caland	Employees	Medium	Medium
Violation of human rights	Burmese people	High	Low

Conclusion

IHC-Caland is an interesting case. It shows that a company's market context has a major impact on its willingness to acquiesce to social demands regarding corporate social responsibility. Companies are able to withstand moral demands for quite a long time, when one or more conditions for an effective reputation manipulation are not met. In this case, the major obstacle to changing IHC Caland's strategy was a dearth of negative feedback from its own employees and customers. Other stakeholders – financial institutions, unions and government – did criticize IHC Caland's policy, but their protest was too indeterminate to provide sufficient incentive to compensate the cost of breaking contracts concluded in 1998 en 1999. However, as we also noted, this protest was not completely in vain. The NGOs' persistence when combined with union involvement (and IHC Caland's need for their cooperation in restructuring its shipbuilding division), the political parties, Dutch government and investors' critical attitude slowly halted IHC Caland's resistance and finally led it to abstain from new operations in Burma.

But how are we to regard IHC Caland's policy and conduct from a moral perspective? We have only assessed them from a utilitarian perspective. Utilitarianism, however, offers no clear conclusion on the moral legitimacy of IHC Caland's Burmese operations, because it is difficult to compare the positive consequences for IHC Caland's shareholders and employees to the negative consequences for Burma's people. These consequences differ in probability as well as in magnitude.

References

Graafland, J.J. 2002. Profits and Principles: Four Perspectives. *Journal of Business Ethics*, 35: 293–305.

Graafland, J.J. 2004. Collusion, Reputation Damage and Interest in Code of Conduct: The Case of a Dutch Construction Company. *Business Ethics: A European Review*, 13: 127–142.

Graafland, J.J. and Smid, H. 2004. Reputation, Corporate Social Responsibility and Market Regulation. *Tijdschrift voor Economie en Management*, XLIX(2): 269–306.

Lane, R. 1994. The Road Not Taken: Friendship, Consumerism and Happiness. *Critical Review*, 8: 521–554.

McIntosh, M., Leipziger, D., Jones, K. and Coleman, G. 1998. Corporate Citizenship: Successful Strategies for Responsible Companies. In: *Financial Times Management*, pp. 61–68. London: Pearson.

Rawls, J. 1999. *A Theory of Justice (Revised Edition)*. Boston, MA: Harvard University Press.

Van de Ven, B.W. and Jeurissen, R.M.J. 2000. Maatschappelijk verantwoord ondernemen en strategie. In: Jeurissen, R. (ed.), *Bedrijfsethiek. Een Goede Zaak*, pp. 98–124. Assen: Van Gorcum.

Part VI
Case E: The Ice Train Accident near Eschede

Chapter 16
Case Description: The ICE Train Accident near Eschede

Michiel Brumsen

Abstract On 3 June, 1998 a serious accident occurred at Eschede involving Deutsche Bahn's (German Railway) prestigious Inter City Express (ICE) train. ICE 884, "Wilhelm Conrad Röntgen" derailed at high speed (approx 200 km/h) and hit a viaduct that then collapsed on the train. The carriages that followed zigzagged like an accordion against the collapsed viaduct. The accident resulted in 101 dead and 88 injured. It sparked the greatest rescue operation undertaken to date in post-war Germany. This train had been synonymous with safety, reliability and progress. How could the accident have happened? At first glance, this accident was an unfortunate, and perhaps hardly foreseeable, failure of a part that unexpectedly proved to be very crucial. Yet, the case can very well be analysed as a situation that could have been prevented had the technology been better organized.

Introduction

On 3 June, 1998 a serious accident occurred at Eschede involving the Deutsche Bahn's (German Railway) prestigious Inter City Express (ICE) train. This chapter investigates the causes of this accident. The direct physical cause was a steel band coming loose from a wheel (see Fig. 16.1), which caused the train to derail, a bridge to collapse, and the train to pile up against the bridge. At first glance, this accident was an unfortunate, and perhaps hardly foreseeable, failure of a part that unexpectedly proved to be very crucial. Yet there are real questions about whether the wheel design was well advised: two different mechanisms, one of which was already known at the time, can be identified which led to the wheel developing a fault. More importantly, because the wheel design was unusual, testing it for faults needed to be done using special machinery. The available testing machinery however generated too many false positives, and for this reason an unsuitable standard testing method

M. Brumsen (✉)
Delft University of Technology, Delft, The Netherlands
e-mail: m.brumsen@zonnet.be

Fig. 16.1 The broken steel styre

was used. The conclusion is therefore that for all kind of organisational reasons, the system within which the wheel was used was not properly equipped to identify, prevent or repair any safety problems that could arise.

Investigation into the Cause, Initial Findings

On-site examination showed that a crossing frog originally located some distance before the place of the accident was absent. Crossing frogs are wheel guides mounted beside rails at switches, crossings and the like; their purpose is to keep the wheels on the track. This part had punctured the floor of the first carriage like a spear. Closer inspection showed that the steel tyre had become detached from one of the first carriage's wheels and was entangled in the undercarriage.

These findings led to the following reconstruction. A few kilometres, and 2 minutes, before the accident the passengers in the first carriage heard a bang. At that moment the steel tyre broke and flew off (Fig. 16.1). Afterwards, the train passed a series of frogs; the steel band tore away a crossing frog that became embedded in the train. That caused the derailed wheels. When the train passed a switch just before the viaduct, the wheels derailed and moved the switch. The third carriage shot toward the adjacent track at 200 km/h. The back of this carriage hit the viaduct's pier and the viaduct collapsed on the fourth carriage. The following carriages crashed in a zigzag pattern against the collapsed viaduct. In the meantime, the locomotive had become detached from the rest of the train. This activated the automatic emergency braking system. The locomotive came to a halt two kilometres further down the line. Only then did the engine driver turn around to discover that he had lost his train. He remained seated there in shock for 2 hours until rescuers found him there.

The Wheel's Design

The design of this train's wheels was special, and most likely played a decisive role. Put more precisely: to understand the immediate technical cause of the accident we must know how the wheel is put together (see Fig. 16.2). It is also important to know something about alternative designs and about the technical, organisational and economic reasons for choosing this design, although we cannot always be sure of these reasons.

There is still no consensus in the literature on which mechanism actually caused the accident. It is certain that it involved a composite wheel, and not a single-piece, i.e. block-cast, wheel. The design of this composite wheel included a rubber tyre over which came the steel tyre that had contact with the rails (Fig. 16.2). The sudden tear resulting in detachment occurred in the outermost, steel tyre. This set off the fatal chain of events. The same design is used in tram wheels, but at a much lower speed[1]. Other high-speed trains use block-cast wheels. After the accident, *Deutsche Bahn* replaced its composite wheels with the block-cast wheels originally delivered with the trains.

An important principle in train transport is that the wheels' rolling resistance has to be very low; that is what makes this type of transport more energy and cost efficient than road transport. Making wheels and rails very hard and rigid contributes to this low rolling resistance. However, one drawback is that the wheel-rail interface is subjected to high material stress. Several recent train accidents can be understood as symptoms of engineers' continuous wrestling with this (Smith, 2003). The basic fact of high material stress resulting from rigid materials and constructions imposes several important requirements: The rails must be laid quite flush and they must have a regular shape. The wheels must be perfectly round. If one of these is not the case, the wheels slam hard on the rails, usually with (additional) material damage as result. Once a wheel has lost its roundness, this surface will always hit the rail with a blow, which only increases the flattening. The extent of the problem depends on other factors including the wheel's suspension; if the suspension is better it will absorb this blow so the wheel will have less to endure. The higher the speed, the greater the forces at play, and so the worse the problem.

The ICE trains had had problems with comfort, especially in the restaurant carriage. The cabins were jolting and noisy, glasses danced along the tables. Wheels containing a rubber tire were put in place of the block-cast wheels in a largely successful attempt to reduce jolting and noise. Because rubber is more pliable than steel, this provided a degree of elasticity: the rolling wheel could undergo greater stress without immediate and permanent out-of-roundness distortion. Rubber can spring back much better than steel. This great increase in

---

[1] A documentary entitled "Eschede – Seconds to Disaster" – broadcast on *National Geographic Channel* – claimed that the Hannover city tram company encountered *fatigue issues* when it used dual block wheels and that it had warned the German Railway about this in 1996.

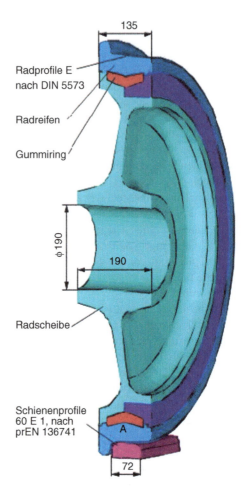

Fig. 16.2 The design of the assembled wheel. (Source: Liu, 2002b)

comfort came at the expense of somewhat higher rolling resistance. The major drawback of this option was that these wheels required more maintenance and better monitoring.

In addition (or actually because of) the higher rolling resistance, at least two problems with the wheels, potentially reducing their operational life. Which of these problems was the deciding factor in the accident is, as we noted, still moot. First, the steel tire around the rubber tire still constantly distorts. Even though the distortion is minor, it still produces symptoms of fatigue. A paper clip breaks when it has been straightened and bent a few times; a steel tire will become fatigued in the same way. The wheel under consideration had done 1.8 million km and thus revolved millions of times. Second, the wheel and its rubber tire become warm from these repeated distortions. Rubber expands much more than steel, but it is hardly

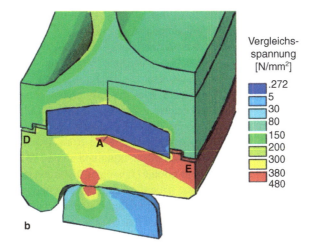

Fig. 16.3 The structure of the wheels used (taken from X. Liu, 2002b)

compressible. Here, the rubber band is "trapped" between the wheel and the steel tire. As the rubber heats up, it exerts a high degree of pressure on the steel tire. Computer simulations (using the finite element method) can now calculate the stress distribution in the material (see Fig. 16.3).

The first mechanism (distortion fatigue) was known; the Fraunhofer Institute, that had studied the design, pointed this out when the dual block wheels were put into operation. The second mechanism (expansion of underlying rubber tire) was not known at that time (See Liu, 2002a). Regardless, the wheels were inspected regularly. On one side, it was sufficiently well known that they had a lot to endure; on the other, everyone could see that the condition of the wheels was obviously crucial. In addition, the wheels had to meet specific standards. The question thus becomes: were these inspections performed? If so, where they performed carefully and correctly? If, again, the answer is yes, were the standards sufficient? Or would it perhaps have been better never to have used this type of wheel?

Safety Inspections

The wheels were inspected daily in a special workshop. First they were assessed for out-of-roundness distortion. Out-of-roundness distortion results in high mechanical strain. Moreover, during these inspections, the thickness of the outer steel tire was measured and the steel tire was inspected for hair cracks.

The measured value had to meet specific standards. The out-of-roundness distortion was not allowed to exceed 0.6 mm; the steel tyre had to be thick enough to keep the total diameter at least 854 mm (the diameter of a new wheel was 920 mm). The test for hair cracks could lead to three different results: (1) wheel is OK, (2) wheel needs additional inspection, (3) wheel needs replacing.

That was the theory. Practice was another story.

The workshop where the inspection was done was equipped with ultrasonic equipment to check the wheels for cracks. There, the train rode through a measurement setup at 6 km/h. In principle, this equipment permitted discovery of cracks not visible to the eye because a surface fracture would reflect sound. However, this equipment was unsound for two reasons. First, it could only detect cracks in the tread. It could not detect cracks arising from within, a distinct possibility certainly given the second mechanism explained above. Worse was that the equipment was so sensitive that in addition to raising an alarm when it found cracks, it also did this for innocuous surface irregularities. That resulted in nearly 20% of the tested wheels falling in the "needs replacing" category. That was impossible given the time pressure in the workshop. That is why the wheels were tested the old-fashioned way: by eye (with a lamp) and ear. This last method consisted in hitting the wheel with a hammer and assessing the sound of the wheel. However, it is unlikely that this method, often used on block-cast wheels, was suitable for this type. The rubber ring against which it is pressed muffles the vibrations in the steel tire. One obvious conclusion is that no suitable testing equipment was present.

Furthermore, the standard for out-of-roundness distortion was simply not applied. A week earlier, on 27 May, there was a 0.7 mm distortion; this grew steadily and, the evening before the accident, measured 1.1 mm – nearly double what the standard allowed. One important reason for this was that grinding the wheel was not a high-priority job. There was a scale with six priority levels for train repairs. Repairing the out-of-roundness had priority level 5. A defective coffee machine had a higher priority. Apparently out-of-roundness distortions were not recognised as safety risks, but at most a matter that reduced comfort or increased wear. That is rather surprising for a composite wheel. It is easy to see that metal fatigue in the steel tyre would cause problems a lot sooner when out-of-roundness subjected the wheel to higher mechanical strain.

Finally, there is the thickness of the steel tyre. At the last inspection prior to the accident, the wheel's diameter was 862 mm. That meant that the tyre met the standard (min. 854 mm). But it is by no means certain that this standard – which permitted a 66 mm decrease in diameter – was adequate. After the accident, Darmstadt's Fraunhofer Institute examined the question and this renown German research institute concluded that a minimum diameter of 890 mm would have been wiser. This would have been a much more demanding standard.

After the accident, all ICE trains were thoroughly inspected. Later all wheels were replaced with block-cast wheels. In the process, (at least?) three other wheels were found to have cracks. Any one of these could have caused a similar accident. This seems to make credible the hypothesis that the wheels' safety inspection was insufficient given their design. We examine this hypothesis further on in this case description.

Other Factors that Played a Role

The Train's Design

Beside the design of the wheel, the design of the rest of the train also played an important role. To start with, there is the design of the undercarriage. Designers of the ICE-1 train (the model of the fatal train) opted to give the train conventional sets of wheels. The superstructure – the casing with cabin – was an entirely new design, but the wheel sets were an enhanced version of conventional trains' wheel sets. However, the suspension requirements for a high-speed train are very stringent because the forces to be handled increase with speed. Many high-speed trains, like the French TGV, use air suspension; ICE-1 used steel multiple leaf springs. This was also probably the reason for the uncomfortable ride on block-cast wheels. You could almost say that the composite wheels with rubber tyres were used because of insufficient investment in designing new air-suspension wheel sets. Understandably, at that point no one wanted to undertake a radical redesign of the undercarriage to increase comfort. The trains were already part of the timetable, and that is a serious barrier for undertaking major modifications.

A second factor that may have influenced the gravity of the consequences is the way the various carriages were coupled in the ICE train. The train folded like an accordion up against the collapsed viaduct, allowing carriages to pile up on top of one another. If the connections had been more rigid, i.e. if there had been fewer hinges – as is the case with France's TGV (Fig. 16.4) – this would probably not have happened. However, whether rigid couplings would have made the accident's consequences less serious is a matter of speculation. Of course, the rescue work would have been easier, but a train that comes to an abrupt halt from a speed of 200 km/h will still probably cause many victims, especially in the forward carriages. The train would probably slide together like a telescope.

Other important elements are the alarm and signalling systems installed in the train. ICE-1 and all other high-speed trains are quite high-tech, with all types of built-in, computerised warning systems and sensors. But there was no sensor for a broken wheel. This kind of system, built into a wheel system, warns when there is unusual vibration. In extreme cases it could set off an emergency stop. In 1995,

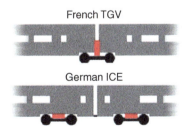

Fig. 16.4 Design of carriage couplings and wheel sets in French and German trains

Gottfried Birlk, a *Deutsche Bahn* employee at the workshop in Mühdorf had suggested building this in, but his suggestion was rejected because of its uncertain reliability and the high cost of further technical improvements to the system (Rhein Zeitung, 1996). However, such a system was certainly within the realm of technical possibility. It is in use today, in Swiss goods trains and in Eurostar trains.

Passengers in the carriage with the broken wheel knew immediately that something seriously wrong had happened; that is clear from survivors' eyewitness reports. Several minutes passed between the time the tyre broke and the actual accident – minutes that could have been used for an emergency stop. The ICE-1 has no passenger-operated emergency brake. Only the engine driver and the conductor can operate the emergency brake. A passenger did try to find the conductor to report that something was wrong, but the latter wanted to find out what was wrong first before operating the emergency brake. At the time of the accident, he had just arrived in the carriage with the broken tyre.

By and large, we can say that designers ignored the possibility that an emergency could arise in the train and that its consequences could be minimised with timely action. The engine driver did, indeed, have several warning systems, but these all had to do with characteristics of the line up ahead. This explains how it could happen that he only discovered after the locomotive had come to a halt that his train had disconnected long ago.

The Track's Design

In many other countries where high-speed trains are used – France for instance – these run on specially built tracks. This has several advantages: The faster the train's speed, the straighter, flatter and more stable the track has to be. Older tracks often do not satisfy these requirements. Moreover, fewer switches and crossings are needed because tracks are seldom if ever shared with other lines. Tunnels are often placed at road crossings.

The tracks for ICE trains were, and are, mixed. The ICE trains ride over normal tracks shared with other types of trains as well as on special high-speed tracks. The route near Eschede was not a special high-speed track; there were four track lines. The ICE trains rode on the innermost two tracks. However, other trains also used these tracks; that is why it was necessary to be able to move trains from the innermost to the outermost tracks and back. This track design played a large role in the accident near Eschede. The switch whose frog the broken steal tyre tore off and where the wheel derailed lay just 300 meter before the viaduct. The switch that the derailed wheel turned lay only 120 meter before the viaduct. It should be clear that if there had been no switches to the adjacent track, the accident would not have taken on the grave proportions that it did. On 21 December 1993, a TGV train on France's Paris-Lille line derailed at 300 km/h. Only two people received slight injuries. The train did run off the track, but nothing much else happened even though the train jolted on a few kilometres alongside the rails before it came to a halt. A similar accident with the TGV occurred in 2001, again without fatalities and just a few

16 Case Description: The ICE Train Accident near Eschede   165

Fig. 16.5 Aerial photograph of the accident. (Source: Delta Universiteitsblad, Delft, 18-3-1999)

wounded. Comparisons between this and the accident at Eschede regularly point to the more rigid couplings between the carriages that we mentioned above.

The presence of switches alone was probably not decisive. What was probably more important was that the switch to the outer rail, the one that the derailed wheel turned, was only 120 m from the viaduct. That allowed a carriage to swing directly against a pier. In addition, the possibility that an accident of this type could occur was apparently not taken into account when the viaduct was designed. It was a fairly heavy concrete viaduct with piers relatively close to the track. If the construction had been lighter, its collapse would have had less serious consequences. Now it was a very solid obstruction for a train moving at full speed. One carriage was completely mashed. In addition to that, the rest of the train folded like an accordion as the picture clearly shows (see Fig. 16.5). More design changes are imaginable i.e. where the piers are further apart and thus farther from the rail; an earthen wall would have provided an additional protective buffer.

Organisational Aspects

In discussing the accident at Eschede, various authors have pointed out that *Deutsche Bahn* was privatised in 1994, or to be more precise: the West German *Bundesbahn* and the former East German *Reichsbahn* were incorporated in an independent company. The question is, to what extent is this relevant to the accident near Eschede.

To start with, the first ICE-1 trains had already been built in 1990. Design and construction of these trains took place a few years prior to the privatisation. At that time, the *Bundesbahn* was running up heavy losses, which could have been one consideration in deciding not to redesign the wheel sets. In addition, it is clear from the preceding that there was no reliable inspection system for steel tires and that the standards for the wheel's out-of-roundness distortion were not met. It is not unlikely that this was due to financial pressure and the consequent heavy workload in the workshops.

Several serious accidents have occurred in the UK since the railways were privatised. There, too, commentators link the increase in the accident rate to privatisation. Actually, overdue maintenance caused several infrastructure-related accidents at the privatised company Railtrack. After the accident near Hatfield on 17 October 2000 and Lord Cullen's subsequent report on railway safety, Railtrack became so submerged in problems that it was put under administration of the transport ministry a year later and converted into Network Rail, a "not-for-profit" company with state aid. This more or less undid the privatisation of rail infrastructure.

Lodge (2002), however, points out that the organisational changes in the UK were very different from those in Germany. In the UK, the people who designed the privatisation were the same ones who had worked on the privatisation of state-owned energy and telecom companies. In Germany, by contrast, it was the work of a commission composed of transport specialists. One consequence of this was that in 1994 the infrastructure remained the property of *Deutsche Bahn* rather than being assigned to a separate company. Unlike British Rail, *Deutsche Bahn* was not subdivided into smaller companies.

Professor Markus Hecht of *Technische Universität Berlin* argued that *Deutsche Bahn* was actually its own regulator (Brinkbaumer et al. 1999). The design of the ICE-1 and particularly of its composite wheels was certified when the *Bundesbahn* was still a state-owned company, despite the Fraunhofer Institute's misgivings. However, at the time of the accident there was a separate regulator. The *Eisenbahn Bundesamt* (EBA – German Federal Railway Authority) was established in 1994 when *Deutsche Bahn* was privatised. The EBA regulates infrastructure companies and railroad traffic companies via a licensing system. The EBA took over supervision of workshop inspection in 1998.

At any rate, there is still the question whether supervision and certification had changed at all since 1994. The EBA was also criticised for not being sufficiently critical of *Deutsche Bahn*, the successor to the *Bundesbahn*. However, this criticism related mainly to the way the EBA treated *Deutsche Bahn*'s competitors and impeded their use of railway infrastructure. Moreover, these were all matters that took place in the years after the Eschede accident.

Finally, there is one last organisational aspect. Up to 2 months before the accident, various conductors had entered eight times into the train's computer that the carriage was jittery. It is striking at the very least that no action was taken on these reports especially when the wheel's measurements showed excessive out-of-roundness distortion. Once again we must note that this type of wheel distortion was apparently not treated as a high-priority safety risk. That is surprising, because this type of wheel had not been tested for high-speed trains, and even more because special testing equipment had been purchased to inspect the wheels for cracks (although it was not used because it was too sensitive). A second observation is that it is all quite well to have a high-tech system where conductors can report matters, but that it is not very useful when it leads to an organisational dead end.

Legal Consequences of the Accident

The accident caused 101 deaths. *Deutsche Bahn* paid their families 30,000 German marks (€15,340) for emotional injury, which caused considerable ill feeling. Some of the wounded got more than a million marks (€512,000). In 2001 six family members of victims (with financial support from around 60 others) filed a test case against *Deutsche Bahn* to obtain higher compensation. The survivors' effort proved fruitless. One of the arguments used was the need to maintain a sharp distinction between compensation for emotional suffering and compensation for incurred loss. The court rejected the reasoning of the survivors' attorney that compensation for emotional suffering should be as great as the total value of the destroyed train divided by the number of victims (which was more than ten times the amount paid out).

Beside this civil case, criminal charges were brought in 2002 against two *Deutsche Bahn* employees and one employee of the wheel manufacturer. All three were involved in certifying the composite wheels for use on ICE. They were charged with 101 cases of criminally negligent homicide. After 53 days, the judge concluded in 2003 that no severe burden of guilt for the accident rested on the accused. This was based on several grounds. First, experts had no principle-based objections to composite wheels, so that their introduction did not run counter to prevailing opinions. Second, a crack that could lead to such an accident could develop very rapidly, i.e. within the time it took to travel a few thousand kilometres, so that it cannot be said that inspection procedures carried out in a manner that could reasonably be described as with due care would have prevented the accident. Finally, that grave errors had been made in calculating wheel strain was deemed unprovable. Taking all this into account the criminal court believed that it should avail itself of the opportunity that German criminal law offers to end proceedings without passing judgment, but still fining the defendants – each for €10,000. Many survivors thought that *Deutsche Bahn*, which they considered guilty of grave negligence, got off scot-free. However, a corporate body cannot be brought to court under German criminal law.

Conclusion

At first glance, this accident was an unfortunate, and perhaps hardly foreseeable, failure of a part that unexpectedly proved to be very crucial. Yet there are real questions about whether the wheel design was well advised. Even more important is that for all kinds of organisational reasons, the system within which the wheel was used was not properly equipped to identify, prevent or repair any safety problems that could arise. If this had been otherwise, use of this wheel design might have been defensible. Furthermore, it is incontestable that the rail design could have been much safer; as France has shown, derailment of a high-speed train need not have such catastrophic consequences. One general comment here is that, while economically attractive, using existing design solutions and infrastructure for such technology can be very risky. The recent derailment in Turkey (2004) of a high-speed train running on older rails and the good reputation of France's TGV for safety both support this conclusion.

References

Brinkbaumer, U.L., Ludwig, U. and Mascolo, G. 1999. Die Deutsche Titanic. In: Goodpaster, K.(ed.), *Der Spiegel, Conscience and Corporate Culture*, 2007, 21/1999, 24th may. Malden, MA: Blackwell Publishing.

Liu, X. 2002a. 'Gummiring im Visier der Forscher', VDI Nachrichten 9th august.

Liu, X. (2002b): 'Neue Erklarung zum ICE-Zugunglucks von Eschede 1998', http://www.gcpd.de/publication/meeting2002/liuxiufei_gcpd2002.pdf (website Journal of the Society of Chinese Physists in Germany)

Lodge, M. 2002. The Wrong Type of Regulation? Regulatory Failure and the Railways in Britain and Germany. *Journal of Public Policy*, 22(3): 271–297.

Rhein Zeitung, 1996. "Neue Sicherheit für die Bahn." *Rhein Zeitung*, 9 Jun.

Smith, R.A. 2003. The Wheel-Rail Interface – Some Recent Accidents. *Fatigue Fract Engng Mater Struct*, 26: 901–907.

Chapter 17
Commentary: Collective Responsibility and the Virtue of Accuracy

Bert van de Ven

Abstract This paper analyses the causes that led to the fatal accident with the ICE High speed train in Germany in 1998. The most remarkable fact of this case is that no one decision or action can be singled out as the main cause of the accident. We are confronted with the so-called problem of the many hands. For this reason special attention is paid to the organisational culture of the German Railway. It is argued that due to a lack of a sense of responsibility and the accompanying virtue of accuracy the German Railway collectively failed.

Introduction

When disasters and major accidents occur, we seem to have a natural tendency to want to know who is responsible. There seems to be a strong desire to find the wrongdoers, because this can reduce the disaster or accident to human proportions; to wit, to an avoidable event resulting from human failure. It is strangely reassuring to know that a disaster did not just befall us, but that evil intent or carelessness played an essential role. We know how to deal with human failure. We punish those who have intentionally done wrong or demand financial compensation for negligence. But what if we find no single culprit, when responsibility rests on the shoulders of many, or when disaster arises from a coincidence of unpredictable factors? Our only option is to accept that accidents happen or that it was an act of nature. However, even when responsibility cannot easily be attributed to a human agent, it often still makes sense to investigate the roles of the different parties in the chain of events that led to the accident. This is certainly true for the accident with the ICE high-speed train (HST). We will start our analysis of the case by discussing whether no one decision or act can be designated as the immediate cause. Then, we will explain what is called the problem of the many hands and how it relates to collective responsibility. Finally, we will examine how collective responsibility impacts

B. van de Ven (✉)
Department of Philosophy, Tilburg University, Tilburg, The Netherlands
e-mail: b.w.vdven@uvt.nl

on the German Railway's management and other employees. We will argue that accuracy is essential to ensuring the HST's safety. Accuracy is related to courage and honesty, but demands that the German Railway's staff display a specific attitude. Furthermore, it must pervade the entire organisation if future accidents are to be prevented.

The Accident's Causes

The factors contributing to the accident with the ICE HST are diverse and complex. This makes it extremely hard to determine who bears how much moral responsibility for the accident. The case description singles out no one decision or action as the main cause of the accident. On the contrary, three factors seem to have contributed to the fatal chain of events. The first was the decision to use composite wheels instead of block-cast wheels. The German railway was aware that composite wheels have a greater rolling resistance than do block-cast wheels. The Fraunhofer Institute had warned the German Railway that the greater rolling resistance would increase metal fatigue. At first glance, the metal fatigue that caused the tyre to break was the immediate cause of the accident. Yet a closer inspection of the case shows otherwise. The choice of composite wheels was as such not a sufficient cause for the accident. The risk of metal fatigue was known. Whether this risk was dealt with in a responsible way depended on whether safety measures were in place to ensure that the wheels were always in an acceptable condition.

A second factor was the high speed of the ICE-trains. The higher the speed, the greater the distortion. That is why using such wheels on HSTs increased the risk. One wonders why the German Railway chose them. Why did it not opt for an air-suspension system like the one used on the French TGV? One reason might be (the case description is inconclusive) that the new air-suspension design was much more expensive when compared to the German Railway's traditional system. The German Railway had originally chosen for a block-cast system. When block-cast wheels caused too much noise and jolting for passengers to enjoy a comfortable journey, German Railway decided to switch to composite wheels. This improved passenger comfort, but increased the risk of metal fatigue. Once the Railway decided to use and develop the traditional system, it became difficult to change course. Time and accumulating expenditures put on pressure. Financial reasons were probably a main factor in the management's decision for the more risky traditional system. Again, this does not imply that this choice was morally irresponsible. It does, however, imply that this choice should have led to greater attention to the safety issues.

The factors described above point to a common problem that lies at the heart of the matter. The German Railway's senior managers had little understanding of how to ensure the new HST's safety. A third factor, i.e. that the German Railway had decided to use the existing rails, instead of rails specially designed for HSTs – a decision that increased the risk of damage to wheels – confirms this. When choosing for composite wheels they should also have set up a strict safety scheme. Because the German Railway's management bore final responsibility for passenger safety, it

17 Commentary: Collective Responsibility and the Virtue of Accuracy 171

should have ensured compliance with such a strict safety scheme. Furthermore, it should have organised scheduled assessments of the safety scheme to detect and deal with risks related to composite wheels. This would have shown senior managers that there was no adequate way to test abnormal distortion in composite wheels. This, in turn, should have led them to set a more stringent norm for the maximum wheel distortion. The low priority given to repairing wheel distortion – lower still than repairing a coffee machine – is further evidence of the failure to attend to safety hazards. This low priority combined with inadequate testing methods resulted in the overall failure of the German Railway's safety procedure.

Two Explanations

A Sociological Explanation

What is the sociological explanation of this inattention to safety problems? There are two aspects to be distinguished in the organisation's collective responsibility. The first has to do with "the problem of the many hands" (Wempe, 1998). A central feature in this problem is that many parties in an organisation, individuals and groups, share responsibility for an event. No one person can be held responsible for what happened. Beside management, technical staff also had a responsibility to respond adequately to the safety hazards. The case description does not state whether engineers were aware that the method for testing the wheel distortion was unreliable. But they should have been concerned about another factor, e.g. the failure to respect standards for wheel distortion. That could explain why, on the evening before the fatal accident, testers disregarded distortion that was twice the acceptable standard. This shows that profound inattention for safety issues stretched from management right down to engineers on the work floor. The result was systematic neglect of the attendant risk. The many hands problem goes some way toward explaining how systematic neglect of safety risks can occur within an organisation. Because many parties share responsibility for safety issues, no single party feels responsible for the outcome of the complex, coordinated action between the organisation's various sections. Another aspect closely related to this emotional detachment is that most employees in complex organisations lack an overall picture of the complex interactions patterns within their organisation. A better grasp (there is probably no perfect perspective) would make greater demands on employees' motivation and sense of responsibility for the whole. Not having this overall picture undermines their commitment to the organisation as a whole. The cognitive problem (no overall view) and employees' emotional detachment reinforce one another.

A second element in collective responsibility, organisational culture, can also help explain this neglect of safety. When a company's core business is to transport passengers, the least that can be expected is that safe performance of this service would be a high priority for management and staff. The right to safety is an important consumer right. Keeping safety risk to a minimum is part of a company's product responsibility. The least that can be expected is that all foreseeable risks to passenger safety be removed or reduced to the lowest level that current knowledge and technology allow. A producer's responsibility extends to product design, its production, and information of its safe use (Velasquez, 1998, 337). For the ICE HST this means that the German Railway failed to assess and deal adequately with safety hazards during the HST's development, and in setting safety procedures. Obviously, the German Railway's organisational culture failed to give proper priority to safety in the list of values guiding action. How are we to explain this lack of responsibility?

What Kenneth E. Goodpaster has called the problem of "teleopathy" (Goodpaster, 2007) offers one possible explanation. Goodpaster coined the term "teleopathy" to refer to an individual's or group's unbalanced pursuit of goals or purposes. The word teleopathy combines the Greek words for "goal" and "disease" to indicate that teleopathy does not refer simply to goal-directed behaviour. It should also not be confused with determination, perseverance and hard work to get things done. For organisations these are virtues, not vices. People have to be able to make decisions, and that presupposes not worrying obsessively and endlessly about the smallest ramification of every goal or purpose. Teleopathy does not qualify all goal directed behaviour as an illness. It refers to a habit of character that values certain limited objectives as supremely well suited for guiding action:

> In its most extreme form, teleopathy involves a suspension of ethical awareness as a practical force in the decision-making process. It substitutes for the call of conscience the call of very different decision criteria: winning the game, achieving the objective, following the rules laid down by some goal-oriented framework independent of ethical reflection (Goodpaster, 2007, p. 28).

The symptoms of teleopathy are (a) *fixation* on tangible goals or purposes without moderation, (b) a tendency to *rationalise* or even deny responsibilities and realities that might impede the accomplishment of those goals or purposes, (c) a general separation of the ethics of business goals from the ethics of everyday life, leading to emotional *detachment* regarding the full human implications of pursuing these goals. An action-ready managerial response is the only way to forestall teleopathy.

Did teleopathy play a role at the German Railway? The case description does not give enough information to tell for sure. All we can say is that there seemed to be a focus on keeping the costs as low as possible to avoid exceeding the budget. This focus on keeping cost down could have led to a fixation on costs overriding safety considerations, which is one symptom of teleopathy. If teleopathy were to a certain degree present at German Railway, it would explain the clear lack of a sense of responsibility for safety issues. Since the German Railway's failure to deal with the safety issues was due at least as much to a poor sense of responsibility as to the problem of the many hands, it is worthwhile to explore ways to prevent this lack of responsibility. In what follows, we will examine this lack of a sense of responsibility from the perspective of virtue ethics.

A Moral Explanation: Safety Risks from the Perspective of Virtue Ethics

How should we interpret the lack of a sense of responsibility shown here? What does it entail? Is it attributable to the entire organisation as well as to the individuals within it? Bovens (1998) called a sense of responsibility a virtue. This virtue refers to a specific stable attitude towards one's tasks and duties. It is reflected in a conscientious way of dealing with issues and with the consequences of one's actions for others. Responsibility as a virtue is also reflected in the proactive assessment of safety risks and in taking initiative to reduce these risks by appropriate measures. It might seem like stating the obvious. Nevertheless, because the German Railway's management did not take appropriate measures to deal with the safety issues, we must conclude that those working for it collectively and individually failed to show that they had such a stable attitude towards safety issues. Safety procedures alone are not sufficient to guarantee attention to safety issues. The entire organisation must give correct priority to safety. This is only possible if the organisation's individual members underwrite the value of safety, and act accordingly. Safety should be part of what Goodpaster has called "the mindset" of an organisation (Goodpaster, 2007, pp. 36–38). A mindset encompasses beliefs and attitudes that govern an organisation's or person's behaviour. Reckless behaviour results when safety is not one of an organisation's values. But when management believes that distorted compact wheels will not lead to serious safety issues, they will still ignore distortion-related risks even when safety is one of the organisation's values. The attitude taken toward beliefs and adequate ways to verify them, thus adds a further complication.

The virtue of accuracy might demonstrate the kind of attitude needed here. According to Bernard Williams accuracy is the central virtue in the pursuit of truth. Accuracy must ensure that what we say is, indeed, true. Whereas sincerity is a virtue that should make us say what we actually believe, accuracy is about the quality of these beliefs. Accuracy's status as a moral virtue is evident when we consider that an accurate person should also weigh the value of additional information against the costs of acquiring it. The cost of gathering information and external (lack of good scientific research or lack of consensus among researchers) and internal (pride, fear of consequences) obstacles to discovering truth make the attitude toward these obstacles the subject of moral consideration.

Williams distinguished two aspects to accuracy. The first concerns the engineers' and managers' will, attitudes, wishes and desires. These became manifest in the trouble they took to discover the truth about safety hazards, and in their resistance to wishful thinking, self-deception, and fantasy. The second aspect concerns the method used to discover the truth. Of course, the two are closely related, since methodological sloppiness does not match well with a desire to discover truth (Williams, 2002, p. 127). It is safe to say that self-deception and wishful thinking did, indeed, play a role in the way the German Railway's employees dealt with the results when they tested the composite wheels. Those who were responsible for safety procedures at the German Railway felt no sense of urgency when it came to repairing wheel distortion. This kind of wishful thinking blinded the whole organisation to the real risks. It was not the first time that sloppiness and wishful thinking have led to disaster. Successive accidents with the space shuttles Challenger (1986) and Columbia (2003) come to mind. The investigating committee report on the Columbia disaster, said that NASA's organisational culture gave lower priority to safety than management's flight schedule goals.[1]

Another example is the notorious disaster with the *The Herald of Free Enterprise* in Zeebrugge in 1987. High Court Judge Barry Sheen concluded as follows regarding management's attitude and the organisational culture:

> All concerned in management, from the members of the Board of Directors down to the junior superintendents, were guilty of fault in that all must be regarded as sharing responsibility for the failure of management. From top to bottom the body corporate was infected with the disease of sloppiness...[2]

Widespread slackness and sloppiness within the organisation have played a decisive role in the disaster with the Herald of Free Enterprise, leading to the death of 193 people.

We cannot say with certainty whether the same degree of slackness and sloppiness at the German Railway was responsible for management's failure to ensure passenger safety. However, we do conclude that there was insufficient sense of responsibility and no will to determine what impact exceeding out-of-roundness wheel distortion would have on the HST's safety. Here the virtue of accuracy would have required finding out how to operate a HST safely. One outcome of a responsible attitude to safety problems is that one is willing and able to recognise the safety issues related to the choice of composite wheels.

Virtuous behaviour does not arise in a neutral environment. Environmental factors have a major impact on the probability that an actor will act virtuously. For the German Railway, this environment consisted of its organisational mindset, i.e. the values and norms that it accepted as valid within the organisation and its beliefs and assumptions about reality. These did much to influence the organisation's members. It is, thus, very important that the German Railway become aware of its organisational mindset and that management take responsibility for the way the organisation introduces measures to reinforce core values like safety. It can foster right attitudes by disseminating them among its employees and then rewarding suitable behaviour while sanctioning violations. Simply adjusting current procedure is insufficient. New risks to safety can emerge at any time in complex technological environments. Where a sense of responsibility and the pursuit of accuracy are hallmarks of an organisation, the chance of discovering and dealing properly with risks grows.

This brings us to our final question how should the German Railway distribute its collective responsibility over its individual employees. We mentioned that the German Railway's management had a responsibility to imbue concern for safety

---

[1] www.caib.nasa.gov (2 February 2010)
[2] www.articles.latimes.com/1987-07-24/news/mn-3866_1_ferry-disaster (3 February 2010)

in its organisational culture and structure. We cannot do enough to stress management's duty to lead by example because its behaviour shows where the real priorities lie. In addition to leading by example, management is also responsible for creating procedures and measures to embed concern for safety within the organisation. Only when that is done is it reasonable to hold individual employees responsible for the way they deal with safety issues. Accuracy and a sense of responsibility should be part and parcel of their professional attitude so that they will give the proper attention to safety risks. The way each one fulfils this responsibility will depend on his/her professional expertise. Collective responsibility means that the individual members of a collective assume the responsibility appropriate to their tasks and duties. For engineers that could mean assuming responsibility for the accuracy of their professional judgement on HST safety. Should they feel that their professional advice and judgement is ignored, they could even be morally and professionally obliged to give public warning. In the end, passengers rely on the German Railway – and all other railway operators – to do all that is necessary to reduce the risks attached to their using the railway system.

References

Bovens, M. 1998. *The Quest for Responsibility: Accountability and Citizenship in Complex Organisations*. Cambridge: Cambridge University Press.
Goodpaster, K. 2007. *Conscience and Corporate Culture*. Oxford: Blackwell Publishing.
Velasquez, M. 1998. *Business Ethics: Concepts and Cases*. Englewood Cliffs, NJ: Prentice Hall.
Wempe, J. 1998. *Market and Morality. Business Ethics and the Dirty and Many Hands Dilemma*. Delft: Eburon.
Williams, B. 2002. *Truth and Truthfulness*. Princeton, NJ; Oxford: Princeton University Press.

Chapter 18
Commentary: Technology as Material Ethics

Tsjalling Swierstra

Abstract In the case of a train disaster, everyone knows that something is amiss and ethical questions will automatically arise on who was responsible for what and to what degree. But more often, it is not so clear if something has gone wrong with our technologies. Then ethics seems not to play a role. This is not correct. I show how many ethical choices were made during the design stage of the train: the final design realizes some values at the expense of others. Each technology apportions responsibilities in complex ways between people and things. And even a well functioning technology has intended and unintended, foreseen and unforeseen, desirable and undesirable consequences that can affect the rights and interests of people, or that are important for what they see as a good life. If we accept that our lives are greatly determined by the technology around us, it is of paramount importance that we more regularly investigate or scrutinize how that technology helps to shape ourselves and our relationships with others.

With technology playing an increasing role in our lives, its ubiquity is so self-evident that we hardly notice it anymore. Actually, our attention is only drawn to technology when something goes wrong. We do not notice a train tearing through the landscape, but we do when it folds itself with a loud bang around a viaduct, as it did at Eschede, Germany, on 3 June 1998. Ethics might well have never addressed the high-speed train if it had not crashed so dramatically. Now, of course, we want to know if someone was responsible for that accident.

Responsibility

Did some miscreant sabotage the rails? No, nothing pointed to anyone's malicious intent to destroy the technology. So were passengers fooling around with the communication cord? Or maybe the train driver was drunk? The case notes reveal that also the *users* were beyond reproach. Was it therefore the *makers* of the train who

---

T. Swierstra (✉)
Faculty of Arts and Social Sciences, Maastricht University, Maastricht, The Netherlands
e-mail: t.swierstra@maastrichtuniversity.nl

made serious mistakes? No, not them either, because no evidence pointed to their not having meticulously followed the design. So was the crash the result of mistakes made by the designers of the train? It would certainly seem to be the case, because they failed to opt for the safest solution to the problem with the suspension. Instead of adapting the undercarriage, as with the French TGV, they settled for a less radical but ultimately unreliable solution of rubber rings in the metal wheels.

Or are we being too hasty with our blame? Technical artefacts are the result of numerous choices. And rarely is the nature of those choices merely "technical". Preparatory calculations of the bearing power of a certain bridge might be a technical affair but the requirement that the bridge will allow people to safely cross to the other side has a clearly ethical importance. The same applies to the requirement that using technical products must not be detrimental to one's health. Or that production and usage of artefacts must fit in an economy oriented towards sustainability. With engineers attempting to design a technology that helps to realize some of these moral values, technical design can thus be understood as "material ethics".

However, it is not always possible to accommodate different moral values in the design. This confronts designers with difficult considerations that can be described as nothing less than a moral dilemma whereby a choice must be made between conflicting values. The train had to be safe, fast, comfortable and affordable, and moreover not to require too much maintenance. In this case, however, the different values appeared to be so irreconcilable that the designers were forced to make "tragic" choices and unsatisfactory compromises. Ultimately, the decision for safety, comfort, speed and affordability was undermined by the demand that the train must not require intensive maintenance. It was exactly this that would later appear to be the weak link.

But are the designers to be blamed for this? If the control and maintenance had been carried out better, nothing would have gone wrong. On condition that maintenance occurred regularly, it was a good and safe wheel. So was it the fault of the maintenance mechanics? After all, they can be called to account for rendering a proper service. But before we blame them for all the victims of the crash, we must ask the question: were the circumstances under which they had to work such that they could indeed carry out a correct control and maintenance? Did they have sufficient grasp of the circumstances under which they had to work? In retrospect, the technical standards of thickness of the steel outer-wheel appeared not to be strong enough, but are the maintenance mechanics to be blamed for this? Maybe those standards were drawn up by a person, or a group, who did not actually work for the company responsible for the train's maintenance. The standards might well have been formulated 20 years ago in a foreign laboratory. And to be a little more concrete: were the maintenance mechanics given enough time to carry out a meticulous control? Were there no managers imposing certain "production requirements" on them: x number of wheels in a specific length of time? If they had insisted the mechanics work against the clock, would they not also be (partly) accountable for the crash? Or were they in turn also being pressurized by higher management? Did the company have sound procedures in place to guarantee that the different responsibilities were clearly allocated, that people were indeed enabled to fulfil that responsibility and that open communication was always possible to address questions concerning protocols, safety criteria and pressure?

We can zoom out even further by asking ourselves if the passenger, i.e. the user of the train, might not also be partly responsible for the disaster after all. After all, people want to be transported increasingly often, for ever longer distances and as quickly as possible. Moreover it must be as comfortable as possible and with as little inconvenience to one's backside as possible. And it must not be too expensive or we will opt for the car. Is it realistic to demand so much? Or is it a feeble excuse to treat the passenger's travel bug solely as an individual preference? Doesn't society as a whole bear some responsibility for the accident? After all, have we not organized the economy in such a way that more and more people *have* to travel to get to work?

The accident can thus not simply be reduced to an individual error here and an individual sloppiness there. The accident is the unintended result of an entire network of actions, routines, choices and decisions. And it is even more complicated than that. Until now we have only spoken about people: users, designers, makers, mechanics, managers, society. But besides people also *things* played a major role in the period leading up to the accident itself. Things do not yield to our wishes just like that; they have a hardness of their own, their own "agenda". It is quite tricky that rubber expands quicker than metal, but that is how it is. It is a fact to which man must adapt. Man is not simply an active subject, just as the technical artefact is not simply a passive one. Things have their own normativity: they can enforce, encourage or tempt us to certain actions. Or they can prohibit our actions: reading a book on a train is acceptable, but not when behind the wheel of a car. This insight is often articulated as: also things are actors.

Why, for example, did the train have to be so fast? This requirement cannot be seen separately from the existence of cars and the fact that there is some kind of competition going on between these two modes of transport. As cars can travel quickly from A to B, the train must follow suit. Of course cars are (still) driven by people and the desire for speed is also a notion in their mind. But at the same time it is not difficult to see that the desire for ever faster transport has in part been created by technology, by the things themselves. The person who drives a car that can go 100 mph will turn into a speedster sooner than someone who drives a car that cannot go faster than 50 mph.

The ethics of technology has learned here from the technology sociologists, historians and philosophers. They have shown how closely knit we, the people, have become with things, with technology. This case is a good example. No comfort without suspension. We delegate an unpleasant task, such as shock absorption, to the rubber in the wheel of the train. We literally allow the things to absorb the shocks. Yet despite the rubber and the steel working well together in the wheel, they also conflict on a crucial point. On the one hand, the difference in hardness between the two materials is exactly what is required to achieve suspension without too much friction, but on the other hand, this combination also creates problems because rubber expands faster than steel. Hence we cannot trust the wheel, this thing, at all. This is why we decide to permanently check whether the wheel still complies with the safety standards. The wheel puts us to work. So it is nonsense to question whether the wheel was safe. On its own maybe not, but the thing/combination "wheel + thorough check" was safe. The wheel did become unsafe due to poor maintenance, but that the check was not thorough cannot just be blamed on people either. The mechanics happened to be using measurement instruments, hence other technical artefacts, which in turn also proved unreliable: they either warned against too many defects or too few. In short, the confusion of things and people results in a continual influencing of the other. In order to combine safety, speed, comfort, affordability and "low maintenance", people and things must work together as optimally as possible. We delegate tasks to the things (absorbing shocks), the things delegate tasks to us (regular checks).

In sum: not only people do things and make demands on the environment but also things do. Not only people answer the question what we must do, but so do things (Tenner, 1996; Verbeek, 2005). Also our ideas about who we are, can be, want to be, can hope etc., are co-determined by technology. For example, it is an old wisdom that travel changes people; thanks to technology, it has become much easier and is thus practised more often. However, does travel still hold the same value now we *consume* distance, as it were, instead of covering it with great physical effort and discomfort? Technology also defines how we know and experience the world. (We experience a landscape totally differently when we walk in it or when we race through it at 185 mph.) For a long time many philosophers felt that this should not be the case – people should not be "subjected" to the machine. It would herald the end of human freedom and dignity. The key question of the old ethics of technology was thus: how do we stay on top of the things, i.e. keep the upper hand? How can we make sure that they serve us instead of our becoming their slaves? We have meanwhile overcome that initial fear and we accept that technology influences us. Hence the old key question has now been replaced by a new one, namely: how do we people deal with the fact that our existence has become inextricably linked with technology?

That is a big question that cannot be answered here. What is clear, however, is that the question "Who is responsible when problems arise from technology?" cannot be answered simply by pointing a finger at one individual or another. Technology nearly always implies large groups of people who contribute from close by or further away to the source of the problem. Those people maintain complex relations – with one another, with things, and with one another through the things. Of course, the ethicist of technology does not reproach the things directly; the ethics of technology addresses people, but its primary concern is not whether one individual or another will behave him-/herself better and bear more responsibility. On the contrary, its concern is that we have a better understanding of how people and things collaborate in complex networks to effect certain results, and how that collaboration can be improved.

Problems

As stated, ethics particularly wake up with a start when problems arise with technology, e.g. because it did not do what was expected of it. We expect a train to carry us quickly, comfortably and safely from A to B. The train at Eschede seriously let us down on all three points. However, if that train had arrived properly at its final destination, would there still have been no reason to look at it from the perspective of ethics of technology? Indeed, yes. An important task of such ethics is to strip technology of its self-evident nature so that we can critically view it afresh. If technology exercises such a large influence on our daily life, it is prudent to dwell on it now and again. A high-speed train can also be ethically interesting when it hurtles safely between the piles of the viaduct. Well functioning technology can also evoke ethical questions.

A technology, for example, often does much more than is clear at first sight. The train "does" more than carry its passengers from A to B. It is also good for the economy, in which fast connections are of the essence. Prosperity is an ethically relevant objective. We also saw that the train was necessary to be able to compete with the car. With its speed, the train contributes to care for the environment – another ethically relevant objective.

Moreover, technology always has unintended, and usually also unexpected, consequences. Some of them desirable. Who could have predicted, for example, that young people would start to smoke less due to the mobile phone? There seems to be little connection between the two until you realize that young people are now spending most of their money on calls. In contrast, there are also undesirable consequences, sometimes caused by abusing the technology. You could certainly use the high-speed train for a terrorist attack, but we do not blame technology itself for this. At the most we will ask ourselves why the safety measures of the train were not better, or why no technological precautions had been taken, such as the possibility to take over the train's steering from a distance if the driver were subversive (or became ill).

But even when we use a technology as it is intended, things can happen that are deemed inexpedient (by some). It goes without saying, that a high-speed train is expected to travel quickly. This implies that it cannot stop at each minor station. The faster the train, the fewer the stations. As the train also carries economic activity in its wake, its high-speed results in some towns flourishing whilst others decline. Who gets or does not get a station? That question touches on the justice of distribution. Or another unintended consequence: the high-speed train allows for commuting long distances, which makes it easier to move out of town. Particularly the more wealthy avail themselves of this opportunity. Yet the better the transport to and from town, the greater the chance of the town becoming run down.

Whether such undesirable consequences actually occur is often open to debate. Maybe the town would have become run down anyway, even without a high-speed train. What is complicated about technology is that the consequences can sometimes occur on the other side of the world or only after a considerable period of time. This increases the opportunity for a reasonable difference in opinion. And to complicate things even further: consequences always occur in interaction with the environment. The train only contributes to the migration of the middle classes from the cities when those middle classes already had a number of reasons to (want to) move. A train only becomes "environmentally friendly" when the environment is threatened by the exhaust fumes of cars. And because the surroundings of technology change often, or because the technology is transported to new surroundings, we can never be completely sure whether we fully comprehend what the consequences of a new technology are.

Sometimes there is also room for discussion on the question whether the consequences are undesirable. What is wrong about people living a pastoral life, when they can afford it, whilst still working in town? Moreover: what is good for some (groups) is not always per definition good for the other. And if the train is good for the environment, does that counterbalance the fact that nowadays more and more commuters are living far out in the country which means that there are ever fewer areas of unspoilt nature? These are all ethical questions that the high-speed train evokes.

Conclusion

Sometimes technology goes badly wrong and there are casualties. Then everyone knows that something is amiss and ethical questions will automatically arise on who was responsible for what and to what degree. But often, much more often, it is not so clear if something has gone wrong and then it seems as if ethics do not play a role. Then we forget how ethical choices were made during the design stage: what value does the design realize at the expense of which other value(s)? Then we forget how each technology apportions responsibilities in complex ways between people and things. Then we forget that even a well functioning technology has intended and unintended, foreseen and unforeseen, desirable and undesirable consequences. Consequences that can affect the rights and interests of people, or that are important for what they see as a good life. And it is a real shame that we always seem to forget that. If we accept that our lives are greatly determined by the technology around us, is it not of paramount importance that we more regularly investigate or scrutinize how that technology helps to shape ourselves and our relationships with others? We already know that to that end we will need all our powers of imagination, because the interactions between technology and environment are often quite unpredictable. Only then can we start to give answers to the key question: how do we want to coexist with which technology?

References

Tenner, E. 1996. *Why Things Bite Back. Technology and the Revenge of Unintended Consequences.* New York, NY: Alfred A. Knopf.
Verbeek, P.P. 2005. *What Things Do. Philosophical Reflections on Technology, Agency and Design.* University Park, PA: Pensylvania University Press.

Part VII
Case F: A Matter of Involvement – Unilever and Indian Cottonseed Cultivation

Chapter 19
Case Description: A Matter of Involvement – Unilever and Indian Cottonseed Cultivation

Wim Dubbink

Abstract On 3 May 2003 a coalition of non-governmental organisations (NGOs) accused the multinational Unilever of being involved in child labour in India's cottonseed industry. The company responded by emphatically denying any direct or indirect involvement in child labour. In the public uproar that followed, the coalition of NGOs and Unilever disputed the truth of almost any fact the opposing party produced, including facts concerning the severity and the extent of child labour; even if all parties agreed that child labour is common in the cottonseed industry and that neither Unilever nor its first tier suppliers have employed children themselves. The concrete demands being made of the multinationals and the grounds upon which these where based, almost got lost in the discussion. Upon closer inspection these revolve around four issues: the extent of Unilever's chain responsibility; Unilever's supposed historical blame for child labour in the cottonseed industry; The reasonableness of Unilever having to assume a positive duty to help fight child labour; And the level of precautions the company must take to prevent indirect involvement in child labour.

Unilever Stands Accused

On 3 May 2003 a coalition of non-governmental organisations (NGOs) accused the multinational Unilever of being involved in child labour (the Dutch newspaper NRC, 2003). The accusation related to the cultivation of hybrid cottonseed in India and the occasion was the publication of a study by D. Venkateswarlu (2003: 1, pp. 18–20), entitled *Child Labour and Trans-National Seed Companies in Hybrid Cottonseed Production in Andhra Pradesh*. According to this study at the turn of the century nearly 25,000 children were employed as child labourers in Andhra Pradesh growing cottonseed on farms that had contracts with a company that – at that time –

W. Dubbink (✉)
Department of Philosophy, Faculty of Humanities, Tilburg University, Tilburg, The Netherlands
e-mail: w.dubbink@uvt.nl

An important source for this paper was the master's thesis by Iris de Wilde submitted to the Faculty of Social and Behavioural Sciences at Tilburg University, August 2006.

was controlled by Unilever's Indian subsidiary, Hindustan Lever. The research was carried out on behalf of the India Committee of the Netherlands (ICN).[1] The other members of the coalition were Oxfam Novib,[2] Amnesty International,[3] the labour union FNV–Mondiaal[4] and the Mamidipudi Venkatarangaiya Foundation (MVF).[5]

The public accusation was the culmination of a process of negotiations that had been going on for some time. At the end of February 2002, the coalition opened discussions with Unilever Netherlands regarding the widespread use of child labour in the Indian hybrid cotton industry and Unilever's presumed involvement, using the tentative research findings as a lever. At the meeting the company emphatically denied any direct or indirect involvement in child labour, as it did in every subsequent meeting. Nevertheless, K. Van der Waaij, director of Unilever Nederland Holdings BV, stated that the company was willing to work on measures to combat child labour. Van der Waaij asked MVF's representative to set up a meeting with the chairman and managing director of Unilever's Indian subsidiary, Hindustan Lever Ltd. (HLL). This meeting took some time to arrange. According to MVF, requests for a meeting with HLL in India were rebuffed. According to HLL, MVF was not willing to come to Mumbai.[6] In the meantime, HLL spun off its seed division into Paras Extra Growth Seed (PEGSL) and sold three quarters of the shares to a US company, Emergent Genetics.

On 24 April 2003, ICN had sent a letter to Unilever's chairman, Antony Burgmans, on behalf of the coalition. It contained the completed research report and a request for a meeting:

> We would like to discuss with you the ways Unilever could help find an answer for the children employed in the production of cottonseed for your company... We would, therefore, greatly appreciate it if you could arrange a meeting with us in the near future. Finally, by way of information, the report will be published soon.

A week later ICN sent the research report to the Dutch newspaper *NRC Handelsblad* which published a story under the headline "Unilever beticht van kinderarbeid"

---

[1] www.indianet.nl.

[2] www.novib.nl.

[3] www.amnesty.nl.

[4] FNV is an important Dutch labour union; FNV Mondiaal is its international department. Its aim is to promote fair labour conditions and labour rights worldwide, among other things by supporting labour unions. (www.fnv.nl)

[5] MVF is an Indian NGO located in the federal state of Andhra Pradesh. By its own account, the organisation takes an "uncompromising stance" against child labour. MVF was established as a research institute on social transformation processes, but since 1991 it has been increasingly transformed into an activist organisation whose aim is to abolish child labour. (www.mvfindia.org)

[6] The data for this case were collected through various interviews and talks conducted by Iris de Wilde and the author with representatives from many of the parties, in particular representatives from Unilever, Oxfam Novib and ICN. For the sake of readability we have chosen not to keep referring to these interviews. All of the parties have explicitly endorsed the final draft of the paper, in the sense that each agrees with all statements attributed to its own organisation. All of the parties expressed doubts about the description of the facts made by other parties.

(Unilever accused of child labour). This led to a storm of publicity. Unilever fell subject to something all quality brands hope to avoid: an association with child labour. The company let *NRC Handelsblad* know that it was certainly willing to work with NGOs to develop efforts that could contribute to ending the use of child labour in Indian hybrid cottonseed production. However, Unilever also stressed that it was unpleasantly surprised by this false accusation and the fact that the report gained public exposure so rapidly. A few days later, Unilever issued a press release in which it rejected the accusation that it had anything to do with child labour.[7]

The NGOs' campaign against Unilever's alleged involvement in child labour used for cottonseed production did not target Unilever alone. The Unilever protests were part of a worldwide campaign to end the use of child labour in Indian cottonseed production that was aimed at involving Western multinationals. NGOs in Switzerland, the US and Germany also took steps against Syngenta, Monsanto and Bayer. The campaign had merely started with Unilever because Unilever's subsidiary was the largest company.

The concrete demands being made of the multinationals almost got lost in the uproar that followed the unwelcome accusations. The NGOs see child labour in India as a complex problem, linked to many structural causes. They want the multinational companies to contribute to solving the problem by countering it in their own supply chain, but more importantly, by contributing to measures that would benefit the industry as a whole, such as measures that could facilitate better education for these children. The ultimate remedy, according to the NGOs, is a higher purchase price for cottonseed. This would allow farmers to hire adults and pay them a living wage, which would leave the children free to go to school. According to the NGOs, the Western multinational companies could be conducive to this process.

Unilever

Unilever, a British-Dutch enterprise, is one of the largest producers of food, household and personal care products in the world.[8] The company was established in 1930 when the Dutch margarine manufacturer Margarine Unie merged with British soap producer Lever Brothers. Unilever has business locations in nearly 100 countries and its products are sold in another 50. In mid-2005, Unilever's activities were incorporated into two divisions – food products and household and personal care products. Its famous food brands include Lipton, Knorr, Hellman's, Slim Fast and Bertolli, while their well-known brand names in household and personal care products include Dove, Vaseline and Pond's.[9] Also in 2005, the company introduced a tri-regional structure to manage its market activities – Europe, North and South

---

[7] Unilever press release, dated 5 May 2003.
[8] www.unilever.nl, visited 21 September 2005.
[9] www.unilever.nl, visited 5 February 2005.

America and Asia/Africa, Middle-East and Turkey – while in a matrix-fashion, innovation and category management fell under the control of two new divisions: food products and household and personal care products.[10]

According to its mission statement,

> Unilever is a company that "meets everyday needs for nutrition, hygiene and personal care with brands that help people feel good, look good, and get more out of life".[11]

The company also claims a closeness with consumers around the world:

> Our deep roots in local cultures and markets around the world give us our strong relationship with consumers and are the foundation for our future growth. We will bring our wealth of knowledge and international expertise to the service of local consumers – a truly multi-local multinational.[12]

The Unilever group has a complicated organisational structure. There are two parent companies – Unilever NV (Dutch) and Unilever PLC (British) – that serve as holding and service-related companies. They are separate legal persons and have separate listings on different stock exchanges. Most of the operating companies are owned by either NV or PLC, with the exception of a few that are jointly owned. Nevertheless, the two parent organisations and all of the group members tend to act as one company. At the level of the parent organisations, this process is facilitated by seating the same persons on the two boards of directors. What is more, the boards are linked to one another by several agreements in which all shareholders of NV and PLC share in the profits of the entire Unilever group. Each operating company bears great responsibility in carrying out its own activities.

Unilever and Corporate Social Responsibility

Unilever is and wants to be known as a company interested in more than shareholder value, or at least a company that wants to earn its profits only within the framework of high standards of conduct.

> Our corporate purpose states that to succeed requires "the highest standards of corporate behaviour towards everyone we work with, the communities we touch, and the environment on which we have an impact".[13]

The company further asserts that

> Unilever wants to make a positive contribution to society not only by producing high-quality products, but also more broadly speaking. We want to be involved in the communities where we operate;... [14] And as a multi-local multinational, we want to play a role in tackling

---

[10] www.unilever.nl, visited 21 September 2005.
[11] www.unilever.nl, visited 07 November 2009.
[12] www.unilever.nl, visited 07 November 2009.
[13] www.unilever.com, visited 07 November 2009.
[14] www.unilever.nl, visited 22 September 2005.

19 Case Description: A Matter of Involvement 189

worldwide environmental and social issues. We do this by working locally and joining with local governments and institutions.[15]

Corporate integrity, also known as "corporate social responsibility (CSR)", or more generally speaking the moral aspect of doing business is thus important for Unilever.[16] That is expressed in the company's presentation. Its "purpose and principles (including the Code of Conduct)" and its commitment to sustainability are prominently displayed on the corporation's website.[17] Furthermore, each year Unilever adds a social report and an environmental report to its financial report.[18] Unilever has also developed a code of conduct and, more exceptionally, a business partner code.[19] The code of conduct describes the standards and principles that Unilever wants to maintain and that the general public may expect of it. Its 2004 business partner code describes the standards and principles that Unilever expects its business partners, particularly its first-tier suppliers, to uphold. The document does not seem intended to motivate partners to *imitate* Unilever, though.

> In keeping with Unilever's partnership approach, we work together with our partners, first to establish how compatible their standards are with ours and then, where necessary, to agree on measures and timescales to achieve the desired performance levels.[20]

CSR is procedurally embedded at Unilever. The company considers cooperation on this matter to be very important and joins in dialogue with internationally operating NGOs (Unilever 2003). The fact that WWF, Oxfam Novib and other NGOs participate in this dialogue shows that they take Unilever's socially responsible role seriously.

Unilever's code of conduct is a brief, two-page document that Unilever thinks contains high and clearly described standards of behaviour. The themes addressed include the environment, staffing, consumers, shareholders, innovation and competition. Its first sentence is characteristic.

> We conduct our operations with honesty, integrity and openness, and with respect for the human rights and interests of our employees. We shall similarly respect the legitimate interests of those with whom we have relationships.[21]

The company explicitly forbids using child labour.

---

[15] www.unilever.nl, visited 22 September 2005.

[16] In Dutch the term for CSR is "maatschappelijk verantwoord ondernemen", a generic term that relates generally to the moral aspects of doing business. In other countries, such as the US, CSR often only refers to some of a company's moral endeavours, specifically those actions related to solving public or social problems (see e.g., Boatright, 2007). We will use the term generically in this paper.

[17] www.unilever.nl, visited 07 November 2009.

[18] www.unilever.nl, visited 22 September 2005.

[19] www.unilever.com/ourvalues, visited 22 September 2005.

[20] www.unilever.com, visited 07 November 2009.

[21] www.unilever.com, visited 07 November 2009.

The business partner code contains ten, briefly stated principles that Unilever expects its immediate partners to respect. Among the code's stipulations are that Unilever's partners must comply with all current legislation in their countries, respect human rights and perform all activities with care for the environment. Regarding employees, the company states that wages and hours must comply with legal regulations. Forced labour is out of the question. A separate item explicitly forbids child labour.[22]

The company views helping to solve global environmental and social problems as one of the important ways it can and should display its focus on moral values. Unilever stresses in various places that it wants to play a role in tackling these problems.[23] Generally speaking, a company can choose between two strategies in giving shape to such involvement. It can develop activities *alongside* its regular activities or it can incorporate them *within* its regular activities, reflecting moral values in its specific moral choices. Unilever does not ignore the first manner, but seems to attach much greater importance to the second.

One of the reasons behind this choice may be the company's apparent belief that activities that can be viewed as being sparked by a moral reason should also be thought of as consistent with commercial reasoning. There are examples to confirm this hypothesis. Several years ago Van der Waaij publicly insisted that commercial reasons were the sole basis for establishing the Marine Stewardship Council (MSC) (Anonymous 2003). The MSC is an independent organisation based in London that issues a quality mark for sustainable fishing. The organisation places heavy requirements on sustainability. Unilever set up the organisation with the WWF because fisheries are dependent on a sustainable supply of fish. Unilever promised that within a foreseeable period it would process only sustainably caught fish.[24]

A possible explanation for the emphasis on a commercial rationale in this type of project is that Unilever – like many other companies (Bird and Waters, 1989) – does not like to state explicitly that it is making choices based primarily on moral reasons. Undisputed or dominant ideas on the type of responsibility a company owes its shareholders can play a role here. Awkwardness in dealing with moral discourse is another factor suggested by empirical research (Bowie, 1999, pp. 120–139). A third possible factor is a cautious approach to mass communication: the more a company publicly boasts of its moral orientation, the higher the public's expectations will be. And Unilever is apprehensive about this:

> As expectations for wider engagement by companies grow, so too are many critics more ready to say when we don't meet their expectations (Unilever 2004: 1).

---

[22] www.unilever.com, visited 07 November 2009.

[23] See www.unilever.nl, visited 21 September 2005, and other sources.

[24] A strategic reorientation that resulted in the sale of virtually the complete frozen foods division put an end to all this.

The Shakti project is another Unilever activity that, like MSC, can be viewed in the context of social involvement or orientation toward moral values and that is also interwoven with the company's own activities. In the project, Unilever's Indian subsidiary, HLL, provides free entrepreneurial training for underprivileged women. These women are organised in self-help groups set up by NGOs and the government. After taking the course, the women can start selling Unilever products through local, small-scale enterprises. This gives them a chance to earn a stable income of around $20/month, nearly double the usual family income (Unilever 2003: 10). A third example is a Dove campaign that attempts to do away with stereotypical notions of beauty. According to the Dove campaign, many modern women approach beauty from a negative self image. Dove wants to show women more definitions of beauty to shorten the gap between their view of themselves and their notion of what is beautiful.[25]

The Hybrid Cottonseed

Cotton is the most important agricultural product in India. Approximately 22,239,500 acres are devoted to its cultivation. This makes India the largest cotton producer, in terms of acreage, in the world. Nearly 40% of the Indian production uses hybrid cottonseed. Hybrid cottonseed is produced by crossing two genetically different varieties of cotton. This is called hybridisation or cross-pollination. The main advantage of working with hybrid cottonseed is that it produces greater yields and higher quality. The hybrid cotton plant is also very adaptable. A final macro-economic advantage of the hybrid variant is that seed production is very labour-intensive and thus provides employment.

Hybrid cottonseed was invented in India in 1970. In the early days state-run organisations saw to its commercial development. Then, economic deregulation and other factors led to spectacular growth in the 1990s and private seed companies jumped on the bandwagon. In time, some of these companies developed their own agricultural seeds. By 2000, 80% of the cottonseed-growing market was in private hands (Venkateswarlu, 2003, pp. 14–17) and concentrated in India's south-eastern province, Andhra Pradesh. One of the reasons for this was the availability of cheap labour. Nearly 60% of the hybrid seeds produced in Andhra Pradesh are sold in other parts of India and in other countries. As with other agricultural products, division of labour has entered into the production of hybrid cotton: some companies produce seed of different varieties of cotton (i.e., basic seeds); others cultivate these varieties, cross-pollinate them and produce hybrid cottonseed; and still others use these hybrid seeds to grow cotton. The problem of child labour is concentrated in the second phase: the production of hybrid seeds.

Farmers are not the only or even the most powerful parties in the cotton production chain. The seed company is a very important player. It has a role at the

---

[25] www.unilever.nl, visited 22 September 2005.

beginning and at the end of the chain. It produces the basic seeds and sells the hybrid cottonseed to cotton farmers. In between, the basic seeds are passed to a seed dealer. Seed dealers, in their turn, sell the seeds to farmers who produce the hybrid seeds. After production, the seed dealers buy back the hybrid seeds from the farmers and sell them back to the seed companies. Seed companies and seed dealers enter into a contract that regulates many matters in detail, such as the type of cottonseed to be produced and the quality and amount. The price at which the producer will buy back the seed from the dealer is also set (buy-back arrangement). The seed dealers also sign contracts with the farmers specifying how to produce the hybrid seeds. The seed dealers sell their seeds to all types of farmers. Some are very large and employ many people, in which case the farmer and labourers are usually not of the same caste. Other farms are much smaller and these usually employ their own families to produce the cottonseed.

This complex organisation of the supply chain is partly the effect of Indian legislation. The seed companies cannot grow the seeds themselves because Indian law does not permit companies to own large parcels of land. In addition, outsourcing is much more advantageous because some labour laws do not apply to small production units. The set up with the seed dealers is a new idea. Before 1990, seed companies often negotiated directly with cottonseed growers. The increasing demand for hybrid cottonseed has led seed companies to work on a larger scale, which made it difficult for them to negotiate directly with farmers.

Child Labour

According to estimates by the International Labour Organisation (ILO), nearly 250 million children between the ages of 5 and 17 were employed as child labourers at the start of the twenty-first century. The ILO is careful to point out that there is a difference between *child labour* and *child work*:

> Not all work done by children should be classified as child labour that is to be targeted for elimination. Children's or adolescents' participation in work that does not affect their health and personal development or interfere with their schooling is generally regarded as being something positive. This includes activities such as helping their parents around the home, assisting in a family business or earning pocket money outside school hours and during school holidays. These kinds of activities contribute to children's development and to the welfare of their families; they provide them with skills and experience and help to prepare them to be productive members of society during their adult life.[26]

Child work is common around the globe and morally unproblematic. Many children, in very different national circumstances, carry out work that is entirely consistent with their education and full physical and mental development.

By contrast, child labour is by its nature morally wrong and a violation of children's rights. There is a large consensus worldwide that child labour is at variance

---

[26] www.ilo.org/ipec/facts/lang--en/index.html, visited 07 November 2007.

19 Case Description: A Matter of Involvement   193

with the right of each child to a normal development that includes education, playtime, care and adequate mental and physical health. Hence, any adult involved in child labour is committing acts that are morally wrong. The same goes for anybody profiting from child labour. The fact that nearly every country in the world has signed and ratified major treaties banning child labour evinces the universal rejection of child labour. Such treaties include the UN *Convention on the Rights of the Child* (1989) and the ILO *Convention Concerning the Prohibition and Immediate Action for the Elimination of the Worst Forms of Child Labour Convention* (1999; No 182), acclaimed by a rare unanimous vote.[27]

But then, how can child work be distinguished from child labour? Drawing on international agreements (UN Conventions 138 and 182), the ILO (2002: x) identifies three categories of child labour, with the latter two being considered among the "worst forms":

(1) Labour performed by a child who is *under a minimum age* specified in national legislation for that kind of work;
(2) Labour that jeopardizes the physical, mental or moral well-being of a child, known as hazardous work;
(3) The unconditional worst forms of child labour, which are internationally defined as slavery, trafficking, debt bondage and other forms of forced labour, forced recruitment for use in armed conflict, prostitution and pornography, and illicit activities.

According to the ILO (2002: x), some 180 million children age 5–17 (or 73% of all child labourers) are now believed to be engaged in the worst forms of child labour. This amounts to one child in every eight in the world. Of the some 171 million children engaged in hazardous work, nearly two thirds are under 15 and therefore require immediate withdrawal from this work and rehabilitation from its effects.

Child labour continues to be a widespread problem and the imperfect implementation of national legislation against child labour contributes to this. More importantly, child labour is not an isolated problem. It is closely related to gender or caste discrimination, poor or powerless governments, lack of freedom, failing political representation, poorly functioning educational systems, poverty, and other socio-political ills. India is one example of a country facing such problems. Many international governmental organisations (ILO, UNICEF) and international NGOs (Plan International, Oxfam Novib and MVF) are working to change this. Some of these organisations focus on specific projects in the countries in question, including campaigns to increase awareness, programmes to establish schools and encourage children to attend them, and anti-poverty programmes. Other organisations focus on raising the awareness of individual citizens and the broader public in countries where there is no child labour. This can put pressure on internationally operating companies that benefit from child labour or are in a position to contribute forcefully

---

[27] www.ilo.org, visited 14 August 2005.

to ameliorating the problem. Examples of such campaigns are those against child labour at the time of the 1998 soccer world championship and the campaign in the 1990s against Nike and other manufacturers of sportswear and sports accessories.

There are also organisations that have programmes aimed exclusively at companies. One example is the ILO's International Programme on the Elimination of Child Labour (IPEC), which targets companies directly. The IPEC operates on the premise that companies have a crucial role to play in combating child labour and it emphasises first and foremost stringent compliance with national legislation on the subject. The most effective way companies can contribute is by "setting high standards on workers" rights and on the use of child labour in their own operations and to seek to extend those standards generally among the business community, including subcontractors'. IPEC believes that there are many reasons for companies to turn away from child labour.

> Employers realize that, apart from obvious humanitarian and social concerns, combating child labour makes good business sense. Children who are left uneducated or are damaged physically or emotionally by early and hazardous work have little chance of becoming productive adult workers. They realize increasingly, too, that public exposure to the use of child labour can cause immeasurable damage to the company image.[28]

Child Labour and Hybrid Cottonseed

It is normal for children in India to *work*. As in other emerging countries, children are expected to help their families by performing tasks. But child labour is also not uncommon in India. There are between 50 and 60 million child labourers in India, 15 million of whom live in slave-like circumstances. According to Venkateswarlu's report, nearly 450,000 children age 6–14 throughout India worked in the cottonseed industry in 2002.

There are several reasons that the organisations involved decided to draw Indian and international attention to the situation in cottonseed production after 2000. Well-known Western companies play a leading role in cottonseed production. They are often more easy to call to account for their role than purely Indian companies. Western companies usually have a business code in place, thereby explicitly indicating that they will comply with given ethical standards. In addition, Western consumers are more critical when it comes to such moral questions and that makes Western companies more vulnerable on this point. Furthermore, in the 1990s, the MVF had explicitly requested that Western NGOs make the battle against child labour in cottonseed production a priority of their activities because it gained little ground in the industry. It claimed that the main reason for this was the seed dealers' aggressive recruitment of children. So, it wanted support from Western multinationals in its conflict with the dealers.

---

[28] www.ilo.org, visited 14 August 2005.

There are also several important industry-specific arguments for choosing to focus on the cottonseed industry. Cultivation of hybrid cottonseed is highly labour-intensive. Cross-pollination must be carried out manually over a 4-month period each year, a task usually assigned to girls. Sowing and harvesting are also often left to them (Venkateswarlu, 2003, p. 8). The farmers prefer children – especially girls – because they are easier to control and cheaper to hire. It is also easier to convince children to work 11 or 12 h a day. In addition, children earn around 30% less than what adult women earn per day and 55% less than adult men. Children earn approximately 10–25 rupees (INR) per day (1 INR was approx. 0.014 EUR or 0.021 USD on 27 Nov. 2009). Some people claim that girls are better able to perform the delicate manual tasks required for cross-fertilisation because of the build of their hands.

A second industry-specific argument is that child labour is increasing in this industry, as a result of the growth in hybrid cottonseed production.

And finally a third reason is that the work children do in cottonseed production can in many cases be classified among "the worst types of child labour". Many children working in cottonseed production are victims of debt slavery or "bonded labour". Indian law prohibits debt slavery but implementation of the law is imperfect.[29] In practice, children are still forced to work to pay off an advance or debt that their parents owe (at excessively high interest rates). Recruiters take the initiative in approaching parents.[30] Given the pittance that the children earn, it inevitably takes their families a long time to pay back the debt. The children are often handed over to a farmer for an entire season or even several years. Matters are exacerbated by the fact that the work itself seriously harms the children's health. One of the major causes of this is the children's exposure to pesticides considered harmful to humans, such as Endosulfan, Monocrotophos, Cypermethrin and Mythomyl. These products cause nausea, headaches, disorientation, breathing problems and other health problems (Venkateswarlu, 2003, p. 33). Furthermore, because of their work in the cottonseed fields, many children get little or no schooling. At least 29% of the children have had no schooling at all. More than half of the children leave the educational system after just a few years to work in the cottonseed fields (Venkateswarlu, 2003, p. 10). Multinationals and cottonseed production.

Western multinational seed companies play a large role in Indian cottonseed production. They usually opt for a construction that involves an Indian subsidiary. Some of the subsidiaries operating under such arrangement are Mahyco (US Monsanto), Syngenta India (Swiss Syngenta), Proagro (German Bayer), Advanta India Limited (Dutch Advanta/ Limagrain) and Paras Extra Growth Seed (PEGSL) (Monsanto). Until 2002, Unilever's Indian subsidiary, Hindustan Lever Limited (HLL), owned PEGSL. After that it passed first to US Emergent Genetics, then to Monsanto,

---

[29] www.indianet.nl, visited 23 August 2005.
[30] www.indianet.nl, visited 23 August 2005.

which bought Emergent Genetics in 2005.[31] Taken together, Western multinationals control 20% of the market; PEGSL alone controls 10%. Venkateswarlu's report projected an increasing role for Western multinationals in coming years; one reason for this is the introduction and use of genetic manipulation techniques.

Unilever's involvement in cottonseed production is a legacy of Unilever's long history in India. Before the Indian economy was deregulated in the early 1990s, foreign investors were obliged to invest part of their earnings in Indian export products (Berkhout, 2003). HLL resulted from the 1956 merger of three of Unilever's Indian subsidiaries. Since then, HLL has strengthened its position on the Indian market and is currently the largest fast-moving consumer goods company (FMCG) in India. Parent company Unilever owns 51.6% of HLL.

Until recently, cottonseed production was also part of HLL. During a strategic reorientation in 2002, HLL spun off its seed division as the subsidiary PEGSL and then sold most of the shares. HLL retained a 26% financial interest in PEGSL, in the form of overdue payments that the purchaser – Emergent Genetics – could not meet at that time. It was agreed that these remaining shares would be gradually passed on to PEGSL over several years. That operation has since been finalised. In the period right after the sale, when Unilever still owned shares in PEGSL, the relationship with PEGSL/Emergent Genetics was purely financial, according to Unilever. Unilever had no management control over PEGSL during that period.

The Indian Report: Disputes as to Its Factual Claims

An important factor in the Dutch conflict between Unilever and the NGO coalition was the report by Davuluri Venkateswarlu. Analytically, the report can be divided into two parts: the empirical (i.e., factual) research into the scope and gravity of child labour in cottonseed production, including a descriptive account of the industry, and an interpretative account of the moral and political involvement of Unilever and other Western multinationals. We will look at the empirical part first.

Venkateswarlu based his study on primary and secondary sources. Much of the secondary research is made up of studies that he had conducted earlier. The primary research is a field study carried out between 1999 and 2001 at 22 farms. According to the report, 12 of them produced for HLL. None of the 22 farms is identified and the report has little to say about the research methodology used. That leads to occasional questions, for instance in terms of determining the gravity and scope of the use of child labour in cottonseed production. The report says that there has been a spectacular increase in child labour in recent years. Altogether in 2000, the report says, this affected some 450,000 children in all of India and approximately 250,000 in Andhra Pradesh. That means that, according to the report, at the turn of the century, nine out of ten workers in cottonseed production were children (Venkateswarlu, 2003, p. 11).

---

[31] www.emergentgenetics.com, visited 23 September 2005.

19 Case Description: A Matter of Involvement   197

Table 19.1 Table copied from Venkateswarlu's report. According to the report this table shows the increase in child labour for the period 1990–2000 (Venkateswarlu, 2003, p. 17)

Year	Total production area of hybrid cotton in acres	Total number of children involved in child labour
1990–1991	6,160	61,600
1995–1996	21,880	218,800
1998–1999	28,000	280,000
1999–2000	30,000	300,000
2000–2001	24,783	247,830

These estimates are based on a sample survey that determined the average number of working children per hectare (1 hectare = 2.47 acres), plus an estimation as to the total number of hectares in use for cottonseed production (see Table 19.1). These figures were also used to make an estimation of the number of child labourers indirectly related to multinationals based in the West, like Unilever (see Table 19.2). It is, of course, worth asking whether these figures can be used without a proper methodological account, especially if they are going to be used as a basis for making accusations.

Regarding the gravity of the child labour, the report says that given the nature of the work and the degree to which children are involved, we cannot mask the various tasks performed by children in cottonseed production as mere children's work as oposed to child labour. It is definitely appropriate to speak of child labour being used for cottonseed production, often in the very grave form of debt slavery. The report illustrates the gravity of the situation with cases like that of a girl named Narsamma (see Box 19.1). Her tragic fate is presented as a case study. But here again, there are problems with its methodology. The story has been written in such a way that it is completely unverifiable. According to the report, real names could not be used for fear of repercussions. While that may be true, it still makes it hard to use such cases to link HLL to child labour practices.

Table 19.2 Number of children (6–14 years old) employed in hybrid cottonseed production in the Indian federal state of Andhra Pradesh on farms that supply Western based companies (2000–2001)

Company	Owner's nationality	Production land used, in acres[a]	Number of children involved
HindustanLever(HLL)[b]	Dutch/UK	2,500	25,000
Syngenta	Swiss	650	6,500
Advanta	Dutch/UK	300	3,000
Mayhyco-Monsanto	American	1,700	17,000
Proagro	German	200	2,000

Table copied from Venkateswarlu's report. According to the report this table shows Unilever's involvement with child labour (Venkateswarlu, 2003, p. 18)
[a] 1 acre = 4,046.86 m^2.
[b] As of 2003: Paras Extra Growth Seed.

Box 19.1: Narsamma case. (Source: Venkateswarlu, 2003)

Narsamma, a 12 year old scheduled caste girl, has been working in the cottonseed fields of an employer in Alavakonda village in Sanjamala mandal (Kurnool district) for last 3 years. Her employer is a local farmer who produces "Brahma" variety of hybrid cottonseeds in two acres for a reputed multinational seed company (Hindustan Lever Limited). She came from a remote village in Prakasam district. Her native village is about 100 km away from her work place. Though her parents own three acres of dry land the income they get from their land is insufficient. They also work as agricultural labourers.

Narsamma had to discontinue her studies after third class to pay back a loan of Rs. 2000 taken by her father from a middlemen who arranges labour for cottonseed farmers. She joined in cottonseed fields in 1998. For first crop season (July 1998–Dec1998) she was paid Rs. 450 per month and now she gets Rs 800. Every year during work season she comes to Alavakonda village along with other children from her native village to work in cottonseed fields. She stays with the employer about 5–6 months (July-December). Employer provides her accommodation and food during her stay with him. She stays in the employer's cattle shed, where all other migrant children are put up. The cattle shed is a small room originally constructed for keeping cattle. It does not have proper ventilation and the floor is dirty without proper cover. Part of this room is covered with cattle fodder. As employer does not have other place to accommodate migrant children he keeps them in this room. During the season when children are accommodated in this room he shifts the accommodation of his cattle to an open place in front of this room.

Her daily routine starts with waking up early in the morning at 5 a.m. and getting ready by 6 a.m. to go to the fields. From 6.30 a.m. in the morning till 7 p.m. in the evening she is in the fields doing various sorts of work. She is engaged in cross pollination till 12 a.m. Around 8–8.30 a.m 15–20 min break is given for taking food. From 12 a.m. to 2 p.m. she is engaged in other works like weeding, picking up cotton kappas, carrying water for pesticide application etc.(pollination and emasculation works are done in specific timings. Pollination work is done in the morning hours preferably before 12 a.m. and emasculation after 3 p.m. During this gap children are entrusted with other works) From 2 to 3 p.m. 1 h break is given for taking lunch, rest and playing with other children. From 3 to 7 p.m. she is engaged in emasculation work. She comes back home at 7.30 p.m. She is free from 7.30 to 8.30 p.m. Takes food at 8.30 PM and spends about an hour or so in the employer's house watching TV. During harvesting season, while watching TV she also does work like separating cotton "kappas".

Recalling the health problems she had faced during the last working season Narasamma stated that "I was ill for two times. First time I had heavy fever

19 Case Description: A Matter of Involvement

> with cold, headache and vomiting because I worked during rain and got wet. That day three of my colleagues were absent and we had to do their work also. To finish the cross-pollination for that day we were requested to work even during raining time and also late hours. Because of that I got fever the next day. It started with cold and headache and finally resulted in heavy fever. I did not go to the doctor. I thought it was not that serious to consult the doctor. My employer brought some medicines for me and I took it. I took 2 days rest and after that I was OK and went back to work. The second time I got severe headache and felt giddiness which was not normal while working in the field immediately after spraying pesticides. I complained to my employer. He suggested her to go home (his residence) and take rest for that day. I went home and took rest for that day. In the evening my employer asked me if I wanted any medicine but I said no. I resumed my work from the next day".

Unilever Netherlands disagreed vigorously with the facts as presented in the report. It did not dispute all of them, however. Unilever agreed that the worst type of child labour can be found in India and in cottonseed production in Andhra Pradesh.

We all know that such things occur there.

For the rest, however, Unilever considered Venkateswarlu's report unsound and thus inadmissible, or at least insufficient, as evidence of its involvement in child labour. With regard to the methodology used, Unilever concurred with the reaction of the Indian Association of Seed Industry (ASI). The ASI is an Indian trade association representing seed companies. Its membership includes prominent multinationals and national Indian companies. According to ASI, we must treat Venkateswarlu's report as an informal document, which lacked adequate instruments for collecting data and based its findings on a tour of 22 seed farmers (0.2% of the population) (ASI 2004).

As for the actual facts presented, Unilever maintained that the researcher seriously exaggerated the number of children involved.

The numbers are based on an unrepresentative sample. We calculated that if Venkateswarlu's figures were correct, the cottonseed industry employed only children.

Unilever also cast doubt on Venkateswarlu's conclusions about the gravity of the child labour within the industry. It noted that children in emerging countries often perform work (as opposed to labour) for their families.

In India, as in other developing countries' agricultural sectors, children frequently work on farms that are run by their families.[32] But the part they play is one of a participant in a family unit, a contributor to the family enterprise outside school time.[33]

---

[32] Letter by Heleen Keep, Unilever, Corporate Relations Department, London, to Dresdner RCM Global Investors (UK) Ltd., dated 3 December 2001.
[33] Letter by M. K. Sharma, vice president of Hindustan Lever, to Mary Cuneen, Anti Slavery International, dated 09 July 2003.

In addition to that, Unilever emphasized strongly that the report did not specifically demonstrate a connection between child labour and plantations linked to HLL. According to Unilever, there is hardly any concrete proof of such a link to be found in the report. It noted, in that regard, that HLL had always been one of the most respected companies in India and that it always set its purchase prices above regular market prices. In addition, Unilever stressed that HLL had long included a provision in contracts with seed dealers that suppliers were not allowed to use child labour. Moreover, Unilever pointed out that the contracts between seed dealers and farmers also contained a provision obliging farmers to comply with Indian law.[34]

HLL always verified whether farmers and seed dealers respected these agreements with regular visitations, oral inquiries and requests for confirmation of their adherence to these requirements. However, in one letter Unilever toned down its claims about regular verification.

> Field visits by HLL staff were not designed to either police or closely supervise the work of the farmers, but were spot checks to test compliance with our requirements.[35]

Nevertheless, the company was sufficiently convinced of its own position, as the following shows:

> If the coalition really had a case against us and really wanted to reach its goals, they should have lodged a complaint against us long ago with the Dutch Ministry of Economic Affairs' National Contact Point (NCP). [The OECD has commanded national governments to set up NCPs as a means of exacting its guidelines for multinational companies. NGOs and others can report infractions of OECD directives to the NCP. The OECD takes a strong stance against child labour.] But the coalition never reported us. Why not? Because it is unable to do so. It has no proof, because there is no proof. Unilever fully complies with the OECD directives.

The Indian Report: Disputes as to Its Moral Arguments

Venkateswarlu's report was more than a statement of facts. It also contained political and ethical argumentation that the researcher used as a basis for concluding that Unilever bore a heavy responsibility in the struggle against child labour and that it fell short of this responsibility in the matter of Indian cottonseed production. Before going into this, it is important to stress that Venkateswarlu admits that the Western multinationals and their first-tier subsidiaries have no children on their own payrolls. The problem arises with the independent farms where the actual cultivation for the Western multinationals takes place (Venkateswarlu, 2003, p. 33).

Hence, the seed companies were not directly involved in child labour. It is also only fair, though, to point out that we should not overemphasise the moral significance of this absence of direct involvement. Moral condemnation can also

---

[34] Letter by M. K. Sharma, vice president of Hindustan Lever, to Mary Cuneen, Anti Slavery International, dated 09 July 2003.

[35] Letter by M. K. Sharma, vice president of Hindustan Lever, to Mary Cuneen, Anti Slavery International, dated 09 July 2003.

19 Case Description: A Matter of Involvement   201

accompany indirect involvement in injustice. A fencer, receiving stolen goods acts immorally; the same goes for someone who knowingly helps a person blackmail someone else. This was exactly what the report was getting at. According to Venkateswarlu, Unilever was a direct beneficiary. Consequently, Venkateswarlu concludes that Western multinationals bear a great responsibility – certainly in the sense that they should be able, and ought, to do something about it:

> The exploitation of child labour in cottonseed farms is linked to larger market forces. Several large-scale national and international seed companies... have involved themselves in subtle ways in perpetuating the problem of child labour. The economic relationships behind the abuse are multi-tiered and complex, which masks legal and social responsibility. (Venkateswarlu, 2003, p. 33)

Venkateswarlu used three arguments to substantiate his position. He stated that seed companies are a powerful party. They can set conditions for farmers in contracts (Venkateswarlu, 2003, p. 33), but they do not do so. They remain passive. Next, Venkateswarlu posited that seed companies pay a low price for cottonseed. According to Venkateswarlu, this price is so low that the farmers have no other option than to hire children. They cannot pay adult wages with the price they get. This is all the more distressing, according to Venkateswarlu, because the seed companies make big profits on the sale of the cottonseed to farmers (Venkateswarlu, 2003, pp. 26–29). Thirdly, Venkateswarlu maintains that the various multinationals, in particular, cannot deny their responsibility because they have committed themselves to acting in accordance with the highest standards of social responsibility. He refers to Unilever's code of conduct as one example. By ignoring the problem, the multinationals' behaviour even falls short of their own standards.

> The activities of these MNCs in the area of cottonseed business in India are certainly not in tune with what they claim about their commitment to socially responsible corporate behaviour. (Venkateswarlu, 2003, p. 24)

Unilever objected to the moral arguments put forward in the report, as well. According to the company, the role of Western multinationals in cottonseed production was being overemphasised. It pointed out that Indian companies controlled 75% of the market. In addition, Unilever disputed the notion that the company could be held fully responsible for everything that took place throughout the supply chain. In various responses, Unilever plainly showed that HLL itself had never hired children and that HLL made certain that this was also the case for its first-tier business partners, in this case the seed dealers.[36] At the same time, the company acknowledged that the situation was less obvious in the rest of the supply chain.

> The situation is less clear in the actual cultivation of cottonseed, but we do not believe that girls are subjected to forced labour to cultivate the cottonseed that we buy.[37]

---

[36] Letter by M. K. Sharma, vice president of Hindustan Lever, to Mary Cuneen, Anti Slavery International, dated 09 July 2003.
[37] Letter by Antony Burgmans, chairman of Unilever, to M. Filbri, Oxfam Novib, dated 18 December 2001.

Unilever also pointed out that it is important to remember that the company itself had no contact with these farmers. It stresses repeatedly that "Unilever has no dealings whatsoever with any of the farmers".[38] According to the company, this has important practical and ethical implications. The practical implication is that

> HLL or the seed organizer (i.e. the seed dealer) has no direct or indirect role in the farmer's practice of either taking help from his family members, or employing labour..... The farmer is not an employee of either HLL or the seed organizer.[39]

The moral implication is that these are independent parties that are each responsible for their own actions.[40]

> (The farmer's) individual practice of using his family members or outside labour cannot be governed by us.[41] In situations in which the linkages are not direct, but diffuse, company involvement is commensurate and respects the many responsibilities of different contributory parties and agencies.[42]

One final argument used to defuse Venkateswarlu's moral claims was that HLL has withdrawn from cottonseed production.

> In 2002 we sold the business to a US company. However, it did not have enough money at the time to take over the whole company. That is why we held 25% of the shares for a while; but we no longer bore any management responsibility.

This response did not convince the coalition. The parties crossed swords in public and privately several times in the post-May 2003 period. At first sight, the discussion seemed to focus on *facts* that the parties disputed. Unilever reiterated repeatedly that its suppliers did not use child labour, while the coalition insisted equally often that it did (albeit further down the supply chain). Whereas Unilever insisted that it paid out higher purchase prices, the coalition had strong doubts about this assertion. The coalition also insisted that these were often cases of some of the worst types of child labour, while Unilever said that we should not ignore the share of cases that were really merely children's work and not child labour.

On the one hand, it is completely understandable that the discussion would concentrate on specific facts. The coalition framed its accusation against Unilever mainly in terms of a factual instance with severe ethical and public relations ramifications; so Unilever reacted by disputing the facts, especially because of their severe implications.

> An accusation of child labour can stick for years. Unfortunately this is also the case even when it is undeserved,

---

[38] Shubhabrata Bhattacharya (25 June 2001).

[39] Shubhabrata Bhattacharya (25 June 2001).

[40] Letter by M. K. Sharma, vice president of Hindustan Lever, to Mary Cuneen, Anti Slavery International, dated 09 July 2003.

[41] Shubhabrata Bhattacharya (25 June 2001).

[42] Letter by Heleen Keep, Unilever, Corporate Relations Department, London, to Dresdner RCM Global Investors (UK) Ltd., dated 3 December 2001.

Unilever repeatedly said. On the other hand, the fixation on the truth value of specific facts is somewhat dissatisfying, morally speaking. The commotion about "facts" distracted attention from four political and ethical issues about which the parties – implicitly – also disagreed. One could say that the Dutch discussion between Unilever and the coalition would remain deadlocked as long as these underlying issues were not settled. That is why we will single out these underlying political and moral issues for attention here.

Moral Dispute 1: Chain Responsibility and Infringement of Rights

The coalition claimed that Unilever should have played an active role in combating child labour throughout the supply chain, even when its only link to child labour was through farmers to whom the company was only indirectly connected. The discussion followed two different lines of argumentation, which were not clearly distinguished. One of these grounded the need for Unilever to play an active role in combating child labour in the morally significant fact that the company had acted morally wrong. It had contributed to the causes of child labour and thus was – in part and indirectly – to *blame* for child labour. Unilever had to step in because it had somehow violated children's rights. The second line of argumentation maintained that it was Unilever's duty to step in and help combat child labour, even though the company itself was not to blame for causing child labour, either in part or indirectly.

Morally speaking these arguments are fundamentally different. In the first case, we are dealing with morally wrong conduct by Unilever that has given rise to a violation of children's rights; in the second, we are dealing with an obligatory duty to help that does not originate in any prior blameworthy conduct. Morality judges these situations differently: it is the difference between being an accomplice in drowning a person and accidentally driving past a pond in which a person is drowning or perhaps even watching a real-life television show in which the camera crew drives past the pond. We will start by discussing the first line of argumentation.

The global discussion on international companies' responsibilities leans heavily on the public discourse about human rights. The UN (2003) expresses its "norms relating to the moral responsibility of transnational companies" completely in terms of not infringing upon and protecting and promoting human rights.[43] The OECD's *Guidelines for Multinational Enterprises* (2000)[44] also refer to respect for human rights. The coalition's first argument dovetailed with this dominant line of thinking regarding respect for human rights. The coalition argued that Unilever infringed

---

[43] United Nations Economic and Social Council, Commission on human rights, Sub-Commission on the Promotion and Protection of Human Rights (2003) Fifty-fifth session. Agenda item 4, *Norms on the responsibilities of transnational corporations and other business enterprises with regard to human rights*.
[44] www.OECD.org.

upon the human rights of the children because of its indirect involvement with the practice of using them as farm labour.

The notion of supply chain responsibility was essential for the coalition in giving this argument credibility. Supply chain responsibility means that an economic agent bears moral responsibility for the entire production chain in which it operates and from which it benefits. If there is injustice at any point along the chain, at least some of the blame falls on all of the links. Supply chain responsibility implies that a company or person can never allow human rights to be violated anywhere along the chain, no matter how indirectly one is involved. If there is involvement, however indirect, then one's behaviour is reprehensible and one can be called to account morally. That certainly applies when one derives some level of economic or other advantage from the abuse, as in a low purchase price. Another compounding factor is when any of the company's actions (again, such as paying a low purchase price) indirectly contributes to prolonging the unjust practice. The coalition's assertion was that because of its supply chain responsibility, Unilever had been involved in and could be called to account morally for child labour.

For the supply chain responsibility argument to work, the coalition had to give an account of what was special about Unilever's position, compared to, say, a regular consumer buying clothes made of the hybrid cotton in Germany or the Netherlands. How could the coalition justify targeting Unilever and not such consumers, as well, when these consumers are presumably also aware of child labour practices in India and Unilever's track record was not quite so bad compared with that of regular consumers? Not many consumers ask regular retailers to prove that their merchandise has been made without using child labour; while only a small percentage buy their clothes in special shops that sell products with a no-child-labour guarantee only. To give muscle to the argument that Unilever bore special responsibility because of its supply chain responsibility, the complainants pointed to four factors. First, Unilever is special because of its power as an economic agent. It has a significant sphere of influence. Second, Unilever is, at the very least, an unwilling accomplice because it passively collaborates in prolonging the practice by offering a low market price for the hybrid seeds. Third, Unilever benefits from the practice for the same reason. Fourth, Unilever is negligent about checking up on its possible involvement (see Moral Dispute 4).

Even though the notion of supply chain responsibility – and its desirability, limits and implications – had not really been made an explicit theme of the discussion, Unilever clearly objected to the idea. The company did not accept the concept of supply chain responsibility. Unilever only accepted full responsibility for its own behaviour and that of its first-tier suppliers; it rejected being responsible for the actions of more distant links down the supply chain. In its 2004 *Social Report* Unilever states:

> Through our new Business Partner Code, we are working with our first-tier suppliers on human rights, labour standards, working conditions and care for the environment (Unilever 2004: 2).

Unilever argued that no economic actor – whose primary aim is to generate a profit and who has to operate under the pressure of a competitive environment – could possibly assume a heavier responsibility than that. The company would collapse if it had to interpret the "sphere of influence" concept so broadly that it applied to the entire chain of production. In addition, the company had to guard against promising things it could not provide.

> As expectations for wider engagement by companies grow, so too are critics more ready to say when we don't meet their expectations.

Despite the company's reservations, Unilever's position should not be taken to mean that it did not want to assume any responsibility at all for the rest of the supply chain. The company repeatedly said that it expected all suppliers to comply with its code of conduct. It also inspected farms and stated that it would immediately terminate contracts with growers where abuses were found.[45] The company insisted throughout, however, on maintaining a distinction between keeping an eye on matters and assuming full responsibility.[46]

Moral Dispute 2: Chain Responsibility and Duty to Help

Oxfam Novib, in particular, used another moral argument to defend the assertion that Unilever was obliged to do its utmost to combat the use of child labour in cottonseed production, even if it did not directly employ children itself. This second argument focused on the principle that moral agents have a duty to help those in need. Morally speaking, there is a striking difference between this argument and the previous one, because the duty to help's appeal to action is grounded much less in blame. In so far as the issue of blame is involved at all, it is not the kind of blame related to prior actions on the part of the agent:

> It is unfortunate that Unilever consistently refuses to take seriously the most important point, which is that Unilever is in a good position to make a difference. It was never our intention to hold Unilever liable for child labour, either legally or morally. What we kept telling Unilever all that time is that it had to adopt the issue of child labour in cottonseed cultivation. They had to make it their problem. This was one reason why we did not want to given Unilever names of individual children. We did not want to reduce the problem to individual cases for which Unilever might possibly be held legally liable. We think that Unilever should assume responsibility for the problem as such, apart from the question of whether Unilever buys directly or indirectly from farmers involved in the practice. Our reason for thinking that Unilever should assume this responsibility is not directly linked to the question of whether Unilever's own suppliers hire children. The point is that Unilever has a relation to this practice, that everyone knows that children are systematically employed in this practice and that Unilever is in a position to make a difference... Unilever says that it is always open for a meeting and that is true and good. However, in the case study we asked Unilever to do something extra this time.

---

[45]Letter by M. K. Sharma, vice president of Hindustan Lever, to Mary Cuneen, Anti Slavery International, dated 09 July 2003.

[46]Letter by M. K. Sharma, vice president of Hindustan Lever, to Mary Cuneen, Anti Slavery International, dated 09 July 2003.

The fact that Oxfam Novib reverted to the duty-to-help argument is quite interesting, but also troubling because the duty to help is, in fact, a very complex principle. Sometimes this duty is very compelling and demands that we take at least some kind of action, even if we still have discretion as to the "what and how". Thus interpreted, it is a duty to rescue and being indifferent to it is, in fact, blameworthy. The standard example is a situation in which a person happens to walk past a pond in which someone is drowning. The passer-by must help. Even though she is not at all responsible for causing the drowning, it is still blameworthy to ignore the situation. Still, she has some discretion in deciding what to do: she can jump into the water, but e.g. when she if not an experienced swimmer, she can also decide to call the police.

There is also much less stringent interpretation of the principle that we are obliged to help others which apply in many other, less urgent cases. As such, the duty to help means that we may not always ignore the needs of others, must take these into account in our decisions and must sometimes act based on this principle. Under this interpretation, we have discretion not only with regard to what and how, but also when. Typical situations where this interpretation of the principle applies are cases in which we are asked to donate money for a charitable cause or when a friend is in need. According to Oxfam Novib the child labour case is one in which the duty to help ought to be interpreted as a duty to rescue. Unilever must step in just like we all would be obliged to act if we came across a pond in which a person was drowning.

The coalition's appeal to an obligatory duty to help is striking in light of commonly accepted views in modern business ethics. Even the idea that companies have a duty to help at all is controversial. Specialists in business ethics like Donaldson (1989) and Elfstrom (1991) posit that the duty to help that is customary among individuals does not apply to companies, or only to a limited extent. The same point of view is confirmed by a recent UN report on the duties of business enterprises, the so-called (United Nations 2003: 19):

> ... [C]ompanies cannot be held responsible for the human rights impacts of every entity over which they may have some influence, because this would include cases in which they were not a causal agent, direct or indirect, of the harm in question. Nor is it desirable to have companies act whenever they have influence, particularly over governments. Asking companies to support human rights voluntarily where they have influence is one thing; but attributing responsibility to them on that basis alone is quite another.

So, Unilever could easily have parried Oxfam Novib's appeal to the duty to help by simply rejecting it. It is noteworthy that Unilever chose not to do so:

> As a company we know that we are not here only to make a profit. Perhaps we do not advertise it as much as other companies do, but for us it is obvious that we must contribute to society. We do this in many ways, some – like the Shakti self-help project – we make public, while we prefer to keep others out of sight.

But Unilever insisted on one thing regarding the duty to help: it was fully optional, at least in the commercial context. Unilever wanted to remain in full control over the what and how of any morally necessary effort:

19 Case Description: A Matter of Involvement

> We want to decide where we aim our efforts. We will decide what we will do when. We believe that we must concentrate on issues related to fish, water and agriculture. We feel linked to these themes. Moreover, they fall within the field of our expertise, putting us in a better position to evaluate projects related to them and to evaluate whether our resources are put to best use.

In other words, Unilever compared the situation in India with the situation in which a person is asked to donate money to a charitable cause. The company also stressed that there were limits to its duty to help:

> We are a company that must operate on the market. We cannot do everything. The most important responsibility for helping people in need lies with the government.

Because of these crucial disagreements about the nature of the duty to help, Unilever in the end rejected Oxfam Novib's argument that it *had* to help fight child labour. But it also made clear that its decision was not grounded in a principled rejection of the duty to help:

> Child labour is upsetting and must be brought to an end as rapidly as possible. However, we bear no direct or indirect blame for the practice. At the same time we choose not to focus our extra social efforts on this issue. There are other, urgent problems, among which sustainability, with which we have closer ties. Of course you may disagree with this choice, but that is no reason to stress only the negative all the time like the coalition does. It tries to make it appear as if we do nothing at all. Actually, we are not doing so badly.

Moral Dispute 3: Historical Blame

One argument that Unilever started using after 2003 to defuse the coalition's claims was that it had since left the cottonseed production industry. According to Unilever, that put an end to its responsibility in the issue. The coalition disputed this. A third moral argument to defend the position that Unilever bore responsibility focuses on this. According to the coalition, withdrawal from the industry did not put an end to the company's responsibility:

> Unilever bears a historical blame because the company contributed – indirectly – to the use of child labour. The blame certainly covers the post-2001 period, when the company could have known what was going on but willingly and knowingly chose to deny all involvement. By helping in the struggle against child labour, Unilever can rectify errors it committed in the past. It is immoral to deny this blame.

Unilever also rejected this argumentation. HLL's withdrawal from cottonseed production in 2002 was a decidedly relevant fact. It put an end to the file entitled Unilever and Cottonseed Cultivation.

> A profit-based company has to set a limit to the moral responsibility that it can assume.

Moral Dispute 4: Prevention

Another ethical question on which the coalition and Unilever differed involved a procedural issue. What precautions should a company take to prevent indirect involvement in child labour (even if it does not recognise supply chain responsibility)? This question grew out of Unilever's admission that the situation on the farms was unclear but that it nevertheless believed that: (a) there was no child labour being used on its farms, and (b) it was morally acceptable to do business with these farmers.

> The situation is less clear in the actual cultivation of cottonseed, but we do not believe that girls are subjected to forced labour to cultivate the cottonseed that we buy.[47]

The ethical question implied in discussions on the matter was: when is it reasonable to believe such a thing, especially if one is going to do business based on that belief?

According to Unilever, it was justified in believing there was no child labour being used on the farms. The company did not blindly accept what it was told but relied on a three-part prevention policy. Unilever required seed dealers to have farmers sign a contract promising to respect all current legislation; it carried out regular inspections throughout the supply chain; and it requested all parties to cite proof of any specific cases found to the contrary.

> We will investigate every case thoroughly to discover whether it is true and which plantations hired these children. We will certainly take measures.

According to the coalition, this was insufficient for validating a reasonable belief that there was no child labour used in the supply chain. The most important argument was that child labour was too closely linked with the entire industry:

> It is very difficult to buy cottonseed in such a way that you buy only from farmers that have nothing to do with child labour. Even if you can do that, accomplishing it requires a lot more effort than just occasional inspections and having all suppliers sign a paper in which they claim to refrain from using child labour.

Furthermore, the coalition also thought it was not acceptable to hold other parties responsible for detecting possible abuses, certainly when the accounts of these abuses would only be taken seriously when the children's full names were listed:

> Given the gravity of the situation, it is unacceptable to leave the task of denouncing abuses to others. What is more, you misjudge the situation in which the children – and their parents – live. Revealing the names of the children makes them very vulnerable to local social pressure and may lead to court cases that take many years and absorb a gigantic amount of energy.... In a case like this one where basic human rights are at risk, it is not up to (others) to prove that Unilever has overstepped itself. It is for Unilever to show more convincingly that it is pristine.

In 2006, the Swiss company Syngenta took the type of preventive measures that the coalition had in mind. Syngenta is still active in the cottonseed production market

---

[47]Letter by Antony Burgmans, chairman of Unilever, to M. Filbri, Oxfam Novib, dated 18 December 2001.

and has recognised supply chain responsibility with regard to child labour for some time. One of the measures that it took to ensure that its supply chain did not use any child labour was to instruct seed dealers to work primarily with small farmers with few employees. The reasoning behind this was that it is mainly the large farmers who systematically employ children sold into debt slavery. Small farmers usually employ their own family members. They, too, will often use children, but the chance is greater that these children will be treated better and be allowed to go to school. In this way child labour is transformed into children's work. Another measure Syngenta took was to sign an agreement with a US NGO called Fair Labour Organisation (FLO) to provide external monitoring of its production chain.

The Aftermath of the Discussion in the Netherlands

The accusations were not the only source of Unilever's displeasure with the case. What disturbed the company also very much was the way the coalition went about its work. In retrospect, many of those involved agreed that Unilever and the coalition communicated poorly between February 2002 and April 2003. Both sides have confirmed that they were willing to discuss the issue during that period but that neither took the lead. Unilever had contacted its Indian subsidiary, HLL, and learned that the latter was willing to set up talks with MVF; the coalition maintained contact with MVF and understood that attempts to contact HLL were rebuffed. The coalition and Unilever no longer discussed the issue themselves, except for one time when Director Van der Waaij asked a representative of the coalition about it. Unilever thought the coalition was negligent; on one Dutch talk show, Chairman Burgmans spoke of "thunderous silence". In the interviews Van der Waaij insisted that

> If the negotiations in India were stalled, they should have told us so. We are always open for a meeting.

The brevity of the period between Unilever being sent the report and the coalition's publicity campaign long remained an open wound for Unilever:

> That the report was sent so quickly to the newspaper NRC is absolutely disgraceful. The coalition should have given Unilever more time. It knew that letters to the chairman first pass through staff meetings. As a result, the issue was in the newspaper before we really had time to take a good look at it.

Since Unilever thought the accusation was unjust and the way it was expressed unacceptable, the company took a hard stance toward the matter.

> The whole affair was a matter of reputation. Unilever has a good name and the coalition wanted to take full advantage of this. The coalition knew very well that anyone linking Unilever or a similar company with child labour was guaranteed to draw media attention. It used this method to try to compel the company to accept a responsibility.

In addition, Unilever contends that not all of the groups in the coalition had pure motives:

> Some groups live from scandals like child labour. Were it not for these scandals, they would lose their inspiration, the ability to accuse others and, not least of all, their source of income. Other respectable parties like Oxfam Novib and Amnesty International were foolish enough to allow themselves to be harnessed to these others. You can't help but wonder whether a coalition that works in such a way is itself operating ethically.

According to Oxfam Novib, the coalition agrees with Unilever that there were lost opportunities in the period from February 2002 to April 2003. The coalition was also willing to admit that the period between sending Unilever the report and notifying *NRC* was very short, "although – even in the business community – some very abrupt deadlines are used". Oxfam Novib noted here that since then they have drafted their own code of conduct entitled *Principles for Cooperation with Companies*.[48] The principle of hearing and being heard is given an important place in the code. Nevertheless, the coalition still has a different perception of the case. According to the coalition, Unilever was negligent, certainly in the period from February 2002 to April 2003:

> One might expect a more alert response from a company facing such serious accusations. Unilever remained too passive and walked away from its responsibility to help eliminate child labour in Indian hybrid cottonseed cultivation. At a given moment, the coalition thought it had to take action. That can include some less friendly tactics. We just wanted to achieve our goal. That is why the national India working group sent chairman Burgmans a letter with the completed research report on behalf of the coalition.

Epilogue

What about the Indian children at the heart of all this? All things considered, the Indian and worldwide campaigns against the use of child labour in cottonseed production are starting to bear fruit. In 2001, the government in the state of Andhra Pradesh passed a resolution ending child labour in all its forms. Other legislation is in the works. The state has also started a campaign to inform parents and children. More than 5,000 cases of administrative measures have been brought against employers. In India, NGOs have also undertaken proactive action against the use of child labour in cottonseed production. This includes information campaigns, establishing schools and setting up centres that prepare children for school.

Especially pertinent for this case is that, partly due to the severe criticism in and outside India, there seems to be a revolution in the thinking of many seed companies, including Western multinationals. After responding with initial reticence, nearly all large multinationals, including Bayer and Monsanto, admit that they cannot guarantee that their production chains are free of child labour and that intensive monitoring is needed to stamp out the practice. ASI (Indian Association of Seed Industry) – to which Monsanto, Syngenta, Advanta, Proagro and Emergent Genetics all belong – decided in 2003 to work with MFV to end child labour. To this end, in 2003 all ASI members accepted the notion of supply chain responsibility and took initial steps in

---

[48] www.novib.nl/mvo, visited 12 October 2005.

2004 against child labour. These include systematic monitoring. Practical arrangements between Syngenta, Monsanto, Bayer, MVF and local groups were negotiated in 2005. A system of penalties is in preparation that would impose punitive cuts in benefits on farmers shown to employ children. Farmers caught repeatedly will find they have no purchasers for their cottonseed. Despite this approach, ASI insists that Venkateswarlu's first report was sub-standard.

All this taken together has led to a significant reduction in the number of children labouring in Andhra Pradesh (Venkateswarlu, 2004, p. 16). Some speak of a 30–40% drop. The only problem with these figures is that the province has suffered from a drought in recent years. There are thus external reasons for the fall in cottonseed production. Another factor is that some seed companies have slowly shifted their operations to other provinces where there are fewer qualms about using child labour.

References

Anonymous 2003, 'Vissticks met duurzaamheid.' NRC-Handelsblad, 27–10–2003.
Association of Seed Industry (ASI) 2004 ASI Position Paper. Child Labor Issue.
Berkhout, B. 2003 'Schuldslavernij in Indiase katoenzaadindustrie.' NRC-Handelsblad, 05–05–2003.
Bhattacharya, S. (2001), "Hind Lever clarifies", Business Line, 25–06–2001.
Bird, F.B. and Waters, J.A. 1989. The Moral Muteness of Managers. *California Management Review*, XXXII(1): 73–88.
Boatright, J.R. 1993/2007. *Ethics and the Conduct of Business*. Fifth Edition. Upper Saddle River: Prentice Hall.
Bowie, N. 1999. *Business Ethics. A Kantian Perspective*. Malden: Blackwell Publishers.
Donaldson, T. 1989. *The Ethics of International Business*. Oxford: Oxford University Press.
Elfstrom, G. 1991. *Moral Issues and Multinational Corporations*. London: Mac Millan.
International Labor Organization (ILO). 2002. A Future Without Child Labor, 90th Session of International Labor Conference, Geneve.
Organisation for Economic Co-Operation and Development (OECD). 2000. *The OECD Guidelines for Multinational Enterprises*, Revision 2000, Paris.
Unilever, Social Report 2004. 2004. Listening, Learning, Making Progress. (Unilever).
Unilever, Unilever Jaaroverzicht 2003. 2004. *Voorzien in de dagelijkse behoeften van mensen, overal*, Unilever.
United Nations, 2003 Social and Economic Council, *Commission on Human Rights Norms on the responsibilities of transnational corporations and other business enterprises with regard to human rights*, August 2003.
Venkateswarlu, D. 2003. *Child Labour and Trans-National Seed Companies in Hybrid Cottonseed Production in Andhra Pradesh* (India Committee of Netherlands) Utrecht. See: www.indianet.nl/cotseed.html
Venkateswarlu, D. 2004. *Child Labour in Hybrid Cottonseed Production in Andhra Pradesh: Recent Developments*. (India Committee of Netherlands) Utrecht. See: www.indianet.nl/cotseed2.html.

Chapter 20
Commentary: The Scope of Chain Responsibility

Jos Kole

Abstract Child labour is dead wrong. The coalition and Unilever agree on that. Yet, they disagree on the scope of chain responsibility, a closely related question of ethical principle. Both parties subscribe to this principle as an important part of corporate social responsibility. The coalition appeals to the principle of chain responsibility to justify its criticism of Unilever and to argue that the latter has a duty to prevent child labour. Unilever, in its turn, asserts that the principle does not apply in this particular case and that the company need not act upon it. It appears that the idea of chain responsibility is open to multiple interpretations. This contribution explores the principle of chain responsibility to explain the difference of opinion between Unilever and the coalition. The first step is to reflect on the meaning of "responsibility". The following is to consider how "chain" denominates this responsibility. The last step offers thoughts on the differing scopes that the parties assign to chain responsibility. Needless to say, these considerations will not resolve the moral conflict. Yet, they may deepen business ethical reflection on the case.

Responsibility

Is Unilever responsible for child labour in Indian cottonseed production? You might think that a simple "yes" or "no" would solve the moral problem underlying this case, but it does not. After all, what does a bluntly positive or negative answer tell us when we have yet to define "responsible"? The term responsibility is frequently used – perhaps even overused; but it occurs in many different settings and senses. Unilever can both be and be held responsible but it can also (and perhaps should) accept responsibility. Furthermore, it may bear responsibility, and may do directly or indirectly or to a greater or lesser degree. Unilever may be called to account for its practice, and so on. On top of this, there is the question whether responsibility

J. Kole (✉)
Ethics Institute, Utrecht University, Utrecht, The Netherlands
e-mail: J.J.Kole@uu.nl

is by definition an ethical notion. Some people consider responsibility the heart of morality.[1]

The common element in this tangle of meanings and uses is that responsibility implies involvement of an actor, in this case Unilever, in some activity, practice or event. Someone responsible for something plays an important and mandatory role in that activity, practice or event. In other words, a responsible actor is tied to something, committed in some way – hence the title of the case. When it comes to moral responsibility, this commitment implies minimally non-indifference to the wellbeing of others beside the actor (cf. Frankena), concern for the quality of human relations, for the good life and a good society. There would be no morality were people to lack this commitment to one another. Business ethics would lose its foundation were companies to be unable to engage in positive involvement (see the other commentary on this case).

Yet "binding involvement" is still only a vague definition for responsibility. What would it mean if the company were obliged to get involved in the fate of the countless children in India who toil in the cottonseed industry? Introduction of a common distinction may clarify matters. On the one hand, responsibility can refer to the actor's *accountability* (liability), but it can also refer to the actor's task or obligation (depending on his role or position in the activity, practice or event). This distinction is sometimes explained as a difference in direction and time. Accountability concerns an activity or event for which one must render account afterwards in terms of one's reasons and motives. One looks back, as it were. Responsibility as accountability is thus retrospective. By contrast, responsibility as *task* or *duty* has a forward-looking character. It gives prior notice that the actor has something to do or that it would be a good thing were the actor to act in a particular way (cf. Online Ethics.org – Glossary, 2009).

Both kinds of responsibility are present in this case study. The coalition holds Unilever (at least partially) accountable for continuation of child labour until the present. Accountability here implies a retrospective reproach or accusation because the coalition assumed that Unilever had had a binding involvement to something immoral. It could not let Unilever get off unscathed.[2] However, Unilever is also responsible in a more positive sense because of its involvement in the Shakti-project, the Ethical Tea Partnership and the Dove campaign. The company apparently considered such binding involvement as its duty and was willing to render account for it in moral terms.

---

[1] The following does not pretend to be comprehensive. There is much discussion in practical philosophy (ethics, philosophy of mind and action) on the nature and capability of (moral) responsibility, especially in relation to the problem of free will (in the context of determinism) and what it means to be an actor. The following considerations intend only to explain chain responsibility and give an idea of its complexity.

[2] According to a famous and authoritative article that deeply influenced philosophical debate on responsibility (Strawson, 1992), someone is responsible if she is the proper object of reactive attitudes like praise and blame, resentment, indignation, hurt feelings, anger, gratitude, reciprocal love, and forgiveness etc. (See Eshleman, 2008). Such reactive attitudes are constitutive of social life.

The two kinds of responsibility are often, but not always, connected. Their being connected in the Unilever case complicates matters and also explains why it is difficult to come to grips with the concept of "chain responsibility". Accountability for something negative that happened in the past (guilt), often leads to a duty to repair the negative situation (repentance). Because Unilever is partly to blame for past and present child labour, it has a duty to correct the situation. Retrospective accountability offers justifying and motivating reasons for this duty. Conversely, a duty can result in holding someone accountable. Unilever publicly denounced child labour and thereby accepted the duty at least to refrain from using child labour in its cottonseed production. The company could choose whether or not to accept this duty. If it did not, it would be held blameworthy. Duty-based responsibility can render Unilever accountable (and guilty of negligence).[3]

The case description's "Duty to aid" section shows that responsibility as accountability is not always connected to responsibility as duty. Having caused a bad situation is not the sole reason for accepting a duty to correct it. Oxfam Novib's argument is that Unilever has a duty to help even though it bears no guilt for child labour. The case description reveals disagreement on the normative force of this special duty. Can others demand or enforce compliance with this duty or should the decision to accept or reject it be left to the actor?

Whether or not others can demand this compliance raises another ambiguity related to responsibility. Others can hold someone responsible, or that someone can accept responsibility. While in the first example a third person ascribes a duty to an actor ("The coalition holds Unilever responsible"), a 1st-person perspective prevails in the second example ("We at Unilever do not accept this responsibility").[4] Duties that a third person believes can be justifiably ascribed to an actor are often narrower (minimum duties) than those an actor voluntarily accepts. We will return to this later.

Of course, there is the question whether it is right or justifiable to ascribe any given responsibility to another person. Is the coalition entitled to hold Unilever responsible for combating child labour? Can an actor deserve praise or blame? Real responsibility is justified responsibility, i.e. responsibility backed by germane and sound reasoning. The discussion between Unilever and the coalition centres on whether the coalition's reasons to hold Unilever responsible are germane and sound. A standard reason for holding an actor accountable for an activity, practice or event is his/her causal role in its occurrence. When it came to causal responsibility, Unilever said there was none; the coalition said there was indeed.

---

[3] Compare this with the strong statement in SER, 2005:61–62: "Accepting chain responsibility should be sharply demarcated from accepting legal chain liability. There can usually be no question of the latter at all." Note that this statement follows a quote from former Unilever CEO Brugmans about Unilever's views on chain responsibility (see below in main text).

[4] One French and continental school of philosophy emphasises the importance of a 2nd-person perspective. The Other holds you responsible (Cf. Emmanuel Levinas's ethical philosophy) in a close I – thou relation (Cf. M. Buber's dialogical philosophy). More recently, moral philosopher Steven Darwall offered a 2nd-person view of responsibility. Yet, Darwall builds on an Anglo-Saxon neo-Kantian analytical philosophy (Darwall, 2006).

Another factor in real responsibility is the actor's free choice. Was the actor freely able to reject the ascribed duty? Could he/she have done otherwise? Although responsibility involves an actor's mandatory commitment, it also requires that the actor be free to opt out. The actor must have a way to refuse involvement. Furthermore, the actor's freedom must include the actual power to act upon his free choice.[5] Suppose that Unilever was forced to participate in a production chain that used child labour ("held at gunpoint") and had no opportunity to leave it. The company could then not be held justifiably responsible. However, it seems that Unilever was able to opt out. Still, Unilever faced pressures that restricted its freedom and may have influenced its degree of responsibility: In addition to moral responsibility, Unilever's economic responsibilities also put pressure on the company. Unilever had to make profit, maintain its market position, compete with other companies, etc. To make matters even more complex, there is a moral dimension to this economic responsibility – e.g. the company has to see to its employees' interests and income. Economic responsibility is not automatically opposed to moral responsibility (as duty) but the two may easily find themselves at loggerheads. In that case, the company has to find a balance. Undoubtedly, there will be those who challenge the company's decisions.

A final factor complicating our case is the connection between involvement and time. The case description recounts that Unilever terminated its cottonseed production operations. At the start of its discussion with the coalition, Unilever was no longer formally part of the production chain. This raises the question of the extent to which Unilever could be responsible (in both senses) at the present for its past involvement.

Chain Responsibility

Chain responsibility enhances the complexity of the many questions that the concept of moral responsibility raises. "Chain" imposes mandatory involvement in the field in which the actor, a business or company[6], operates. Quoting Cramer & Klein we may describe a "chain" here as follows:

> Each firm operates in one or more product chains. Each chain transforms raw material into products and supplies these to clients. It derives its unique structure and composition from the companies involved. An oversimplified representation of such a chain is, for example, the chain supplier 1 > supplier 2 > producer > retailer > client. In practice, the structure of chains is often much more complex. Besides, one product chain (for example office supplies) can cover a diversity of products. The effectiveness of a chain depends on the

---

[5] In role responsibility, the actor takes responsibility (renders account) for activities and events not of her choosing or causation. One example: A state secretary must assume responsibility for the errors of officials in her department.

[6] Chain responsibility can also involve the client, to the extent that she is taken to be a link in the production and supply chain. Action groups appeal to the chain responsibility of clients when they, for example, call people to buy Fair Trade products like coffee.

relation between the chain's links. Frequently, one or only a few parties dominate the chain. Due to their dominance, they can influence the other companies in the chain. (Cramer and Klein, 2005 :p. 14, transl. JJK).[7]

The case description explains the product chain in which Unilever operated. This chain can be considered an agricultural chain, as opposed to an industrial one (Cramer 2005 : p. 14–15). Agricultural chains tend to be more transparent than industrial chains because it is easier to track agricultural products to their basic substance. Our case shows that source seed is the primary material. The case description reconstructs a rather transparent chain[8] from producing farmers (who often employ children) via seed companies (with a mediating role as seed broker) and Unilever subsidiary Hindustan Lever Ltd (HLL) to parent company Unilever. Agricultural chains often have an hourglass design. While there are many players at the beginning and end of the chain, there are only few in the middle. The latter usually hold the most power to control the chain. The cottonseed production chain starts with many farmers who produce seeds and ends with many customers who grow cotton. Seed companies, among them HLL, occupy the narrow waist. That is why the Venkateswarly report ascribes so much chain influence to Unilever. The company is to have had such powerful control over the chain that it could have banished child labour. The coalition criticised Unilever for a lack of benevolent chain control. Put differently, Unilever could and should have done more than it did to eliminate child labour and in that respect was negligent.

How does chain responsibility connect to the distinction between backward and forward responsibility? Unilever is not *directly* responsible in a liability sense. Neither Unilever nor its subsidiary employed children. The coalition acknowledged this. Yet, Unilever and the children are links in a chain[9] that the company dominates through its subsidiary (HLL). For that reason, the coalition holds Unilever *indirectly* responsible. In its view, there is an indirect causal relationship between Unilever and child labour, even though it is hard to prove this. The case description defines chain responsibility as follows:

> Chain-wide responsibility implies that an economic actor bears moral responsibility for the *entire production chain* in which it operates. (Italics JJK)

The coalition would like this view because it would enable them to hold Unilever indirectly accountable for everything that happens throughout the entire cottonseed production and growing chain. At the bottom of the chain, a poor farmer has his children work from dawn to dusk growing cottonseed. The seed returns to the Unilever's

---

[7] The quote continues as follows: "Due to increasing globalization of the economy, product chains get an increasing global character. It heavily depends on the complexity and diversity of the chain, how a company takes its corporate social responsibility. Meanwhile the factor of power plays an important role as well." (Cramer and Klein, 2005:14, curs. and transl. JJK). Note that chain responsibility is taken here as a 1st-person obligation as in the SER, 2005 recommendation.

[8] Links in the chain are reasonably evident, but their degree of interdependence is subject to discussion.

[9] At least until Unilever formally ceased growing cottonseed.

Indian subsidiary via a seed broker.[10] So in the coalition's view Unilever ends up with dirty hands one way or the other.

This view of chain responsibility introduced by the writer of the case study and implicitly presupposed by the coalition seems too strong. Holding Unilever accountable for the entire chain seems to witness to an overstrung morality. It appears unreasonable to lay the burden of responsibility for the entire chain on only one of its links, even when this link is the dominant company in the chain. There are also pragmatic reasons to doubt such overstrung morality. If the hurdle is set too high, no one will be able to jump it. Chain responsibility becomes an all-or-nothing issue. One either jumps the highest hurdle and becomes fully accountable for all that goes wrong in the chain, or one fails. Unilever does not accept full (indirect) responsibility for the entire chain. Yet, it would be unjust to accuse Unilever of a complete lack of commitment to what happened in and went wrong with the chain.

It seems more sensible to understand chain responsibility as a graduated rather than as an all or nothing concept. Unilever can to a certain degree be held retrospectively responsible for what happened and happens in the cottonseed growth chain and prospectively for what should happen there.[11] The exact extent to which Unilever should consider itself liable and duty-bound to eliminate child labour is a matter of practical wisdom and judgement. Ethical dilemmas cannot be resolved with indisputable mathematical accuracy.

When Unilever Netherlands was still formally involved in cottonseed growth, its CEO Anthony Burgmans expressed a less absolute view of chain liability in another context.[12] That view may also explain Unilever's position in its discussion with the coalition (as described in the case):

> Food chains are long and very complex nowadays. The chain goes from seed providers and crop protection producers through farmers and auctions to those who fabricate half-products, manufacturers, wholesale and retail chains, and, at the end of the line, consumers who have to store and prepare the food properly. *It is completely impossible to make one chain player responsible for the whole chain.*
> *Chain responsibility is thus each player's responsibility for that part of the chain that he surveys and controls.*" (Burgmans, 2000, 30, italics and translation JJK)

Burgmans clearly does not want to jump the highest hurdle. Yet, Unilever does not deny that it shares responsibility as one of the links in the chain. It also appears as if Burgmans also reverses the viewpoint. The focus changes from liability for what

---

[10] The case description shows that Unilever and the coalition also disagree about the facts of the matter. Facts are very important in ethical reflection, but they hardly if ever appear in moral deliberation in their pure form, i.e. without bias, without implicit evaluation or interpretation. The weight given to facts in a moral conflict often depends on the ethical views of the one doing the weighing. So the quarrel about facts is actually a mock battle in the moral conflict between Unilever and the coalition.

[11] Chain responsibility as chain liability may not be plausible from a legal perspective (see note 3). Yet it can be, to a certain extent, from a moral point of view.

[12] Burgmans was speaking about food supply chains and the risk of crises in such chains when consumers no longer trust food safety.

happened in the past to responsibility for what should be done (duty responsibility). Burgmans continues, saying:

> This implies in particular that each player in the chain takes its own responsibility for quality and safety; compliance with laws and regulations, and immediate and complete information to the government, the business partners, and the public if something goes wrong. Each of us has the *duty* to ascertain that his suppliers acknowledge this responsibility and actually live up to it (*op. cit.*, italics JJK).

In Unilever's view, chain responsibility is neither endless nor absolute, but it is not absent either. There is a degree of chain responsibility that seems to extend to links close to the actor. However, if each chain player accepted its own limited responsibility, the entire chain would benefit. In this view, chain responsibility is a combination of the limited individual responsibilities of each chain player and collective responsibility of all the chain partners.

> There is also a collective responsibility of the chain partners. This can take shape, for example, in agreements that each partner exclusively collaborates with well-known, trustworthy and certified suppliers. After all, we know too well that the biggest risks are with parties who aim at fast money and do not have long-term interests in the chain. (*op. cit.*, italics JJK).

This combination of chain partners' collective and individual responsibilities sounds plausible. For companies, it seems more feasible than the black-and-white view of chain responsibility and this also explains why the coalition has a good reason for sidestepping it. Even for companies, however, this type of chain responsibility is problematic. It requires a kind of regulation and coordination that are difficult to arrange in practice. Surprisingly, Burgmans assumes that chain players will not be able to coordinate their collective responsibility by themselves. He said:

> We, as market parties, cannot cope with this alone. We need a powerful governmental organisation that guarantees an "equal playfield" for all. Clear, pan European norms, rules and criteria that correspond with views and requirements from elsewhere in the world. For example, rules that enable chain control. A governmental organisation that takes care of smooth, uniform and predictable admission procedures for ingredients, products and processes.
> The same governmental organisation should also be able to maintain the rules. And, it should be able to manage a crisis adequately and with proportionate measures, both at a national and supranational level. (o.c., italics JJK).

Burgmans' appeal to a "powerful governmental organisation" on national and supranational levels is somewhat paradoxical in the context of chain responsibility. Globalisation is sapping government power, which is why chain responsibility was invoked. As it appears now, the viability of that same idea depends on "powerful governmental organisations." At least, that is Burgmans' view. Without national governments' support and enforcement, companies and players in the production chain seem incapable of collective moral self-regulation. Suppose we could apply Burgmans' words to the cottonseed growing chain. We could pose the critical question whether Burgmans might not be ignoring the influence his own company has as one of the chain's dominant players. Was he not shifting responsibility to the governments? Or, did Unilever have less power to influence the chain than the coalition ascribed to it?

Scope: Between Minimal Duty and Optimal Ideal

To what extent is Unilever co-responsible for child labour in India? And, to what extent should it strain to change the deplorable situation of children in the cottonseed growing industry? Ultimately, the answer to the first question is mainly important for its impact on the second question. The greater the accountability, the more compelling is the duty to... um, yes, to do what exactly? Responsibility as obligation is still undetermined when the content of the duty is left undefined. One could say, "You should accept your responsibility in this situation!", but that does not say what you should do. How does concerned commitment morph from conviction to action?

Burgmans offered one answer. A company should make arrangements with other adjacent players to move them to adopt and implement the same high principles of corporate social responsibility in their businesses. The case description mentions Unilever stating that chain partners should be monitored for compliance with such arrangements. Chain partners should include compliance with these agreements in contracts, although it is not directly clear how judicial force could impact on child labour: Should HLL unilaterally terminate contracts with chain partners that hire children? This is the intention. Yet, as mentioned above, in daily business, the weight of moral considerations is always balanced against other, economic, considerations. Unilever is oriented toward dialogue, the coalition toward confrontation. The latter puts pressure on the company. Yet, to what extent can chain responsibility be enforced?

One can simply choose to keep one's hands clean by not having anything at all, be it directly or indirectly, to do with child labour in the cottonseed growing industry. From one perspective, this is what Unilever actually chose to do later on when it withdrew (for whatever reason) from the sector. We could call this an illustration of "non-maleficence" (the moral "do-no-harm" principle). Although that moral effort is important, it is still a minimal morality that aims at bare survival and preservation of a lowest acceptable quality for human coexistence. To be sure, this moral minimum is not negligible. Quite the contrary, it offers the basic substratum for good life to flourish. However, we need more than a moral prevention of harm and evil. We also need to roll up our sleeves and work for the optimal good. In other words, we need beneficence – doing good – alongside non-maleficence – doing no harm. There is a big difference between "refraining from indirect use of child labour" and "the sustained efforts to improve the living conditions of these children, their parents and their social context to such an extent that the actual causes of child labour are removed". That latter is an ideal, expressing a goal that is hardly if ever fully realisable. The coalition aims at this ideal and wants to jump a high hurdle. It would like to see Unilever and other companies do likewise. Unilever, however, has more modest moral ambitions.

Compliance with duties normally leads to safeguarding a decent moral minimum, while aspiration to ideals aims for the best and highest. Both duties and ideals belong to morality but each has its own dynamic and characteristics. They differ in an important respect. Usually, there is a broad consensus – intersubjective agreement – on minimal duties. This implies that participants in moral life (people, companies, NGOs) can require one another to perform these duties. Often, this reciprocal claim exerts a very strong coercive force on moral actors; one example is the prohibition against killing. Minimal duties can also be ascribed from a 3rd-person perspective. Conversely, there is usually far less agreement about the ideals we should strive for to secure optimal coexistence. People regularly feel greater personal commitment to ideals than to principles. From a 1st-person perspective, ideals can have highly inspirational effect on people. Yet, it is hard to require commitment to such ideals from a 3rd-person perspective.[13] You can encourage others to pursue your ideals but it is difficult to hold them accountable when they do not. This is easier to do in the case of recognised duties.

The coalition's disagreement with Unilever can be explained, at least in part, by their diverging views on the interpretation and scope of chain responsibility. That scope can be either minimal or optimal. It is difficult to make chain responsibility obligatory when the stakes are set high. The "duty to help" in the coalition's second argument (see case description) seems to belong to the domain of the moral optimum; it is hard for a 3rd person to enforce cooperation. It would be praiseworthy if Unilever as 1st person accepted this responsibility. Yet, it is also understandable that the company wants to demarcate the scope of the responsibility and obligations it assumes. Unilever wants to decide for itself in which domains it will exercise its corporate social responsibility. Perhaps, the coalition would have achieved more with a less offensive strategy. Perhaps, it would have achieved more had there been better communication. Nevertheless, the coalition was morally justified in putting heavy moral pressure on Unilever since child labour is dead wrong and all possible "auxiliary troops" should be mobilised to fight it. We may not settle for less.

References

Burgmans, A. 2000. 'De kwaliteitsgarantie in de voedselketen' in SER 2000. 50 jaar Wet op de Bedrijfsorganisatie. Verslag van de bijeenkomst Met raad en daad, 26 May 2000.
Cramer, J. 2005. 'Duurzaam ondernemen in internationaal perspectief' in: FSR Forum, jrg.7, Nr.3 (April), pp. 18–24.
Cramer, J. and Klein, F. 2005. 'Ketenverantwoordelijkheid staat nog in de kinderschoenen' in: Milieutijdschrift ArenA, May, nr.3, pp. 14–15.
Darwall, S. 2006. *The Second-Person Standpoint. Morality, Respect and Accountability.* Cambridge, MA: Harvard University Press.

---

[13] People can feel compelled by the power of their own attraction to ideals, but this is less transferable to others than is the normative force of a minimal duty.

Eshleman, A. 2008. "Moral Responsibility", in *The Stanford Encyclopedia of Philosophy (Fall 2008 Edition)*, Edward N. Zalta (ed.), See http://plato.stanford.edu/archives/fall2008/entries/moral-responsibility/. Last viewed on 9-10-2009.

Online Ethics.org - Glossary 2009. 'Responsibility' http://onlineethics.org/CMS/glossary.aspx?;letter=R Last viewed on 9 October 2009.

SER 2005. Chapter 5: Cooperation and Chain Dependency in: Social and Economic Council of the Netherlands [SER]. *Corporate Social Responsibility. The Dutch Approach,* pp. 59–66, Assen (The Netherlands).

Strawson, P. 1992. Freedom and Resentment. In: Watson, G. (ed.), *Free Will*, (7th edition), pp. 59–80. Oxford: Oxford University Press.

Chapter 21
Commentary: Child Labour, Companies, and Precautions

Robert Heeger

Abstract The report on the cottonseed production in India will probably leave few readers indifferent. The fact that children are still forced to labour at the age of six to fourteen will probably in most of us cause a spontaneous moral reaction: those who make use of child labour do wrong. This thought is associated with a feeling of disapproval. That we react this way indicates that, regarding this issue, certain moral norms are important for us. One such moral norm has traditionally been called the "principle of non-maleficence". This principle states that we must not harm persons or other living beings or, more generally, that we must not bring about evil. Child labour is an evil. We ought not to employ children. But the report is also about indirect involvement in child labour. We are indirectly involved when we, for example, buy goods from someone who makes use of child labour. We then contribute to the continuation of child labour for that person. An objection to such conduct is that it clashes with another norm which in ethics usually is called the "principle of beneficence", for this principle says that we ought to prevent or to remove harm or evil and that we ought to promote good. Moral norms pithily express demands which we, morally speaking, must not ignore. If we refer to moral norms such as the principles mentioned, this has two favourable consequences. First, the norms can support our spontaneous moral reaction to child labour. Second, and above all, they can help us to think through the moral problems of the case. The moral problems of the case which I will focus on emerge from the discussion between the coalition of NGOs and Unilever. The first issue is whether the moral norms of not causing harm, of preventing harm and removing harm actually apply to a company. Is it possible to claim that moral norms which are valid for persons also have validity for companies? I will sketch two lines of reasoning that lead to conflicting results. The second issue is about a company's precautions. Assuming that the moral norms do apply to a company, what precautions should a company take in order to prevent involvement in child labour? In conclusion I will make two suggestions about precaution policies.

R. Heeger (✉)
Ethics Institute, Utrecht University, Utrecht, The Netherlands
e-mail: rheeger@theo.uu.nl

Do the Moral Norms Apply to a Company?

In the present case, the issue of whether moral norms apply to a company arises especially in two places. First, it crops up where the coalition of NGOs *accuses* Unilever *of reprehensible behaviour* because it allegedly refrains from taking its "chain responsibility." The coalition reasons as follows. Even though Unilever and its direct suppliers don't employ children, the cottonseed producing farmers do. As a buyer of the cottonseed Unilever plays a dominant role in the production chain: the company has the power to determine the conditions under which the production elsewhere in the chain takes place. Thus, the company is indirectly involved in child labour there. On this matter it can be morally challenged because a company in this position shows reprehensible behaviour not only if it employs children itself but also if it allows others in the production chain to do so. What the coalition is finding fault with in Unilever is, in terms of the introduction above, that the company does not comply with a particular moral norm. It fails to remove the harm or evil of child labour for farmers elsewhere in the chain. But is it permissible to bring this forward as a moral shortcoming of a *company*?

The issue of whether moral norms apply to a company also comes up where the coalition states that Unilever *has a moral duty* to help combat child labour in the cottonseed production as a whole. The coalition expects Unilever to take this responsibility since the company has relations with the practice of cottonseed production and is in a position to do something about this practice. Thus, the coalition puts forward the moral norm that Unilever must help with removing the harm or evil of child labour in the entire cottonseed production. But is it permissible to claim that a *company* has such a moral duty?

This question is not easily answered. The same goes for the question as to whether it is permissible to accuse a company of morally reprehensible behaviour. It is not immediately clear what answer to choose, because one's answer is also dependent on an issue that should be dealt with beforehand: the issue of whether a company can be considered to be a *bearer of moral responsibility*. Is it possible to maintain that the activity of a company can be judged in moral terms (such as "moral duty" and "reprehensible behaviour"), or must one say that the activity of a company is outside the scope of these terms? To answer this question I will sketch two lines of reasoning which lead to conflicting results because they have different points of departure. The first line of reasoning, which can be called "classical", starts out from the responsibility of a person; the second line, from responsibility in political ethics.

A Company Compared with a Person

Traditionally it is seriously doubted whether the activities of a company can be compared with the actions of a person, morally speaking. Moral duties or moral criticism cannot be addressed to a company because a company differs too much from a human being. We can rightly draw another person's attention to her moral duty, and we can rightly accuse her of morally reprehensible behaviour only if certain conditions are met, but a company doesn't meet these conditions. What these conditions consist in becomes clear if we ask ourselves "when are we allowed to accuse someone of morally reprehensible behaviour?" Our answer will reasonably include that we are allowed to do this only if the other is *morally responsible* for this behaviour, and whether he is indeed responsible depends in turn on at least two requirements. First, it is necessary that he acts *intentionally*, that is, his action is not just a reflex or compulsory, but he knows what he is doing and has the ability to reflect on the reason or the aim of his action. Second, it is necessary that he acts *voluntarily*, that is, he is not exposed to impermissible pressure or coercion. Such requirements of moral responsibility have been discussed at length in the ethical literature (Van den Beld, 1982; Scanlon, 1998; Taylor, 2003).

Few will deny that also a company performs actions. It is a collective actor of a particular kind. It is not just a cooperation of many individuals but also an independent actor with its own aims, a distinct structure, and decision-making procedures of its own, and who provides its managers and employees with specific rules and social roles which make their activity within the company distinct from acting in their private life. However, an independent actor like that does not meet the above requirements of acting intentionally and voluntarily. It doesn't act intentionally (in a literal and not in a purely metaphorical sense) because it cannot "know" what it does and cannot "reflect on the aim" of its action. This can only be done for it by individual persons or by groups of individuals. Neither can one say that it (in a literal sense) acts "voluntarily" because the distinction between acting voluntarily and acting involuntarily refers to a situation where a person tries to make up her mind and where others either can or cannot exert pressure on her or coerce her. Whenever a person tries to make up her mind, this presupposes that she can act intentionally, namely that she can reflect on the reasons or aim of her action. That others can exert pressure on her or can coerce her presupposes that she has something to lose that she doesn't want to lose, for example life, liberty or property. An independent collective actor, however, cannot reflect on the aim of its action and cannot worry about what it may lose. Only individual persons can do this, for example, the representatives within the collective. But if a company as an independent collective actor doesn't act intentionally and voluntarily, we can not say that it is a moral actor since the two necessary conditions are not fulfilled. From this it follows that we are not allowed to accuse a company of morally reprehensible behaviour. Likewise it follows that we cannot rightly attribute moral duties to a company.

If we keep to this line of reasoning, we must conclude that the action of a company cannot be judged in terms of moral duty and reprehensible behaviour. The activity of a company is outside the scope of these terms. This implies that the moral norms of not causing harm, preventing harm and removing harm do not apply to the activity of a company as a whole.

A Company in a Well-Ordered Society

From the point of view of political ethics the result of the classical line of reasoning is unacceptable. One important objection is this. If one asserts that the activity of a company as an independent collective actor is exempt from moral assessment, then one must also keep silent about the fact that a company can cause enormous harm to humans and other living beings. But to keep silent about this is morally wrong. Political ethics, on the other hand, provides reasons why a company too can be confronted with certain moral norms, like those of preventing harm, removing harm and not causing harm. There are three reasons that should be mentioned in particular. First, in a well-ordered society the consequences of companies' actions must be controlled. Second, for that purpose it is indispensable for society to approach companies also on matters of moral duty and morally reprehensible behaviour, because coercion alone, by authority or by law, is both undesirable and insufficient. Third, even without being coerced, a company can accept certain restraints of its freedom of action and modify its behaviour accordingly.

Let me explain these reasons in more detail. They are rooted in a normative theory of society as a fair system of cooperation (Rawls, 1972, 1993; Scanlon, 1998). To be viable a society must be well-ordered. A well-ordered society must solve the basic problems of coordination. In order to achieve this, it must define what each relevant actor owes others, and it must ensure that he fulfils his obligations to others. The first reason above emphasizes that a company is such a crucial actor that the consequences of its activity must be kept under control. The second reason concentrates on the necessary means. To exercise control by governmental or legal coercion alone would be inadequate. It would be undesirable because a meticulous supervision by officials would cripple a free market economy. It would, furthermore, be insufficient because the law has its limits and is moreover often poorly enforceable. Therefore, society must keep companies under control also by means of morality, not least by addressing moral duties and criticism to companies. The third reason says that this is in fact possible. Moral norms such as those of not causing harm, preventing harm and removing harm can be put forward to a company. This is not undermined by the fact that a company is an independent collective actor. For such an actor has the capacity to govern itself in many respects. This includes the ability of a company to freely acknowledge certain constraints, for instance certain duties, and to bring its actions in line with these constraints. A company can take such decisions by means of persons who work for it and who fulfil their specific roles within or on behalf of the company.

It is quite possible to defend these reasons. Therefore, we can rightly assert that the moral norms of preventing harm, removing harm and not causing harm are applicable to a company's activity and that a company is, at least in this sense, a bearer of moral responsibility.

What Precautions Should a Company Take?

Assuming we can agree to what has just been asserted, what does that imply for a company policy on child labour? What do the norms require a company to do? Let me focus on one norm which seems to be particularly important for an anticipatory policy of a company: the norm of preventing harm. This norm says that a company should take precautions concerning child labour. But this prescription is still insufficiently determined. It needs to be specified so that it can express *what precautions* a company should take.

The main reason for specifying the norm is a moral one. The norm needs to be specified in order that one can stipulate which actions are stringently obligatory, and in order that one can know that one's action is in accordance with the norm. If a moral norm is to point out what is stringently obligatory, then it must have boundaries which keep it from spreading out everywhere. Norms without boundaries demand too much and are excessive. This has with good reason been asserted in ethics. One argument is this. If one ignores the fact that a stringently obligatory norm has boundaries, then there is the danger that one's duty turns into an obsession, that is, the norm becomes so dominant that one thinks there is nothing else one is allowed to do but to follow that norm (Fried, 1978).

How should the norm of preventing harm be specified then? What precautions should a company take? If one would demand from a company, say Unilever, that it takes precautions to prevent all child labour in India, one would in all probability assert a norm without boundaries. The scale and complexity of the problem of child labour in the Indian subcontinent are far too big. But what are we to think of the demand that a company should take precautions to prevent getting involved in child labour in the cottonseed production? If one makes this demand, then one probably respects the boundaries of a stringently obligating norm, because one may assume that a company such as Unilever is not devoid of means to prevent involvement in child labour. For instance means to induce other parties in the production chain to change their behaviour. Let me, therefore, focus on this latter specification of the norm.

Two Proposals Regarding Precaution Policies

If one is allowed to demand *that* a company take precautions in order to prevent getting involved in child labour, then the question arises *what* the company should do. This question comes up in the case where the coalition of NGOs criticizes Unilever's prevention policies as insufficient. The criticized policies fall into three categories: the seed agents must get the farmers to sign a contract committing them to comply with all existing regulations, Unilever carries out regular checks in the production chain, and Unilever calls upon all parties to bring forward concrete occurrences which show that children perform labour, in which case Unilever will take measures. The coalition considers these policies inadequate, and this for two reasons. First, child labour is so closely linked with the whole sector that much more is needed than carrying out occasional checks and signing forms on which the suppliers declare to refrain from using child labour. Second, it won't do to burden other parties with the responsibility to detect possible abuses.

This disagreement raises the question as to what precautionary policies a company such as Unilever should pursue. Let me make two suggestions, one about obtaining information, the other about taking measures. The first suggestion is that a company should try to find out whether it is in danger to get involved – directly or indirectly – in child labour. In this matter policies begin with the question, "When is there *sufficient reason* to investigate whether one is getting involved in child labour?" A cautious interpretation of the precautionary principle – familiar in particular from environmental policy – suggests itself. There is sufficient reason, if one has *a reasonable suspicion*, although one has no conclusive scientific evidence yet. The rationale behind this policy is this. If one takes action only when one has conclusive evidence, then it will often be months before one can respond effectively, and this may be too late (Gremmen & Van den Belt, 2000). The precautionary principle also gives rise to a further question, to wit: has one done enough in order to get to know what one should know? This question concerns the carefulness of the investigation. Carefulness is important because superficial information may leave a company in ignorance about the facts. To mention some examples, abuses may not be reported for fear of the consequences, contracts may be signed but not observed, or child labour may remain invisible during incidental checks because the age of the children is being misstated. If a company is to acquire the necessary knowledge, it would probably have to choose a *case by case* approach, it would have to get over the possibly great difficulties of systematic inspections – from physical violence to deceit – and it would have to work together with other – local, national or international – organisations.

Precautionary policies are of course not limited to obtaining information. They must also include measures to be taken in cases where a reasonable suspicion has been corroborated by inspections. That is the subject of my second suggestion. This suggestion amounts to the following. It is insufficient to lay down in *contracts* that the parties concerned shall not make use of child labour, and in case of non-observance to break off the cooperation. For to compel a supplier to dismiss children would only shift the problem. The children would lose their income and would probably be forced to take other, possibly more dangerous, jobs. Therefore, further measures must be considered. First, a company must look for a *well thought-out solution*. This requires that the managers must be made conscious of the just mentioned complexity of the child labour problem. Second, a company must try and find such a well thought-out solution by choosing an *integral approach*. Something must be done in order that the children can support themselves, can be educated, etc. This must be done in cooperation with the parties concerned as well as with other organisations, such as other companies, local government and NGOs.

References

Beld, A. 1982. *Filosofie van het menselijk handelen*. Assen: Van Gorcum.
Fried, Ch. 1978. Right and Wrong as Absolute. In: *Right and Wrong*, pp. 7–29. Cambridge: Cambridge University Press.
Gremmen, B. and Belt, H. 2000. The Precautionary Principle and Pesticides. *Journal of Agricultural and Environmental Ethics*, 12: 197–205.

Rawls, J. 1972. *A Theory of Justice*. Oxford: Oxford University Press.
Rawls, J. 1993. *Political Liberalism*. New York, NY: Columbia University Press.
Scanlon, T.M. 1998. *What We Owe to Each Other*. Cambridge, MA: Harvard University Press.
Taylor, J.S. 2003. Autonomy, Duress and Coercion. *Social Philosophy and Policy*, XX(2): 127–155.

Part VIII
Case G: Rise and Fall of Silicon Valley in Flanders – Lernout & Hauspie Speech Products

Chapter 22
Case Description: Rise and Fall of Silicon Valley in Flanders – Lernout & Hauspie Speech Products

Marc Buelens and Eva Cools

Abstract The early years of Lernout & Hauspie (L&H) were turbulent. The company crawled from one financial crisis to the other. At the beginning they repeatedly had to go to friends, acquaintances, distant acquaintances, local businessmen (butchers and bakers) and farmers. A prime minister, a provincial governor and various mayors, even the heir to the throne all spoke in public and often showed their unconditional support with financial resources. In 1995, L&H became listed on the US Nasdaq technology exchange. Starting in 1996, the company started along the takeover path. Among the companies it acquired were its two most important US rivals, Dictaphone Corporation (7 March 2000) and Dragon Systems (27 March 2000). The company displayed spectacular growth and drew new investors. In 1997 Microsoft invested $45 million to acquire nearly 8% of the shares. Later it became clear that the board at L&H grossly underestimated one factor: the last two takeovers meant that nearly half their turnover was generated in the USA. L&H's management was clearly no match for the US press and analysts that smelled blood. The financial operations were far from transparent and most experts became convinced that L&H was a clear case of fraud. Bankruptcy became unavoidable.

The Founders

Jo Lernout, then 39, and Pol Hauspie, then 36, founded the public limited company Lernout on 10 December 1987. Two years later the company changed its name to Lernout & Hauspie Speech Products (in Flanders mostly known as L&H). Friends and acquaintances helped set up the company; it had €300,000 in capital, but not all of that was in a bank account. There was "creative" contribution in kind consisting of know-how. This kind of contribution is rare when setting up

---

M. Buelens (✉)
Vlerick Leuven Gent Management School, Ghent University, Gent, Belgium
e-mail: marc.buelens@vlerick.com

a company; civil-law notaries do not accept it without reason; at the very least it requires a report from an external accountant. The first shareholders were promised that they would be paid back within 18 months. So from the company's very start, Jo Lernout and Pol Hauspie had to be on the lookout for new investors. This became a constant theme running through the story (De Witte et al., 2002). They repeatedly found themselves with their backs to the wall financially. They repeatedly had to go to friends, acquaintances, distant acquaintances, local businessmen (butchers and bakers) and farmers. L&H was once called a "14-year search for money" (Van Apeldoorn, 2001).

The founders' had an ambitious goal for L&H from the very start. They wanted to make it the world leader in speech and language technology. L&H's mission was to supply all imaginable speech and language technology applications. Moreover, L&H intended to supply these core technologies for all imaginable types of processors and for multiple languages. To carry out this mission, Jo Lernout and Pol Hauspie signed licensing contracts with three Belgian laboratories that held world-class status in speech and language technology at that time. Later, L&H would sign more licensing and joint venture contracts and would hire international experts. The many takeovers that started in 1996 would turn the company into the world leader in speech technology in the second half of the 1990s.

By appealing to farmers, political leaders, bankers, bicycle racers, local businesses and housewives, Lernout and Hauspie served an educational role, first in the immediate vicinity, later in the province of West Flanders and finally, throughout the Flemish region. Flemings had to learn to invest in venture capital. Doubters were proven wrong at all technology trade fairs. Many, common people and professional investors alike, invested unconditionally and took substantial financial risks to invest even more. Investing in L&H became a sign of patriotism for people in the province and the region. Moreover, the project was nearly certain to provide a nice yield. And who would think of doubting... a royal prince, a prime minister, a provincial governor and various mayors, even the heir to the throne all spoke in public and often showed their unconditional support with financial resources.

Jo Lernout is a visionary, a salesman. The man has a compelling vision. With a BA in science he had enough technical and scientific training to understand the technical background of speech and language technologies. As experienced salesman at Wang, as driven personality, as honest local boy, he was able to convince everyone that the future of speech technology had already started. Whether in the smallest church hall, the best-filled convention centre or most highly educated auditoriums, it was always the same: Jo Lernout was the top of the bill. Disarming, never arrogant, clear as crystal, he set his listeners dreaming by taking them on a trip along the endless applications for speech technology. Surgeons, drivers, even housewives: how have they all managed to survive without speech technology? We will all soon be talking to our refrigerators and our cars. We will be able to speak on the phone with the Chinese because super-powerful software will translate our words into Mandarin and back again. Jo Lernout gave awesome demonstrations of speech and translation technology that worked, of voiceXpress packages and virtual management assistants. The future had really begun. Moore's law, which states that the capacity of a computer chip doubles every 18 months, is indeed a law of nature and the consequences can scarcely be grasped. It is as plain as the nose on your face that computers will soon be smarter than people. Then we will *have* to talk to them because language is humanity's natural medium for communication.

Pol Hauspie's interest was clearly on the financial side. He had an office for software accounting (HPP: Hauspie Pol Poperinge) in Poperinge, the city that made him an honorary citizen in 1999. That office was a formidable competitor for some of Wang's products. That is how Jo Lernout came to meet him. They gradually became real friends and dreamt of a new company. The unconditional bonds of trust certainly do not date from the 1st day. Before they set out together in 1987, they took a few days off together in the Ardennes woodlands at Pol Hauspie's suggestion. They became better friends as their contacts and shared activities increased. "We're brothers", Pol Hauspie would often repeat. Where Jo Lernout was known as a shrewd salesman, everyone knew that Pol Hauspie was the prototypically rock-solid, meticulous, one-hundred-percent-reliable, nose-to-the-grindstone worker, the model of the idealistic, authentically Catholic native of West Flanders. Pol is intensely religious and very active in his church choir.

Rooted in the Vicinity

Lernout and Hauspie had their roots in the broad neighbourhood around Ypres. As soon as they raised enough cash, they did all they could to put their home province on the world map. L&H would sponsor the most wide-ranging projects from a local basketball club to a language technology park called Flanders Language Valley. But above all, they were driven by a higher calling. They wanted to increase employment in that out-of-the-way part of Flanders. On 21 January 2001, honorary citizen Pol Hauspie addressed the Poperinge municipal council. He called upon them to support him in his efforts to provide employment in the area. Later, long after the debacle, Jo Lernout commented:

> We were a company that almost anachronistically wanted to provide employment in our home area. (Claeys, 2005)

The two entrepreneurs' ties with the area are legendary. This is a company set up by West Flanders natives, with West Flanders capital and a West Flanders mentality: work hard and smart, take well calculated risks. Looking back at the collapse of his company, ever hard-working Jo Lernout said:

> I come from a family where all were intensely religious, Catholic and self-employed. I inherited a strong work ethic from my parents. In good times and bad, the message was keep on working. (Claeys, 2005)

Jo and Pol, as everyone called them, because of course everyone in the area knew them, remained modest, meticulous workers who had invested in the future technology. They held up a mirror for their area. Everyone could see that what Jo and Pol did was good. The people in the area were grateful. Jo and Pol were awarded the most prestigious honours that West Flanders had to give: following in the footsteps of eminent writers Hugo Verriest and Stijn Streuvels, political leaders Achilles van Acker and Dries Vlerick and eminent business leaders Anton Beeckaert and Jan Lannoo, they became "Knights of West Flanders" in 2000 in service of the local secret societies like *De Swighenden Eede* and *t Manneke uit de Mane*.

The First Step Is Always the Hardest, and Certainly for L&H

L&H's early years, right after 1987, were turbulent. The company crawled from one financial crisis to the other. Jo Lernout recalls that at one time they could not pay their staff and a bailiff threatened to impound the company's assets. The persistent stream of crises elicited from Jo Lernout the oft-cited statement:

> the grass is always greener on the edge of the abyss. (De Witte et al., 2002)

Jo Lernout and Pol Hauspie had a dream but no money. They continually had to look for investors, because R&D was expensive. L&H became one long round of pass-the-hat in which they often had to use their personal assets as guarantee. To attract investors, Jo Lernout and Pol Hauspie also had to do more than tell a nice story. Potential investors also wanted to see some tangible achievements. The pressure to prove that the technology works meant that L&H initially developed products that were really no more than gadgets, like a talking Christmas tree decoration. Jo Lernout and Pol Hauspie tried a different approach to carry out their mission. Instead of working on practical applications for end users, L&H turned to the development of basic technology. L&H wanted to develop a standard, preferably a world standard. But the direction they were heading never changed completely. The manoeuvring act only got more daring. Money remained a problem. At the same time, more institutions invested in speech technology, including the Flemish government and an investment company that it controlled. As with so many technology companies, most of these investors put their hopes in the future. Analysts considered speech and language technology the next technological wave in what could be a market worth millions of dollars (Maremont et al., 2000). L&H became the focus of the biannual Flanders Technology International trade fair. As of 1997, plans for Flanders Language Valley started to ripen. Jo Lernout and Pol Hauspie dreamt of attracting other companies that also work on speech and language technology. In that way, they hoped to give back something to the area and create two thousand jobs in and around Flanders Language Valley. The 60-acre industrial site opened at the end of 1999. A cluster of companies built on the talents of polyglot Flemings would definitively put Ypres on the world map. Jo Lernout and Pol Hauspie were convinced that language technology was *the* up and coming thing and that Flanders was the ideal place for developing this new industry because Belgium was a multilingual country with extensive language teaching.

In 1995, L&H became listed on the US Nasdaq technology exchange. L&H's flotation was a natural step in the company's evolution and seemed to be a success from the start. The introduction on the NY exchange not only stilled the voracious hunger for financial resources, it made L&H international and respectable all at once. However, listing on the Stock Exchange and the accompanying enormous expectations of investors at home and abroad, put the management under very great pressure to report better figures each quarter. Above all, it put the company under the surveillance of the Securities and Exchange Commission (SEC), the US exchange authority.

At that time, L&H still had not turned a profit and its sales were hardly more than a few million euros. Sales would rise exponentially in the subsequent years. The share price swung spectacularly from $11 at the time of flotation (1 December 1995) to $16 at the end of the 1st day then to $45 and $92, to between $75 and $80, back to $25, up to $72, only to crash first to $28 then to $13 and finally to nearly zero.

Gold Fever

The 1990s were known for an economic mentality that – in retrospect can no longer be considered reasonable, but that investment banks, consultants, business schools and, especially, the financial economic press all accepted at the time. It became clear later that all the conditions for a bubble were present, but at the time few seemed to be concerned about this. On the contrary, those who listened to prophets of doom in 1995 missed out on tremendous stock market yield because they apparently still did not understand that a "new" economy had arisen.

Internet and ICT caused a shift in economic and financial thinking. Nasdaq and Easdaq (the European counterpart of the US technology exchange) are two new exchanges set up solely for technology shares because these shares had their own dynamism. For them, growth was much more important than dividends. Operational profit was considered a misleading indicator. The link between share price and profit figures was considered broken. It was crucially important to be the first to develop new products, the fruits of new technology. Only at a later stage did sales become important. And only after that did profit become pertinent. Once the product had a near monopoly, the profits would be gigantic. These expected profits were capitalised on the market in anticipation.

Investors did not speculate on profit or dividend but on the increase in share value. The more and the faster the products were developed and brought to market, the greater the share value would become. Capital gains of 200% and 300% in just a few months were no longer just a dream. It could happen. It had happened. It would happen again. Gold fever was rampant. The first to lay claim to a vein could sell the claim the next day at considerable profit, long before the first ounce of gold was extracted.

Companies bought other companies and paid in shares in the new merger. Everyone won, because the mere announcement of the merger sent share prices up. The seller got an extra amount on top of the sales price, the buyer did not have to fork out any cash. New investors entered the market goaded on by the perception of permanent price gains. But good news was needed every quarter: new products that passed tests, new investors clamouring to get in, another company bought, and the sales of new products that far exceeded grandest hopes. When the supply of good news faltered, share prices could take a nosedive turning the company into a takeover target.

Sometimes a Little Less Scrupulous...

In January, 1997, readers of the weekly business magazine *Trends* voted Jo Lernout and Pol Hauspie 1996 managers of the year, a prestigious and striking distinction. Their comment was:

> From an ethical perspective, we never overstepped the line. If we had done that, we would have ceased to exist, because then the trap would have sprung shut. Anyone examining our balance in September 1995 before the Nasdaq launch would have seen that we carried a cumulative net loss of $72 million on our books. Our operating capital was in the red. Yet our greatest asset didn't show up in the balance: the loyalty of customers, suppliers and staff. You can't assign numbers to such things. Yet they are crucial. If you make a mistake there, you've had it. (Buelens, 2002; Kay, 2003)

Later, Lernout will adapt his outlook to the perception of the rest of the world:

> It can be asked whether all aspects of the way we treated our shareholders was by right and factually ethical. (Trends, 1997)

The founders seemed on occasion to be not scrupulous enough in their choice of staff and associates. In 1993, L&H contacted Maurits De Prins, a very controversial businessman and former head of Super Club, a video chain store. In 1996, they set out with Ray Kurzweil, best known from his books *The Age of Intelligent Machines* (1990) and *The Age of Spiritual Machines* (1999). But in 1993 Kurzweil Applied Intelligence was discredited when accountants discovered evidence of fraud in the books. A lot of the turnover turned out to be imaginary. In 1996 before L&H set out with Ray Kurzweil, *BusinessWeek* wrote the following in response to the proceedings against several former senior staff members at Kurzweil Applied Intelligence:

> Ethical experts say the decision to keep phony revenues in the records may arise from a misguided sense of loyalty. "Executives in this type of situation often have an emotional investment in the company... They have all this wonderful stuff to offer the world. So they rationalize. They say, 'We'll do this temporarily, and that will give us time to make it all come out right'. But instead, they dig themselves in deeper". (Claeys, 2005)

Then they recruited Gaston Bastiaens in 1996. He was known in the technology community mainly for his failures (Apple's Newton, Philips' CD-I) and for contested transactions at software company Quarterdeck.

Later, Lebanese-Armenian businessman Harout Khatchadourian proved to be involved in financing L&H. He put in $36 million. His name struck a sour note in Flanders. He may have been involved in a possible case of tax fraud related to the Beaulieu textile empire via a secret system of fake commissions set up by his father Aram Khatchadourian. Even now this case has not been brought to court. Nevertheless, the association of the name Khatchadourian with L&H surprised everyone in Flanders.

A Growth Company Needs a Lot of Money

L&H constantly needed a large flow of money. Starting in 1996, the company started along the takeover path. Among the companies it acquired were: Mendez Translations (10 September 1996), a Spanish, German and Italian translation agency (5 November 1996), Berkeley Speech Technologies (27 November 1996), Kurzweil Applied Intelligence (16 April 1997), Gesellschaft für Multilanguage Systeme (28 May 1997), and above all its two most important US rivals, Dictaphone Corporation (7 March 2000) and Dragon Systems (27 March 2000). Few people seemed concerned that Dictaphone Corporation had debt to the tune of €450 million. Later it became clear that the board at L&H grossly underestimated one factor: the last two takeovers meant that nearly half their turnover was generated in the USA. That meant that detailed accounts had to be submitted to the SEC, the US stock exchange watchdog. L&H's management was clearly no match for the US press and analysts that smelled blood. The last shred of goodwill was lost when L&H insulted stock exchange analysts ("if you're too stupid to understand...")[1] and made statements that came back like a boomerang, "there is nothing wrong in being smart" (Maremont, 1996; De Witte et al., 2002).

Cooked Books or High-Tech Finance?

As L&H grew it became obvious that the butcher and baker were no longer sufficient to satisfy the company's nearly insatiable need for fresh capital. Pol Hauspie was co-designer of a series of complex financing plans. The founders used a complicated holding structure to keep a firm grasp on all this (De Witte et al., 2002). Jo Lernout and Pol Hauspie set up L&H Holding, a company under Belgian law. Its purpose was to organise supervision of L&H and to keep it rooted in Flanders. L&H Holding was involved in investments in the networks around L&H. According to Jo Lernout, this was Pol Hauspie's strong point:

> He is very creative. Legally it's all right, and it helps you survive. (Merchant et al., 2003)

In addition they set up numerous financial structures outside of L&H, the best known being language development companies (LDCs). The LDCs held licences to develop L&H's basic technology for use with a specific language group. For instance, LDCs were set up to develop speech recognition systems for Arabic and Hindi. Were L&H to do this work themselves, it would increase costs and push down the bottom line

---

[1] See also: www.businessweek.com/1996/38/b3493123.htm last viewed 19 Oct. 2009.

on the income and expenditure account. When a language development company did the job and paid royalties to L&H, L&H booked a nice turnover instead of a loss. For their books to be in order, the LDCs had to be financially independent of L&H and L&H could not do the developing. Gradually people began to suspect that neither was the case.

Credit default swaps, i.e. selling part of the risk on a loan, and other techniques were used to keep various credit risks off the balance sheet. Artesia Bank, L&H's principal banker, provided a €28 million bridging facility in 1998 and 1999. It was later suspected that this money was used to book phony sales. Loans were also turned into sales via a detour to South Korea; contracts were antedated which raised turnover and the bonuses linked to them. These and other practices were later bandied about in the media. No one was ever sure whether they simply lied about these and other constructions or whether they thought these were normal constructions for a growth company in the new economy. For the purely juridical side of the case – were the financing mechanisms used legal or fraudulent? – we must of course wait for the court's decision (Maremont et al., 2000).

On 27 July 2000, L&H Holding sold no fewer than 625,000 shares to Gaston Bastiaens, who held operational management of the company from 1996 to 2000. He paid €40 per share, while the market price was €30. Bastiaens borrowed $25 million from Artesia Bank Nederland to buy the shares. The revenue from the sale accrued to Jo Lernout, Pol Hauspie and Nico Willaert, a less visible personage behind the scenes at L&H, someone with good contacts (e.g. the royal family). The sum was directly placed in short-term investments (De Standaard, 2003). A series of transfer operations, possible double use of guarantees and shady reinvestments give the impression that L&H wanted to use the same money twice. It was later uncertain which bank owned the sum, because several pledges proved worthless after the bankruptcy. This situation put several banks in serious difficulty. The minimum that can be said is that the transfer operations were far from transparent; later the media would severely criticize it and it would result in a court case. Nevertheless, the company displayed spectacular growth and drew new investors. In 1997 Microsoft invested $45 million to acquire nearly 8% of the shares. Bill Gates came to offer his personal support when Flanders Language Valley opened. Everyone seemed to be there: Belgium's prime minister, Flanders' minister president, leading industrialists and even Prince Philip, the heir to the throne. In 1999, Intel invested $30 million. Anyone who had any doubts about Jo Lernout and Pol Hauspie was clearly someone with no feeling for facts.

A Fine Piece of Research Journalism

While L&H's figures for 2000 were not examined too closely in Flanders, they raised some hard questions in the US. The books showed that 52% of L&H's first quarter sales in 2000 came from South Korea. In a year's time, sales increased by a factor of 607. Two *Wall Street Journal* reporters went to Korea to document the spectacular growth. They came across remarkable data. One company said it had not bought anything from L&H but *sold* to it. Three other companies had to that point never bought anything. Three others had bought, but for much less than claimed. Still another said that it bought no products, but that a joint venture with L&H had bought them. L&H tried to show that it was all a misunderstanding; it commissioned auditing company Klynveld Peat Marwick Goerdeler (KPMG) to perform a special audit. Later, once Gaston Bastiaens was dismissed because he lost confidence after the revelations, the new management asked PricewaterhouseCoopers to examine the books again.

John Duerden, formerly of Dictaphone, took Bastiaens' place in 2000. He, in turn, left amid a full-blown crisis in January 2001 to make room for Philippe Bodson, the epitome of Belgian management. When Bodson learned of the fraud discovery, he said he

> "was very impressed by the level of sophistication" of the fraud and "the amount of imagination that went into it."[2]

Flanders quickly divided into a camp that retained and a camp that lost faith in L&H. The local area remained loyal; local political figures continued to voice their support. Those who remained loyal started to believe in a conspiracy theory. They thought the US government did not want a Belgian company to own critical technology. In this theory, speech recognition, given the numerous military applications, had to be brought under full US control. L&H had to be eliminated. Under such circumstances, they thought, it was easy to find a Korean stick to beat down a pup in West Flanders. Jo Lernout did not support this theory, "I don't think there was any conspiracy. No one forced us to the takeover of Dictaphone – a US company with a large turnover and high debt ratio – just to make it easier to bring us down" (Carreyrou, 2001).[3] However, in later interviews, Lernout dramatically changed his tone, attributing the downfall of his company to a CIA-conspiracy.

Lawyers in the Lead

After the economic turbulence came the legal turmoil. On 21 September 2000, the US Securities and Exchange Commission (SEC) launched an official investigation into L&H's financial reporting. On 9 November 2000, L&H distributed two press releases. In the first they admitted that "some errors and irregularities were found" in the accounts for 1998, 1999 and the first two quarters of 2000. The second announced the resignations of Lernout, Hauspie and Willaert. The court in Ypres instituted a preliminary investigation on 12 November 2000. At L&H's request, two accounting firms examined its figures: first KPMG then PricewaterhouseCoopers. KPMG seemed to be both judge and party. The office served as external accountant

---

[2] See also: www.businessweek.com/datedtoc/2000/0038.htm last viewed 19 Oct 2009.
[3] See also: www.tomcoyner.com/auditors_investigation_finds_70.htm last viewed 19 Oct 2009.

and at least one key staff member had received an important position in the network around L&H. KPMG ascertained that the management systematically passed on misleading information. The report that PricewaterhouseCoopers released on 6 April 2001 said that 70% of the income attributed to L&H's Korean department was imaginary. On 26 April 2001 the Belgian Justice department ordered the founders' arrest – in genuine US style complete with handcuffs – on suspicion of forgery, falsification of annual financial reports and price manipulation. They were kept in preliminary detention for 9 weeks. The company's operations continued under a temporary court-ratified composition; it worked on setting up a credible recovery plan.

October 2001: The Curtain Falls

Commercial court judge Michel Handschoewerker had to conclude that the recovery plan was de facto a liquidation plan.

> Under those circumstances, the court cannot offer the company protection against its creditors. (De Standaard, 2003)

Bankruptcy became unavoidable.

The bankruptcy hit many small investors like an uppercut. Political leaders maintained a discrete silence. Banks that appeared to have granted loans without any real collateral now licked their wounds. Suits were prepared in Asia, the US and Belgium. Employees were let go. The local community was traumatised. Flanders Language Valley became a ghost town.

The questions around Flanders' most visible and spectacular bankruptcy continue to spark controversy. L&H has left many Flemings with permanent scars. Is the L&H debacle a classic example of run-away entrepreneurship? Or is it simply large-scale fraud? The courts still have to decide on the legal aspects. But can we point to a place where, ethically seen, things began to go wrong? No one has ever asserted or seriously defended the idea that Jo and Pol were thieves from the start. They undoubtedly had 100% faith in their dream. Is there a correlation with the hiring of new people? Without doubt. But a correlation is not a causal link. Why did a company so closely associated with the local social and economic fabric come to such a brutal end?

May 2007: The Trial

The fraud trial started at the Ghent appellate court on 21 May 2007. Hundreds of angry investors attended the 1st day. The financial press was mainly interested in the fact that financial services group Dexia and accounting firm KPMG were among those charged. Twenty-one persons were charged with accounting fraud and manipulating share prices. It was claimed that some 50,000 people lost money. The courthouse was deemed too small and the trial took place in a convention centre.

Prosecution spokesman Dominique Debrauwere told journalists,

> The revenue was dramatically overstated between 1997 and 2000 and this led to investors and potential investors being misinformed about the true state of the company's finances. (Scheidtweiler, 2002)

In January 2008 Pol Hauspie pleaded guilty, much to the dismay of Jo Lernout who still claimed his innocence: the technology was real, and the sales were genuine. The company was the victim of a CIA-conspiracy. Lernout remains the strongest believer. He told the court: "Google could have been in Flanders" (Lernout, 2005).

The trial's complexity (340,000 pages), the number of accused, and endless procedural matters proved a hindrance. The verdict is expected for the fall of 2010.

References

Buelens, M. 2002. *Managementshock*. Tielt: Lannoo.
Carreyrou, J. 2001. Lernout Unit Book Fictitious Sales, Says Probe. *Wall Street Journal*, 9 April, p. B2. See also: http://www.tomcoyner.com/auditors_investigation_finds_70.htm last viewed 19 Oct 2009.
Claeys, R. 2005. Had ik geweten dat het zulke proporties zou aannemen, ik had het wellicht niet aangedurfd. *Trends*, 13 January, p. 86.
De Standaard. 2003. Gerecht brengt rol van banken in L&H affaire in kaart. *De Standaard*, 21 Jun., 24.
De Witte, R., Van Aelst, L. and Van Peteghem, L. 2002. *De L&H Files: Lernout & Hauspie, het verhaal en de geheimen*, p. 45. Tielt: Lannoo.
Echikson, W. and Moon, I. 2000. How to spook investors, *BusinessWeek*, 18 September, p. 69. See also: http://www.businessweek.com/datedtoc/2000/0038.htm last viewed 19 Oct 2009.
Kay, J. 2003. *The Truth about Markets*. London: Allen Lane.
Lernout, J. 2005. België heeft het kind met het badwater weggegooid, *Trends*, 13 January, p. 85.
Maremont, M., 1996. Anatomy of a fraud, *BusinessWeek*, 16 September, p. 28. See also: http://www.businessweek.com/1996/38/b3493123.htm last viewed 19 Oct. 2009.
Maremont, M., Eisinger, J. and Carreyrou, J. 2000. Muffled voice: How High-tech Dream at Lernout & Hauspie Crumbled in Scandal, *Wall Street Journal*, 7 December, p. A1. See also: http://www.tomcoyner.com/how_high.htm last viewed on 19 October 2009.
Merchant, K.A., Van der Stede, W.A. and Chen, X. 2003. Case Study: Lernout & Hauspie Speech Products. In: Merchant, K.A. and Van der Stede, W.A. (eds.), *Management Control Systems: Performance Measurement, Evaluation and Incentives*. Harlow: Pearson Education Limited.
Scheidtweiler, J. 2002. L&H-machine kwam een jaar geleden tot stilstand, *De Morgen*, 24 October, p. 20.
Trends, 1997. Verkiezing Managers van het Jaar. *Trends*, 9 Jan. p. 45.
Van Apeldoorn, R. 2001. *De Windmakers: het Lernout & Hauspie-drama*. Kalmthout: Biblio.

Chapter 23
Commentary: Law Versus Community

Luc van Liedekerke

Abstract We analyse the L&H case from three perspectives macro, meso and micro. The macro perspective concentrates on the impossible growth strategy that was the strategic background for the dotcom bubble. The meso and microlevel concentrate on the central role of local community commitment in the L&H case. It opened up a morally blind spot with respect to legal rules that from a local perspective were judged to be a pure administrative burden and not a proper source of information for investors. Combined with a failing oversight role by auditors and banks alike, the moral blind spot turned into a massive investment fraud.

Introduction

On the 9th of February 2006, US company Nuance Communications acquired Dictaphone. What appeared to be a purely US transaction left many Flemings with a bitter taste. Nuance Communications is the former Scansoft that ran off with all the L&H technology after its spectacular $40-million downfall. Scansoft succeeded in doing what L&H never managed to accomplish, but at the same time it demonstrated that Lernout and Hauspie's vision was indeed correct. First, the industrial product they were offering – speech technology – is an essential element in the information storage and processing industry. And secondly, the L&H business strategy – consolidation via takeover – is crucial for a company's long-term survival in this field.[1] Why did Scansoft succeed were L&H failed, why did things go so spectacularly wrong for L&H? We will answer this question on three levels: micro, meso and macro. At the macro-level we concentrate on the high risk growth strategy that caused the dotcom bubble. At the meso level we demonstrate how strong local

---

L. van Liedekerke (✉)
Centre for Economics and Ethics, Katholieke Universiteit Leuven, Leuven, Belgium
e-mail: Luc.Vanliedekerke@econ.kuleuven.be

[1] This is also evident from a lecture *The Rise and Fall of L&H* that Professor Dirk Van Compernolle gave as part of a series entitled *Seminars about Language Engineering Applications*, at KULeuven's Department of Metallurgy on 26 February 2002.

community commitment interfered with respect for the law. At the micro level we discuss the level of personal responsibility in the debacle. The interaction between the three different levels of analysis allows us to better understand how the leaders of this company developed a morally blind spot that led to massive fraud and thousands of victims.

Manias Panics and Crashes: The Macro Level

In a book entitled *Manias, Panics and Crashes*, historian and economist Charles Kindleberger examines several historical examples of euphoria in the financial sector; each of which had quickly turned to panic and ended in a fatal crash. That also is the story of the technology bubble that dominated financial markets in the 1990s. This macro-context serves as backdrop for L&H's drama. Growth – the top line – not profit is what counted. Being the biggest was most important because the only options were to eat or be eaten. The wave of mergers depended on a seldom-witnessed stock market surge. Shares created a fast growing mountain of capital for companies on the hunt for takeovers: Enron, Worldcom and L&H. They all followed the same strategy. This strategy also seemed inevitable. Anyone not joining the rush was overtaken and taken over. Nevertheless, it was an extremely dangerous strategy. A fast growing accumulation of share capital can collapse as quickly as it has been created; everything depends on the quarterly figures. These have to give the right signals to analysts and other financial pundits. Given the economic cycle, the strategy was bound to collapse for fundamental reasons. Sooner or later there comes a time when good results slacken and turn into feeble results. But by then everyone on the way down the takeover path has become so dependent on share price that any drop in that price can put the company's continuance at risk. And suddenly several people found themselves at the wrong side of the law, fudging accounts because it seemed unthinkable to abandon the growth path. Audit firms, which at that time were still trying to butter their bread on both sides and which often earned more with consulting than from auditing, had first-hand experience of this dilemma and would not be quick to halt the forward momentum of growth companies that provided them with so much work. So they designed new, creative ways of keeping accounts that enabled them to disguise economically disappointing results or even to turn them into positive results. It tempted companies like Enron and L&H to continue the impossible strategy. In this sense the role of banks and auditors is morally questionable. Both play a delegated monitoring role for anyone investing money in these growth companies yet both allowed bookkeeping to get off track in order to save the firm and their capital investment and consulting fees.

Loyalty to West Flanders: The Meso Level

Unlike their Protestant Dutch neighbours, Flemings are not champions in rule-following. The reasons are rooted in history. One result of having been dominated by foreigners for centuries seems to be that Flemings offer little protest against their rulers' caprice. They manage dextrously and cautiously to side-step legal regulations, instead.[2] For Flemings, legal regulations are external givens to be regarded with distrust. What is true of Flemings as a whole is supremely true of the West Flanders natives, an area commonly described as Belgium's Texas. The L&H story was a dyed-in-the-wool West-Flanders tale. The founders are natives of West Flanders in heart and soul; the venture capital came from West Flanders; many employees were from West Flanders and L&H explicitly preferred to recruit locally even though it was an international technology company. Jo Lernout sprouted from a family of fourteen children, was a picture of simplicity, and up to this very day is still a local hero. Pol Hauspie is intensely religious, introvert, stubborn and hardworking. Both are ambitious, both take risks and are stubbornly persistent: another series of characteristics to which West Flemings gladly own up. These two driving forces introduced a tightly woven, family atmosphere into a company that looked upon loyalty as the highest value.[3]

That Flemings look askance at legal regulations does not mean that rules are unimportant in Flanders. Flemings have a strong culture the rules of which do not necessarily coincide with what is written in the law. When there is a conflict, insiders will quickly tend to refer first to their own rules and look to the legal rules originating outside the local community at a later stage, regarding them at best as open to creative interpretation. This "we-they" perspective is a constant in Jo Lernout and Frieda Joris's book (2005). It describes political leaders in Brussels as "the swellheads in Brussels" (Lernhout and Joris, 2005: 105) and outside shareholders are thanked for their capital but are expected to abstain from posing inconvenient questions. "We in West Flanders are the boss here" (Lernhout and Joris, 2005: 139) and this at a time that those in West Flanders held no more than 10% of the shares. It seems anachronistic, but this high-tech company, this international rising star remained totally local right to the very end. Venture capital requires faith and this faith was rooted in a West Flanders identity that was engrained in the company and its financiers. There was never a critical voice from within; critical voices that did not speak with a West Flanders accent went unheard or met with disbelieve. That, too, is part of a strong local culture.

When the painful truth about L&H slowly came to light, it was a great shock for all of Flanders but above all for the area around Ypres (L&H's home turf). A variety of denial strategies arose immediately. Many people kept believing that L&H's downfall was orchestrated by the CIA because the acquisition of Dictaphone put sensitive information under Flemish control. And Jo Lernout took hold of those ideas with both hands. His book reads like a settling of the scores with John Duerden and Philippe Bodson – the two outsiders, the first from the US, the second representing those swellheads in Brussels. It also reads like a conspiracy story that explains why L&H was not permitted to survive. "For America it was not only a disgrace

---

[2] At one time the Belgian underground, or "black", economy was estimated to equal 25% of Belgium's GNP, a European record.

[3] During start up L&H found itself on numerous occasions without the resources to pay its personnel on time; but that was no reason for employees to leave the company. Loyalty reigned.

that two Belgians owned that [speech technology for espionage services], it was also unthinkable that defence secrets could be leaked to Ypres" (Lernhout and Joris, 2005: 136).

Personal Responsibility: The Micro Level

> From an ethical perspective, we never crossed the line. If we had done that, we would have ceased to exist, because then the trap would have sprung shut. Anyone examining our balance in September 1995 before the NASDAQ launch will see that we have a cumulative net loss of $72 million on our books. Our operating capital was in the red. Yet our greatest asset didn't show up in the balance: the loyalty of customers, suppliers and staff. You can't assign numbers to such things. Yet they are crucial. If you make a mistake there, you've had it (Trends, 9 January 1997:7; translation by author).

These are the words of Jo Lernout and Pol Hauspie. It was January 1997, L&H was growing at full speed. It is typical that Lernout and Hauspie equate ethics here with loyalty to customers, employees and suppliers, i.e. to the company's local core in West Flanders. In their view, ethics does not have meaning on the balance sheet. And that's where matters take a wrong turn. The strong internal company culture bended the externally imposed accounting regulations without second thoughts. This approach will ultimately collide with the US financial environment that is much more stringently rule-conscious and rule-driven. The first accusations, that came as early as 1999, were easily disposed of. A side effect of the acquisition of Dictaphone was that L&H became subject to even stricter accounting requirements. The company proved unable to cope with the new transparency.

Even now Jo Lernout regards himself as an honest person who had no bad intentions and who had no intention to deceive anybody.

> "Pol [Hauspie], Louis Verbeke and I were overconfident boy scouts. We ran around in short pants and were not qualified to sit down at the table with the big boys in suits," (Lernout, 2005: 139)

Again we are confronted with the self-legitimizing picture of the simple, somewhat naive but thoroughly honest boy scout from West Flanders and the nobs from Brussels and the USA. It is clear that in his mind the real bad guys are not the boy scouts but the men in suits that succeeded in ousting the boy scouts. Yet from the start the veracity of the company's accounts was an easy target.[4] As was the lot of external shareholders who relied on these figures. The occasionally suspect employees that Jo Lernhout and Paul Hauspie attracted were all masters in obfuscating the message in the accounts. Some were directly involved in ongoing fraud investigations. It is impossible to escape the impression that the founders intentionally sought such fixers, an element that casts a serious doubt on the founders' true intentions. They claim loyalty to their local community, yet at the same time they

---

[4] Even in the first act the capital balance was dressed up with non-cash contributions (consisting of knowledge), an unaccustomed technique in Belgian deeds of incorporation.

lured thousands of small investors from their region into investing their capital into an extremely risky investment without ever revealing the true nature of the risk.

The legal outcome of this affair will doubtless churn up a few spicy details, but the perception in Belgium at the time this article was written is that the two founders were not really intentional deceivers. But moral failures in business seldom start out from vicious, intentionally deceiving individuals. The banality of evil is a well-known topic in ethics. By not taking rules serious from the start moral blindness grew inside the company and its leaders. Surrounding themselves with people with a track record of dubious transactions did not help and when the auditors not only turned a blind eye but actively helped to develop accounting techniques balancing on the edge of legality moral blindness grew into active misleading of shareholders.

Conclusion

Driven by their ambition, native stubbornness and unceasing financial distress, L&H's founders flouted economic truth. The strong culture of West Flanders in which the company and its founders were rooted was probably the most important factor in the development of the moral blind spot that persists even now, as Jo Lernout's book shows. But we also should not underestimate the macro context. In the distribution of macro-economic roles, banks and especially auditors exercise a supervisory function on behalf of the thousands of small investors. This role was not properly fulfilled. The L&H drama took place in a decade in which nearly all financial players, from banks to consultants and auditors, took full advantage of creative accounting techniques that allowed them to take part in the stock market hype. These techniques were common knowledge and there was little hesitation in using them. It shows how the quality of the institutional structure surrounding the market can open up a space for moral failure.

Artesia, L&H's principal banker energetically supported the new accounting techniques. KPMG audited the books with one hand while giving financial advice on financial tricks with the other. It all seemed quite alright. Only when the Enron bomb burst in the US a collective awakening in the financial world came about, a shift from hype to horror. As a consequence, the banks and the auditor, KPMG adopted another perspective in their reports, one that showed that all L&H's accounts made up one protracted lie. Later KPMG implicitly admitted guilt by offering US$115 million settlement to all investors who had purchased L&H shares via US NASDAQ. Those who bought shares in Belgium were left in the cold. Thus far the banks have gotten off unscathed, although there are clear indications of their facilitating role.[5]

---

[5]They vigorously supported L&H's creation of fictive customers and when things turned sour, small investors were urged to retain L&H shares at a time that the banks had already sold theirs (Huwart, 2005:37).

In the meantime, Jo Lernout, the company's figurehead, has sought greener fields in Asia, first with an artificial guinea pig named Gupi, now by selling Belgian chocolates in the Philippines. Here again he sees growth opportunities. He keeps a diary of his experiences in the Philippines for the people back home in his village, Geluwe. Updates can be read on Radio Geluwe's website. Despite the company's dramatic collapse, despite the many thousands of victims that saw all their savings evaporate, some still believe in the icon of West Flanders reliability. Ethics are impossible without a strong root in culture, but a strong culture can at times be a serious obstacle to ethics.

References

Huwart, J.Y. 2005. L&H et les Banques. *Tendances*, 17 November, p. 37.
Lernhout, J. and Joris, I. 2005. *Jo Lernhout. Mijn verhaal*, Antwerp: Houtekiet, p. 336.

Chapter 24
Commentary: Lernout & Hauspie – Chronicle of a Bankruptcy Foretold

Dick de Gilder

Abstract Although the downfall of Lernout & Hauspie seems an amazing story, it is not unique. I argue that several characteristics of the case can be found in other dark tales of organisational failure. What makes such cases complicated is that several related destructive processes seem to take place at the same time. Charismatic leadership seems to have played a role, blinding Lernout's followers – as well as Lernout himself – for the risks associated with the decisions he took. The decision making processes at Lernout & Hauspie themselves were prone to increasing risk taking and escalation of commitment. However, although the internal organisational processes were unsound, the company was dependent on external and – in principle – independent stakeholders such as banks and accountants. But even the external stakeholders failed to sound the alarm bell, probably because they were not as independent as they should have been. With such situational ingredients, it is like waiting for a drama to unfold.

Introduction

The most bewildering in the case about Lernout & Hauspie (L&H) is that the series of decision described made the company's demise virtually inevitable. It is hardly imaginable to assume that the accounting tricks, the slight of hand with expenses and income, the magnitude of the debt would not be discovered sooner or later. The fact that American journalists were the first to ask hard questions meant only that the misappropriations came to light sooner than when the exchange authorities had started the investigation. This prevented the management from becoming more entangled in the web of its own design and may have thus prevented still greater financial suffering. Despite the impression that the events are incomprehensible, I will try here to suggest explanations for the management practices that played a role in the case.

D. de Gilder (✉)
Department of Organization Science, VU University, Amsterdam, The Netherlands
e-mail: tc.de.gilder@vu.nl

Lernout & Hauspie's discomfiture is not an isolated instance, just as the practices that have come to light are not. Since early 2000 several large, often internationally operating companies have gone under or, almost as the result of a miracle – that usually comes in the form of a financial injection from banks or governments – just avoided bankruptcy by the skin of their teeth. Among these are Enron, Tyco, Worldcom, Ahold and Parmalat. That a supermarket chain and food industry company are present in this list shows that questionable management practices and financial acrobacy are not restricted to technologically advanced companies.

Not only have very different types of companies gone over the edge, corporate misconduct is not unique to one period of time (Kindleberger, 2000). We should not believe those who claim that corporate misconduct was limited to the 1990s with its takeover crazes and the technology bubble. The management literature discusses many examples of equally questionable strategic decisions by equally self-willed, often charismatic leaders. Think of the decision by Jürgen Schrempp, chairman of the board at automaker DaimlerChrysler, to acquire aircraft manufacturer Fokker at a time when Fokker was already in financial hot water. After DaimlerChrysler lost a billion, it decided that it would no longer finance Fokker's debts; once it did that, Fokker went bankrupt. That this takeover had more than simply a rational history was evident from Schrempp's famous assertion that he considered Fokker his "love baby" (for other examples see Conger, 1990). Questionable decisions by senior managers seem to be more a recurrent theme than a characteristic of a past period.

One problem in reconstructing the events described in the Lernout & Hauspie case is that there is never enough information, if only because the management did not take into account that its case would be included in a book. Not all pertinent information was preserved; later interviews with key figures will probably reflect a distorted picture of past time, even when those interviewed intend to be completely open. Possible explanations for events are necessarily post hoc, with all the hazards that entails. There is the inevitable question whether L&H would still exist as independent company if different decisions had been made or if there had been more and larger investors at an earlier stage; perhaps it would have become part of a multinational, probably Microsoft which was interested enough in L&H technology to invest in the company. However, this question is unanswerable. We know the outcome and the probable causes, but we will never know what would have become of L&H if matters had gone differently. That certainly does not mean that the exercise is not worth the effort. Reconstructions of disastrous events and the consequences of decisions, e.g. as in groupthink research, has produced much valuable information in the past on possible underlying causes. At the same time, it must be recognised that although specific recommendations have been made to prevent groupthink from recurring, it has by no means disappeared.

Possible Explanations

So, what are the possible explanations of, the possible causes for, the L&H debacle? The case invites closer inspection of three elements. (1) Jo Lernout's display of visionary or charismatic leadership (cf. Conger, 1990); (2) the decision-making related to the approval of the financial constructions and the dubious bookkeeping, in which Pol Hauspie seems to have had an important role (cf. Armstrong et al., 2004); and (3) the role of various stakeholders surrounding the company: shareholders, small and large private investors, banks and accountants. I think it likely that the last element, the stakeholders' role, is the most characteristic for the L&H case, but also for other companies that seem to have gone along the same route, e.g. Enron and Ahold (cf. Trinkaus and Giacalone, 2005). While risky or even dubious management decisions, like the effects of charismatic leadership on followers, can be found in all periods, bankers' and (small) shareholders' risk acceptance and the passive and active cooperation of accountants in dubious management practices are probably unique to this case or even for this juncture in time. At the same time we must note that the three elements cannot be separated. Without visionary leadership, L&H would probably not have been able to convince stakeholders of the need to accept its management decisions, but in accepting the management practices, the takeovers and the bookkeeping, stakeholders probably increased Jo Lernout's charisma. Without visionary leadership the large takeovers that contributed to L&H's downfall would probably have been impossible.

The Dark Side of Leadership

When we look at leadership, it appears that Lernout is in fine company. Heads of large companies and important political leaders have made equally far-reaching, nearly incomprehensible decisions or perpetrated fraudulent deeds that also almost inevitably had to come out into the open. Again, the CEOs at Enron and Ahold are good examples. US President Nixon (Watergate scandal) and German Chancellor Helmut Kohl (illegal party financing) showed that such practices are not the preserve of companies or personal financial advantage.

In an attempt to understand such behaviour, the approach to leadership known as the dark side of leadership tries to make a convincing case that the aforesaid practices often have to do with the view of the senior manager, with his/her style of impression management and hazardous management practices.

Lernout is described as a visionary leader. That is also evident from the mission and aspiration of L&H's founders. This could hardly be more ambitious. They wanted to become the world leader in speech and language technology. The founders were willing to go far to reach that goal in being very active in signing joint venture agreements, but above all in taking over major competitors. And, thanks to the takeovers, they even reached their goal. L&H became the largest company in speech technology, but paid dearly for it. We may justifiably ask whether the objective was not so decisive for the course of action that business operations suffered from this. That is the two-edged sword of vision and ambition. On one side, they are needed as seedbed for the extraordinary effort required, and thus for attaining an elusive goal; on the other, the goal can become so burdensome that all resources are used up in an attempt to reach it. It is characteristic of visionary leaders that they consider personal goals more important than the market's or stakeholders' goals. As Conger (1990, p. 44) put it,

> they might construct an organizational vision that is essentially a monument for themselves....

Lernout's method can be considered a shift in goal. We can appreciate that someone wants to conquer the world with his company, with – what he/she considers – the best products on the market, and in that way to maximise profit. It is more difficult when size alone becomes the primary goal since this usually coincides with enormous losses. When a leader has convinced himself that the end justifies the means, he/she loses contact with reality. It is equally characteristic for visionary leaders that they do a poor job of assessing, or even downplay, the risks they take. In the case of a co-owner of the company, personal effort may perhaps be greater because failure puts his/her own financial future and personal reputation at risk. The downfall of L&H is a typical example of what Conger (1990) calls a Pyrrhic victory. Attaining the goal robs the organisation of the ability to survive in the long term. L&H cut off the branch on which it sat.

Reputation probably plays a more important role here than usual. Its anchoring in Flanders, personal contact with shareholders and financers, the call to friends, neighbours and acquaintances for financing would make the damage to reputation resulting from failure all the greater. More cosmopolitan managers would have fewer such ties and would consider the immediate surroundings less important. Reputation then depends solely on performance, not on the immediate environment. There are no personal ties to financers. That is one less worry; but that is not always an advantage. It permits a more business-like approach, but local anchoring can also give an extra incentive for a major effort. When does this become a burden for the company? When you do not dare to rectify wrong decisions, when you make promises you cannot keep because people you know personally would call you to account, would be disappointed in you?

Charismatic leadership exists by grace of followers, thanks to the personal *relationship* between the leader and his/her followers. Since this is a relationship, it works in both directions and is important for both parties. Followers are ready to make great efforts to serve their leader, but the leader must also have a lot to offer if he/she is to keep these followers. The pressure to satisfy followers' expectations can be enormous. Football coaches, top-notch football players and political leaders all know what this is. The stakes are enormously high and the chance of disappointment equally great.

Decision-Making

Strategic decisions and leadership go together in every organisation. Yet research into group decision-making shows that group processes can affect the decisions taken, that there are general aspects of group decision-making that need not have anything to do with leadership. In this type of research a decision-making problem is presented to a group and to individuals. Research shows that the outcomes of group decision-making processes often differ considerably from a situation in which one individual must make a decision. One of the phenomena reported is "risk shift", i.e. groups tend to make riskier decisions than individuals, even when these individuals are first asked to decide separately and then later to make a definitive group decision. Explanations for this include (a) diffusion or obscuring of responsibility: people who make a group decision can more easily point to another group member when the decision turns out to be wrong (In any case, you are not solely responsible for the decision.) and (b) group members that like risks tend to dominate decision-making: they do more talking and have relatively more opportunities to convince others of their views.

What is clear in the L&H case is that decisions became increasingly risky. Unfortunately, we cannot discover the group dynamics that affected decision making here. It is striking, however, that L&H's management team and entourage came to include people with a suspect reputation. It is not very fair to keep hounding people for past mistakes. We must also be cautious in declaring people morally guilty when competent legal authorities have judged them not guilty. But it is noteworthy that just these people were engaged, or that just they felt drawn to L&H. Why were they the first ones considered suitable to become involved in L&H's business strategy? Armstrong et al. (2004) record that risky decisions and unethical behaviour increase with the size of the group. Again, we cannot identify a causal relationship, but the case suggests that the most far-reaching misappropriations took place after these persons joined the entourage. In one sense, appointing people with a suspect reputation is already a risky decision.

The risky shift was not the only element to affect decision-making within L&H. There were also the well-described escalation of commitment, the tendency for groups and individuals to persevere in unsuccessful past actions and decisions and to keep investing in them. The quote in the case relating to the process against former senior managers at Kurzweil Applied Intelligence is a very adequate summary of what escalation of commitment means. Four elements sustain this: (a) investments already made in a company or project (this can range from money to personal reputation, see above) (b) an inappropriate notion that opportunities will have to change in the future because things cannot always go wrong (This is the gambler's fallacy, applied to gamblers who think that their next wager is in some way related to their previous wagers e.g. when people at a roulette table believe that after a series of black numbers the chance increases that the next number will be red) (c) lack of attention for the environment (wearing blinders) because the goal has become too important personally and (d) the high cost of ending the project. Once a risky course has been set, or when the first unethical deed has been done without repercussions or even with success, it becomes more difficult to turn back and admit to the unethical behaviour. The sad part is that the start of the unethical actions often occurs with the company's assumed interest in mind and seldom because this is taken as guideline for future actions. A good example of escalation of individual commitment is Nick Leeson whose conduct of business single-handedly caused Baring bank's bankruptcy. Like many gamblers, he bet larger and larger sums to make up for past losses. L&H's conduct also appeared progressively more reckless; a recklessness of comparable scope was found at Enron and Parmalat.

Stakeholders

The literature describing total management failures often refers to their leadership and strategic decision-making. A strikingly constant element in this is that it seldom involves unethical behaviour or fraudulent deeds. Nearly every case was about a visionary leader's wrong assessment and/or unsound decision-making based on incomplete or incorrect information from the organisation's environment. These can, of course, be as disastrous for an organisation as the actions at L&H and other companies, but they are not punishable offenses. Disciplinary action usually follows: the company goes bankrupt or else the council of supervisors or the shareholders dismiss the management. Conspicuous at L&H (and at Enron and Parmalat) is that none of the stakeholders seem to have offered any resistance against the way L&H conducted its business until it was too late. Everything seemed permissible. What would have happened had one of the stakeholders been more alert to what L&H's management was doing? Were they blinded by Lernout's visionary leadership or was it something as intangible as the spirit of the times, given the parallels in other companies? Perhaps small shareholders cannot be expected to understand all a company's ins and outs, but this *is* to be expected of the council of supervisors, banks and accountants. That banks were willing to invest without proper collateral is worrisome, especially for stakeholders in those banks (De Standaard, 2003: 21). Again, it is striking that several banks were involved, each of which must have made independent assessments about financial support for L&H. Above all, highly reputed accountants KPMG should have raised questions about L&H's financial doings. Apparently the annual financial statements were approved year after year either because no one discovered what was going on or because they did not want to expose the misappropriations (possibly from fear of losing a large account). Thus, the judgment is that either they were incompetent or they share responsibility for L&H's downfall. KPMG is not alone since two other accounting firms with – until then – good reputations also fell short in the accounting scandals related to Enron and Ahold. The last chance to correct the management was thus lost. One may rightly ask whether matters could not have ended otherwise.

References

Armstrong, R.W., Williams, R.J. and Barrett, J.D. 2004. The Impact of Banality, Risky Shift and Escalating Commitment on Ethical Decision Making. *Journal of Business Ethics*, 53: 365–370.

Conger, J.A. 1990. The Dark Side of Leadership. *Organizational Dynamics*, 19: 44–55.

De Standaard. 2003. Gerecht brengt rol van banken in L&H affaire in kaart. *De Standaard*, 21 June, p. 24

Kindleberger, C.P. 2000. *Manias, Panics and Crashes: A History of financial Crises*, p. 304. New York, NY: Wiley Investment Classics.

Trinkaus, J. and Giacalone, J. 2005. The Silence of the Stakeholders: Zero Decibel Level at Enron. *Journal of Business Ethics*, 58: 237–248.

Part IX
Case H: Construction Fraud

Chapter 25
Case Description: Construction Fraud

Johan Graafland and Luc van Liedekerke

Abstract Due to the actions of a whistleblower The Netherlands was confronted with a massive case of construction fraud involving almost the entire construction sector. Price fixing, prior consulting, duplicate accounts, fictitious invoices and active corruption of civil servants were rampant practices. This case description concentrates on price fixing and prior consulting which were long standing industry practices that only became illegal in 1998. We trace the history of price fixing in the construction sector and the institutional factors that pushed the sector into price fixing. We consider several institutional proposals to solve the issue as presented by a parliamentary investigation committee as well as the building sector itself.

Introduction

On 6 December 2001, the Dutch House of Representatives set up a temporary committee to investigate construction fraud.[1] Construction fraud can be defined as "all illegal and untrustworthy operations by construction companies and subcontractors; which aim to undermine market forces in the construction industry and reduce exposure, increase profitability or ensure continuity" (Priemus, 2002). The widespread fraud with which the Netherlands suddenly seemed to be infected provoked exasperated cries. Jan Marijnissen chairman of the Dutch socialist party gave breath to widespread feelings of disbelief among the Dutch by saying:

> has The Netherlands really turned into a land of fraud? (*NRC*, 2004i)

J. Graafland (✉)
Tilburg Sustainability Center and European Banking Center, Tilburg School of Economics and Management, University of Tilburg, Tilburg, The Netherlands
e-mail: j.j.graafland@uvt.nl

[1] In 1953, (De Vries Commission), 1971 (Standing Committee on Economic Competition) and 1982 (Consultative Body on Regulating the Tendering System) the government also set up commissions to weigh proposals for solving problems in the construction industry. The new parliamentary committee delivered its report in 2003 (Tweede Kamer, 2003).

May be not, but still it is possible that within relatively corruption free countries particular industries become permeated with fraud and corruption. For instance: around the same time Norway, Sweden, Denmark and Finland struggled with large scale price-fixing scandals in the asphalt industry; a core element of the construction industry. None of these countries are known for being particularly prone to corruption yet all of them were confronted with significant fraud cases (Cobouw, 2002).

Is it due to the particularities of the construction industry's structure that it is susceptible to fraud? Or is it due to the people working in the industry? Are they unusually susceptible to the temptations of fraud? Those involved insisted for a long time that there was no question of fraud and certainly no question of immoral conduct. They say that even should some practices have been unacceptable, we must view these in their proper context. To offer one example, Joop Janssen, former CEO at Heijmans construction company, said that construction fraud came down to a question of culture (Van Empel, 2002).

> The construction industry is technology-driven. A bridge may not collapse. So the bridge has to have sturdy columns and for these you need technical skill. That is why the construction industry attracts a particular type of person. People who work in the construction industry are used to fixing things themselves. They choose freedom over red tape and paperwork. (Tweede Kamer, 2003)

During the preparatory investigation, Joop Janssen told Marijke Vos, chair of the parliamentary investigative committee that

> You people [the politicians] just don't understand it. You have no idea how the industry's culture works. These are customs that have become ingrained over decades. Justifying one's actions is not part of the industry's cultural component ... Construction workers are real he-men. (Tweede Kamer, 2003)

According to the construction industry itself we have to look for the explanation of the typical characteristics of the industry outside the industry itself. In the end the government provoked the wide spread use of price agreements and other typical practices. In the same interview as quoted above, Joop Janssen drew attention to the fact that many of the fraudulent practices arose because clients – usually the government – did not reimburse the cost of tendering – thus provoking the fraud. Others explain this by drawing attention to the unique Dutch construction industry's institutional context. On one side you have an army of bureaucrats that manage more than half of the money in the industry, on the other a strong corporatist culture in which cartels and consultative interest groups are deeply rooted. In this context, secret agreements or deals, passing a job on to a colleague, a pre-arranged price and made-to-suit tender specifications will naturally take place. These and other statements show that fraud in the construction industry is not self-contained. Several contextual factors appear to have contributed to the situation. The objective of this case description is to provide this contextual information and prepare the ground for a judgment on the ethical quality of the construction business and building contractors' conduct. But first, we must know what construction fraud is.

What Is Construction Fraud?

Construction fraud is typically understood to encompass three activities. First is the so called "informal consultation" or "prior consultation" preceding each official tender. During this consultation – legally forbidden since 1998 – contractors come together to decide who will do a given job. The contractor with the lowest price is given a chance to acquire the job. But the others do not leave empty handed. This contractor adds two so-called "corrective elements" to the pricing procedure: reimbursement for calculation expenses and a price mark-up euphemistically labelled "price improvement" by the sector. The reimbursement for calculation costs is a fee that the chosen construction company pays to competitors to cover the cost of tendering. Price mark ups are increases to the lowest price to reduce the lowest submitter's exposure. Koop Tjuchem's – later revealed – duplicate accounts showed that the price mark-up resulting from prior consultation came to approximately 8.8%.[2] On an annual industry volume of 15 billion euros, that equals nearly 1.5 billion in excess profits. This refutes the building contractors' argument that prior consultation is only intended to reimburse calculation costs, because calculation fees – when they were standard procedure – came to only 2% of the contract price (Hé, 2003). Building contractors and their individual members were not the only ones to benefit from these price increases. Some of the money flowed to trade associations like the Amsterdam Contractors Association (AAV). It used the money it received to pay for gratuities for its members, e.g. an annual trip on the Rhine or a vacation flight with a leased DC9 (*NRC*, 2004h).

Issuing and collecting fictitious invoices is a second aspect of the construction fraud. Claiming costs not incurred adversely affects principals and increases profit margins inappropriately. An article in the Dutch daily *NRC Handelsblad* attests that Strukton issued 13.1 million euro in fictitious invoices on a tunnel project. This money was siphoned out to other projects, to make up for the losses there (NRC, 2002e). Keeping duplicate accounts allowed this practice to go unnoticed.

A third aspect of the construction fraud involved the building companies' attempts to obtain information on budget ceilings. "Grubbing official" and other terms were used as euphemism for the corrupt civil servants in provinces and municipalities and at the Directorate-General for Public Works and Water Management that provided this information (*NRC*, 2002d). Among their rewards were visits to bordellos or written-off leasing vehicles (called passing on a car). Colluding construction companies could use information on budget ceilings to raise their prices to that level. Contractors called this doing business Italian style. You read the bids during the prior consultation to determine the lowest price. The lowest bidder would get the job but the price of his bid is raised to the budget ceiling as revealed by corrupt officials. The difference between the budget ceiling and the price of the lowest

---

[2]There is still an element of competition because the principal choose the tender with the lowest price. Anticipating the price change when securing a contract, companies that want to acquire a job bid under cost in the prior consultation. This mechanism makes it doubtful whether the price change resulting from the prior consultation was ever really 8.8%.

bidder is split into equal shares. When for instance ten companies took part in the prior consultation, each got 10%. This reduced exposure and increased profits.

Besides these three activities, we can also classify other acts as fraudulent, among them construction companies' tax fraud and employees' use of company materials while moonlighting. Like other labour intensive industries (hospitality, consumer goods repair), construction is known for moonlighting (Graafland, 1990). The parliamentary committee set up to investigate the fraud chose not to include these types of activities in its definition of construction fraud.[3]

Although the construction fraud's three aspects – prior consultation, fictitious invoices and bribing civil servants – are linked, the rest of this article will focus on the first facet.

Who Are the Parties Involved?

Construction fraud had an impact on several stakeholders. The most important are the building contractors and the various government authorities. We can classify these by level. Building contractor are involved

- on a meso level: construction industry trade organisations, e.g. Building Netherlands (formerly AVBB [the Coalition of Dutch Construction Industry Organisations])
- on the company level: entire individual contracting companies
- on a personal level:
  - individual managers responsible for drafting quotations and securing orders for their companies
  - members of the building contractors' board of directors
  - the building contractors' employees that undergo the indirect consequences (e.g. greater profits, more sales, more jobs) of their employer's participation in building fraud
  - directors of the construction industry's trade organisations.

Government bodies affected include:

- the European government, mainly as legislator
- the Dutch national government, as legislator (Competitive Trading Act) and monitor (Economic Investigation Service – Netherlands Competition Authority [NCA]) and as purchaser of major infrastructure projects

---

[3]Construction is also known for high absenteeism (EIB, 2001a). In 1998, 32 of every 100 employees received a disability payment (EIB, 2001b). The workload is heavy and has even grown in recent years (EIB, 2001c). Nevertheless, recent benchmark research shows that construction companies are no worse at socially responsible business practices than metallurgy or financial service industries (Graafland and Eiffinger, 2004).

- local and/or regional governments as regulators (issuing permits, approving zoning and municipal land-use schemes) and as purchasers of the building contractors' products
- individual public officials acting on behalf of local, provincial or national governments and entrusted with awarding jobs to building contractors.

Other stakeholders involved in or affected by the construction fraud or its consequences are the building contractors' other customers, their shareholders,[4] their accountants[5] and society as a whole (including tax payers).

The Background

The construction fraud had a long history. It is difficult to ascertain exactly when it started. For decades the Dutch government had officially recognised the practice of prior consulting and had supported it. Several possible causes influenced the rise of construction fraud. In this section, we treat causes relating to the nature and production of the construction industry's product. After that we will examine the institutional aspects of the construction market and the history of prior consultation, with attention to the government's role.

A basic characteristic of the construction industry is that nothing can be produced ahead of time. A commission always precedes production. This makes it difficult for building companies to deliver production gradually during cyclical fluctuation. Because building contractors produce capital goods for other companies and because business investment is much more sensitive to trading cycles than are consumer goods, construction companies are extra sensitive to discontinuities. Another factor that restricts opportunities for a balanced scheduling of building activities is the dependence of government contracts on political decision-making, which after consuming much time and causing great delays often expects haste in implementation. Such reasons lead building contractors facing empty order books to work at a loss to avoid the expense that results from a great variation in turnover, e.g. the cost of laying off staff in slow periods and hiring new staff when business picks up.

A second characteristic is that construction is site-dependent. A production process and organisational framework have to be created for each job. This increases the need to work with familiar partners. The building contractors, the various

---

[4]One consequence of the construction fraud's becoming known was that construction company stock prices fell by up to 15%. When it became obvious on 14 February 2004 that there were price agreements in other segments of the earth, road and water works industry (following upon news of other shadow accounts), stock prices of companies involved fell sharply once more (*NRC*, 2004a). The literature on the subject also shows that a lack of corporate responsibility is detrimental to a company's share price. See: Soppe (2000), Rao and Hamilton (1996), Davidson III et al. (1994), Graafland and Smid (2004).

[5]Testimony before the investigatory committee shows that accountants did not draft the fictitious invoices. "There had long been no real auditing", according to Deloitte & Touche's Veenstra (*NRC*, 2002d).

subcontractors and related companies (architects, etc.) know one another and cross paths regularly. All contractors cultivate relationship management. They nurture and maintain contacts, meet at service clubs, etc. This expands opportunities to make deals.

A third characteristic is that construction projects tend to be unique, to require large investments and to have a long technical and economic lifespan. This is particularly true of major infrastructure projects like tunnels, etc. Each project is different, which means a unique price must be set. Drafting bids for such projects is expensive; and according to the industry, calculation expenses need to be reimbursed. Furthermore, something can always be overlooked when compiling a budget. This helps explain the great difference in bids during tendering. Principals often lack the expertise needed to assess price bids. The need to check whether the calculation was truly correct can also justify the pre-prior consultation.

Moreover, the lack of mass production means the risk of unexpected setbacks during construction is relatively large. However, the market structure (see below) requires building contractors to agree to a price before they can produce and calculate the actual cost of the product. Add to that the customer's requirements cannot always be rendered with adequate detail (in specifications and drawings), which means they must be completed or modified during construction. Uncertain factors like weather, soil conditions at the building site, etc. reinforce the construction industry's unforeseeable character. One consequence is that the final cost is sometimes very different from the agreed price. Some projects are very profitable, while others run a loss. That makes it very important for a building contractor to reduce exposure to risks. The so-called "price improvements" were one way of doing so. The average profit margin in the building industry is far from high, around 2–3% of turnover.

Institutional Characteristics of the Construction Market

In addition to these characteristics related specifically to the nature of the product, the construction market also differs from other markets in the structure of competitive relations within the industry (Van Waarden, 2003).

First, the construction market is known for its public tenders. This stimulates price-based competition. The details of the planned building are largely fixed in the principal's tender specifications and drawings. This separates design from implementation. Moreover, in the Dutch situation the principal typically did not require a detailed description of how contractors plan to carry out the task. The whole tender revolved around the price. All other criteria – e.g. quality – carry less weight. The lowest price was the most important criterion against which the principal compared submissions.

As soon as they have been awarded a job, contractors tried to cut costs by substituting cheaper material for expensive types. In this way cuts in prices lead to cuts in quality. Another strategy used to compensate inadequately low prices is to calculate a higher profit margin on work in excess. When additional work is needed during the construction, the contractor is in a much stronger negotiating position because he is dealing with the principal in a one-on-one meeting and because the principal cannot call in another contractor (except at very high cost). Moreover, the contractor can profit from his superior knowledge. The contractor knows the site's modalities and circumstances better than the principal does. That is why a project's final cost is often much higher than the tender price. Each disparity or omission on the estimate is an occasion to claim work in excess. The result is that relations in a project quickly sour. This, too, adds to the construction industry's poor image.

Second, the construction industry has a low concentration ratio. In the Netherlands, there are more than a hundred thousand construction companies, each with a rather narrow specialty. High market segmentation is the result. Entry requirements are relatively low. Construction workers and machines can be hired-in easily for a single project. Temporary employment is not unusual; there are many self-employed workers in the industry. In comparison to other industries, investments are relatively low. "If you've a shovel and a customer, you can start up a construction company in the Netherlands" (Van Empel, 2002). One result is that competition can sometimes be especially heated. This set-up produces a buyers' market.[6]

Another factor reinforcing competition is that the national government is a powerful player when it comes to commissioning infrastructure work. It has been argued that the dominant position of the government as principal in the industry has contributed to the construction fraud (Priemus, 2002). The government commissions 90% of all ground, road and waterworks. This leads to an imperfect construction market in which the government holds a powerful position vis-à-vis a large group of contractors. That makes it easy for the government to play one off against the other. There is a danger that the construction companies compete to undercut one another. As monopsonist, the government is seldom, if ever, willing to pay a calculation fee.[7] Contractors have to see for themselves how to earn back the cost of often very extensive calculations. Another widespread problem is the way government agencies go about like hawkers asking for quotations from construction companies and then use this information (and the expertise it represents) to demand lower prices from competitors.

> The government window-shops at various construction companies then combines the cheapest and most innovative aspects from various tenders into a contract awarded to the lowest bidder (Van Empel, 2002).

---

[6] That contractors often work with many sub-contractors does little to make construction procedure comprehensible for the principal.

[7] A perfect market has a multiplicity of suppliers and takers, none of which can exert substantial influence on the market price because of their small share of it. In a monopoly, one supplier provides goods/services to a multiplicity of customers and can exert significant (upward) influence on market prices. In a monopsony, one taker buys goods/services from a multiplicity of suppliers and can exert significant (downward) influence on market prices by playing one supplier off against the other.

This means that building contractors have to bear heavy calculation costs without their effort being rewarded with a contract. This removes all stimuli for innovation in the industry. Moreover, according to many in the industry, the government in this way provoked fraud.

Historical Background

The Dutch government had permitted prior consultation since 1953 to prevent construction companies from collapsing under heavy competition. The road-building contractors combine *Wegenbouw Aannemers Combinatie* (WAC) was established in that year. Under the guidance of an independent chairman, it offered a forum for prior consultation that met government-approved rules. Dozens of small building cartels have followed its example since then. Earthworks, dredgers, every job category had its own cartel to set prices and distribute contracts. In 1963, all the separate construction cartels joined one umbrella organisation the association of cooperative price-regulating organisations, (*Samenwerkende Prijsregelende Organisaties* (SPO)), with the government's approval. 28 cartels representing more than 4,000 construction companies joined this umbrella organisation which was officially allowed to organise a prior consultation process in close cooperation with the government.

The vulnerability of this formal prior consultation became evident from the ease with which it could lead to other, illegal, types of prior consultation. Contractors often met one another away from the independent chairman for consultations before the formal meetings. At this pre-prior consultation, contractors agreed to higher amounts than the official calculation fee. This was illegal. Yet it was widespread. The independent chairmen reported it regularly.

> Once, I arrived at the meeting at an hotel but I found the front door locked. So I went around the back and found the meeting room full. (*NRC*, 2002a)

and

> At a meeting at Gouden Karper hotel I saw that the parking lot was already completely full. Apparently the pre-prior had just finished, because on the way from my car I saw several contented contractors. (*NRC*, 2002a)

As of 1987, tendering methods followed rules in a set of uniform pricing regulations with the government's approval. Companies wanting to submit a bid had to register with the SPO. The SPO organised the prior consultation that designated one contractor to negotiate with the principal and that set the calculation fee.

Five years later, large-scale pre-prior consultation was still widespread among road builders. But on 5 February 1992, the European Commission prohibited construction cartels and imposed a fine of 24 million euro on the Dutch contractors' cartel. The Commission judged that prior consultation disrupted free competition because cartel member companies had an advantage over non-member companies. The Dutch government and the construction industry were outraged, but in 1996 the

25 Case Description: Construction Fraud

European Court of Justice upheld the prohibition of construction cartels. The uniform pricing regulations proved to contravene Art. 85 of the EEC Treaty. Dutch contractors had to submit to free competition. Accordingly, in 1998, the Dutch Competitive Trading Act forbade prior consultation.

Because of this long historical background and the engrained culture it produced, companies found it difficult to do away with prior consultation on their own. In November 2001, a Dutch television programme showed that many construction companies ignored the prohibition against cartels and still made price-fixing agreements. Dutch newspaper *NRC Handelsblad* ran a headline on 15 August 2002 that said, "Price-fixing prohibition fails. Contractors wanted to get out of illegal system" (*NRC*, 2002c). Reporting on the period between 1998 and 2001, this article described how major exchange-quoted Dutch contractors (e.g. HBG, Heijmans en Volker Wessels Stevin) tried several times to obey the law and exit the illegal price-fixing system. Because attempts to follow the law resulted in "a drastic fall in orders", according to HBG CEO J. Veraart, contractors decided to return to pricing agreements and prior consultation on bidding. In Veraart's words,

> Too many parties took part in bidding. You couldn't withdraw from the system on your own. We were all trapped in the system. (*NRC*, 2002a)

Another contractor, Scheurs, also recounts that he could not escape the system.

> I was obliged to work within this system because all the others did so. I had to issue invoices with incorrect descriptions. Were I not to take part in the tendering fee system[8], my fellow submitters could very easily have underbid me thanks to the tendering fees that they received. (*NRC*, 2002a)

Van Well and Nelissen, directors at Dura Vermeer, defended the long continuance of illegal practices by referring to individual contractors' difficult position.

> Individual contractors could not set up market-wide arrangements... To be sure, our first responsibility is to the 3600 families that earn a living at this company. (*NRC*, 2004g)

They, too, point to the construction industry's culture.

> Betraying colleagues was an enormous cultural turnaround in the industry. (*NRC*, 2004g)

Van Well and Nelissen mention attempts to break out of the system in 1992 and 1996. In the end, it did not work. Because the Dutch government had defended the prior consultation system in Brussels for so many years, it was not thought of as a punishable act but rather as part of risk management and care for the company's continuity.

And some government officials too continued to play the game. Deloitte & Touche gave a sad picture of the municipalities' ability to resist fraud.

> According to Deloitte & Touche, local governments had service networks of government officials that leaked information to contractors; they were known for maladministration, incomplete specifications and sloppy tendering procedures. Moreover, Deloitte & Touche

---

[8] A surplus charge was the extra margin added to the tender during illegal prior consultation.

also noted that few municipalities had a policy on ethics. Successive studies into malpractices in the Directorate-General for Public Works and Water Management produced the same picture. (*NRC*, 2002d)

The Industry's Response and the Aftermath

On 9 November 2001, the construction fraud received prominent coverage on Dutch television. In one broadcast, Ad Bos, former director at Koop Tjuchem, told an interviewer about Koop Tjuchem 's duplicate accounts. These duplicate accounts showed widespread involvement of contractors in illegal prior consultations. The duplicate accounts covered the period 1988–1999 and contained forbidden agreements related to 3,445 bids for a total tender value of 3 billion euro. One example: in a job for the Ministry of Defence's Infrastructure Agency, Koop distributed almost 1 million euro over thirteen other contractors. That amount was included in the 7 million euro contract price. Sometimes this type of payment came after just one phone call. Another example: in a job for the province of Limburg, Koop Tjuchem agreed over the phone with the KWS/Bloem-Hoensbroek combine that Koop would get 1% of the 2-million-euro contract price. Koop got this money without taking part in the official tender (*NRC*, 2003).

Building contractors were initially hesitant to respond to this publicity. CEOs of large companies denied knowing anything about such practices because they were not personally involved in attracting commissions. Managers who did admit to being involved in illegal prior consultation often sympathised with it. As contractor Henk Burggraaf said

> I didn't sit there for financial gain. I wanted to protect my market... Maybe it is against the law, but I didn't see it as a crime.

Even when paying fines, contractors remained aloof from any notion of guilt. As J. Koelman (who represented Strukton, on the board of directors at the KSS/Strukton/HBG combine) said

> That would look like pleading guilty. And I refuse to admit to even one fault. (*NRC*, 2002d)

He knew that construction companies sent fictitious invoices, but he saw fictitious invoices as something different from falsified invoices.

> Nothing dishonourable happened. (*NRC*, 2002d)

Wim van Onno, CEO at BAM NBM, a large Dutch construction company, also rejected accusations.

> The whole construction industry rotten? That's not correct. (*NRC*, 2002b)

BAM co-director de Vries even said

> But we love competition! What really irritates me is the implication that we are just fat lazy builders tossing jobs back and forth. (*NRC*, 2002b)

25 Case Description: Construction Fraud

Martien Heijmans, division head at Heijmans Infrastructure, noted that

If continuity and employment are your first concern, you cannot be the only one to withdraw from something that pervades the entire industry (Hé, 2003).

Another case of duplicate accounts surfaced in February 2004. It showed that construction fraud was not restricted to large government projects. Between 1995 and 2001 dozens of companies had made price-fixing agreements for the construction of office buildings, schools and hospitals. It appeared that senior managers at participating companies were well aware of what was going on since they were the ones to make the agreements (Financiele Dagblad, 2004). Predictably, political officials responded with indignation. The government sent the construction industry an ultimatum that same month. Construction companies were given until 1 May 2004 to submit their duplicate accounts and report other violations to the Netherlands Competition Authority (NCA). Anyone caught after that deadline would be excluded from tendering procedures.

The government's ultimatum had its impact. BAM, one of the leading companies in the industry, said in Dutch newspaper *NRC*,

We decided to reverse course to avoid having to operate defensively; we are working with all our cards out on the table. (*NRC*, 2004b)

Other large Dutch construction companies – Heijmans, Ballast Nedam, Volker Stevin, Dura Vermeer and Strukton – also decided to give the Netherlands Competition Authority (NCA) the information it requested (*NRC*, 2004b). In March and April, a growing number of companies submitted their duplicate accounts to the NCA. By 1 May, the number rose to 400 builders. They represented 70% of construction turnover. Large clients, among which Philips, Shell, ING and ABN AMRO, followed the government lead and threatened to exclude mala fide builders (*NRC*, 2004c).

While the threats increased in tone and number, the attitude in the construction industry finally changed. Whereas initially the construction industry refused to admit guilt and took on the attitude "let them prove that we did something wrong", people slowly started to pass the buck. Directors at Dura Vermeer builders apologised publicly (*NRC*, 2004g), but added that in their view, the construction fraud did not harm the Dutch economy. They thought that the cartel agreements had not increased prices. In addition, individual companies took various measures to reduce the chance of construction fraud. One result was that Heijmans introduced a code of conduct. Before the construction fraud, CEO Joop Janssen opposed such a code of conduct (Janssen, 2001). Companies also incorporated mechanisms that would warn senior managers of any unacceptable activities in the company. Examples for Heijmans include having an external controller to supervise bidding procedures and obliging Heijmans managers to sign a document stating that they did not participate in illegal prior consultation (Graafland, 2004). Most companies claim to have cooperated with the NCA's investigation. Nearly 350 of the 400 roadwork companies that the NCA prosecuted for their role in the construction fraud chose for the accelerated penalty procedures that the cartel authority created to deal with the construction fraud. According to the NCA, massive interest in a rapid settlement showed that the construction companies wanted to put their house in order (*NRC*, 2004e). Another factor in this high response is that authorities gave companies a 15% discount on fines when they signed up for the accelerated procedure (see below).

Institutional Measures

The parliamentary committee investigating the construction fraud made several suggestions for reforming institutions in the construction industry in its report.[9] As it was a whistle blower who had brought the case before the media, one of the first suggested measures was strong whistle blowing protection next to clearer tendering laws. Further suggestions included not paying calculation fees for standard jobs and basing awards on lowest price. A designing fee could be offered for difficult or innovative work. Builders also considered it reasonable to base selection for standard projects on the lowest price. These suggestions elicit various comments. What is a standard project? A standard project implies that the commissioning party provides a complete set of specifications and that the construction company need do no more than implement these. But how many hospitals or fire stations are identical? Moreover, how efficient is this way of working? After all, a standard project leaves no room for innovation during construction.

Another suggestion in the committee's report is that the government should do more to enforce the law. One way of doing so would be to give a greater role to public spending watchdogs like the *Algemene Rekenkamer* (the Dutch General Accounting Office). Government authorities should institute codes of conduct that explicitly state what it expects of its employees. More guarantees could also be built into the tendering procedure, e.g. by extending contacts with companies to more than a few individuals and by instituting job rotation. Moreover, government authorities should appoint a trusted third party and set up whistle-blower regulations.

A third proposal in the committee's report was that implementation risks should rest on those who can do most to control them. That is not always the contractor, on whom it now rests. One way to do this is public private partnership. According to Jan Holleman (chairman of AVBB, the Coalition of Dutch Construction Industry Organisations), large, complex projects can best be carried out with all parties cooperating from the drawing board right through to implementation and management, with a proper distribution of risks and duties. When road laying encounters delays because permits hold up work, the government, not the contractor, should bear the cost (Ter Veer, 2002). Cees van Staal, publisher of *Building Business*, expected a lot of the innovative commissioning practice with shared risks or mixed financing (Ter

---

[9] You can download the Dutch report from www.bouwfraude.nl (access is restricted to customers of Bedrijvenweb Nederland B.V.).

Veer, 2002). The UK has had positive experience with this. The objective should not be the lowest possible price for the customer, but quality through cooperation. This option for public private partnership can sometimes have better results than a public tender in which only the lowest price is chosen. Research in the UK showed that proper interaction and shorter building time lowered investments by 13% when contracts encourage teamwork.

For that, contractor and customer must trust one another. Not everything can be nailed down tight ahead of time. This way of working will require a new open culture. To promote this open culture, Jan Holleman argued for clear codes of conduct and for new training courses in the building trade that focus on social and communicative skills and that produce broadly oriented managers that, unlike today's nerds, are able to work within partnerships.

Two other institutional measures that aim at healthy competition and restoring trust between contractors and customers include setting up a Coordinating Council (*Regieraad*) and a Foundation to assess the Integrity of the Construction Industry (*Stichting Beoordeling Integriteit Bouwbedrijf*).[10] The Coordinating Council's task is to launch change in the construction industry so that it can again claim to be healthy, transparent and innovative. The Coordinating Council has suggested specific renovations to shape this change in various parts of the building industry like earth, road and water works, utilities and homebuilding. The coordinating council's purpose intends to stimulate all parties to assume responsibility for their tasks.

In October 2003, Building Netherlands set up a Foundation to Assess the Integrity of the Construction Industry (abbreviated SBIB in Dutch). The SBIB's goal is "to encourage the drafting, managing and monitoring of disciplinary codes intending to ensure the construction industry's integrity in bidding for contracts and in competing in the Netherlands".[11] The SBIB supports construction companies' integrity policies, makes them visible for third parties and monitors compliance with this integrity. Its activities concentrate on the introduction of and compliance with business codes. The SBIB lists companies with a business code in a public register and provides information on the criteria set for mention in the register. Furthermore, SBIB monitors compliance with provisions in the business codes and imposes penalties when needed. To this end SBIB has established a supervisory committee consisting of independent external experts in business ethics and competition. This committee handles complaints about violation of codes by companies listed in SBIB's register and offers binding advice to SBIB on penalties.

---

[10] The Ministries of Economic Affairs (EZ), Housing, Spatial Planning and the Environment (VROM) and Transport, Public Works and Water Management (V&W) established the Coordinating Council for the Construction Industry on 6 February 2004 (www.regieraadbouw.nl).

[11] www.sbib.nl

Penalties

The NCA designed a special penalty system for building fraud. It had three different discounts on the fines that the NCA imposed on construction companies:

- The clemency arrangement gave a discount on the fine for companies that voluntarily reported cartel arrangements to the NCA (NRC, 2004e). This largest discount reached around 50%.
- Companies that signed up for rapid settlement got another 15% discount (NRC, 2004d).
- Companies received an additional 10% discount when they reached a financial arrangement with the customers they duped (NRC, 2004e).

Normally, the penalty could reach 10% of the tainted turnover. Those handling the construction fraud assumed the penalties would reach 10% of a year's turnover. That paved the way for a rapid settlement of construction cases and cut penalties down by 75%.

NCA imposed the first fine, for €100 million, on 22 companies in December 2003. In a second round, following at the end of 2004, it imposed another €100 million on 344 construction companies. In 2005, it fined 155 companies €40 million; in 2006, fines on 596 companies brought in €70 million. Although the amounts may seem large, the European Commission expressed doubts in a letter to the NCA on the preventive efficacy of fines that it considered relatively low given the turnover concerned (NRC, 2006). At the same time as, and parallel to, the construction fraud in the Netherlands, the European Commission investigated the creation of cartels in the asphalt industry elsewhere in Europe. The commission fined 14 companies €267 million on a €500-million turnover over 8 years. NCA, by contrast, imposed a €233-million fine on the road and waterworks industry, which come to 0.7% of 2001 turnover (€34 billion). The NCA's argument for this relatively mild approach is that the intention could not be to decimate the industry. Were it to follow the Commission's lead, it would have imposed a monster fine of a few dozen billion euros which would have wiped out large parts of the entire industry.

In addition to the NCA's fines, construction companies also faced civil claims from customers that thought they had paid too much, and claims from the tax service as well as investigation of criminal action. In these affairs, too, we see that the government sought to punish not destroy. The public prosecutor for instance apparently "forgot" to specify in the summons that the focus was on the *intentional* aspect of participation in illegal consultation prior to bidding. That meant that the contractors were charged with breach of the Competitive Trading Act rather than with criminal behaviour. A breach far less serious in Dutch law and with a shorter period of limitation. The public prosecutor's procedural "error" had a major impact, because a conviction for prior consultation could have led to exclusion from government contracts nationally and throughout Europe (NRC, 2004f).

Conclusion

The Netherlands is a country that scores consistently very high in the TI corruption perceptions index. It is therefore no surprise that the massive nature of the construction fraud, involving almost the entire sector came as a serious blow to the country. We have tried to analyse how such a massive derailment could come about. Essentially old practices continued while the world moved on and because bad habits are so hard to eradicate the entire sector found itself in due time at the wrong side of the legal divide. It is interesting to see how the self-understanding by the sector moved on as the scandal exploded. While there was clear moral blindness and even denial of any wrongdoing at the beginning, by the end of the crisis most participants recognised their mistakes and new standards were put in place. Moral learning took place as the industry leaders moved from denial of fault to acceptance that something had gone wrong and finally pro-active construction of a new institutional structure where better moral standards can grow. It is a sobering lesson for every country on top of the CPI index.

References

Cobouw. 2002. "NCC kiest met bekentenis eieren voor zijn geld". *Cobouw*. 7 February.
Davidson III, W.N., Worrell, D.L. and Lee, C.I. 1994. Stock Market Reactions to Announced Corporate Illegalities. *Journal of Business Ethics*, 13: 979–987.
EIB (Economisch Instituut voor de Bouwnijverheid) 2001a. *Ziekteverzuim in de bouwnijverheid in 2000*, Amsterdam.
EIB (Economisch Instituut voor de Bouwnijverheid) 2001b. *Arbeidsongeschiktheid in de bouw*, Amsterdam.
EIB (Economisch Instituut voor de Bouwnijverheid) 2001c. *Werkdruk bij uitvoerders en werkvoorbereiders*, Amsterdam.
Empel, F. 2002. Bouwers zijn anders. *Bouwers*, 2: 10–12.
Financiele Dagblad. 2004. "Bres in het Kartel." *Financiële Dagblad*, 25 February.
Graafland, J.J. 1990. Tax Policies and Interaction Between Hidden and Official Economy. *Public Finance/Finances Publiques*, 45: 70–89.
Graafland, J.J. 2004. Collusion, Reputation Damage and Interest in Code of Conduct: The Case of a Dutch Construction Company. *Business Ethics: A European Review*, 13: 127–142.
Graafland, J.J. and Smid, H. 2004. Reputation, Corporate Social Responsibility and Market Regulation. *Tijdschrift voor Economie en Management*, XLIX: 271–308.
Graafland, J.J. and Eijffinger, S. 2004. Corporate Social Responsibility of Dutch Companies: Benchmarking, Transparency and Robustness. *De Economist*, 152(3): 1–24.
Hé 2003. De bouw uit de schaduw. *Hé. Magazijn voor medewerkers van Heijmans b.v.*, 3(nr. 1).
Janssen, J.P.M. 2001. *De maatschappij mij een zorg? Bronnen van waarde voor maatschappelijk ondernemen*. The Hague: NCW.
NRC. 2002a. "Rijk negeerde jarenlang bouwfraude". *NRC*. 23 March.
NRC. 2002b. "BAM De hele bouw rot? Dat is onjuist". *NRC*. 10 July.
NRC. 2002c. "Bouwers wilden af van illegaal systeem". *NRC*. 15 August.
NRC. 2002d. "Ook ministers hebben selectief geheugen". *NRC*. 17 September.
NRC. 2002e. "Rijk 'eigen' aannemers eerst". *NRC*. 2 December.
NRC. 2003. "Rechtszaken bouwsector tegen NMa". *NRC*. 16 January.
NRC. 2004a. "Bouwsector weer in opspraak geraakt". *NRC*. 16 February.
NRC. 2004b. "Bouwbedrijf legt stukken op tafel." *NRC*. 23 February.

NRC. 2004c. "Ikea sluit bouwers uit." *NRC*. 14 April.
NRC. 2004d. "Megaboete dreigt voor wegenbouw." *NRC*. 14 October.
NRC. 2004e. "Geen miljarden, maar miljoenen". *NRC*. 15 October.
NRC. 2004f. "Vormfout hier, voormalig minister Netelenbos daar." *NRC*. 9 October.
NRC. 2004g. "Na de boete volgt de bekentenis". *NRC*. 13 May.
NRC. 2004h. "Persoonlijk gewin bij bouwfraude". *NRC*. 23 October.
NRC. 2004i. "Is Nederland een fraudeland geworden?". *NRC*. 28 February.
NRC. 2006. "Schuldbesef bij bouwfraude nog steeds gering." *NRC*. 9 November.
Priemus, H. 2002. Opgaven voor de parlementaire enquête bouwfraude'. *Economisch Statische Berichten*, 87(nr. 4345): 84–87.
Rao, S.M. and Hamilton III, B.J. 1996. The Effect of Published Reports of Unethical Conduct on Stock Prices. *Journal of Business Ethics*, 15: 1321–1330.
Soppe, A.B.M. 2000. Heeft ethiek een prijs op Beursplein 5? *Economisch-Statistische Berichten*, 85(nr. 4280): 912–914.
Tweede Kamer der Staten-Generaal, Eindrapport Parlementaire Enquêtecommissie Bouwnijverheid. 2003. *Vergaderjaar 2002–2003, 28244*, nrs. 5–6, Den Haag, SDU.
Veer, P.T. 2002. Bezem erdoor, snel weer aan het werk. *Bouwers*, 2: 3–6.
Waarden, F. 2003. Bouwenquête beperkt bestek. *Economisch Statische Berichten*, 88(nr. 4393): 36–39.

Chapter 26
Commentary: The Moral Assimilation of the Market

Bert Musschenga

Abstract In my commentary on the case of fraud in the construction industry I first address the extent to which prior consultation and price-fixing agreements – although illegal – can be defended morally. Then I examine whether universal participation and the heavy price paid by those who did not cooperate were sufficient excuses for participating. Finally, I review the recommendations of the parliamentary committee investigating the building industry and other measures intended to put the construction industry in order.

Introduction

As Graafland showed, until recently numerous unacceptable practices took place in the construction industry. Bribery and fictitious invoicing came on top of prior consultation and price-fixing agreements. It was striking that leading figures in the construction industry who appeared before the parliamentary investigatory committee displayed little sense of guilt. There was no shortage of excuses: Everyone did it. If you did not follow suit, your colleagues avoided you like the plague and you were never included in anything. Prior consultation and price-fixing agreements were necessary because businesses had to protect themselves against high risks on the construction market and against government's monopoly as commissioner of large infrastructure projects. Moreover, construction industry leaders aroused the impression that prior consultation and price agreements did not lead to higher prices; the commissioning government's interests were not endangered. I will first address the extent to which prior consultation and price-fixing agreements – although illegal – can be defended morally. Then I will examine whether universal participation and the heavy price paid by those who did not cooperate were sufficient excuses for

B. Musschenga (✉)
Faculty of Philosophy, VU University, Amsterdam, The Netherlands
e-mail: aw.musschenga@dienst.vu.nl

participating. Finally, I will review the recommendations of the parliamentary committee investigating the building industry and other measures intended to put the construction industry in order.

Prior Consultation: From Legal to Illegal

The free market idea is one of the pillars of our economic system. Free market means that the market parties' efforts to pursue their own interests are unrestricted. According to philosopher Christopher McMahon (1981), certain conditions must be met if the economic system is to flourish. These conditions give rise to imperatives that economic actors' behaviour must satisfy. McMahon calls them efficiency imperatives. They are the heart of what he calls the implicit morality of the market. This market morality is less than the everyday or common morality that orients our relations to others. The parties are not obliged to offer one another help or assistance, certainly not when that would require sacrifice. They are also not obliged to refrain from actions that could be disadvantageous to some unknown other. On the market, it is morally permissible for one company to drive another out of business. However, companies are forbidden to mislead one another or third parties about the characteristics and value of goods bought and sold. They must also refrain from practices that restrict free competition. The morality of the market regulates and restricts what parties can do to further their own interests. This last requirement is the most important for our subject.

Because not all entrepreneurs have internalised the morality of the market to such an extent that they spontaneously meet its requirements, we must take into account that, where possible, they will make agreements on prices or the division of the market. As Adam Smith noted,

> "People of the same trade seldom meet together, even for merriment and diversion, but the conversation ends in a conspiracy against the public, or in some contrivance to raise prices." (Smith, 1776, Vol. I.x, Part II).

That is why it is necessary that the morality of the market be established in legislation and that adequate monitoring and adequate sanctions bolster compliance. Besides being against the law, prior consultation on assignments and price setting also contravene the morality of the market. Every upstanding entrepreneur should feel guilty about this, certainly when he is caught red-handed. So how are we to explain that so little guilt was on display during the parliamentary inquiry? Are building contractors morally worse than other entrepreneurs? Although the construction industry is thought of as a wild west in which business has its own rules, I do not want to assume this from the start. The building contractors' story was that the construction market has several specific characteristics that make it understandable and justifiable for entrepreneurs to think it necessary to institutionalise prior consultation when tendering for a contract. Whether that story is correct remains to be seen. But even when it should prove true, bribery and fictitious invoices cannot be justified. For that reason these practices will not be addressed here.

Graafland writes that the Dutch government had permitted prior consultation since 1953 to prevent construction companies from collapsing under heavy competition. It even regulated it up to 1998 when pressure from Brussels forbid prior consultation based on the Competitive Trading Act. He also wrote that legal prior consultation easily led to illegal types of prior consultation – pre-prior consultation – in which entrepreneurs paid one another higher amounts than the official reimbursement for calculation costs. Prior consultation went underground in 1998. Then Prime Minister Lubbers predicted that in 1992, when the European Commission prohibited construction cartels. The difference between legal prior consultation and illegal pre-prior consultation evaporated. Since then, the government has had no idea about what arrangements companies reach. Knowing the construction industry, it was unwise of the government to expect that companies would immediately obey the law. If the Dutch government saw good reasons to permit prior consultation before 1998, these reasons did not disappear with the legal prohibition in 1998. They persisted in the entrepreneurs' view, and the latter acted accordingly.

Is it true that the construction market has specific characteristics that could justify exceptions to the morality of free competition? Let us review a few frequently mentioned characteristics. The first is the high risk of miscalculations. In calculating the price quoted in the construction tender there are so many uncertain factors that there is a serious risk of forgetting or underestimating items; a company could then founder when it is awarded the contract. Prior consultation offers an opportunity to compare tenders and eliminate such errors. However, economist Van Damme (2002) denies that miscalculations and erroneous estimates are specific to construction. A second characteristic is government's dominant position as commissioning authority for infrastructure projects. As Graafland noted, government acts like a hawker when it combines the cheapest and most innovative aspects from various tenders into the contract awarded to the lowest bidder. The question here is whether this characteristic justifies an exception to free competition. Economist Van Damme argued that in some situations it can be reasonable for a monopoly-holder to agree not to hawk. If contractors fear that the contracting authority (government) will use their tenders to squeeze out still better prices, they will bid differently than when they can be sure that it will be their one and only bid. This strategic modification can definitely work against the supplier. A third characteristic is the cost of preparing a quotation. It takes much time and thus much money to draw up a tender submission, certainly for unique and complex projects. Experts can see there is a problem here, but do not agree on the solution. Legal expert Chris Jansen (2001) argued that the commissioning party should be obliged to reimburse quotation costs incurred in vain. Economist Van Damme, relying on economic model analysis, rejected this suggestion. He preferred a tender with prior selection.

When we can believe the experts, construction is by no means a market with unique characteristics. We can find these same characteristics in other markets. On the other side, the construction market diverges so far from the ideal of a perfect market that its regulation requires government's constant attention.

Civil Disobedience?

If my reasoning is correct, the government is at least partly responsible for sending prior consultation underground. The government simply submitted to Brussels' prohibition of Uniform Price Regulating Regulations and other arrangements without seeking a timely alternative arrangement. In addition, the government apparently failed to monitor adequately implementation of the 1998 Competitive Trading Act. Can we regard the consultation's going underground as a justifiable act of civil disobedience? Civil disobedience is not merely citizens disobeying a law or government policy with which they disagree fundamentally. If I block access to a facing plot because I do not want my open view to be impeded by construction, this is not an act of civil disobedience. Civil disobedience is an act of resistance against something considered unjust. Removing my open view harms my personal interests but is not necessarily an unjust act. Imagine that the 1998 Competitive Trading Act were unjust to the construction industry. The current normative theory on civil disobedience imposes strict requirements for the justification of acts of civil disobedience (See Rawls, 1971, etc.). You must first have tried to amend the law by normal methods. Furthermore, you must be able to justify the act of civil disobedience by invoking the conventional, public understanding of justice. In addition, your resistance must be overt and you must be willing to bear its consequences (fines, imprisonment). Now, I do not know whether entrepreneurs have lobbied against the Competitive Trading Act or how strong and extensive their lobby was. It is clear that the prior consultation did not continue in public and that the entrepreneurs were not at all willing to bear the consequences of making illegal agreements. Even when building contractors had good reasons to complain about the new Competitive Trading Act, their response – i.e. taking prior consultation underground – cannot be called a justifiable act of civil disobedience.

Moral Responsibility and Moral Culpability

The building constructors' taking prior consultation underground is not a justifiable act of resistance. To what extent is inadequate government action a moral excuse for the deed? A few years ago, while descending along a narrow mountain road in Switzerland I had a road accident because the car slipped when I tried to stop for an oncoming car that appeared unexpectedly from around a mountain curve. The local authorities had spread gravel on the roadbed that had softened from the heat, but it had neglected to put up signs to warn drivers of this. Had I known that, I would have driven more slowly. I was responsible for the accident, but the government's failure to give adequate warning was a mitigating circumstance. Earlier on I suggested that government shares responsibility for sending prior consultation underground. Can government's neglect be considered a mitigating circumstance? Because I was not warned of the gravel on the road, I did not adjust my driving style. There was a causal – albeit indirect – relation between my not being warned and the accident. There is also a causal relation between the new law and permitting prior consultation to go underground. It was a freely taken, conscious decision. There are no grounds for the assertion that the entrepreneurs could not have done otherwise. These grounds would probably be there were it possible to show that, given the specific characteristics of the construction industry, many bankruptcies would undermine free competition in the industry. If that situation meant putting the implementation of infrastructure works in danger, the common good would be put at risk. But to my knowledge that has not been demonstrated.

Imagine that this were the case, we would then have to ask whether persisting with prior consultation would be a suitable response. It is certainly not true that the entrepreneurs' concern for the wellbeing of their companies and the entire industry left them with no other choice but to continue with prior consultation. There will doubtless have been companies that did not agree with this but who participated from loyalty or because they feared the others would not work with them if they refused. Given the stories in circulation, this fear does not seem unfounded. But the number of companies that, after the discovery of the construction fraud, claimed that they continued with it because it was so difficult to withdraw seems greater to me than the number that had really objected to going underground. Between 1998 and 2001, according to Graafland, several large construction companies tried to comply with the law, but gave up. The social pressure and sanctions of others proved too heavy, even for large construction companies. Given this, to what extent can we object to a particular entrepreneur's participating? Can we expect an entrepreneur to risk his company to keep the law?

In some countries it is impossible to obtain certain papers (travel documents, permits and the like) without paying bribes. Does that make paying morally less culpable or even excusable? It is obvious that the one paying helps to maintain the bribery system. But those without power or influence have little choice. If they want or need to go abroad, they have to pay to obtain the documents. Perhaps companies needing a permit are better able to insist upon issuance without paying a bribe. The moral culpability of bribery depends on the payer's ability to resist. The situation is different when demanding a bribe, except, perhaps, for those unable to support a family on their public sector pay. It is difficult to keep one's hands clean when one's children are hungry. Two elements play a role in assessing the culpability of going along with bribery. First, how serious are the consequences of not going along, for yourself and those who depend on you? Second, are you able, alone or with others, to take action to halt these practices? Multinationals could join forces and refuse to invest in a country where government refused to eliminate bribery. Some companies, among them Shell, have undertaken to do this. Nevertheless, these practices will not cease when government is unable to take a firm position and impose adequate sanctions.

Are Dutch construction companies that participate in prior consultation and price-fixing comparable to companies that pay bribes in countries where bribery is part of the culture? There is at least one important difference, i.e. government's role. Government in countries with a culture of bribery tolerates these practices or does too little to halt them. In the Netherlands, government was long unaware that prior consultation persisted. It could have known that sooner had there been efficient monitoring. But once it became known, government did take action. Companies could have done more than not participate. They could have notified government about the prior consultation. But that did not happen. To my knowledge, the aforesaid large companies did not do this. They could have notified the government anonymously, even without withdrawing from the prior consultation. Their sense of loyalty to their colleagues was probably too strong to allow them to tattle to the government. In the end, individuals were responsible for making these fraudulent practices public. That not one company – not one management board or board of directors – tipped the government, even secretly, bears witness, in my opinion, that the unwillingness to participate was not very strong even in companies that did not favour taking the prior consultation underground. Perhaps we should really blame the companies less for still going along with the prior consultation and more for their appearing not to take any action to halt the practice.

Getting Matters Organised

In the period when the construction fraud took place, civil servants and contractors acted dishonestly. That does not mean that they were ethical failures in all senses. Socio-psychological research has shown that the situation and context in which people act exerts great influence on their behaviour. A crooked contractor can quite easily be an honest member of his church's management committee. Perhaps the man would have been a splendid entrepreneur if he had had a business in the IT industry. There are probably few people who act morally entirely by their own will power. People adapt easily to their social environment. They seek guidance for their conduct in other's deeds. The conduct and attitude of others in their social environment is a more important orientation than codes or legislation. To remain on the right track, people need others who look over their shoulders and offer criticism and correction where necessary. Given this background, how should we regard the measures taken after the construction fraud?

The parliamentary committee investigating the construction industry noted in its final report that it saw no reason to treat construction differently from other branches of business. There, too, open and honest competition and healthy market mechanisms come first. There can be no question of a reimbursement from contracting authorities for calculation costs. We think it reasonable to give a design fee to a select number of candidates for complex and innovative projects. The committee seems to share the same opinion as economist Van Damme. As commissioning authority, the government's tenders must meet European principles of objectivity, non-discrimination and transparency; in granting contracts it must strive to spread risks evenly. Contracting authorities must make unambiguous arrangements about risks – be they setbacks or windfalls. They may not decide too quickly to have the contractors bear all the risks. The committee also believed that the anticipated integration of the various European procurement directives would offer sufficient opportunities for establishing regulations that do justice to the characteristics unique to the industry. Furthermore, the committee found that the government, as supervisor, had to exercise its role proactively to maintain its credibility. That appears to be an implicit criticism of the way the Netherlands Competition Authority (NCa) worked.

As a result of an evaluation of the Competitive Trading Act and the NCa, the government suggested a few improvements in October 2003. These improvements followed from the entrepreneurs' inadequate cooperation in the investigation of the construction fraud. The NCa was given the authority to enter the homes of private persons after review by the examining magistrate of the Court of Rotterdam. The power to seal business premises and objects and to remove documents temporarily was also strengthened. In addition, the NMa's ability to impose sanctions was extended. It was assigned the authority to impose fines on private persons, because of their role in the corporate structure, as commissioning authorities or senior managers.

What did the industry do? At the end of 2002, the Coalition of Dutch Construction Industry Organisations (AVBB, now called *Bouwend Nederland* [Building Netherlands]) presented a new version of the code of conduct for construction companies; it was intended to restore and maintain confidence in the industry. The code's keynote is that honesty is a core value to be anchored in the companies' actions. Companies signing the code can be held accountable for compliance with it and stand open to review. Infractions are penalised, in extreme cases with expulsion. The AVBB wanted government to make adherence to the code mandatory for those tendering for government contracts. In that case, expulsion would mean that a company would be prevented from obtaining government contracts for at least 3 years.

It is also important to shed light on all fronts. The investigative committee clearly stated that regardless of the construction industry's distinctive characteristics, there was still no reason to digress from the principles of free competition. The government, in its role as commissioning authority was clearly told that it must spread risks fairly. In issuing its new code, the AVBB clearly showed which rules contractors had to follow in economic transactions. Supervision over the industry was also tightened. Now we need to transform the construction industry's morally degenerate climate. That will only come about when entrepreneurs internalise the morality of the marketplace.

References

Jansen, C.E.C. 2001. Aanbesteding en offertekostenvergoeding. In: van den Boom, W.H., Jansen en J.V. Meijnen, C.E.C. (red.), *Aanbesteding en aansprakelijkheid*, pp. 69–104. Den Haag: Boom.
McMahon, C. 1981. Morality and the Invisible Hand. *Philosophy and Public Affairs*, 10: 247–277.
Rawls, J. 1971. *A. Theory of Justice*. Oxford: Oxford University Press.
Smith, A. 1776/1976. *An Inquiry into the Nature and Causes of the Wealth of Nations*. In: Campbell, R.H. and Skinner, A.S. (eds.). Oxford: Oxford University Press.
Van Damme, E.C. 2002. Bouwfraude in breder perspectief. In: Nielissen-Breukers, D.D., Nielissen, D.A.J.F., Jonker, L.E.J., *Juvat-dag 2002*, pp. 53–71. Nijmegen: Wolf.

Chapter 27
Commentary: Fraud, Excuse and Responsibility

Marcel Verweij

Abstract During the Parliamentary Enquiry on Fraud in the Dutch Construction Industry, CEOs gave various responses to the accusation that their companies were involved in fraud. Some responses only offer explanations of what had happened, but other responses were aimed to take away the blame that fell upon the companies and their executives. In this comment I distinguish excuses and justifications given by CEOs. The distinction helps to clarify the responses and to assess whether they are persuasive.

Introduction

In this case study, the CEOs of construction companies appeal to several arguments to ward off accusations of fraud. How convincing are their responses? It is interesting to note that several responses can be understood as excuses, while others as justifications for their actions. That applies especially to prior consultations in which agreements were made on tenders and reimbursement for calculation costs. Bribery and distributing favours to officials could be considered beyond excuse and justification and will not be discussed in this chapter. Rather, I will limit myself here to CEO's comments on prior consultations and reimbursement of calculation costs. First I will explain the various types of responses from an ethical perspective, then I will assess whether these responses, notably the excuses and justifications, are convincing.

Explanation

First we can distinguish between explanations, excuses and justifications. In part three of his presentation, Johan Graafland gave several clear explanations of how construction fraud could emerge and continue: the government used to stimulate

M. Verweij (✉)
Ethics Institute, Faculty of Humanities, Utrecht University, Utrecht, The Netherlands
e-mail: M.F.Verweij@uu.nl

prior consultations, and then there were also various characteristics typical of the construction market. This government involvement and the fact that all parties – at least those participating in the consultation – could agree with the state of affairs *explains* why CEOs did not feel that they were doing anything wrong. It is also understandable that this long-established practice did not disappear from one day to the next when it was forbidden in 1998. While these aspects offer an explanation for the persistence of prior consultation and the distribution of tendering fees over the candidates, it does not exonerate the building contractors. When you are accused of fraud, merely explaining what happened e.g. by drawing attention to a variety of economic and cultural factors that encourage this behaviour is no help. Rather, you have to show that your role is so minimal, innocuous or even correct that moral criticism is not, or not entirely, correct.

Excuse

In making an excuse, you admit that the contested act or practice was incorrect, but also argue that you did not *perform a deed* in the full sense of being fully responsible. Perhaps, you did not know what you were doing; it may have been an accident; maybe you acted under duress. You admit that it was wrong, but you do not accept full responsibility for it. Another defence is to deny that what you did was wrong. In that case, nothing can be held against you; your actions were morally correct – at least that is what you assert. This last defence is a justification, not an excuse.

The first and most insistent excuse given in the case study comes from the CEOs who deny any involvement. They argue that they were not directly involved in the procedure for acquiring orders and thus could not have known of the practice of informal prior consultation. Even if this defence were plausible, it is not a very comfortable excuse for a CEO. After all, is she not supposed to be informed about the way orders are acquired? Of course, a CEO cannot keep abreast of every external contact each of the company's employees has, but this is an exceptional case. The prior consultation came after a long established practice had recently been declared illegal, which should have led to a thoroughgoing change in the way orders were acquired. Were not the CEOs in the best position to take the lead in this situation? In his classic essay *A Plea for Excuses*, J.L. Austin wrote,

> "... few excuses get us out of it completely: the average excuse... gets us only out of the fire into the frying pan – but still, of course, any frying pan in a fire."(Austin, 1961)

Excuses usually go only so far in getting you out of a mess. One CEO's excuse that he was not informed of the prior consultation only draws attention to another problem. As CEO he should have been informed. It is not strange that none of the CEOs and directors put forward standard excuses like "I didn't know what I was doing" or "it happened by accident". For a director that is usually a sign of certifiable ineptitude.[1]

A much more appropriate type of excuse is that individual companies or CEOs could do little to change the practice. "You couldn't withdraw from the system on your own. We were all trapped in the system." This defence is complex. It contains elements of excuse (it was wrong, but I am not or am only partly responsible) and of justification (I was fully responsible, but what I did was not wrong). We can consider it an excuse when there is an element of compulsion or threat. In criminal circles, it can happen that parties that do not want to cooperate in fraud are threatened and punished. One entrepreneur, whom colleagues forced to participate in price agreements and distribution of tendering fees, cannot be held fully accountable for the fraud. Extortion, compulsion and other criminal practices did not come to light in the construction fraud. It was the system, the collective practice of agreements and competition that forced companies to comply with the practices, not one mastermind criminal or group of companies whose double-dealing coerced others to participate in fraud.

But is this defence a valid excuse? Apparently all entrepreneurs took part more or less freely. They may have wanted things to work differently, but none of them could change the situation alone, so prior consultation and reimbursement for calculation costs persisted. The excuse is found mainly in stressing that the group as a whole was responsible; that implicitly tones down one's own responsibility. This mitigation can be put forcefully by asserting that the government or trade organisations, not the individual companies, were the ones primarily responsible for regulating the market. If the government or branch organisation should have changed the illegal practice, there is less reason to reproach entrepreneurs or CEOs. This shifts a large portion of the responsibility. Most quotations from building contractors do not shift responsibility to another party; rather they describe how the entrepreneurs kept a stranglehold on one another. When a company cannot escape from this – i.e. has no control over its own actions – it has a reasonable excuse. However, it seems that several companies were able to escape the practice, but that CEOs thought this irresponsible. There is no longer any question of an excuse – but perhaps the CEOs held a stronger trump?

Justification

Because the companies made agreements on tendering and reimbursements, refraining from fraud was detrimental. A few large companies tried to break with price-fixing agreements. However, the attempts ran aground when these companies

---

[1] Philosophers tend to distinguish two conditions for moral responsibility: knowledge and control. The less knowledge one has about the consequences of one's actions, and the less control one has over one's actions, the less one can be held responsible for those actions or their consequences.

saw that operating legally led to a drastic fall in orders. Operating legally came at a very high price. Some CEOs implicitly couched the high price in moral terms:

> "Let's be clear: our first responsibility is to the 3,600 families that earn a living at this company." (NRC, 2004)

This defence is not purely an excuse; it also *justifies* committing fraud. The presupposition is that a company is supposed to provide jobs and incomes for its employees. The company has to stay healthy, and for that it needs a well-filled order book. When the construction company gets fewer orders, problems arise that could mean having to let workers go. For CEOs this is not purely an economic question; they have a special moral responsibility toward their employees. If they can prevent a slump for the company – and thus for its employees – they have to do so. Choosing to desist from illegal practices could endanger the company – and that is what CEOs are supposed to prevent. In short, although fraud is immoral, it now appears that not committing fraud also raises moral problems. In this reasoning, CEOs saw themselves caught in a conflict of duties. On one side their leadership role requires them to see to it that the company obeys the law and does not commit fraud. On the other they have to see to the wellbeing – here the employment – of their employees. The moral conflict implies that they cannot do both at once. It is legally and morally necessary to reject fraud and hence to stay away from prior consultation. Yet without prior consultation, the company cannot acquire the orders it needs to keep up employment. If there is no way out of this dilemma, CEOs will have to decide which obligation gets priority. It is conceivable that a CEO can give convincing reasons why his/her obligations to employees should come first. In that case, he/she will have given adequate moral justification for choosing to commit fraud.

There is nothing wrong with the structure of this argument. But what about its content? Has the notion of a conflict of duties given CEOs a cogent moral justification for the way their companies acted in the construction fraud? That is open to doubt. First, there is the question whether companies were really unable to stop prior consultation and distribution of tendering fees. A few large companies tried to back out of the fraud, but the only result was that they lost new orders. Companies, individually, could not change the practice; in any case, they could not change it solely by deciding on their own to cut ties with it. Yet the major players could have at least joined together to raise the issue in talks with the government. From a moral perspective, it is too easy to say that this would have been seen as "squealing on your colleagues" or that it was difficult because not all civil servants had clean hands (remember that government was also the main provider of contracts), although these arguments are not without value.

A second problem is whether the dilemma (what comes first, the law or my employees) is really as sharp as is suggested. Companies that decided not to take part in prior consultations and that refused to take their cut of the tendering fees saw their order books shrink. That is undeniably detrimental for a company. But it does not mean that employees must be made redundant forthwith. The dilemma is not that a CEO has to choose either to commit fraud or fire 150 workers. Not committing fraud means that there will be fewer orders and, if that cannot be turned around, something will have to be done. Involuntary redundancies can be a part of this, but there are other ways to counter a decline in earnings. One of the possibilities is, again, proactively thwarting and undermining prior consultations by raising the question with the government.[2] Although it can be said that by working on construction fraud the CEOs protected their employees' jobs and wellbeing, it is clear that there are other ways to keep jobs.

A third problem concerns how far CEOs should go to protect their employees' jobs. This concern can be considered a special moral responsibility. It is an obligation that the entrepreneur has toward his/her own employees, but not toward others.[3] Can this responsibility reach so far that it can justify fraud? Thomas Scanlon says that the general moral framework of what people owe one another puts limits on special obligations.[4] In non-consequentialist theory, one can defend the idea that negative obligations not to harm or mislead others place limits on positive moral obligations to foster good (be this the common good or the good of a group of people for which you bear special responsibility).[5] In addition, the Netherlands has a robust social safety net of unemployment benefits, so that neither employee nor employer need fear that redundancy will lead to intolerable poverty. That, too, puts a cap on an employer's moral responsibility. The responsibility does not extend so far that a company must contravene moral and legal norms to protect its employees.[6]

Nothing Dishonourable Happened

Some building contractor CEOs simply deny that they did anything wrong.

> "Maybe it was against the law, but I didn't see it as illegal".
> "That would look like pleading guilty. And I refuse to admit to even one fault."
> "Nothing dishonourable happened."
> "I didn't sit there for financial gain".

These are justifications, not excuses. But are they adequately grounded? It is plausible that the CEOs that spoke these words wanted to distinguish between what

---

[2] The dilemma could also be phrased in this way: either I report the fraudulent practice and betray my colleagues, or I fire my employees. In that case, squealing seems justified.

[3] For special obligations, see Jan Vorstenbosch's contribution in this volume.

[4] Scanlon gave the following example to illustrate the limits of special obligations: helping friends in need is part of our moral concept of friendship. But if the help given consists of robbing a third person's kidney to save one's friend, this does not fit in our moral ideas of being a good friend: "... friendship also requires us to recognize our friends as having moral status as persons, independent of our friendship, which also places limits on our behavior." (Scanlon, 1998: 165)

[5] Cf. Philippa Foot "It is interesting to see that, even where the strictest duty of positive aid exists, this still does not weigh as if a negative duty were involved." (Foot, 1967: 15).

[6] The argument that the company participated in fraud to protect their employees, might be overly opportunistic. After all, many companies also get rid of employees to increase profitability.

the law requires and what morality demands. They may have broken the law, but they did not believe that they acted immorally. The fact that for years all parties had considered prior consultation and splitting tendering fees as normal and acceptable practices, once again becomes meaningful. In that light it is understandable that the CEOs would feel that the legal prohibition of the cartel by law (to comply with European policy) lacked all moral foundation. CEO Dick van Well of Dura Vermeer apologised profusely for breaking the law, but said that the clients were never cheated, and that the cartel agreements did not raise prices. If clients are treated fairly, how can a practice aimed at benefitting all and in which all have a say, raise moral problems?

A deontological answer to this question is that moral norms need not be based purely on the consequences of an act, or on implicit or explicit agreements. Some practices are morally wrong simply because they violate principles meant to create a fair market. The factual premises in the reasoning also raise questions. Was it true that the cartel did not lead to higher prices? Koop Tjuchem's duplicate accounts, as described in the case study, show that 10% of a 15 million-euro contract was divided over companies that did no work on the building. Money also went to companies that did not even participate in the tendering. Companies involved in the preparatory stages divided up the tendering fees, even when they did not submit a tender. Arguably, such practices will have higher prices as an effect.

A second question is whether indeed no one suffered harm. Illegal price-fixing agreements and sharing tendering fees could only be fair when everyone could profit from them. But it is not evident that each building contractor could and did get in line. In a community where the most important parties know one another well and make agreements, there is a serious chance that other, new or smaller companies will be excluded and thus be harmed by the illegal negotiations.

The construction fraud demonstrates that the construction community has many norms about what is honest, honourable and fair, but that these do not necessarily coincide with the general moral principles that the rest of society takes for granted. Dura Vermeer CEO Van Well noted that the construction industry had the illusion that the rest of society had the same sense of standards as the construction industry. "Apparently that is not the case." (NRC, 2004).

What was accepted within the construction industry proved, upon closer inspection, to be socially undesirable and unacceptable. But that is not a convincing excuse, let alone a moral justification for fraud.

References

Austin, J.L. 1961. A Plea for Excuses. In: *Philosophical Papers*, pp. 175–204. Oxford: Clarendon Press.
Foot, P.H. 1967. The Problem of Abortion and the Doctrine of Double Effect. *Oxford Review*, 5: 5–15.
NRC. 2004. "Na de boete volgt de bekentenis". *NRC*. 13 May.
Scanlon, T.L. 1998. *What we owe to each other*. Cambridge, MA: Belknap Press.

About the Authors

Michiel Brumsen was assistant professor of Ethics and Technology at Delft University of Technology. He now teaches history at a secondary school in Flanders.

Marc Buelens is full professor at the Vlerick Leuven Gent Management School, Gent.

Eva Cools is post-doctoral research associate at the Vlerick Leuven Gent Management School, Gent.

Gemma Crijns is advisor on CSR and network coordinator of the Partnerships Resource Centre at Rotterdam School of Management, Erasmus University, Rotterdam.

Frank G.A. de Bakker is associate professor of Strategic Management at the Department of Organization Science of the Faculty of Social Sciences, VU University, Amsterdam.

Dick de Gilder is associate professor of Organizational Psychology at the Department of Organization Science of the Faculty of Social Sciences, VU University, Amsterdam.

Frank den Hond is associate professor of Strategic Management at the Department of Organization Science of the Faculty of Social Sciences, VU University, Amsterdam.

Wim Dubbink is associate professor of Business Ethics and Philosophical Ethics at the Department of Philosophy of the Faculty of Humanities, Tilburg University, Tilburg.

Rosalie Feilzer was at the time of writing studying Social Science at the VU University, Amsterdam. Now she is a consultant, working at a management consultancy firm.

Johan Graafland is full professor of Economics, Business and Ethics at the Tilburg School of Economics and Management and member of the Tilburg Sustainability Center and the Tilburg European Banking Center, Tilburg University, Tilburg.

Robert Heeger is emeritus professor of Ethics at the Ethics Institute, Faculty of Humanities, Utrecht University, Utrecht.

Pieter Ippel is professor of Law at Roosevelt Academy, a 'liberal arts and sciences-college' of Utrecht University, Middelburg.

Edgar Karssing is associate professor of Business Ethics at the Nyenrode Business University, Breukelen.

Jos Kole is senior research fellow Ethics at the Ethics Institute of the Faculty of Humanities, Utrecht University, Utrecht.

Peter Koslowski is Professor of Philosophy, especially Philosophy of Management and History of Philosophy, VU University, Amsterdam.

Bert Musschenga is Professor of Ethics at the Faculty of Philosophy, VU University, Amsterdam.

Tsjalling Swierstra is full professor of Philosophy at the Faculty of Arts and Social Sciences, Maastricht University, Maastricht.

Bert van de Ven is assistant professor of Business Ethics and Philosophical Ethics at the Department of Philosophy, Faculty of Humanities, Tilburg University, Tilburg.

Mariëtte van den Hoven is senior lecturer and coordinator of the Professional Ethics Program at the Ethics Institute, Faculty of Humanities, Utrecht University, Utrecht.

Frans-Paul van der Putten was at the time of writing researcher at Nyenrode Business University and is currently a research fellow at the Netherlands Institute of International Relations Clingendael, The Hague.

Luc van Liedekerke is associate professor of Business Ethics at the universities of Leuven and Antwerpen and director of the Centre for Economics and Ethics, KULeuven, Leuven.

Henk van Luijk was emeritus professor of Business Ethics at Nyenrode Business University, Breukelen.

Marcel Verweij is associate professor and coordinator of the International MA Program Applied Ethics, Ethics Institue, Faculty of Humanities, Utrecht University, Utrecht.

Jan Vorstenbosch is associate professor of Applied Ethics at the Department of Philosophy of the Faculty of Humanities, Utrecht University, Utrecht.

Raoul Wirtz is program manager executive education at the Executive & Management Development Center of Nyenrode Business University, Breukelen.

Index

A

Accountable, 16, 26, 178, 214–215, 217–218, 221, 283, 287
AIDS, 31–61, 70–75, 80–81, 89, 91, 93, 98, 100–101, 106, 108
Autonomy, 25, 50, 80–81

B

Bribery, 132, 277–278, 281, 285
Business
  community, 4–5, 7, 9, 11, 35, 125, 132, 194, 210
  ethics, 3–9, 19–30, 57, 117, 144, 206, 214, 273
  partner, 72, 74, 79, 137, 189–190, 201, 204, 219

C

CEO, 6, 39, 44, 108, 128–132, 142–143, 149–150, 215, 218, 253, 262, 269–271, 285–290
Chain responsibility, 203–210, 213–221, 224
Child labour, 100, 185–187, 190, 192–211, 213–218, 220–221, 223–228
Civil
  servant, 14, 263–264, 282, 288
  society, 134
Code
  moral, 6, 142
  of conduct, 129–132, 148, 150, 189, 201, 205, 210, 271, 283
  of ethics, 5–8
Community, 4, 5, 7, 9, 11, 35, 53, 123, 125, 132, 134, 144, 194, 210, 238, 242, 245–250, 290
Competition Authority, 264, 271, 283
Compliance, 25, 58, 136, 142–144, 171, 194, 200, 215, 219–221, 273, 278, 283
Conflict, 51–52, 69, 73, 75, 91, 108, 116, 122, 127, 132, 137, 178–179, 193–194, 196, 218, 223–224, 247, 288
Consumer, 38, 40, 59, 88–90, 117, 123, 125, 128, 132, 143–144, 172, 188–189, 194, 196, 204, 218, 264–265
Contract, 69, 112, 114–115, 119–155, 192, 208, 227, 263, 267–268, 270, 278–279, 290
Control, 8, 13, 15, 24, 34, 36, 67–68, 74, 136, 178, 188, 195–196, 206, 217, 219, 226, 241, 247, 272, 287
Corporate governance, 6, 143
Corporate responsibility, 8, 35, 265
Corporation, 15, 22, 57, 66, 90, 136, 189, 239, 248
CSR, 7–8, 87, 189
Culture
  corporate, 262
  organisational, 23, 171–172, 174–175

D

Discrimination, 42, 143, 193, 282
Dubbink, W., 11–16, 19–30, 185–211
Duty
  imperfect, 56, 58
  perfect, 56, 58

E

Environment, 4, 7–8, 16, 28, 51, 83–84, 87, 89, 91, 93, 105, 112, 121, 128, 132, 142–143, 174, 180–182, 188–190, 204, 248, 254–256, 282
Ethics, 3–9, 12–14, 16, 19–30, 51, 57, 59, 61, 109, 115, 117, 143–144, 172–173, 177–182, 206, 214, 223–227, 248–250, 270, 273

293

F
Fraud, 11, 233, 238, 240–242, 246, 248, 253, 256, 259–290

G
Goodpaster, 172–173

I
Institution, 3–9, 15–16, 19–30, 80–84, 88, 91, 103, 105, 107–108, 133, 144, 149–151, 153, 189, 236, 249, 262, 265–268, 272–273, 275, 278
Integrity, 6, 50, 80, 189, 273
Internet, 88, 101, 123, 237

J
Job, 27, 67, 81, 125, 149, 152, 162, 228, 236, 240, 254, 262–266, 268, 270, 272, 288–289
Justice, 20, 22, 40, 59, 181, 201, 204, 242, 269, 280, 282
Justification, 9, 19, 28, 280, 285–290

K
Kant, 56, 105, 215

L
Law, 6–8, 16, 37, 82, 100, 113, 122–123, 141–144, 150, 152, 167, 192, 195, 200, 226, 234–235, 239, 245–250, 269–270, 272, 274, 278–281, 288–290
Least developed countries, 34, 42–44, 48, 122
Legitimacy, 89, 91, 103–109, 137, 153
Loyal, 14, 238, 241, 246–248, 281–282

M
Management
  change, 6, 8
  ethical, 24–25
  reputation, 6, 117, 152
Market
  construction, 265–266
  imperfect, 267
  price, 200, 204, 240, 267
  regulation, 136
Marketing, 41, 65, 67–68, 93
McMahon, 278
MNC, 201
Moral
  duty, 48, 55, 58, 224–226
  obligation, 14, 16, 34, 40, 44–45, 47–53, 82–83, 145, 289
  question, 44–45, 194
  reason, 190
  requirement, 40
Morality, 7, 12, 15–16, 22–25, 29, 51–52, 58, 60–61, 117, 136, 142, 203, 214, 218, 220–221, 226, 278–279, 290

O
Organisation
  studies, 7

P
PG, 67, 70–71, 74, 81–82, 92, 99, 101, 115, 117
Poverty, 36, 65–66, 193, 289
Power, 9, 20, 27, 33, 39, 66, 91–92, 105, 108, 122, 134, 136–137, 143, 149–150, 152, 178, 182, 191, 193, 201, 204, 216–217, 219–221, 224, 234, 267, 281–283
Price fixing, 28, 262, 269, 271, 277, 281, 287, 290
Privatisation, 165–166
Profit, 6–7, 26, 29, 36, 38, 40, 43, 48, 51, 57, 59, 67, 82–84, 87, 91, 109, 126, 148, 168, 204, 206–207, 216, 237, 246, 254, 263, 266–267, 290
Promotion Girls, 63–93, 95–117
Property, intellectual, 36–37, 44
Public tender, 266, 273
  public private partnership, 272

R
Rawls, 21, 152, 226, 280
Reputation, 4, 6, 8, 76, 88–90, 93, 108, 117, 124, 130, 132, 134, 147–153, 168, 209, 254–256
Respectable companies, 7, 128
Responsibility
  collective, 169–175, 219
Rights
  human, 28, 83, 91, 116, 121, 123, 125, 128–132, 135–137, 142–145, 150–152, 189–190, 203–204, 206, 208
  patent, 35, 40, 47
  prosperity, 181
  women, 4
Risk management, 6
Risk safety, 162, 166, 171–175
Rules, 6, 12, 21, 24–25, 27, 51, 71, 113–114, 116, 131–132, 141, 143–144, 172, 219, 225, 247, 249, 268, 278, 283

S

Sex
   safety, 36
   tourism, 70
   worker, 66–67, 71, 80, 83, 107
Sexual harassment, 98–101, 113
Shareholders, 48, 51, 57, 68, 87, 123, 129–130, 132, 134–135, 149–153, 188–190, 234, 238, 247–249, 253–254, 256, 265
Side effects, 108, 111–117, 248
Social
   capital, 26
   injustice, 40
   norms, 71
   pressure, 76, 133, 149, 208, 281
   responsibility, 6–8, 41, 43–44, 89, 104, 106, 109, 113, 117, 130–131, 135, 148, 153, 188–191, 201, 217, 220–221
Stakeholders, 38, 57–58, 74, 84, 89–90, 103, 107–109, 133, 144, 147–153, 253–254, 256, 264–265

T

Tax Fraud, 238, 264
Technology, 44, 168, 172, 177–182, 234–239, 241, 243, 245–248, 252–253, 262
Teleopathy, 172

Trade
   ethical, 8
   fair, 216
Trade Union, 73, 121–122, 125, 127–129, 131–133, 135, 137
Trust restoring, 273

U

United Nations, 203

V

Values, 21, 24, 40, 49–50, 59, 76, 103, 105, 107, 109, 147, 151, 161, 167, 172–174, 178, 180, 182, 188, 190–191, 203, 237, 247, 270, 278, 283, 288
Van Luijk, 3–9, 11–16, 83, 132–133, 145
Virtue, 14–15, 68, 147, 169–175

W

Wage, 23, 29, 70, 75, 83, 85, 93, 99, 107, 114–115, 187, 190, 201, 255
Whistleblowing, 272
Women
   abuse, 100
   promotion girls, 63–93, 95–119
   self-help, 191, 206
WTO, 36–38, 144, 238

Lightning Source UK Ltd.
Milton Keynes UK
UKOW06n1456220816

281226UK00001B/19/P